Circulating Queerness

Circulating Queerness

Before the Gay and Lesbian Novel

Natasha Hurley

University of Minnesota Press

Minneapolis | London

The University of Minnesota Press gratefully acknowledges the generous assistance provided for the publication of this book by the Faculty of Arts and Office of the Vice-President (Research), University of Alberta.

Portions of chapter 2 were previously published as "Reading Anthologically: The Queer Traffic in Literature," *English Studies in Canada* 36, no. 1 (2010): 81–108.

Published by the University of Minnesota Press
111 Third Avenue South, Suite 290
Minneapolis, MN 55401-2520
http://www.upress.umn.edu

Printed on acid-free paper.

The University of Minnesota is an equal-opportunity educator and employer.

Library of Congress Cataloging-in-Publication Data
Names: Hurley, Natasha, author.
Title: Circulating queerness : before the gay and lesbian novel / Natasha Hurley.
Description: Minneapolis : University of Minnesota Press, [2018] | Includes bibliographical references and index. |
Identifiers: LCCN 2017055863 (print) | ISBN 978-1-5179-0034-2 (hc) | ISBN 978-1-5179-0035-9 (pb)
Subjects: LCSH: American fiction–19th century–History and criticism. | Homosexuality in literature. | BISAC: LITERARY CRITICISM / Gay & Lesbian. | SOCIAL SCIENCE / Gay Studies.
Classification: LCC PS374.H63 H87 2018 (print) | DDC 809.3/9353–dc23
LC record available at https://lccn.loc.gov/2017055863

For my family, in and out of law:
a queer lot, in one way or another

CONTENTS

PROLOGUE
On the Queer Worlds of Books

Ah, his books! The library of almost every man of like making-up, whose life has been largely solitary, so concentratedly from the inside, is companioned from youth up by innermost literary sympathies of his type.
Edward Irenaeus Prime-Stevenson, "Out of the Sun"

WHEN EDWARD PRIME-STEVENSON wrote "Out of the Sun" in 1913, he took for granted the ways in which sexuality as a social "type" was marked "by innermost *literary* sympathies." By his account, the genesis of this sense of an inner sympathy, which today goes by the name *homosexuality*, was not (primarily) sexological or psychoanalytic but the effect of books. The story begins with Dayneford, on the last day of his life, surveying his library:

> Dayneford stood now before his bookcase, reading over mechanically the titles of a special group of volumes—mostly small ones. They were crowded into a few lower shelves, as if they sought to avoid other literary society, to keep themselves to themselves, to shun all unsympathetic observation.[1]

Books, "mostly small ones"; books accumulated and organized on shelves; books that "companioned" one "from youth up"; beautiful books with arabesque covers, translated into English from an astonishing range of languages and cultural contexts.

Tibullus, Porpertius and the Greek Ant[h]ologists pressed against Al Nafsaweh and Chakani and Hafiz. A little further along stood Shakespeare's Sonnets, and those by Buonarrotti; along with Tennyson's "In Memoriam," Woodberry's "The North-Shore Watch," and Walt Whitman. Back of Platen's bulky "Tagebuch" lay his poems. Next to them came Wilbrandt's "Fridolins Heimliche Ehe," beside Rachilde's "Les Hors-Nature"; then Pernauhm's "Die Infamen," Emil Vacano's "Humbug," and a group of psychologic works by Krafft-Ebing and Ellis and Moll. There was a thin book in which were bound together, in a richly decorated arabesque cover, some six or seven stories from Mardrus' French translation of "The Thousand Nights And A Night"—remorsely separated from their original companions. On a lower shelf, rested David Christie Murray's "Val Strange" and one or two other old novels; along with Dickens' "David Copperfield," the anonymous "Tim," and Vachell's "The Hill," companioned by Mayne's "Intersexes," "Imre" and "Sebastian au Plus Bel Age."[2]

This global library of books standing alongside each other, socializing together, enables the protagonist of a once-lost American short story, the old man Dayneford, to see in them the accretion of his queer life, broken down into often contradictory pieces, with only a provisional coherence, across time, space, and book gutters. The *bookworlds* on these shelves, whose genres vary even as they somehow add up to a single life in fiction, offers us a spatially organized, mosaic view of a character's inner life—a map, essential to the transition from an externally defined to an internalized narrative of sexual subjectivity itself. What Prime-Stevenson both exemplifies and describes is not just the representation of queer life *in* literature, but the ways in which the traffic in literature participates in the generation of sexual types. "Companioned from youth up" by this library, Dayneford understands his self-composition through it: as a protagonist, his "making-up" is an effect of literary circulation. In a single-sentence-spanning library, books themselves come together (and stay apart) as if they were the members of a subculture:[3] an extrasubjective world that makes the subject imaginable to himself and available—that is narratable—to us.

I argue in this book that one way of understanding what is literary about queer history is to track the force of literary objects and representations as accumulated, interactive, side-by-side engagements
of texts with other texts that make it possible to conceive of queer
subjectivity itself as a simple abstraction: the "type" that Dayneford imagines literature has made him. But rather than take as my
object of study the figure of the subject of sexuality as a matter of
textual representation, I examine instead the textual conditions of
its possibility. In other words, I'm interested in what we learn about
the form that subjectivity takes when we track it through the making of protagonists at the heart of literary worlds. To that end, I look
backward from the emergence of what I take to be the largest-scale
literary world to figure such protagonists—the novel—to investigate
the rhetorics and textual accumulations that make these characters
and their worlds possible. These protagonists who now appear to us
as queer, lesbian, gay, or bisexual often first emerged in print as New
England spinsters, Uranians, similisexualists, South Sea Islanders,
inverts, or chums—many of whom are defined not by their inner
sympathies at all but by their locations. So it is, then, that I turn to
tracking the mise-en-scènes of homosexuality—within and beyond
books—that give life to the queer novel. My point is not to trace a
clean line of ascent. Nor is it even to choose sides in debates about
the resonances and discontinuities in the before-and-after portraits
of sexuality's crystallization as identity. Rather, it is to consider the
unpredictable force of circulation that knits and unravels both types
and genres of world-making, both of which present themselves to us
at once as inevitable and unpredictable, familiar and yet unreadable
in the face of modern sexuality's status as a property of the self.

Most of the books in Dayneford's library, after all, may never
have been intended as works of queer literature as such. But through
performative acts of reading and collection, these books on the
shelves frame and reframe each other, possessing an agency of their
own. Collecting texts makes selves and worlds. Prime-Stevenson's
description of the books on Dayneford's shelves as a historical model
of queer "making-up" has fascinated modern-day anthologists of
the history of gay fiction. Mark Mitchell and David Leavitt's *Pages
Passed from Hand to Hand: The Hidden Tradition of Homosexual*

Literature in English from 1748 to 1914 and James Gifford's *Glances Backward: An Anthology of American Homosexual Writing, 1830–1920* both open with Dayneford's Books.[4] Gifford's monograph on American homosexual writing, which seeks to parse types of literary homosexuality, is even titled *Dayneford's Library*.[5] For these editors and writers, the passage exemplifies something fundamentally reflective of the history of gay writing.

The je ne sais quoi that mobilizes the unruly and productive circulation of books stands no less as an active force for writing by and about queer women, whose literature by the turn of the century also began to index the queer conditions of its own development—even if that writing has not supplied us with quite as nice a commentary on its own origins as Prime-Stevenson offers us. Natalie Barney, the maven of Paris's expatriate lesbian salon culture, declared: "To misquote is the very foundation of original style. The success of most writers is almost entirely due to continuous and courageous abuse of familiar misquotation."[6] "Familiar misquotation"—a conscious, if slanted, repackaging of intertextuality—is for Barney essential to the emergence of the literary style she cared about, a mode of textual engagement underwritten by circulation and fostered under conditions of lesbian literary sociability, where, as several scholars have pointed out, books serve as sites of alternative reproduction.[7] Whereas Prime-Stevenson attributes a peculiar sort of willfulness to books themselves in circulation, Barney locates that willfulness in stylistic displacement and biting wit. In a similar vein, Louie Crew and Rictor Norton describe the historical scene of homosexual writing as follows:

> One can write and then eschew publication, as did E. M. Forster with *Maurice*. One can arrange for private printings, as did many of the writers from 1890 to 1920. One can reverse the pronouns prior to publication, . . . call one's lover Narcissus and transform oneself into a simply country swain, . . . leave pointers via Greek mythology, . . . talk about aesthetics and spiritual friendship, . . . tell a tale of woe and kill off a major character in the last chapter, thereby providing evidence of redeeming social value. One can do just about everything—except utter the truth.[8]

Following Crew, Norton, Roger Austen, and others, we have tended to read these formal decisions as sites of closeted writing that somehow withhold the truth.[9] Even if that were true (which would mean accepting as axiomatic a modern reading practice that laminates a current worldview onto a historical one only to find it lacking), what remains undeniable is that the literary road to queer truth-telling is a matter of stylistic detours, private printings, mythological mediations, eschewals, pronoun play, and aesthetic way stations. At stake here is what Kevin Ohi and Jordan Stein later describe as the queerness of style[10]—where style, as Stein puts it, allows us to access a history of sexuality that "fail[s] to be represented at the manifest levels of discourse," even for texts that strike readers today as "so gay."[11] For today's readers, style may seem to lack the manifest content we expect of it, but only if we are confident that truth, figured as an interior self, is already there to begin with. Otherwise the flourishes of style also should be read as a history of making selves and sentences, sympathies and worlds that have not yet existed as such.

The history I have in mind thus includes but also exceeds the sentence-level analysis of style to account for the traces and sedimentations of a book history approach to sexuality. The sociability that Prime-Stevenson identifies in Dayneford's library comes to be literalized, for instance, in the pages of anthologies. (Almost all the books he lists here appear in Edward Carpenter's 1902 anthology *Ioläus: An Anthology of Friendship*, a collection of texts very much like Prime-Stevenson's own 1908 anthology *The Intersexes*.)[12] Barney hosts a similar scene of literary sociability in her Paris salons. These authors gesture here to a mode of understanding queer literary production that has been obscured by the vocabulary of homosexuality's emergence at the end of the nineteenth century and, later, by scandals around Oscar Wilde's *The Picture of Dorian Gray*. While Barney gestures to a text's sentence-level distorted archive of its own precursors, Prime-Stevenson describes a queer sociology of texts wherein books exert an influence on each other, an exertion akin to subjectivity that exceeds the agency of both authors and readers. These sentence-level and extratextual circulations are central to the queer literary worlds that come to life in the pages of American fiction by the turn of the century.

In a sense this study constitutes a material manifestation of the Foucauldianism that has long underwritten queer theory's entrenchment in literary criticism. The simple abstraction of homosexuality (as well as the category of the "gay novel" that eventually emerged) disguises the complex literary routes and paths that made the abstraction visible as such—paradoxically, as a mode of interiority or a property of the self, whose process of emergence renders opaque the social life of its seemingly inevitable march to emergence. In Michel Foucault's famous pronouncement, "The nineteenth-century homosexual became a personage, a past, a case history, and a childhood, in addition to being a type of life, a life form, and a morphology."[13] What we understand less well are the discrete ways that language comes to make this story. Foucault argues that "there was a steady proliferation of discourses concerned with sex—specific discourses, different from one another both by their form and by their object: a discursive ferment that gathered momentum from the eighteenth century onward." And he points us in particular to "the multiplication of discourses concerning sex in the field of exercise of power itself: an institutional incitement to speak about it, and to do so more and more; a determination on the part of the agencies of power to hear it spoken about, and to cause *it* to speak through explicit articulation and endlessly accumulated detail."[14] Institutions and "agencies of power" incite the multiplication of sexual discourses, but they also act as the primary audience for them. What might it mean if this incitement to speak about sex and to accumulate details about the forms of intimacy it generates also produces new audiences for these new sexual "personages" and "life forms"?

"Proliferation," "gathered momentum," "multiplication of discourses," and "accumulated detail": these features of linguistic "ferment" all evoke questions of scale that have long been implicit but undertheorized in our attention to the history of sexuality. As David Halperin notes, "The history of sexuality, as Foucault conceived it, . . . is not a history of the representations, categories, cultural articulations, or collective and individual expressions of some determinate entity called sexuality but an inquiry into the historical emergence of sexuality itself."[15] This question of scale poses a problem at the level of evidence for the literary critic schooled in the art of textual close reading of putative minor literary texts. Queer theorists embraced this challenge, in part, through the universalizing approach advocated by Eve Kosofsky Sedgwick in her landmark work *Epistemology of the Closet*.[16] Rather than track queer life as a minoritized phenomenon, critics following Sedgwick sought to understand the centrality of the spectrum of homosocial relations and desire to the social more generally. We positioned ourselves to notice the social asymmetries generated in the name of what Michael Warner termed *heteronormativity*.[17] One conscious effect of this approach was to shift the terrain of inquiry that had been defined by gay and lesbian studies as well as by some branches of second-wave feminism to open up questions about the material and discursive status of queer life. Another, at least within the field of literary study, was to shift focus back to literary history writ large to ask not after gay or lesbian characters or authors but to queer the very ways we read texts. How to navigate the historical flux and status of identity categories themselves became (and arguably remains) a significant site of scholarly preoccupation.[18] Debates about whether presexological texts anticipate modern sexuality or stand in contrast to it, however, overlook perhaps how the debate itself is a symptom of the ways all taxonomies knit and unravel themselves in the face of their circulation. Consider the bitterly ironic fate of the term *queer,* a concept built precisely as an anti-identitarian category that now circulates both as its own identity category and, in some circles, as a derisive signifier of queer theory's own limits. These debates within the field of queer scholarship in a sense revolve around the question of which queers literature and theory invoke. Whose worlds and worldviews find themselves outside the circuits of queer theory? Whose literary circuits become central and how? What, in short, counts as a world at all when it comes to the "ferment" of discourse? Who gets to stand as the example for the universalization of queer life?[19]

The question of scale has emerged as an explicitly salient one for literary criticism more generally over the past decade: through proposed expansions of reading methods (Franco Moretti's "distant reading," Stephen Best and Sharon Marcus's "surface reading," and Heather Love's focus on "description"); through the work of the digital humanities and its large-scale data models; through returns to the limits and possibilities of "world literature"; and through attention to sociological networks. These approaches are only beginning to circulate within the field of queer literary studies. The reading methods of queer theory come up twice, for instance, in Best and Marcus's introduction to their special issue on "surface reading": first as the example par excellence of symptomatic reading ("a queer symptomatic reading might interpret the closet, or ghosts, as surface signs of the deep truth of a homosexuality that cannot be overtly depicted") and later as an example of surface reading itself (Sedgwick's "reparative reading" stands as an example of "receptiveness and fidelity to the text's surface").[20] But we have no "graphs, maps, or trees" of queer literary history (Moretti), no "sociology of [literature's] associations" (Bruno Latour).[21]

In her turn to description and the history of sociological analysis, Heather Love comes closest to articulating such methodologies for queer literary analysis by way of an engagement with deviance studies and description in queer texts. She even goes so far as to characterize Lauren Berlant's scholarly oeuvre as one defined by investments in scale-oscillation, though Berlant doesn't use quite this language. In *Cruel Optimism,* what Berlant identifies as her method is "to track the becoming general of singular things": "the singular becomes delaminated from its location in someone's story or some locale's irreducibly local history and circulated as evidence of something shared," and she seeks "to give those things materiality by tracking their resonances across many scenes."[22] In my own approach to the queer novel, I share both Love's interest in description as a methodology of reading and Berlant's attention to "resonances" of phenomena "across many scenes." In this way both Love's and Berlant's work—and indeed a great deal of the work of queer studies—can be seen to shuttle back and forth between large-scale explanations of phenomena and attention to small-scale examples of those phenomena.

My approach to circulation in, and of, the queer novel thus takes its inspiration from these scholarly approaches (replete with multiple taxonomies for categorizing it) less as an outcome than as a large-scale historical laboratory that allows me to track the many vectors of literary circulation that facilitate its emergence.

Circulation counterposes itself with the concept of direct transmission (as well as its refusals or failures).[23] As a genre that narrates a literary world and has a history of ingesting other genres and sites of discourse, the novel seems perfectly suited to reading the accumulations and condensations of queer history that go into its making. Two large case studies of the circuits that lead to arguably queer novels, each of which tracks a long literary web, constitute the heart of this book. One of these webs tracks encounters between American travelers and the inhabitants of South Sea Islands as a scene for the narration of same-sex and nonmonogamous eroticism. This web includes texts by Herman Melville, Charles Warren Stoddard, Bayard Taylor, and Walt Whitman, as well as missionary writings on the South Seas. The other tracks the figure of the New England spinster and includes texts by Catharine Maria Sedgwick, Rose Terry Cooke, Sarah Orne Jewett, Edith Wharton, and Henry James.

The "worlding" of sexuality—through networks of association, the collecting of texts, the scope of narrative worlds, and the shifting terrains of place and race types that the above texts exemplify—galvanizes a view of queer literature that is explicitly American (if we tie affiliation to the authors' citizenship) while also showcasing the multiform debts these writers display to other locations and literary traditions. Dayneford's library, despite its status as the collection of an American writer, is not, after all, the exclusive domain of American letters. This contradiction alerts us to the unboundedness of American literature of this period, focalized through the conceit of a national literature while also fully registering the American fantasy of that unboundedness. This paradox points in turn to another problem of scale and world-making that attends both the literary history of sexuality and the scholarship that undertakes it: both have come to be organized not so much by American literature per se but from the vantage points of American academic circuits. American scholars of world literature including Emily Apter, Wai Chee Dimock, David Damrosch, and Gayatri Chakravorty Spivak have taken aim at the "world" of world literatures, pointing to its entanglements with market economics, its impossible politics of translation, and planetary devolution.[24] The "worlding" of literature, in short, comes up quickly against its limits, which again are a matter of scale. World-making is a concept dear to queer theorists, myself included, who are indebted to and moved by what Michael Warner calls the "world-making project of queer life," with consequences for the present moment that he describes as follows:

> Because gay social life is not as ritualized and institutionalized as straight life, each relation is an adventure in nearly uncharted territory. . . . There are almost as many kinds of relationship as there are people in combination. Where there are patterns, we learn them from other queers, not from our parents or schools or the state. Between tricks and lovers and exes and friends and fuckbuddies and bar friends and bar friends' tricks and tricks' bar friends and gal pals and companions "in the life," queers have an astonishing range of intimacies. Most have no labels. Most receive no public recognition. Many of these relations are difficult because the rules have to be invented as we go along. Often desire and unease add to their intensity, and their unpredictability.[25]

Warner flags the continued proliferation of categories, the persistence of "uncharted territory" as a metaphor for sexual adventure, and the simultaneous locality and widespread applicability of the processes by which worlds are made and complicated. The unnamed bar friend could be in any bar; the tricks, under global capitalism, could be almost anywhere. World-making is itself a powerful, multi-tentacled beast of a fantasy in its execution. Its optimistic force also circulates beyond itself and in so doing asks us to consider its limitations. In attending to another era's experiments in proliferation and invention, to its deployments, tricks, and complications of labels, and to its fictions, I hope to hold on to the productive force of world-making and to recognize the ineluctable appeal of taxonomies while recognizing, as well, their discontents.

INTRODUCTION
Circuits, Lies, and the Queer Novel in America

Tell all the Truth but tell it slant—
Success in Circuit lies

Emily Dickinson

ROGER AUSTEN'S *Playing the Game: The Homosexual Novel in America* (1977) remains the only account of the history of the homosexual novel in America to date, a book that aims to "offer a corrective to the past decades of shabby treatment that much gay fiction has received" and to "reacquaint" gay readers "with many of the older, less well known novels."[1] At a time when secrecy was the byword of queer life, the name of the "game" that Austen saw being played around American fiction about homosexuality was homophobia. Taking his epigraph from Emily Dickinson, the same quoted above, Austen's focus was on the capital-T "Truth." Not only were critics averse to writing about gay fiction, but the historical conditions themselves had not been fit even for generating it: "The main reason for the dearth of explicitly gay novels in America from the nineteenth century up to 1920 is that sexual perversion was regarded as hardly a fit subject for fiction." To catch the literary study of homosexuality up to the "many studies [that] have been written about the special contributions made to our national literature by the more respectable minorities" means to counter homophobia, which "has been played with appalling success on all sides."[2] Austen took it as his mission to do for the gay male novel in America what he believed Jeannette Foster's capacious account *Sex Variant Women in Literature* (1956) had done for the lesbian novel: "cover" its history in documentary fashion.[3]

Almost half a century later, it seems hard to appreciate the terms of Austen's intervention as anything but ancient history. The rise of queer theory and the expansive scholarship on queer fiction it has produced in recent decades make it hard to remember a time before MLA-goers in dapper-colored jackets graced the front page of the *New York Times,* and Eve Kosofsky Sedgwick was crowned "the soft-spoken queen of gay studies" by *Rolling Stone* magazine.[4] But the Dickinson epigraph foregrounds something more about Austen's approach that percolates almost imperceptibly throughout his archive and recalls us anew to the gay and lesbian studies recovery projects that queer theory largely left behind. This approach highlights a different keyword from those Dickinson lines, *circuit.* Others, writing at the same time as Austen, with his same investments in shedding light on the "truth" of homosexuality in fiction, focused on the "slant" style of truth, though its slant is as much a matter of circulation as it is of style. Writing itself, in this account, is both a scene of displacement and the effect of creative literary recirculations and refused circulations. As Austen saw it, the truth of sexuality may have been withheld, but the matter of literary history consisted in the circuit itself. Writers shared texts with approving nods and winks, developed knowing vocabularies, and carefully curated their own archives of relevant texts. In Austen's still commonplace understanding, the homosexual novel came into view just after the concept of homosexuality itself. But this emergent literary subgenre metabolizes a much longer literary tradition obscured by our commonplace understanding of identitarian sexuality. Success in *circuit* lies, even if it refuses the kind of truth Austen sought to proclaim. At play in these circuits, sexuality becomes a scene of condensation, of withholding, and of anthological consolidation.

But success of circuits also *lies*: our fantasy of networks continues to be one of endless connectivity and proliferation. But networks exclude just as they cluster. One circuit overwrites or re-places another. The residues of earlier histories persist less as sites of secrecy than as the signs of forgotten or discarded worlds. Vestigial vocabularies are left behind or exposed as quaint anachronisms. Analyzing circuits is not so much about recovering and re-creating the moments in which one worldview seemed to give way to the other as it is being attentive to the residues of what is, in the process, being left behind. In one sense this book looks back to the minoritized logic that queer theory, beginning with Eve Sedgwick, hoped to leave behind in its attention to a universalizing logic whereby queer life subtends the social *tout court*.

In returning to the history of what Austen called "the homosexual novel in America," I am offering in this book a rejoinder both to Austen's work and its successors, elaborating on the methodology of circulation, accumulation, and condensation implicit in his archival approach but never fully characterized as a methodology for understanding the history of queer fiction. I argue that queer texts entextualize their own history, framing and reframing other queer texts in their circulation, curation, and consumption by reading publics. In this sense, my approach to the history of the queer novel begins where Austen's epigraph ends—with a focus on literary circuits—so that I might then end where Austen's study began: at the point of the gay and lesbian novel's American emergence, at the end of the nineteenth century.

Austen and others since him have tended to think of this history in terms of "firsts": one version of the story claims that the first gay novel was Bayard Taylor's *Joseph and His Friend: A Story of Pennsylvania* (1870); a recent paperback reprinting gives the honor to Charles Warren Stoddard's *For the Pleasure of His Company: An Affair of the Misty City* (1906); another account points to Edward Prime-Stevenson's *Imre: A Memorandum* (printed privately in Naples in 1906, but written several years earlier). Alongside these, Henry James's *The Bostonians* (1885–86) tends to be the agreed-on point of origin for the lesbian novel in America. All of these narratives read forward from such putative inaugural moments in the genre. Although queer theory has sought to interrupt such normalizing narratives of taxonomy and identitarian history, no study of the history of the queer novel in America has been undertaken since Austen's. Rather than take the homosexual novel as a category of literature whose life span is to be traced in the wake of its emergence, I examine the conditions of literary circulation that gave it life to begin with.

Despite all the scholarly work that has complicated our origin stories about queer literature, it can somehow still seem that once homosexuality had been recognized as such, novels were written about it shortly thereafter, and the genre has never looked back. Today, despite the decline of the queer bookstores that once served as distribution hubs, arbiters of taste and market categories, and community gathering sites, the very literary categories these locations helped popularize persist. Annual events, such as the Lambda Literary Awards for gay, lesbian, bisexual, and transgender fiction,[5] have become gala affairs; libraries have dedicated specialists for queer literature; and universities regularly feature courses on queer writing and/or the LGBT novel. But even within this seemingly dedicated march to the novel's centrality in queer writing (as well as much queer scholarship), this broad history conceals marked shifts in the terms of self-identification, social belonging, and the narration of queer history as an effect of literary and social circulation. Once taken for granted, such terms as *invert, Uranian, romantic friendship,* and *Boston marriage* persist today mostly as quaint anachronisms. Meanwhile, new terms, like *transgender* and *genderqueer,* have emerged alongside relatively more established terms like *gay* and *lesbian,* in large part because *gay* and *lesbian* have reached certain limits. Queer theory emerged precisely in tension with the seeming coherence with which such terms announced themselves, offering trenchant critiques of the ways the circulation of *gay* and *lesbian* undermines such coherence.[6] In its wake, the *queer* of queer theory has come to circulate against its own aims: as a cooler term of identity. Having become almost synonymous with its homosexual precursors, *queer* has in turn come under fire from transgender theorists and queers of color who see in the term a too-easy synonym for white gay men. Queer theory finds its academic self both reaching a point of saturation and generating intense debates among its most important thinkers. Seen in this way, we might think of queer theory not just as a set of concepts, a political orientation, and a mode of reading, but as an isolated historical interval in the still-unfolding field of sexuality studies. The force of this unfolding might well be characteristic of a long history of sexual type complication wherein terms emerge, proliferate, reach the limit of their purchase, come under fire, and stand simultaneously as sites of fierce attachment, exclusion, and ambivalence.

Literary texts have long found themselves central to the historical formulation, understanding, and transformations of modes of sexuality. They are considered archives of social usage as well as avatars of queer futures to come and laboratories of linguistic experimentation. Perhaps for this reason, Christopher Looby has gone so far as to argue that "sexuality is essentially a literary phenomenon" and that "its history must perforce be a literary history."⁷ Looby is inspired in part by Ian Hacking's concept of "dynamic nominalism," whereby "people spontaneously come to fit their categories." "The claim of dynamic nominalism," Hacking insists, "is not that there was a kind of person who came increasingly to be recognized by bureaucrats or by students of human nature, but rather that a kind of person came into being at the same time as the kind itself was being invented. In some cases, that is, our classifications and our classes conspire to emerge hand in hand, each egging the other on."⁸ Literary categories of sexuality don't just follow the sexological or scientific inventions of those categories: they are co-constitutive. Similarly, we might observe that the history of queer literary criticism can be tracked through successive readings of key texts, like Radclyffe Hall's *The Well of Loneliness*, Oscar Wilde's *The Picture of Dorian Gray*, or even Henry James's *The Turn of the Screw*. But what neither Hacking nor Looby accounts for is the force of the dynamism in nominalism itself, which highlights the performative character of literary circulation, as literary texts participate in producing the frames of reading reference that we use to interpret them.

If we take a longer view of the matter, however—by positioning the late nineteenth-century-emergent gay and lesbian novel alongside its literary precursors from, say, a hundred years earlier— we begin to see that it's not just nominalism that has been dynamic. The very object of our reading has not even always existed as such.

We are confronted with generic change, particularly with respect to scale and temporality, within that literary history of sexuality. When the novel itself was emerging and developing as a genre through the eighteenth century, it was sparsely populated by minor characters or fleeting episodes of desire expressed between members of the same sex, whom scholars, from our vantage point today, have begun to recognize as prototypes of modern queer characters.[9] The force of minor characters and their relationship to larger textual worlds remains underdiscussed within literary theory. In his study of the phenomenon of the minor character, Alex Woloch refers to characterization more generally as the "bête noir of narratology." He makes the case for its significance through attention less to protagonists than to what he calls "*character space* (that particular and charged encounter between an individual human personality and a determined space and position within the narrative) and *character system* (the arrangement of multiple and differentiated configurations and manipulations of the human figure—into a unified narrative structure)."[10] I take seriously in this book the concept of "character space" as a key means of understanding the terms on which minor queer characters were understood in their historical moment, while also extending the idea of that space beyond the pages of the book to track the recursive evolutionary process by which circulation over time helps minor characters develop into types of protagonists—where, ironically enough, they begin as flat types and evolve into central characters with complex interiorities.

The further back in literary history we look, the less consciously coherent same-sex sexuality and gender nonconformity (each of which tends to overlap with the other) appear to modern eyes. Less consciously coherent, that is, if what we are looking for is the language of sexual identity that takes hold by the end of the nineteenth century. This seeming incoherence has its own formal features and its own historical logic, whose specificity scholars have documented quite well. We can see the episodic quality of same-sex encounters, the colorful presence of secondary characters, and the unnamed homoerotic intensities in the context of the rise of the novel in the English literary tradition across a range of texts: Delarivier Manley's "new Cabal" of women in *The New Atalantis*;

Mary Wollstonecraft's treatment of female friendship in *Mary, A Fiction*; Tobias Smollett's Captain Whiffle and the Earl of Strutwell; shorter fictional pieces like Henry Fielding's *The Female Husband* and Daniel Defoe's "The Apparition of Mrs. Veal"; the anonymously written *Love Letters between a Certain Late Nobleman and the Famous Mr. Wilson*. While recognizing the historical significance of such texts, queer theoretical approaches to them tend not to linger either on their episodic quality or their minor characters' status as minor. In a study of the centrality of the episode to early American literature, Matthew Garrett calls for a consideration of "the way literary-critical interest in plot has built upon episodic form even as it has displaced attention from the conceptualization of the episode itself."[11] Such a call is relevant as well for any form-sensitive account of the literary history of sexuality.

Same-sex characters tend to be minor characters in longer works or central characters only in shorter works, and in both cases their adventures are short in duration, their characters potentially complex but thinly realized. By the end of the nineteenth century, these minor characters had evolved into protagonists and their episodic encounters had either multiplied or developed into novel-length narratives with the texture of entire worlds. The sodomite had not only become a species (in Michel Foucault's famous pronouncement); he now had an entire narrative world as his backdrop. This evolution is at once sociological and stylistic, an unfolding by fits and starts not just of queer protagonists but of complete narrative worlds in which those protagonists make sense. It is this process of development that this book takes as its focus.

Central to understanding this process is an understanding of the role literary circulation plays in generating the detailed narrative worlds that novels require and an insistence that literature itself (and not just the categories into which literature is divided) participates in producing—and transforming—the terms by which it comes to be understood. Mark Mitchell and David Leavitt insist that "today the study of pre-1914 homosexual literature is still a matter of pages passed from hand to hand."[12] But what grounds this assertion at the level of form and within historical literary practice? By the beginning of the twentieth century, creative recirculation and literary accumulation had come to be recognized as central to queer literary life. Indeed, one might argue that not just rereading but recirculation—the reading, collection, disordering, and reordering of books—persists as the very lifeblood of queer theory's engagements with literature today.

While the forms of literary circulation that writers like Natalie Barney and Edward Prime-Stevenson highlight are significant for queer literary production generally, as I discussed in the prologue, they have particular significance for thinking about the queer novel as a laboratory to consider the history and scale of queer worldmaking. In a crude sense, novels are accumulations of words: episodes, characters unfolding over time, narrated in prose style. Even configurations of late nineteenth-century homosexuality as "unspeakable" or as "the love that dare not speak its name"[13] rely on such accumulations to make visible the textual gaps and slippages that scholars have argued amount to a late nineteenth-century idiom of sexuality.[14] Novels require these words so that they can showcase change in their characters over time and situate those characters in described environments that often include other characters. Novels, to borrow a phrase from Andrew Marvell, require "world enough and time" so that they can elaborate precisely what his poem could not: the conditions under which a particular manner of sociosexual relationship might flourish and reach a fuller articulation than the spare condensation of poetic lines seemed to offer him.[15] To the degree that a gay and lesbian novel requires not just a character, a subplot, or an episode but a protagonist, we can recognize that accounting for the development of this novel exceeds an account of the emergence of homosexual subjectivity. A protagonist requires a fully realized social world in prose—a world in which that protagonist makes sense, a world in which her movement and change unfold across time and in social space. A protagonist thus requires not just an understanding of complex psychology or subject formation (otherwise the protagonist might be indistinguishable from the speaker of a lyric poem) but an understanding of the novel's accounting of change and movement as the kind of world-making project I described in the prologue.

Frequently, that world also requires detailed narration and

description of setting from a perspective beyond that of the protagonist. Although there may always be examples from other genres that press on the novel's generic limits[16] (for example, the detailed world-making of Walt Whitman's prosaic poetry or the lyricism of epistolary novels), the ways that words are literally organized on the page—the novel's organization as a book object—as well as what Ian Watt long ago called its "formal realism" contribute to our recognition in the everyday language world of the novel's dimensions.[17] That the novel has a history of finding itself at the limits of other genres is one of its distinguishing features. Literary and social circulation collectively create the conditions under which the novel continues to reinvent itself, often in terms that enable us to see new novel categories. A focus on literary circulation also allows us to see the extent to which the production of what now seems so clearly to be queer literary consciousness in American literature may have been an effect of literary cultural practices—patterns of style and representation as well as habits of collecting and reading—without actually being the goal of any particular authors or writerly subculture.

In that sense, I read the queer traffic in American literature as an effect of rogue circulation: the circulation made visible when a text or artifact moves through the world in unpredictable or unexpected ways. Rogue circulation is at once a textually material instantiation of what Judith Butler framed as the relationship between imitation and gender insubordination (an effect of disruptions in the circuit) and a way of understanding those disruptions as positioned firmly within the cultural conventions that frame some things as roguish, in the ways that Jacques Derrida has described.[18] Circulation assumes the repeated exposure of texts to various audiences across time and space, as well as the possibility that those texts may themselves be replicated to maximize that exposure. As Butler argues, such repetitions, even when they assume replication or imitation, create the possibility for rupture or difference.[19] The "rogue" as Derrida imagines it, however, marks something clandestine within view of norms of law. Adapting Derrida's concept of the "rogue" (*voyou*) to consider rogue circulation forces us to consider not only the status of the rogue vis-à-vis structures of law but the status of circulation vis-à-vis the literary public sphere. Michael Warner has argued that writing that circulates in public, addressed implicitly therefore to strangers, "cannot go astray."[20] And yet it can certainly seem to. Writing's unconventional circulations are an effect of larger literary, cultural, and historical norms, even if its movement through the world does not necessarily confirm those norms. Textual circulation is thus paradoxical insofar as it facilitates the queer circulations and accumulations of literature that are key to the writing (and reading) of novels we may now call "queer" by the end of the nineteenth century in America, but those novels also carry with them residues of earlier type vocabularies and worldviews that fail to align fully with our modern sense of sexuality as such.

A circulation approach to understanding the literary cultures of sexuality that make way for the queer novel allows us to interrupt the still prevailing teleological approach to identitarian forms of sexuality and the literary genres defined by them. Circulation is at once generative and regressive, forward-oriented and backward-looking, progressive and conservative. Theorists of circulation including Warner as well as Benjamin Lee and Edward LiPuma, and Elizabeth Povinelli and Dilip Gaonkar, have pressed the materialist stakes of cultural circulation in terms of circulation's productivity. Lee and LiPuma speak, therefore, of "cultures of circulation": "Circulation is a cultural process with its own forms of abstraction, evaluation, and constraint, which are created by the interactions between specific types of circulating forms and the interpretive communities built around them." What they term "structured circulations" allow for an understanding of the forms of collective agency that emerge from within a "new stage in the history of capitalism."[21] Thanks to Marx, circulation finds itself interlaced with capitalism (even if capitalism and circulation don't resolve into each other). In the first volume of *Capital,* Marx keenly observed the overlap between the two: "Capital cannot . . . arise from circulation, and it is equally impossible for it to arise apart from circulation. It must have its origin both in circulation and not in circulation."[22] However productive and generative circulation may prove to be, any heroic tale of circulation must be tempered by the rather obvious fact that rogue circulations are no less positioned within capitalist and cultural norms than more conventional mass circulations, particularly in nineteenth-century America.

Scholars of nineteenth-century American literature and culture have long been engaged with circulation as a contradictory force for making (and unmaking) social worlds and collectives.[23] Although this work has not typically been the domain of queer literary critics, it highlights the importance of circulation for understanding the literary, economic, and cultural history of the period. With the field-defining work of Roger Chartier and Robert Darnton, "circulation" has been the byword of book history. Darnton's well-known "communications circuit" foregrounds the history of the book as a matter of circulation per se.[24] Chartier's focus on "the order of books" meanwhile emphasizes the dialectical relationship between reading and printing: while books aim to install order, communities of readers constitute sites of encounter between a text and its reception; "reception invents, shifts about, distorts."[25] Historians of the book have engaged in spirited debate over these concepts, complicating both Darnton's model and Chartier's dialectic.[26] Work on the history of the book in America has focused especially on the force of readers and on reading contexts that exceed institutional parameters. The five-volume compendium *A History of the Book in America* includes discussions of women's book clubs, libraries, benevolent societies, and readers of writings in German.[27] But to my knowledge, there has been no study of what we might call queer book history—only piecemeal attention to aspects of that history through the treatment of canonical writers, through attention to Comstock laws that curtailed circulation of obscene materials in the post, and in the scant records of private collections. Not merely a matter of small-scale community sharing of texts, but of secret book collecting and accumulation alongside the reading and publishing within the mass circuits of literary magazines and newspapers; not merely interpretive communities that changed the meaning of shared texts (or texts that were also read by other reading communities), these collectors, quoters, and collators of books—as well as poems, type keywords, excerpts of books, cutouts from serial publications, mise-en-scènes, and snippets of reviews—distorted the order of books as if they operated as one large-scale scrapbook or commonplace book. Dayneford's library, Charles Warren Stoddard's scrapbooks and story collections, old maids from across genres, intertextual references to earlier print examples—all served as sites where the queer life of print was nested and digested.[28]

This order and disorder that constitute the queer life of print cannot be disarticulated from the matter of political economy. Mark Simpson has tracked the contradictions attending social mobility in the American nineteenth century in his study *Trafficking Subjects*. In his words, "the politics of mobility" are the "contestatory processes that produce different forms of movement," forms invested not just with "social value" or "cultural purchase" but also with "discriminatory power."[29] In light of the ways nineteenth-century America was marked by the emergence of new forms of social circulation, new technologies of human movement, and an increase in domestic literary production—as well as prohibitions governing all these things—the "contestatory processes" central to circulation find themselves also at the heart of a growing body of literary criticism. But this body of scholarship has not yet attended to the paradoxical productivity of circulation for an analysis of the century's emergent queer categories of literature.

The case studies at the heart of this book have all been understood to contribute to, anticipate, and in some cases inaugurate the literary subgenre of the gay and lesbian novel, even as they carry with them the residues of earlier formal, social, and literary norms: Herman Melville's *Typee*; Charles Warren Stoddard's *South-Sea Idyls* and *For the Pleasure of His Company: An Affair of the Misty City*; Henry James's *The Bostonians*; texts about the old maid in New England: Catharine Maria Sedgwick's "Old Maids," Mary E. Wilkins Freeman's "A New England Nun," and Sarah Orne Jewett's "Martha's Lady"; Gertrude Stein's *Q.E.D.*; and Henry Blake Fuller's *Bertram Cope's Year*. One of the most striking things about this group of texts is, first of all, their authors' sense of their centrality to American literature more generally. In imagining the conditions of their own circulation and distribution, none of these authors aspired to write minor literature. Nor did they consciously address themselves to coterie reading publics—even if some, especially Stoddard, emerged out of such coteries, and some have since been read primarily among members of sexual subcultures or other limited reading publics. James, for example, famously described *The Bostonians* as "a very *American* tale, a tale very characteristic of our social conditions";[30] Melville calculated *Typee* "for popular reading, or none at all."[31] Both are also heavily indebted to the fantasies and materialities of primitivism and race in America: James to those of post–Civil War America, Melville to those of American economic expansion in the Polynesian Islands. Yet all of the texts in this study have since come to be seen in terms of minor literatures as their circulation has evolved.

Not only did this very diverse group of authors *not* anticipate how they might circulate under the aegis of queer literature, they actually look backward to other texts and contexts as they acknowledge the literary circuits in which they participate and to which they respond. In other words, they recirculate (and thus reframe) their own reading material in their writing. Stoddard imagines himself in conversation with the poetry of Whitman and the travel narratives of Melville—who himself cites missionary accounts of the South Seas in *Typee* in order to expose the missionaries' shortcomings (an exposure he later edits out in an American edition of the book). Meanwhile, Catharine Maria Sedgwick can invoke what she sees as literary history's overwhelmingly thin treatment of the old maid and compare it to the richer detail her characters observe around them; and James aspires to write description in a manner consistent with Alphonse Daudet's "pictorial quality." In doing so, all of these writers develop various modes of metacommentary on the cultures of literary circulation they frequent whereby they acknowledge the very parts of other texts that help them to construct their own literary projects. At the same time (and thirdly), this body of texts invokes a culture of social circulation in which these acts and forms of literary circulation make sense. Each text highlights typologies and ideologies of location that resonate with our modern understandings of sexuality without being fully consonant with them. Consider the very titles of the following texts: *The Bostonians, Typee,* "A New England Nun," *The Country of the Pointed Firs, For the Pleasure of His Company: An Affair of the Misty City.* By defining characters in terms of place rather than interior identity, these texts focus on sexuality as a mode of located sociability, not as a property of the self. At a time in American literature when writers were highly concerned with literary nationalism and what it meant to be American within a broader climate of English letters, it seems perfectly understandable that these American writers would likewise be concerned with the difference location makes.[32] But articulating what they offer to an understanding of the literary history of sexuality requires rethinking the focus on self-identity, since these texts expand parameters of social type depictions. Place types are not psychological types or identity types in the same way that "gay," "lesbian," "homosexual," or even "queer" suggests; they invite us to see identity as determined from the outside in, not from the inside out. To read these texts in terms of the subsequent emergence of sexuality as a property of the individual is thus to miss the ways in which they actually cannot be fully rationalized in the context of emergent identitarian forms of sexuality. It is to miss, in other words, what is unique about their literary contribution to the history of sexuality and what is specifically sexual about literary circulation at this historical moment more generally.[33]

Still, it is no coincidence that the fictional works I describe here appear at a time when identitarian categories of sexuality are only beginning to coalesce. But it is more useful to suggest that the gay and lesbian novel emerges at the intersection of two different, yet connected, processes of cultural development: sexual type evolution and the emergence of a subgenre for the novel. Examining the emergence of a subgenre defined by homosexuality, however, requires that we attend not just to the depictions of interactions, desires, or identities of characters but to the formal productions of social worlds in which those characters make sense as protagonists. What I am suggesting, then, is that the queer novel is also a world-making project, and that this project is not just the product of newly emergent sexual identity categories. Homosexuality doesn't just come to be named and then have novels written about it, even though the emergence of the very terms *homosexuality* and *inversion* did obviously shift the vocabulary we have for describing the novels in which they appear. It can be recognized in abstract terms only when enough concrete details have accumulated to make the abstraction possible as such. If anything, we might say that rather than the gay and lesbian novel emerging in the wake of the very term *homosexuality*, the detail-accumulating, world-making project of the novel may well have made homosexuality possible as an abstraction— where the naming of the abstraction amounts as much to a moment of discontinuity as it does to one of continuity. Abstractions after all are marked by their skeletal conceptual structure, which evacuates detail while tacitly acknowledging its presence.

The very structure of this abstraction we call *homosexuality* is, we have long known, saturated by the cultural logic of racism. From the careful scholarship of Siobhan Somerville, Sander Gilman, Jaime Hovey, Lisa Duggan, Mark Rifkin, Kobena Mercer and Isaac Julien, and many others, we have come to understand that the very making of homosexuality as an abstraction was, to use Somerville's phrase, "deeply intertwined" with typologies of race.[34] Gilman points out, for instance, that late nineteenth-century textbooks characterized all black female sexuality as deviant and lesbian: "By 1877 it was a commonplace that the Hottentot's anomalous sexual form was similar to other errors in the development of the labia . . . leading to those 'excesses' which are called 'lesbian love.'"[35] Hovey has suggested that by the early twentieth century, "sapphic primitivism celebrates a 'foreign' sexuality as dark, other, earthy, and outside bourgeois codes."[36] (Gertrude Stein, Hovey argues, deploys this primitivism to narrate the white lesbianism of her characters in *Q.E.D.*) Duggan's research connecting the narratives of lesbian love murder to narratives of lynching in the late nineteenth century would suggest that the intersection between race and sexuality was not so much "foreign" but "typical in a particularly 'American' way." This "American way" consolidated itself, as Duggan puts it, over and against an increasing range of racial, class, and gender diversity, "radically condens[ing] such particularities into a mutually constituting network of binary categories of identity."[37] According to Rifkin, this late-century shoring up of straight, middle-class whiteness is the central work of settler colonialism, which has long functioned both to displace and overwrite Indigenous culture in North America.[38] Mercer and Julien's insistence, in 1988, that "the prevailing Western concept of sexuality . . . *already contains racism*" reads now like an understatement.[39]

The archive of texts at the heart of this study affirms the

centrality of the logic of race and racism for emergent long fictions about homosexuality. Melville's and Stoddard's writings about the South Seas subscribe fully to the logic of primitivism and Western fantasies of nonheterosexuality in Indigenous cultures; James's inspiration for his fundamentally American tale *The Bostonians* owes as much to Honoré de Balzac's "Woman with the Golden Eyes" as it does to New England local color writing. Gertrude Stein's "angular spinster" has a "nature of the tropics," and Helena, the "lady" of Sarah Orne Jewett's "Martha's Lady," is exoticized through her Indian accessories and worldly travels. Indeed, arguably the earliest theorist of American queer literature, Edward Prime-Stevenson, in his characterization of what he called "American Philarrhenic Literature," insisted on its racial character:

> The North-American (by such term indicating particularly
> the United States) with his nervosity, his impressionability, his
> complex fusion of bloods and of racial traits, even when of
> directly British stocks, is usually far more "temperamental"
> than the English. He has offered interesting excursions at least
> towards, if not always into, the homosexual library. His novels, verses and essays have pointed out a racial uranianism.[40]

It remains the case, nonetheless, that however central race was to the conceptualization of homosexuality, our earliest archives of queer fiction are the records of white dreamers. The history of queer worldmaking through print by racial minorities in nineteenth-century American literature has yet to be written, even if its representation within African American writing has begun to emerge. In *The Delectable Negro,* Vincent Woodard points out that "no study on black masculinity in the nineteenth century focuses on homoeroticism."[41] Woodard's book goes some length toward uncovering such an archive through a cluster of examples foregrounding cannibalism as a queer mode of expression.[42] By his account, the dearth of historical sources, however, has as much to do with the ways modern vocabularies of sexuality obscure our view of the past. Our current understanding would suggest that not until the Harlem Renaissance do we begin to see a discernible network of queer print production and circulation among racial minorities, and most histories and critics of queer literature tend to identify the earliest examples of the queer novel in African American writing as James Baldwin's *Giovanni's Room* (1956) and Ann Allen Shockley's *Loving Her* (1974). But attending less to the ways historical accounts of sexuality align with or seem to anticipate modern ones and more to the outdated, vestigial, or defunct modes of describing sexuality might yield new archival discoveries as well as new ways of reading known texts.[43] It seems inarguable that the literature studied in this book is underwritten by homophilic racism, where fantasies and ideologies of race as encoded in place types are central to the imagination of sexuality in texts as diverse as *Typee* and *The Bostonians*. The density of historical meaning that attends seemingly innovative texts nonetheless mires them in (and so mobilizes, even vestigially) the regressive ideological frameworks that coexist with them.

Attending to circulation as a way of reading texts positions us not only to examine textual proliferation by way of circulation but also to recognize the ways networks themselves stand as sites of exclusion and even oppression. Not the least of these sites of asymmetrical ideological reinforcements concerns class. After all, those who could print their texts privately (Prime-Stevenson), host literary salons (Stein, Barney), and move freely around the world (James, Melville) did so either because they were comfortably wealthy or could earn money in industries that required travel. Rather than treat circuits as cultural structures per se, then, I see circulation as a methodology: a way of doing materialist genealogy that is as attentive to its own minoritizing effects as it is to the affirmation of dominant cultural mores.

Circulation also helps us chart what may otherwise seem to exist as a chicken–egg paradox at the level of genre, when it comes to understanding the relationship between the complexities of sexual types (including race and place types) and literary categories (the gay and lesbian novel). Utterances, Mikhail Bakhtin has argued, connect the history of society to the history of language, and "not a single new phenomenon (phonetic, lexical, or grammatical) . . . can enter the system of language without having traversed the long and complicated path of generic-stylistic testing and modification."[44] In this sense, the subgenre we now call the gay and lesbian novel is less

an "invention" than a generic reconfiguration where contents previously associated with other speech genres enter the domain of the
novel. In their efforts to create narrative worlds that both consolidate and exceed considerations of the identity, sexual practices, or
desires of individual characters, these authors, like so many American writers, focus quite literally on the place of sexuality. The novels
here appear to anticipate sexuality as we have come to know it,
but they do so by looking backward, not forward, to other texts—
poems, stories, newspapers, and even other novels. When these
books refer to other texts, they sometimes embrace them, sometimes
parody them, and sometimes consciously recognize the shortcomings of type abstractions, and we can see them (and perhaps their
authors as well) pushing up against the very literature with which
they are in conversation. Sometimes, they make no conscious recognition of those precursors at all, allowing their form itself to archive
the history of its generation—even as this act of archiving amounts
as well to an act of exclusion. These narrative worlds become the
mise-en-scènes of same-sex intimacies and thus amount to a literary
laboratory, allowing writers to test the ways literature generates and
dismantles sexual types. What gives life to these expanding narrative worlds and their attendant processes of type complication is
literary circulation: the circulation of texts within the larger, extratextual, social world, and the intratextual social circulation of
characters within the fictional worlds they populate.

   The virtue of making sense of both type complication and
novel production in terms of literary circulation is that it allows us
to account for both continuity and discontinuity within the literary
history of sexuality (and, indeed, in literature more generally). It
allows us to see the ways earlier sexual types likewise participate
in making visible later sexual types without simply seeing earlier
types as historical analogues for later ones. The New England "old
maid," for instance, may be "queer" in that she is outside heteronormative marriage structures, but she is not necessarily lesbian in
her attachments—despite the fact that imagining communities of
unmarried women does help to develop narrative worlds where sexual sociability between women is possible. As writers complicate the
old maid figure by testing one representation of her against another,

the terms of unmarried female sociability begin to shift and change. But the fact that old maids and lesbians seem to exist alongside each other in texts like "Martha's Lady" suggests that the one category does not replace the other historically, however much they might also overlap in a text like *The Bostonians.*

Attending to literary circulation also allows us to measure accumulations and condensations of language, whether detailed descriptions or abstract types, over time. Writers can literally accumulate the words necessary to convey novelistic worlds with all the space and time they need, but literary evolution of increasingly detailed narrative worlds makes possible a paradox in type production (of which the homosexual is just one example): that the emergence of an abstract type may owe its birth to the accumulations of concrete details.[45] How otherwise could we call Melville's *Typee* a gay or queer novel? The same literary and social mechanisms that facilitate the recognition of a novelistic subgenre also facilitate the emergence of a new language for sexual types. After all, sexologists and early psychoanalysts frequently relied on literature to yield examples for the diagnoses they made.

In my analysis of the ways literary circulation gives life to these expanding narrative worlds and the sexual types that populate them (whether they are native South Sea Islanders, old maids, bohemians, Typee bachelors, or Bostonians), I situate my work in response to several (sometimes overlapping) bodies of scholarly literature: treatments of the novel across the history of gay and lesbian studies and through the lenses of queer theory, theories of the novel, and theories of cultural circulation. Each of the sections that follow situates my analysis in response to these bodies of scholarship.

Laying out the ways my approach responds to the work of these scholarly fields, I proceed to outline the structure of my argument, which spans five chapters and focuses on four key types of evidence. Of primary concern in each chapter is intertextuality, which I see as formal metacommentary on a text's place in a particular context of circulation vis-à-vis other texts. Fleshing out the significance of this metacommentary necessarily entails looking also at what might strike us as extratextual evidence—the material conditions of the text's circulation that situate it within the history of the book. The fact that the old maid figure appears frequently in literary magazines, for instance, and the many pages of snippets from earlier reviews that appear at the beginning of the first American edition of Melville's *Typee* are two examples. The objects in which each of these texts circulates, and the other texts that frame them, offer us insight into the conditions under which texts circulate in their own moment, and often beyond. The third evidentiary focus that spans this study is textual description, which, as I explain below, I take to be both a site of textual accumulation (because it often appears literally in many words) and a site of textual condensation (accumulating words deceptively masks any sense that words from earlier contexts have been left behind). James may claim in his notebook that he wants to write description like Daudet, but unlike other writers in this study he conceals his acknowledgment of any overt debt to Daudet in the pages of *The Bostonians*. Finally, I look at the language of place types, whose status is somewhat more complicated since place types operate as sites of textual accumulation when authors aim to complicate them (as Catharine Maria Sedgwick does in "Old Maids"), but which operate also as sites of textual condensation when they are invoked as abstractions (as in *The Bostonians*).

Collectively, my analyses of these bodies of evidence aim to further our understanding of the ways these cultural and textual objects both embed the conditions of their circulation and expand beyond themselves as they continue to circulate past their initial moment of publication. They participate in the making-legible of queer novel-ty, often in ways their authors could not have predicted in advance, even as these texts both abandon and metabolize dense histories of race, kinship, and class typologies.

Novel Homosexuality

Pathbreaking work from an earlier generation of scholars in the field of gay and lesbian studies as well as more recent theoretical approaches within queer studies make this study possible. Consistently underrecognized recovery work by generations of gay and lesbian studies scholars has permitted the circulation of some literary works that might otherwise have been lost to modern view. Meanwhile critics from the perspective of both gay studies and queer theory have generated new readings of canonical texts and authors. The subgenre of anthologies, bibliographies, and documentary histories I highlighted earlier has proven indispensable to my work in the pages of this book.

At the same time, the stubbornness with which homosexuality as an identity category has taken hold of our scholarly imagination has, until recently, tended to obscure our view of the role of literary form not just in reflecting but in producing queer life. Identity politics, at the level of authorship and at the level of content, have dominated the terms in which scholars have long thought about the gay and lesbian novel. We can see this in the most basic descriptions of the genre, written by scholars of queer literary history, as well as in more recent readings of novels that offer critiques of identity politics. Michael Stanton defines the gay male novel as

> a form of fiction in which male homosexuality is central—not always a central problem but certainly a central concern. That said, few other absolute statements are possible. The protagonist of such a novel is likely to be gay, as are at least some of the lesser characters. Feelings of love arise; sexual acts occur; conflicts with the straight world—parents, teachers, friends, employers—happen. One way to trace the emergence of the gay male novel is to measure the frankness with which such things are described.[46]

Although Stanton does acknowledge the queer content of earlier novels like *Fanny Hill,* the "frankness" he sets up as the defining feature of such novels' descriptions can be observed only by recent standards of explicitness. Sherrie Innes, whose account of the lesbian novel goes back only as far as modernism, summarizes the prevailing scholarly thinking about the subgenre in similar terms: "Exactly what features make a novel 'lesbian' are difficult to specify. Critics have different ideas about how to define the lesbian novel, but most agree on two points: The author must be a lesbian, and the central character or characters must be lesbians."[47] Innes excludes novels by men (like James's *The Bostonians* and Compton Mackenzie's

Extraordinary Women) as well as novels written by heterosexual women (like Mary McCarthy's *The Group*).[48] Like Stanton, Innes focuses on the identity of the central character of the novel (as well as the identity of the writer)[49] while other formal features that might define the novel fade into the background.

There are important historical reasons for critics' insistent embrace of the political significance of the gay and lesbian novel. Much of the scholarly work that recovered and built bibliographies of queer texts[50] happened before the advent of anti-identitarian queer theory and the universalizing approach to anti-homophobic inquiry advocated by Eve Kosofsky Sedgwick.[51] One effect of this universalizing approach has been a scholarly focus not just on the significance of homosocial and homosexual bonds to social relations more generally but also on the fundamental queerness of canonical texts themselves. Robert K. Martin, for instance, when asked if he had considered editing an anthology of gay and lesbian literature in America, quipped, "It already exists. . . . It's called *The Norton Anthology of American Literature*."[52] While I generally support this universalizing approach to queer life, one of its casualties has been a diminished status for the body of seemingly minor literature (texts not included in the *Norton Anthology*) that an earlier generation recovered as "gay" and "lesbian." Another effect of the universalizing approach has been to accept genre itself as an archive of queerness rather than an organizing principle of queerness. Even those scholars engaged in recovery projects (like Austen) have often had to affirm the very existence of the gay and lesbian novel, rather than chart it as one possible outcome of historical forces, just in order to make the claim for its political significance. Austen clearly identifies the homophobia against which he battled in his work: "The very existence of the homosexual novel," he observed, "is steadfastly denied. The reading public has been led to believe that while gay men dabble in poetry and write interesting plays and trenchant essays, the few novels they have written about themselves and their milieu have always turned out to be seriously flawed and second-rate."[53] In a footnote to the above quotation, he cites personal correspondence with Leslie Fiedler to defend his claim.[54] Famous for his diagnosis of an "innocent homosexuality" at the heart of American literature,

Fiedler is said to have written that "he should not be thought of as having taken an 'adversary position' toward gay literature in America, yet at the same time he clings to the insistence that it has not been 'useful' to recognize the homosexual novel as a 'special sub-category' of American fiction."[55] The critical history of both the gay and the lesbian novel echoes Catharine Stimpson's eloquent claim that homosexual writing can never be neutral: "Few, if any, homosexual texts," she writes, "can exemplify writing at the zero degree, that degree at which writing, according to Roland Barthes, is '. . . basically in the indicative mode, or . . . amodal . . . [a] new neutral writing . . . [that] takes its place in the midst of . . . ejaculation and judgements; without becoming involved in any of them; [that] . . . consists precisely in their absence.'"[56] Even when Julie Abraham seeks to critique what she sees as "the hegemony of the lesbian novel" and its "heterosexual plot," she takes for granted not just that the lesbian novel already exists as such but that its "hegemonic" status is in fact a mark of cultural power.[57]

More recent scholarly studies that trade less in the language of identity politics and more in considerations of sexual queerness (so as to invoke sexuality as a nonnormative mode of sociability) have shifted the focus from political urgency toward considerations of literary form. Influenced by deconstruction, psychoanalysis, and poststructuralist theory, these analyses have tended to focus on rhetorical form and on the representations of social worlds within texts. Arguably the most influential of these analyses belongs to Eve Sedgwick. In "The Beast in the Closet," she charts fin-de-siècle homosexuality as a "thematics of absence" by looking at preterition and prosopopoeia, while in *Between Men* she examines the triangulation of homosociality whereby women become objects of exchange between men. D. A. Miller's "Anal Rope" likewise offers up an approach to reading "connotation" (what is both there and not there), while Lee Edelman's *Homographesis* explores the extent to which language itself—its inscriptions and descriptions—functions to defer the certainties of meaning.[58] Form—the form of the unspoken and the form of language itself—has preoccupied queer theorists from the beginning, but genre is taken for granted.

Given the attentiveness to analyses of form within queer theory, it is somewhat surprising that no study of the formal emergence of the queer novel has yet been undertaken, especially since no genre of literature has been quite as central to the rise of queer theory. The very first sentence of *Between Men* explains that "the subject of this book is a relatively short, recent, and accessible passage of English culture, chiefly as embodied in the mid-eighteenth- to mid-nineteenth-century novel."[59] In another germinal queer theoretical work, *The Novel and the Police,* D. A. Miller points to the putative social utility of the novel to justify his own generic focus when he argues that "perhaps no openly fictional form has ever sought to 'make a difference' in the world more than the Victorian novel," its point being "to confirm the novel-reader in his identity as 'liberal subject.'" To understand the Victorian novel's relationship to its age, he argues, "is thus to recognize a central episode in the genealogy of our present."[60] Both Sedgwick and Miller take the novel as their site of exploration in arguments that highlight the centrality of homosocial and homosexual bonds to the imagination of cultural life more generally. They chart shifts in the historical and linguistic representations of homosexuality, but they generally take the novel to be a stable form. Similar points of focus define analysis of lesbianism. Valerie Rohy focuses on the rhetorical structures of lesbianism, while Kathryn Kent analyzes identity formation. Even the text that most approximates a study of the prehistory of the lesbian novel—Lisa Moore's *Dangerous Intimacies: Toward a Sapphic History of the British Novel*—sees its history, not the novel, as "Sapphic." (A similar adjective placement marks the title of another book by Eve Sedgwick, her edited collection of essays *Novel Gazing: Queer Readings in the Novel,* in which *queer* modifies *readings,* not the novel itself.)[61] Whereas *queer* marks an orientation toward a text (a mode of reading) in these works, only recently has scholarly attention turned back to the question of queer genres.

Christopher Looby sketches out quite nicely the dilemma that attends any analysis of the queer novel. The following passage is worth citing at length for its perspicacity. On the one hand, he argues,

> the novel might seem well suited to queer sexuality. The novel
> has a long history of discreditation as a low genre, both on

the basis of its ostensible formal appeal to dangerous readerly absorption and emotional vagrancy and because of its frequent attention to sexual intrigue, disgrace, deviancy, and so forth. Why, then, shouldn't the novel be a perfectly apt genre for exploring the newly organized field of erotic deviancy described by the rubric of the "homosexual" around the turn of the century? If the novel could do well by countless adulterers, courtesans, seducers and other sexual reprobates, why wouldn't it be perfectly capable of accommodating stories of pansies, dykes, and the like?[62]

And yet the lack of fit, as Looby then observes, is the stuff of commentary in some queer novels themselves. As he continues,

From another perspective, however, the novel's long affiliation with conventions of romance—and especially its deep investment in narratives of courtship, marriage, and reproduction— might tend to render it recalcitrant when faced with erotic scripts that ran counter to the novel's historically heteronormative bias. The novel had been very good at representing threats to marriage, sexual fidelity, and social reproduction, but it had done so (one could argue) in an essentially disciplinary way. The norms were articulated and reinforced precisely by virtue of the novel's dramatization of what threatened them. Could the novel really do anything with queer sexuality other than add it to the list of disgraceful threats to heterosexual propriety? Could the novel actually defamiliarize received categories of sexual experience, and thus serve the interest of sexual redescription and the remaking of experience? The *question* of the queer novel, the question of its very possibility, had to be confronted by writers who, whether themselves queer (under some description) or not, meant to bring novelistic art to bear upon historically emergent queer sexual experience.[63]

These paragraphs, which appear in Looby's overview essay on the modern gay novel for *A Companion to the Modern American Novel,* constitute the most up-to-date theorization of the queer novel as a literary form. Although other scholars take the queer novel as an object of inquiry, Looby consciously theorizes it. In the wake of such scholarly analysis of queer rhetorical structures and the emergence of queer modes of literary analysis, the moment thus seems right to bring these facets of queer literary study to bear on the rise of the queer novel, which has depended, I argue, on both the gradual production of queer rhetorics and queer readings across literary history. Following the lead of Jordan Stein, moreover, it seems important to consider the queer novel in terms of "the history of sexuality [that] can and should be written in relation to texts and experiences that fail to be represented at the manifest levels of discourse or—especially in the case of literature—of thematics."[64] A circulation approach to the history of the queer novel is well positioned to consider the dialectial relationship between the seemingly inevitable manifest content of the queer and less visible conditions of its possibility.

By embracing the cumulative work of queer archivists and bibliographers, while also assuming that gay and lesbian identity is not a determinant (but perhaps a product) of literary circulation, my investigation thus inhabits a space of inquiry that these earlier analyses collectively open up without fully exploring. This investigation of the conditions under which the gay and lesbian novel emerges as such would not be possible without either the important political and archival work of early gay and lesbian studies scholars or the more recent efforts by queer theorists both to expand and critique the limits of that work and of the dominant narratives that organized early queer theory itself. I have relied often on early bibliographies and anthologies like *The Intersexes* and *The Lesbian in Literature* to piece together a dynamics of textual circulation that many scholars of gay and lesbian studies set in motion. The texts they collected themselves continue to circulate in more recent collections and bibliographies but often seem to have been left behind in the readings of canonical texts that have tended to constitute the focus of queer theoretical analyses. Equally indispensable to my study, however, are the insights and reading practices produced out of these queer theoretically informed readings since they have made it possible to read the textuality of sexuality without assuming the primacy of identity politics.

The existing body of scholarship on gay, lesbian, homosexual, and queer literature is itself an excellent case study in how discourse can shape the conditions of its own circulation. The very shifts in vocabulary that mark the literary study of homosexuality (including the reclamation of *homosexuality* as term of description rather than damnation) reveal the dynamic nature of sexual types. The terms we use as well as their grammatical position in a sentence direct and shift our focus: whereas scholars suggest that we focus on gay characters or lesbian authors, queer reading directs our attention to the way we read more than the character we read or the author who writes. Language both creates and shapes our focus on particular textual objects. Just as circulation allows us to chart relationships between psychological/sexological sexual categories or earlier sexual place types, so too might circulation allow us to understand how more recent sexual type categories that variously overlap and oppose each other, like "gay," "lesbian," "homosexual," and "queer," emerge out of a complication of the others, or slip together in maddening, if also productive, ambiguity.[65] It is for this reason that I suggest, in chapter 1, that the reception history and scholarly treatment of *Typee* reveal that the text has an "acquired queerness."

The "queer" of queer theory emerged as a way out of the impasse of identity politics, and its spirit embraces the slippage that takes place in my chapters. However unnecessarily, queer theory has nonetheless produced an impasse of another kind in its own circulation. In literary studies, queer theory's focus on primarily canonical texts overlooks the cultural significance of texts with less universalizing impulses. The work of Charles Warren Stoddard is an interesting case in point: he was astoundingly prolific; he knew and socialized with every major literary figure of his time; and his writing has been included in virtually every anthology of gay male writing produced in the past one hundred years. But he has been interesting primarily to gay and lesbian studies scholars, not to queer theorists, whose largely deconstructive analytic style has not found in his work evidence of the kind of line-by-line formal cleverness they value. He is interesting in my analysis because, first of all, he is credited with writing one of the first gay American novels, and second, because he has been so roundly criticized as a bad writer, despite his own canonicity within gay literature. My point is that each emergent sexual typology, even in critical idiom, opens up one avenue of inquiry and closes down another, accumulates details while also condensing and leaving out others. Through such processes of accumulation and condensation, marked by intertextuality and even appropriation, fiction such as Stoddard's comes to echo nothing more or less than the novel's own generic history, as described by its most important theorists.

Novel Textuality

To understand the emergence of the gay and lesbian novel in terms beyond the emergence of homosexual types, we need to understand something more about the literary genre that is the novel: the conditions under which it has emerged and sustained its novelty as well as the conditions under which it (and, if its own history is any indication, other genres as well) produces its own spin-offs in the form of subgenres. As Claudio Guillén has suggested, genre is "a problem-solving model on the level of form." It is, he explains, "an invitation to the matching . . . of matter and form" where "matter" is understood to be not content but language that is "already shot through with formal elements"; "all previous forms, that is, become matter in the hands of the artist at work."[66] Bakhtin, known primarily for his theory of the novel's polyglossia, makes a similar claim. I highlighted this claim earlier in this introduction, but it is worth recalling in this context: utterances, he argues, connect the history of society to the history of language, and "not a single new phenomenon (phonetic, lexical, or grammatical) . . . can enter the system of language without having traversed the long and complicated path of generic-stylistic testing and modification."[67] Michael McKeon deploys these insights in his own account of the origins of the English novel, in his observations that inconsistency in the categories of "truth" and "virtue" are essential to the rise of the novel, where vestiges of older forms persist in the newer ones.[68] Novels in this sense are thus products of historical and dialectical accumulation. They are parasitic upstarts, in Marthe Robert's estimation, that somehow never really manage to overthrow the forms they ingest.[69]

But the dialectical process of accumulation described above necessarily entails a process of subtraction, or leaving behind, or condensing some forms and details while embracing others. Taking a longer view of the novel's polysemous, multivocal, and omnivorous formal features, theorists such as Northrop Frye, Walter Benjamin, and Sigmund Freud highlight the significance of devolution and condensation to the rise of the novel. Each of these theorists highlights an area of concern for our consideration of the relationship between accumulation and condensation or displacement as it relates to the rise of the gay and lesbian novel: Frye concerns himself with the ways literary form archives its own history of development; Benjamin highlights the significance of the shift from oral culture to print culture for the rise of the novel; Freud meanwhile sees in textual transmission a model of psychic displacement (thereby offering his own theory of textual accumulation). For Frye, first of all, realism (which Ian Watt sees as a defining feature of the novel) itself reveals the displacement of fiction from pure mythic structure. This form, Frye suggests, allows fiction (and by extension the novel) to adapt or adjust itself to contexts by invoking earlier forms through imitation or parody. In both the "low mimetic" mode and the "parodic" mode, Frye suggests that fiction archives its own generic history at the level of formal displacements.[70] As texts gesture to their continuity with earlier forms of writing, they also register breaks or discontinuities with those earlier texts.

Benjamin, on the other hand, sees in the novel a process of displacement—of the oral story into print culture: "What distinguishes the novel from the story (and from the epic in the narrower sense) is its essential dependence on the book. The dissemination of the novel became possible only with the invention of printing."[71] To understand the rise of the gay and lesbian novel, therefore, it is important to describe what might be particular about the role print culture plays in its emergence: to take account of the text not just in terms of its meaning but in terms of the object by which it circulates. Benjamin assumes the novel's dialectical relationship to print culture, whereas Frye argues for fiction's dialectical relationship with prior forms.

Freud, finally, is something of a special case, since what he offers us for an understanding of novelistic development can be gleaned only by reading him somewhat against the terms of his own argument. In the following passage, he concerns himself with psychic displacement, that is, with the recording of dreams and dream-thoughts in language:

> The first thing that becomes clear to anyone who compares the dream-content with the dream-thoughts is that a work of *condensation* on a large scale has been carried out. Dreams are brief, meagre and laconic in comparison with the range and wealth of the dream-thoughts. If a dream is written out it may perhaps fill half a page. The analysis setting out the dream-thoughts underlying it may occupy six, eight or a dozen times as much space.[72]

What interests me here is less Freud's psychoanalytic theory of dream life than his implied theory of language accumulation. He highlights a difference between the two records of psychic activity: writing down the thoughts about the dream (or conveyed in the dream?) literally produces more language than writing down the mere dream. In making this distinction, Freud assumes that condensation applies only to writing down the dream itself. But we can also recognize that the dream-thoughts are subject to condensation as they are written down. Freud means to argue that the dream-thoughts, being the psychic origins of the dream, constitute an origin for the dream story in a psychic reality. This reality seems to exist prior to the writing of both the dream story and the dream-thoughts. But if we consider Bakhtin's and Guillén's points about all language belonging to earlier formal incarnations, the very act of writing down the dream-thoughts translates them into linguistic form while also transforming them and leaving significant details behind. In this sense, the dream-thoughts are also subject to condensation. They are more detailed accounts of the psychic conditions that produce the dream, even if they take up "a dozen times as much space." Freud's recorded dream-thoughts are novelistic insofar as they go beyond the plot summary of the dream to include a description of the dream-life context in which the dream story unfolds. Drawing an analogy between Freud's dream-thoughts and the novel allows us to see how textual accumulations are themselves condensations: accumulations, perhaps, of condensations. Similarly we might say that as long as the gay and lesbian novel, like any other novel, is the product of textual accumulations borne through acts of literary circulation, these accumulations cannot be said in any way to be historically or formally complete. As detailed as they are, they leave things out or shift our focus so as to enable us to view some things more fully than others. To the extent that it examines the prehistory of the gay and lesbian novel in terms of literary form and print cultural archives, and attends to textual detail as both accumulation and subtraction, my work here treats the rise of the gay and lesbian novel in terms similar to the rise of the novel more generally. But like any subgenre of the novel that emerges after the novel itself,[73] it is distinct because it can count the novel as a precursor to its own emergence. Unlike the novel at the point of its own emergence, its subgenres can (and perhaps must) acknowledge earlier novels as influences on their own development. In this way, the novel's subgenres can be said to behave like minor literatures. Gilles Deleuze and Félix Guattari point out that "a minor literature doesn't come from a minor language; it is rather that which a minority constructs within a major language." They suggest that minor literatures emerge as "assemblages," the results of what they call "deterritorializations" and "reterritorializations" of pieces of the dominant literatures.[74] A good example of how Deleuze and Guattari's theory works in the reterritorialization of sexual culture can be seen in Didier Eribon's *Insult and the Making of the Gay Self*.[75] Eribon traces the role of insult and the reclamation of insulting terms (like *faggot* and *dyke*) within queer cultures. Expanding this analogy to the context of the gay and lesbian novel, we can say, therefore, that the novel is not just the result of literary circulation (as it was at its moment of emergence in the eighteenth century) but an influential agent of circulation. Under these conditions, characters or episodes that may be minor or not fully developed in terms of subjectivity in one incarnation, like Melville's Kory-Kory in *Typee,* might nonetheless inspire more developed characters in later novels, as Kory-Kory does when Stoddard creates Kána-aná in *South-Sea Idyls*. Circulation does not insist that we develop teleologies of generic development; instead, it suggests that we cannot predict in advance how even the most flattened, insulted, or derogatory depictions of cultural life may give life to fuller, more complex incarnations of literary genres and social types alike.

Circulation, Sexuality, and the Novel

I have been insisting that circulation is the motor of textual accumulation and condensation, that which makes possible the warp and woof of narrative worlds necessary for the emergence of the gay and lesbian novel. Yet the word *circulation* rarely appears in the above theories of the novel's development, despite its implicit centrality. It is necessary to Frye's sense of devolution, essential to Benjamin's account of print culture's transformation of stories in novel form, and the condition under which Deleuze and Guattari can imagine the deterritorializations that make a minor literature possible. The role of circulation is just as implicitly central to the history of sexuality. Another name for the literary accumulation and condensation that lead to the visibility of the queer novel is discursive proliferation. Our dominant model for thinking about such proliferation of sexual discourse (including, even, the very term *proliferation*) comes from Foucault (although his sense of discourse is not especially attentive to questions of genre). In the first volume of *The History of Sexuality,* he argues that, in spite of efforts to repress discourse about sexuality, "at the level of discourses and their domains . . . practically the opposite phenomenon occurred. There was a steady proliferation of discourses concerned with sex—specific discourses, different from one another both by their form and by their object: a discursive ferment that gathered momentum from the eighteenth century onward."[76] Foucault points particularly to "the multiplication of discourses concerning sex in the field of exercise of power itself: an institutional incitement to speak about it, and to do so more and more; a determination on the part of the agencies of power to hear it spoken about, and to cause *it* to speak through explicit articulation and endlessly accumulated detail."[77] As important as Foucault's insights have been within the history of sexuality, we are only just beginning to explore how it is that discourses "gather momentum" or "multiply"—often in ways Foucault's paradigm itself does not imagine (as I will explain in the chapter on *Typee*). For this reason, the literary history of sexuality can use more thinking about the role that circulation plays in discursive proliferation as well as genre formation.

Some of the best theoretical work conceptualizing the relationship between language and circulation appears in the field of linguistic anthropology, which concerns itself in detail with the processes of "entextualization," the ways in which culture comes to be translated into discourse that can circulate through the world in objects.[78] Greg Urban insists on what he believes to be "a fundamental principle of culture, viz., discourse tends to shape itself in such a way as to maximize its circulation."[79] But what is promising about his theory is the sense that it offers us a nonpsychoanalytic way of thinking about the limits of individuals' control of the language they use (and which, if he is right, also uses them). He goes further to make the case for situating meaning-making beyond the agency of people and within the agency of discourse itself:

> Referential or semantic meanings are relevant to a broader public. They are also efficacious—they can get people to do things. Yet, they are ghostlike, circulating along piggy-backed on discourse forms, but themselves intangible, unseen.
>
> Even the hardest headed skeptics among us must agree that there is something God-like about referential meanings. Discourses modify themselves so as to maintain or increase their circulation. But by what agency do they do so? You can say that agents are individuals. Individuals modify and manipulate discourses as they circulate. They are the bedrock source of change. Yet, at least insofar as the cold pole of tradition is concerned, individuals only modify what has diffused to them from others, what has seeped down over time. Circulating discourses are the end result of innumerable revisions and tinkerings and refinements. Only at the hot pole of experience can they be thought of as individual products, and even there the suggestive power of prior discourse is at work. To say something new, one must use old expressive forms, which have crystallized at the cold pole of tradition.[80]

Urban admits that there may be a certain amount of agency in the sheer act of writing down discourses ("at the hot pole of experience"), but this agency does not amount to the power of invention. So much historical tinkering has gone into those "old expressive forms" that the forms themselves carry a history that can change only gradually over time. Central to tracking such change over time, in the context of linguistic anthropology, is the evidence of "metalanguage" (which preoccupies Benjamin Lee in *Talking Heads*) and "metaculture" (which Urban makes the focus of another book called *Metaculture*). These analyses, which inspire my own methodology, take seriously as evidence the language that frames language, including, for the purposes of my study, not only what Gérard Genette has called "paratexts," but reviews, discarded textual editions, texts' internal references to the conditions of their own production and circulation, as well as literary criticism and commentary itself.[81]

Important as well to my analysis of the emergence of, and shifts within, sexual and literary types is the work of Charles Sanders Peirce, whose own work on types is historically contemporary with the emergence of these specific types themselves. Peirce explains the relationship between token and type as follows:

> A common mode of estimating the amount of matter in a . . . printed book is to count the number of words. There will ordinarily be about twenty *the*'s on a page, and of course they count as twenty words. In another sense of the word "word," however, there is but one word "the" in the English language; and it is impossible that this word should lie visibly on a page or be heard in any voice. . . . Such a . . . Form, I propose to term a *Type*. A Single . . . object . . . such as this or that word on a single line of a single page of a single copy of a book, I will venture to call a *Token*. . . . In order that a Type may be used, it has to be embodied in a Token which shall be a sign of the Type, and thereby of the object the Type signifies.[82]

Counting words, estimating their formal capacity for circulation "on a page" or "in any voice": these are central to Peirce's theory of Form and Type. The dialectical relationship between token and type is not merely a matter of translatability (such that a token can embody its type), but it implies a matter of scale. Peirce's theory forces us to think not only about the relationship between example and concept but about the portability of the type and the token. Language assumes the role not just of representing type but of making it portable and available for the accumulations necessary for the emergence of type. In this sense, his theory exceeds literary hermeneutics—as a matter of interpretation—without ever abandoning interpretation itself.

To think about literary circulation is also, then, to think about its significance in nonhermeneutic ways in addition to empirical ways. Hans Ulrich Gumbrecht advances such a nonhermeneutic model for studies in the humanities. He does not eschew the value of interpretation but, rather, suggests that "aesthetic experience [is] an oscillation (and sometimes . . . an interference) between 'presence effects' and 'meaning effects.'"[83] He urges us to see how materialities of culture amount to a presence in the world and thus exert power over us. He develops this theory further with respect to studies of textuality in another book, *Powers of Philology,* in which he explores the terrain of philology as an examination of text as object, where its materiality, however related it may be to what it tries to say, becomes an object of exploration in its own right. Gumbrecht does offer us a program for reading texts line by line (as Benjamin Lee does when he describes the metalinguistics of narration).[84] For him, being content not to know how exactly presence works at the moment it is felt is a key part of the aesthetic experience. But because he insists on the power of the text's materiality (what he would call its sheer presence), like Urban above, he has had to account for the seeming religiosity of his theory (the godlikeness of referential meaning). Ascribing agency to cultural objects[85] has long been the domain of metaphor itself—where figures of speech create the illusion of agency (dismissed by some as pathetic fallacy, for instance). But if we hold open the possibility that the discourses carry with them histories of their own formations and tinkerings, we can begin to understand more fully the long paths of stylistic testing that generate discourses—as theorists of the novel have attempted to do.

Understanding the power attributed to discourses may raise some eyebrows if we try to imagine whether discourse has the same kind of agency that human beings have—and whether this means we attribute less agency to humans as a result. If we pause to think about it in a slightly different register, however, we see that our culture's core liberal values are everywhere peppered with the insistence that words and books do things in the world—an assumption that has not yet tempered the belief in human agency. We can see the force of this belief in the ways we think about children's literature, for instance: no body of literature is so charged with forming the very audience its existence presupposes. Children are encouraged to give themselves over to (some) discursive forces; this is the condition under which, paradoxically, we teach them that they have agency. Warner advances a more adult version of this argument when he studies "cultural meaning of printedness"[86] in eighteenth-century North America leading up to and just beyond the moment of the Revolution. If, as Warner reasons, an entity no less invested in the idea of political agency than the Unites States is produced through print and print circulation, then perhaps it is possible to see that acknowledging the agency of discourse is the condition under which politics itself can happen.

We have already seen the example of Prime-Stevenson's attribution of agency and sociability to books in the passage I cited at the beginning of this book: "crowded into a few lower shelves, as if they sought to avoid other literary society, to keep themselves to themselves, to shun all unsympathetic observation." Strategic misquotation, in Natalie Barney's phrasing, is but another way in which texts reflexively index the conditions of their own making. Each of the following chapters aims to understand further the ways discourse entextualizes the conditions for sexual type development (and complication) and the long history of circulations and tinkerings that makes the queer novel visible as such.

In chapter 1, a case study of Melville's *Typee,* I chart two distinct but intertwined aspects of queer literary history generated through readings of the text: Melville's descriptions of sexual encounters—between men and among men and women; and the long critical history of identifying sexual social patterns in the text. The first of these can be traced through Melville's record of his intertextual engagement with missionary texts, indexed through his quotation and citation of those texts. The second aspect is an examination of the ways in which Melville's engagement with the specifically sexual aspects of missionary texts resonates with other texts the more his own sexually charged texts circulate. I argue that

Typee has gradually acquired its status as a queer text as it participates in a long process of queer type development. Central to that development are the metacultural and paratextual framings of the text that register the terms of its circulation, many of which can be tracked not only through reviews and revisions of *Typee* but through what happened to the now largely unread first American edition of the text, which was redacted at the request of Melville's editor, in an effort to quell controversy over its treatment of sex and religion. Only in retrospect, however, can we see exactly how Melville's text actively participates in this queer production. Melville could probably never have predicted the ways in which *Typee* would interact with later discourses of sexuality, which suggests in effect that his text exerts an agency that outlives him, if not his reputation.

Like Melville, Stoddard, the focus of my second chapter, reads backward and consciously deploys an intertextual metalanguage to reference the context of literary circulation in which he participates. His discourse holds on tightly precisely to texts like *Typee* that provide him with a language of self-understanding and literary expression. As mentioned earlier, Stoddard's writing has led some to describe him as the first gay novelist in America, a fact that looks forward from Stoddard to others who would later write such novels. I read Stoddard instead through his engagement with, and connections to, the writers who have come to define his literary moment (like W. D. Howells, Mark Twain, and Joaquin Miller) and whose writings ultimately help Stoddard define himself. Stoddard reveals himself to be a sentimental collector of texts, in his life and his writing. His archival tendencies ultimately allow him to see the extent to which literary discourses (his own and others) have produced him—something we can see in Stoddard's unfinished but novelistic scrapbooks toward the end of his life.

The next two chapters of this book observe the processes of textual accumulation and condensation I've been describing as metatextual indices of textual circulation in nineteenth-century appearances of the old maid, who is often seen as an analogue for the modern lesbian. In chapter 3, my archive covers a century of literary representations of old maids from late eighteenth-century periodicals like the *American Magazine*, through stories, essays, poems, and novels by Sedgwick, Nathaniel Hawthorne, Freeman, and Jewett, up through Edith Wharton's 1924 novel *The Old Maid (The 'Fifties)*. They collectively test the seeming lifelessness of the old maid across a range of genres and contexts, and infuse the old maid figure with the kind of transformative energy necessary for us to imagine the lesbian as a possible effect of her circulation in literature. To understand how the old maid makes visible the later lesbian, I argue that we must, perforce, recognize her as a historically distinct figure, not a lesbian euphemism.

My fourth chapter on James's *The Bostonians* describes how in the space of one novel James dramatizes the processes of sexual type production and social circulation that I have been documenting in American literature throughout the nineteenth century. The form of his narration conveys the ways type language converges on individuals like Basil Ransom and Olive Chancellor, from outside the self, while James's descriptive language, harking back to French sources, carries with it a history of sexuality that is piggybacked on the form itself. James's eponymous "Bostonians"—Olive Chancellor and Verena Tarrant—effectively evolve into themselves throughout James's novel, an evolution masked by the title's deft assumption that they have *been* themselves from the very start.

The concluding chapter explores the afterlife of nineteenth-century place types and the world built through and around them to investigate how a circulation-based approach to literary history might reframe how we think about queer interiority at the beginning of the twentieth century. Structured as a series of short commentaries on the representation of protagonists' interiority at the turn of the twentieth century, this chapter suggests that once it has become possible to imagine same-sexual sociability at the heart of an entire narrative world, the terms of queer literary experiment begin to shift: they move inside the sentence and inside the character. This chapter comprises three short essays: one that rereads Jewett's "Martha's Lady" to emphasize its status as a transitional moment in the portrayal of queer interiority as an effect of place and race types; another on the similarly refracted interiority presented in Fuller's *Bertram Cope's Year*; and a third on the interior landscapes at play in Stein's *Q.E.D.* The accumulation of detail that has created these queer worlds, I argue, at once helps to make homosexuality possible as an abstraction—and erases, at the level of content, the visibility of its own history and creativity, while treating the form itself as the repository of this creative history of circulation. Psychoanalysis and fiction alike are engaged with the project of how to narrate the inner life of the sexual subject. Focusing less on the problem of world-making, they repurpose the frameworks of landscape and place types to characterize the inner life of characters as topoi and reduce to traces the complex histories of social and literary circulation that preceded them. They assume the very scope of writing that these earlier texts made possible—all while seeming to conceal the very conditions under which their own concerns with interiority and plot came to be filled with ironic possibility to begin with. In short, I read these queer novels' concern with interiorities both showcased (in Jewett and Stein) and withheld (Fuller) as evidence of the ways these texts archive, almost imperceptibly, the conditions of the history of circulation that gave rise to them.

A second story I want to tell through these examples concerns more precisely the limits of circulation itself. This book thus concludes with a coda that acknowledges some of the paths not taken. As I have already acknowledged, circulation offers us a fantasy of ever-expanding accumulation and inclusion, one that borrows liberally from our ubiquitous network imaginaries. The text webs I chart here are fundamentally incomplete. Literary networks then as now are limited by access to social and financial capital. At the same time that circuits are hubs of cultural productivity, they stand also as networks of exclusion and sites of sometimes regressive cultural reproduction. While queers have long treasured our cultivation of stranger sociability, our practice of doing literary history would do well not only to embrace the productive and unpredictable forces of circulation, but to be reflexive in the face of their inevitable exclusions and sensitive to the nonreproductive histories of queer life.

1

ACQUIRED QUEERNESS
The Sexual Life and Afterlife
of *Typee*

IN THE MIDDLE of "In a Transport" (1873), one of Charles Warren Stoddard's *South-Sea Idyls*, the narrator describes his arrival at Nouka Hiva, near the Typee valley. He surveys the landscape, marking its "scorching soil," "groves of rose-wood," "strips of beach that shone like brass," and "the cocoa-palms that towered above the low, brown huts of the natives." But off in the distance lies a location whose descriptions in print have conferred on it a kind of mystical status, if also a tragic one:

> Far up the mountain, hung above a serene and sacred haunt, and under its shelter was hidden a deep valley, whose secret has been carried to the ends of the earth; for Herman Melville has plucked out the heart of its mystery and beautiful and barbarous Typee lies naked and forsaken.
>
> I was rather glad we could not get any nearer to it, for fear of dispelling the ideal that has so long charmed me. Catching the wind again, late in the afternoon, we lost the last outline of Nouka Hiva in the soft twilight, and said our prayers that evening as much at sea as ever.[1]

For some nineteenth-century travelers, the allure of the South Seas was primitive life itself; for others, it was ripe with potential for investment or religious conversion. It is clear that the attention itself was destructive for the people and the islands, but no less resistible for that. For Stoddard and his narrator alike, the attraction of that "serene and sacred haunt" encompassed a located mode of sexual sociability between men. It is, the narrator says in the next sentence, "the ideal that has so long charmed me."

What Stoddard and his narrator saw in the Marquesas Islands and wrote about has been described variously as uncivilized, sentimental, Uranian, gay, primitive, homosexual, innocent, childlike, inverted, effeminate, and just plain schlocky. Some of these descriptions have themselves been both scrutinized as colonialist and reclaimed as queer. What appealed most to Stoddard about life in and writing about the South Seas went by none of these judgments or names as such, even if it remains difficult for us to imagine how it could not have. So accustomed are we to having at our disposal (and for our disposal) the shorthand vocabularies of identitarian sexuality—or even of queerness—that it becomes equally difficult to grasp the dimensions of a lifeworld where people lived and operated without those linguistic categories as we know them today. Stoddard's nod to Melville's *Typee* suggests that one way of developing frames of reference for understanding these lifeworlds was to read and write through the words and worlds of others, assembling them side by side as if to create the illusion of both texts and people traveling in the company of others. His nod to Melville also registers the extent to which modalities of homoerotic reading, writing, and sociability—modalities that now seem obvious precursors to identitarian sexuality—operated within much more complex codes of recognition that are difficult even to describe to readers today without using language like "homoerotic," "queer," or "homosexual."

The crystallization of sexuality-as-property-of-the-self obscures the linguistic vagaries of its emergence of such. For instance, when it was published in 1846, *Typee* was not initially understood to be about sexual or intimate relationships between men by any audience or reviewer. First published in England as part of John Murray's Home and Colonial Library series, Melville's putatively autobiographical tale plots his adventures with natives in the islands of the South Seas. The book is so ironic in tone that the plot itself is difficult to convey: dismayed by life aboard their ship, the narrator (known to the natives as Tommo, but to readers presumably as Melville)[2] and his friend Toby abandon their vessel only, subsequently, to be "captured" (debatably) by a community of natives in the Typee valley. Tommo lives with the Typees for four months before staging his "escape" back to America. The book takes us through Tommo's approach to the Marquesas Islands on board his ship, his first contact with a seemingly generic group of South Seas natives, and, for the bulk of the narrative, life among the Typees.[3] It concludes with a very fast escape from a situation the book only ambivalently conveyed as captivity.

Heralded for its titillating accounts of a sailor's life in captivity and excoriated by religious groups who deplored its representation of missionaries, the book had every chance of success: a perfect storm of sexy controversy and religious outrage fueled its literary circulation. In fact, *Typee* became the most successful thing that Melville ever knew he published.[4] By the time he died, Melville had outwritten his own early circulation: his prodigious literary output, including several volumes of sea novels, failed to secure audiences, and he subsisted only on the outdated, if persistent, reputation of his first book as a controversial piece of travel writing. When he died, he was eulogized only as the author of *Typee*. *Moby-Dick* was collecting dust somewhere in a warehouse, while the manuscript of *Billy Budd* had never even made it to the printer.

If we told the story of *Typee*'s success by looking forward from its moment of publication—that is, if *Typee*'s earliest readers could speak back to us today (or perhaps even to Stoddard)—they (and we) might be just as mystified as contemporary readers who take its queer status for granted. As Robert K. Martin points out, although Melville responded to a tradition of writing about the South Pacific as the exotic ideal that Stoddard identifies, his rendering of "male beauty and same-sex male relationships" was "unreadable by Western observers," as "the acts of invasion, conversion, and colonization had already transformed that which was being observed."[5] Western readers lacked the appropriate frames of reference for making sense of the queer scenes before them and only later would they (we) come to understand something of this dynamic. One problem that critics have observed is that Melville's characters are drawn as types, both fetishized and colonized through the gaze of the book's narrator, Tommo. As Michael Snediker puts it, Melville offers us only characters "who *nearly* seem like characters, and whose desire for other characters, concomitantly, only nearly seems like desire." As a result, Snediker continues, "In *Typee,* we encounter a surfeit of nominally homoerotic bodies, all of which lack an interiority capable of erotic complexity or motivation; the text circuits between an astonishment that precludes observation to observations incapable of interpretation beyond superficial significance."[6] What Martin and Snediker identify are challenges not just for understanding the history of homosexuality but for the reading of sexuality's written history. They flag for us the assymetries of historical reading as well as the challenges of reading sexual types under the expectations of reading interior life.

By the end of the nineteenth century, as new language emerged to describe sexual types, frames of reference were less of a problem for Western readers. But this was not just because of the birth of sexology and the emergence of a vocabulary for understanding perverse, queer, or same-sex sexuality as is often taken to be the case.[7] Readers and writers were beginning to assemble and publish books and anthologies that brought together longer histories of same-sex sexual worlds. In this process, Stoddard would not be the only queer writer to see an earlier sexual *je sais quoi* in Melville's work. Passages from Melville's *Typee* and its sequel *Omoo* appear in Edward Carpenter's 1909 collection *Iolaüs: An Anthology of Friendship,* one of the earliest collections of writing about intense, eroticized sociability between men. E. M. Forster, Hart Crane, Robert Duncan, and Tennessee Williams would also come to see in Melville's sea novels a much less "innocent homosexuality" than Leslie Fiedler famously diagnosed as the condition of American literature and which numerous scholars since have discussed.[8] In this process, Stoddard may well have been the first to finger the circulation of Melville's writing as a transformative cultural and literary force. Having "plucked out the heart of its mystery," Melville helped carry both Stoddard and Typee's "secret . . . to the ends of the earth" leaving it "naked and forsaken" (more "naked" than "forsaken" for Stoddard).

In light of what happens to and through *Typee* as it circulates, it seems clear that the book, like so many texts in the Melville canon, has an acquired queerness: acquired, that is, through the ways it resonates with readers and texts that circulate after it has been published or through coterie-style readings; and queer in the variety of overlapping ways that *queer* has come to mean in the time since *Typee*'s publication (sexually nonnormative, socially strange, homosexual, and just plain perverse). In *Melville Unfolding,* John Bryant attributes Melville's negotiation with queer life to his engagement with the writing process itself.[9] Bryant traces in Melville's manuscript textual deletions and emendation, for instance, that he reads as evidence for Melville's process of repressing and acknowledging his own desire. According to this logic, Melville's queerness can be read as an effect of the drafting process. Whereas Bryant foregrounds Melville's agency as writer and reviser of *Typee* as a "fluid text," my argument in this chapter addresses itself to the force of the text's circulation as *Typee* participates in producing the frames of reference—particularly the queer hermeneutics—by which it comes to be read. Insofar as *queer* has come both to organize and depart from a whole range of sexual types and to complicate their taxonomies, the sign/word/idea itself might indeed be taken to reference the slipperiness of nonnormative sexual life under the conditions of modern circulation. *Queer* diagnoses a relationality to others and a departure from them in the movement of people and language through the social world.

But to say that *Typee* has an acquired queerness is not to say that later queer readers of *Typee* (interpretive communities, if you will)[10] made up or projected onto the text something that isn't there (although for all I know some might have). Rather, what I would like to argue here is that we can recognize *Typee*'s significant contribution to the emergence of queer sexual types only after they have already become legible as such. By way of increased networks of literary circulation, expansion of social circulation (through the steam engine, boat travel, etc.), new ways of reading and new frames of reference reorganized a lot of what came before, snapping into focus and stabilizing (provisionally, at least) what had often been more messy and amorphously described in prior literary incarnations. To the extent that Melville was writing something queer, he was, to use Cindy Patton's phrase, "thinking without a proper name"—describing a world and a mode of sociability that we can still read and see but that was never organized under the conscious sign of the queer.[11] Attending to *Typee*'s histories of sexual and social circulation—between and beyond its pages—we can begin to understand how it is that queerness becomes legible through the proliferations of sexual language that take place when the parts of some books are placed alongside parts of others; when social groups and writers cohere through acts of reading texts; when one author cites another in an effort to produce a new frame of reference through a consolidation of what has come before. All of these things happen through and to *Typee,* making it an ideal case study of the ways a text participates in the ongoing proliferation and circulation of its own reputation.

What is surprising about the case of *Typee* are the ways its circulation history complicates the dominant model we have for thinking about the proliferation of sexual discourse. Foucault observed that despite efforts to repress discourse about sexuality, the opposite basically occurred, as institutions incited sex "to speak through explicit articulation and endlessly accumulated detail."[12] Central to this model of discourse, proliferation is the operation of the repressive hypothesis, connected—typically for Foucault—to the institution of the Catholic Church and the discursive structure of repression and confession. In the history of *Typee*'s acquired queerness, however, the agencies of power that cause sex to speak in these ways are not religious as they are for Foucault. Only in the recirculation of religious language in nonreligious texts, like Melville's, does Protestant religious language come to do what Foucault claims is typical of the discursive structure of the Catholic confessional.

Melville's accumulations and proliferations of sexual detail in the text operate through his direct quotations from missionary accounts and ethnographies about South Seas life, by writers such as Charles Stewart, Captain Porter, and James Cook. According to the Foucauldian model, one might expect that in the effort to repress and reform the sexual behavior of the South Sea Islanders, the missionaries (whose writings on the subject were prolific) would generate more discourse about their sexual practices and behaviors. One might also expect that Melville would benefit from a bounty of details that these accounts provide in cautionary apostrophes as they generate descriptions of undesirable behaviors. In their attempts to exercise power and catalog vices to be eliminated, they might be expected to foreground the sexual practices and social structures of the Marquesans "through explicit articulation and endlessly accumulated detail." But the missionary and travel writing to which Melville responds does not offer him much by way of "explicit articulation and endlessly accumulated detail"—as we shall see. That they do not measures the difference between a French textual tradition significantly influenced by the rhetorical structures of Catholic confession and an English-American textual tradition that focuses more on the positivism of Protestant conversion narratives, which are far more likely to foreground the optimistic piety of the missionaries than detailed catalogs of the natives' vices.[13] And the fact that they do not suggests that Melville's model of discourse proliferation does not quite correspond with the one Foucault lays out. What Foucault attributes to institutions, *Typee* exemplifies through its circuits of literary and social circulation.

That Melville accumulates so much of the textual detail that is available to him and then augments those details with a few of his own may well be one of his finest accomplishments in this text: he consolidates details that are otherwise dispersed in others' accounts. In the spirit of Foucault, we might describe Melville's *Typee* as one "countereffect" of earlier efforts to "tighten up rules of decorum" on the islands. But *Typee*'s textual history reveals how complicated discursive proliferation is, across time and through the space of textual circulation—even as it exposes how thin our understanding of this complication is. Foucault describes "a discursive ferment that gathered momentum from the eighteenth century onward,"[14] but we are only beginning to develop methods for understanding how texts "gather momentum" and how detail "endlessly accumulates" in the context of understanding the literary history of sexuality.

The fact that *Typee* both exemplifies the accumulation and abstractions of sexual type detail within its pages and later becomes central to others' accumulations and abstractions makes it an excellent case study of precisely this problem. It tells a story that has, since its publication, sparked great debate about Melville's representation of sex and sexuality, all while promising that this story conveys detailed descriptions of South Seas life. The text allows us to discern different rates of accumulation and proliferation for sexual discourse—where what we now recognize as heterosexual encounters appear, quite literally, in more words than what we now recognize as homosexual encounters. It also allows us to see the persistence of the controversy *Typee* has always invoked for its representations of licentious behavior in the South Seas and to connect the persistence of that controversy to the later recognition of the sexual eroticism between men within the pages of the book.

The pages that follow tell a story of *Typee*'s circuitous, paradoxical, and often evaporating contributions to the history of sexuality. That story begins with the book's initial publication, reception, and controversy, paying particular attention to the ways the form of Melville's writing helps to produce its divided readership and reputation. This requires looking at two distinct although thoroughly intertwined aspects of queer literary history that are produced through *Typee*: (1) Melville's descriptions of sexual encounters—between men and among men and women; and (2) the history of recognizing sexual social patterns as such through readings and interpretations of *Typee*. Central to this first section of the discussion are the effects generated through his own accumulation and subsequent citation (and placing side by side), at the beginning of his novel, of sexual encounters in earlier accounts of life in the South Seas. Melville thus uses the accounts of others to scaffold his own presentation of a social world in the South Seas, which is profoundly nonnormative in terms of sexual and gender behaviors. This nonnormativity, arguably the book's earliest form of queerness and its most controversial, enables its later forms of nonnormative sexual sociability to become visible. *Typee* even produces a model for understanding how circulation and literary form in tandem produce the frame of reference required for reading other kinds of queer literary life before they emerge as such.

By looking at how Melville situated his own reading in his writing and at how others' reading and interpretation of Melville have situated his writing, this chapter explores how essential historical contexts of reading, analysis, and textual circulation have been to the transformations in *Typee*'s (and Melville's) cultural significance and to the consolidation of broadly sexual and specifically queer historical types. Only through hindsight, perhaps, can we recognize these details as part of an ongoing world-making project, wherein queer histories of life in both the South Seas and the Anglophone reading world are mutually constituting. The emergence of homosexuality as a literary phenomenon obscures the complexities and vagaries of a history of sexuality that belie its own settling into a defined phenomenon. I want to show here how *Typee*'s rise to and fall from literary grace offer us purchase on a rich textual and social history that the commonplaces of sexuality-as-identity often leave behind.

Melville and the Missionary Position

There has never been a time when sex did not permeate discussions about *Typee*. What is already well known about the history of the text's printing in America demonstrates the case nicely. In response to the success (and controversy) of the 1846 Murray first edition, publisher John Wiley expressed interest in printing a new American edition. Wiley balked, however, at what some reviewers had called the "voluptuousness" and "racy" parts of the text and at Melville's critical attitude toward missionaries. As a condition of publication, he demanded that the book be expurgated of controversial sexual and political content. Editors of *Typee* today do not acknowledge the revised edition (the first American edition) as authoritative,[15] despite the fact that it would enjoy numerous printings in America—all while the original text continued to circulate in England. Melville did make the revisions Wiley wanted—sometimes eliminating entire chapters—all in an effort to increase the book's circulation.

Still, the sanitized text did not really shake its sexy reputation. Perhaps realizing this fact, Wiley even came to depend on it. In his paperback release of *Typee*, he (Melville) ultimately drew on the authority of countless reviewers who had already defined *Typee* by precisely those features to which Wiley objected in the text. This is a fact of the book's history that current editions of *Typee* tend not to include (perhaps because they place so little authority in the revised edition to begin with). Wiley could not resist adding a lengthy advertisement to the front of the revised edition: nine lavish pages of excerpts from reviewers (two sections of reviews, from Britain and America) who repeatedly described the book as both "charming" and "racy."[16] These deleted pages, however, amount to clear evidence of the ways a metacritical language about the text indexed and replayed the text's (deleted) "voluptuousness" and helped create the conditions of its circulation. Ironically, these reviews highlight as virtues the very textual vices that Wiley demanded be expurgated, producing a paradox that ultimately became invisible. Readers were told that this was a "racy" book (perhaps in more ways than one—even though race would not yet have been understood in quite this way), even though some of its most racy elements had become muted in the pages following the reviews. Thus was the book framed and marketed for readers who had yet to encounter the contents between its covers.

American reviews of *Typee* were generally split roughly into two groups. Literary figures such as Washington Irving, Nathaniel Hawthorne, Margaret Fuller, Ralph Waldo Emerson, and Henry David Thoreau all applauded the text's literary merits. Readers sympathetic to (or familiar with) the extensive missionary work taking place in the South Seas were outraged. The terms of the first group's assessment tended to focus on questions of style while the terms of the second on veracity. What they could agree on was that the text was rather naughty. Hawthorne, for instance, pointed out, "The narrative is skilfully managed, and in a literary point of view, the execution of the work is worthy of the novelty and interest of its subject."[17] Almost in spite of himself, however, he had to acknowledge the potential outrage of a more "staid" audience:

> The author's descriptions of the native girls are voluptuously
> colored, yet not more so than the exigencies of the subject
> appear to require. He has that freedom of view—it would be
> too harsh to call it laxity of principle—which renders him tol-
> erant of codes of morals that may be little in accordance with
> our own; a spirit proper enough to a young and adventurous

sailor, and which makes his book the more wholesome to our staid landsmen.[18]

"Laxity of principle" meanwhile worked just fine as a description of the work for Melville's detractors, particularly those averse to his representation of Christian missionaries. These detractors spoke powerfully enough to convince Wiley that sales might suffer. The most scathing of such critiques in America was William Oland Bourne's. In the *New York Christian Parlor Magazine*, Bourne lambasted the book with a litany of its shortcomings. He could not get over what he saw as its lack of realism, its contradictions, and the extent to which Melville could possibly have seen the Marquesans' vices in a virtuous light. According to Bourne, *Typee* is objectionable in part because it lauds the innocence of the "barbarians," which it values above "civilized society . . . excuses and wilfully palliates the cannibalism and savage vices of the Polynesians, or is guilty of . . . ignorance of [its] subject." Most reprehensibly, however, it is "redundant with bitter charges against the missionaries . . . and broadly accuses them of being the cause of the vice, misery, destitution, and unhappiness of the Polynesians wherever they have penetrated." Bourne concludes that Melville either never "saw the Marquesas" or that he wrote "a sort of romantic satire at the expense of the poor savages."[19] And these are but excerpts from the diatribe. Unable to bear thinking about where or what the Polynesians' happiness might have "penetrated," Bourne sees licentiousness as inaccuracy. This clues us to his preference for missionary accounts, which seem more accurate to him for *not* including these details. Protestant readers like Bourne, in other words, do not expect to see the Foucauldian "repressive hypothesis" at work in their religious writings.

Ultimately, Melville capitulated to the people who would look on his "freedom of view" unfavorably. In a letter to John Murray, the text's first publisher, he wrote that he would be willing to revise the text, so as to adopt "some slight purification of style": "the book," he says, "is certainly calculated for popular reading, or for none at all. . . . Proceeding on this principle then, I have rejected every thing, in revising the book, which refers to the missionaries. . . . Certain 'sea freedoms' also have been modified."[20] An exquisite irony thus attended this careful "calculation for popular reading." Calculating for popular reading meant eliminating some political and sexual content, but that very content persisted in the apparatus surrounding the text, not to mention the word-of-mouth reputation the text already had.[21] The very terms on which *Typee* enjoyed wide circulation led it to have a cultural life despite Wiley's effort to restrain the sexual and religious terms of that cultural life in his desired revisions. The reviews of *Typee*, and Melville's response to them, show us that in attempting to disarticulate Christianity from sexuality, the text's history (if not the first edition of the text itself) reveals their close relationship to each other. The fact that Melville was both licentious and critical of the missionaries catapulted his book even further into public consciousness. In short, it went viral.

The controversy surrounding Melville's treatment of both sex and the missionaries continued to fuel sales of *Typee* and led to the publication of further editions of the book (two in 1846, the first and then the revised editions; 1847; 1850; 1861; 1892; 1900) and thus also facilitated the circulation of all these seemingly indigestible descriptive details. Further, the success of *Typee* generated something of its very own category of spin-off literature, all examples of which seem to claim some derivation from *Typee*: other first-person accounts of "going native claiming to be true stories,"[22] Christian adventures in the South Seas,[23] adventure fiction,[24] and even a whole subgenre of children's literature.[25] *Typee*'s status as a cultural touchstone is a large part of what has enabled the book to be subject to such sustained and complex readings of its sexual representations for so long.

But knowing about the *Typee* that its nonreaders could have heard about without even having read the book allows us to understand only half of the fascinating story it offers us about sexual circulation. The other half of this story concerns Melville's staging of his books as the *product* of literary circulation. This part of the story sees Melville's text not merely as the object (some might say victim) of circulation around which a range of other stories and meanings cohere, but also as an exemplar of the ways and means by which discursive and literary proliferation operate, as one text calls on a set of others to produce a frame of reference and mutually reinforce each other.

The original problem for Wiley was with passages like the ones in the opening pages of the book, in which Tommo the narrator introduces and then exemplifies the nature of initial contact between Westerners and the natives of the South Seas. The text has us believe that the moment of cultural contact between Westerners and South Sea Islanders is a moment of sexual contact. To convey this to us convincingly, Melville scaffolds his narrative by invoking at the beginning a series of separate but parallel accounts of first contact between Westerners and Marquesas Islanders as they are conveyed by other travel writers and missionaries. In doing so, he establishes his narrator and prepares his readers for such contact before describing his own. Unlike the epigraphs at the beginning of *Moby-Dick* that precede the text without entering fully into the narrative itself, these opening anecdotes are folded into Tommo's prose at the start. The effect, as we will see, is overwhelming: repetition and assembly of disparate pieces of text create the sense that there is an obvious type of South Seas cultural, sexual initiation. Moreover, from this beginning Melville reveals the extent to which he participates in, builds on, and further extends the influence of the generic type. In front-loading these disparate pieces of text from other writers (pieces of text that do not usually find themselves at the beginning of other missionaries' travel narratives), Melville mobilizes for his own writing a machinery of generic influence whose momentum of generic type development extends well beyond the initial publication of *Typee* in 1846.

Before he even starts piecing these episodes together in his own story, it becomes clear to us that there is a set of expectations extending outward from the very name of the place Tommo is about to encounter. He believes he knows exactly what to think, for instance, when the captain finally assents to drop anchor near the Marquesas after six months at sea: "The Marquesas! What strange visions of outlandish things does the very name spirit up!"[26] What he expects is "strange" and "outlandish"—a telling index of the awkward relationship between the precise backward-looking configuration of expectation and the murky forward-looking strangeness that expectation courts but cannot fully anticipate: the name itself presumably carries a history that generates an image of what is to come. The very syntax of Tommo's initial descriptions seems sure of its ordering of words and yet also peculiarly incoherent at the sentence level. What he knows about the place, in particular order, one assumes, are its

> naked houris—cannibal banquets—groves of cocoa-nut—coral reefs—tattooed chiefs—and bamboo temples; sunny valleys planted with bread-fruit-trees—carved canoes dancing on the flashing blue waters—savage woodlands guarded by horrible idols—*heathenish rites and human sacrifices.*
>
> Such were the strangely jumbled anticipations that haunted me during our passage from the cruising ground. I felt an irresistible curiosity to see those islands. (13)

We see here not just the extent to which stories have come to structure Tommo's expectations and fuel his "irresistible curiosity"; we see also a picture of how Tommo's mind organizes these "strangely jumbled anticipations," laying out those semiconnected noun groups into a sequence of scenes he will see. The stories he knows are represented provisionally through a series of nouns, both connected and disjointed by the long dashes between them (strikingly similar to the chapter headings throughout the book that summarize the content of each short episode). This representation of the men's combined curiosity, desire, hunger, and water-weariness may be embodied in the ship itself—"Poor old ship! Her very looks denote her desires: how deplorably she appears" (13)—but it is Tommo (not the ship) who in offering up the descriptions we see allows us to see his previously disconnected nouns acquiring verbs and contexts.

Before the ship and its sailors actually experience their own moment of contact with the island and its residents, we get more exposition and examples from the travel of others—sometimes through gestures, sometimes through direct citation and elaborate retellings. We are referred, for instance, to William Ellis, whose *Polynesian Researches* Tommo describes as "interesting accounts of the abortive attempts made by the Tahiti Mission to establish a branch Mission upon certain islands of the group" (14). He "cannot avoid relating" a "somewhat amusing incident [that] took place in connection with these efforts" (14). The incident involved "an intrepid missionary" introducing his wife to the natives so that she might have some influence over their religious conversion. First thinking her to be a "prodigy," the natives are fascinated with the fact that she is clothed, so they, in Tommo's words, "sought to pierce the sacred veil of calico in which [she] was enshrined, and in the gratification of their curiosity so far overstepped the limits of good breeding, as deeply to offend the lady's sense of decorum. Her sex once ascertained, their idolatry was changed into contempt" (15). Lest the language of piercing the veil of calico prove too euphemistic, Tommo states the case plainly: "To the horror of her affectionate spouse, she was stripped of her garments, and given to understand that she could no longer carry on her deceits with impunity" (15). Then, to round out the first chapter of the book, Tommo skips ahead to his own later experience "between two and three years after the adventures recorded in this volume" (15) to offer yet another example of female licentiousness, this time on the part of a Nukuhevan Queen, who "singled out . . . an old *salt*" (16), extensively tattooed:

> She immediately approached the man, and pulling further
> open the bosom of his duck frock, and rolling up the leg of
> his wide trowsers, she gazed with admiration at the bright
> blue and vermilion pricking, thus disclosed to view. She hung
> over the fellow, caressing him, and expressing her delight in a
> variety of wild exclamations and gestures. (17)

By the time Tommo gets around to describing his own first encounter with the Marquesans, we have some sense of what to expect.[27]

Not surprised are we when the first item on Tommo's fantasy list, "naked houris," is also the first to be checked off: as the *Dolly* approaches the beach, it sails "right into the midst of . . . swimming nymphs, and they boarded us at every quarter" (24). The synecdoche tells the story. Ship and men alike are boarded by the nymphs, "their jet-black tresses streaming over their shoulders, and half enveloping their otherwise naked forms" (24). Thus, in an orgy—and an exfoliation of detailed description—"the 'Dolly' was fairly captured" (25). The sheer word count of the details helps force Melville's (and Tommo's) point:

> Our ship was now wholly given up to every species of riot
> and debauchery. Not the feeblest barrier was interposed

between the unholy passions of the crew and their unlimited
gratification. The grossest licentiousness and the most shameful inebriety prevailed, with occasional and but short-lived
interruptions, through the whole period of her stay. Alas for
the poor savages when exposed to the influence of these pol-
luting examples! Unsophisticated and confiding, they are easily
led into every vice, and humanity weeps over the ruin thus
remorselessly inflicted upon them by their European civilizers.
Thrice happy are they who, inhabiting some yet undiscovered
island in the midst of the ocean, have never been brought into
contaminating contact with the white man. (25)

In a seeming reversal of the colonial dynamic, Tommo acknowledges the complicity—the "contaminating contact"—of "the white
man."[28] Nonetheless, the sexually licentious native women fully
inhabit their role as the sexual aggressors.[29] (Not surprisingly, the
second sentence of the above passage is among those that Melville
deleted at Wiley's insistence.)

What Tommo calls the "abandoned voluptuousness" of "the
Marquesan girls" (25) becomes overstated in Melville's text through
this accumulation of parallel examples—each presumably drawn
from a separate account or experience of contact with the natives
of the South Seas. Such an accumulation creates the overwhelming
sense that all encounters with South Sea Islanders are sexual in exactly this way. This is also the kind of overstatement that Melville
attempts to downplay, at Wiley's insistence, for the revised edition
of the book. In the revised edition, therefore, Melville lightens his
description of the above scene by cutting the repetitive accumulations he originally built up.

The kind of textually accumulated sexual normativity that
Melville constructs on behalf of the South Seas natives and the text
written about this are paradoxically nonnormative for his English
and American readers. This paradox is a driving force for the text's
circulation, since the book creates momentum for itself by way of that
titillating disconnect. The ways that predictable abnormality is produced textually, however, raise interesting problems concerning just
how Melville crafts and describes sexual encounters throughout—
but also beyond—his text. They also establish an antagonism with

the Christian missionary accounts that he depends on, even when his resistance falls apart. He creates a narrative system against which the experiences he is about to relate can be tested and judged. In this case, Tommo's experiences seem to confirm what other storytellers have observed. Elsewhere in the text—when, for instance, Tommo tries to figure out whether he has met up with Typees or Happars, and when he attempts to determine whether he's being fed pork or human flesh—Melville uses this same strategy of testing Tommo's experience against the stories he has heard in order to demonstrate the ways in which experience itself exceeds (and builds on) them. These kinds of moments thus invite us to consider how important Melville's accumulated and selective reading of printed experiences (his own and others) is to the representation of his narrator's experiences, and to the proliferation of sexual discourse in his own text. They also allow us to recognize that some sexual discourses are more distinctly marked as paradigms than others. Some descriptions of sexual behavior—like those that open the book—are quite detailed and through their linguistic exertion enable us to see how sexual discourse proliferates unevenly in *Typee*, depending on the nature of the sexuality in question.

It seems undeniable that Melville relies on common images and fantasies of Western first contact with South Sea Islanders; the question is, how did they come to seem so common? The critical literature on Melville's text has already made much of this focus on the colonial encounter between the desires and expectations of sailors and missionaries and the putative sexuality of South Sea Islanders. Among the most significant contributions to the critical literature is T. Walter Herbert Jr.'s *Marquesan Encounters*. Not unlike Melville himself, Herbert reproduces, side by side, some of these first contact moments from Porter (whom he describes as "a spokesman for the Enlightenment") and C. S. Stewart ("a Calvinist"); both are referenced by name in *Typee*, conveying the sense that Melville's book is, at least at the beginning, an account of accounts.[30] The examples that Herbert supplies help to explain his argument; he traces the cultural features common to a group of quite disparate texts and argues they can tell us something about the culture that those texts represent—and about the "civilization" that has produced them.

Herbert is thus reading for a pattern of examples, reading those examples with and against each other, so as to articulate the complicated status of sexuality in conceptions of civilization. It is precisely through the sexual mores expressed in these writings that Herbert diagnoses the centrality of sexuality to civilization in Melville's text.[31] In Porter's account, for instance, Marquesan men "invited us to shore and pointed to the women and the house near which they were standing, accompanying their invitation with gestures which we could not misunderstand; and the girls themselves showed no disinclination to grant every favour we might be disposed to ask."[32] When this approach fails, "the old chief directed the young girls to swim off to us: but on the appearance of reluctance, the young men led them toward the water, where they were soon devested of every covering and conducted to the boat amid the loud plaudits."[33] When the women finally reach the boat, the seamen are perfect gentlemen, who "threw [the women] their handkerchiefs for a covering."[34] Stewart, on the other hand, records that both men and women swam to his ship naked and "the officers by their swords very courteously pointed out the steps at the gangway to them."[35] Nonetheless, he continues, "I doubt not it is the first [ship] in which they have ever known any restriction to be placed on the grossest licentiousness," and "the vessel was thus cleared of noise and nakedness and the perfumes of cocoa-nut oil and other strong odours, which had greatly annoyed and disgusted us."[36] By drawing on these details and citing them in close proximity to each other, Melville creates the sense not just that naked native women always come out to greet sailing ships but also that this is the first detail to which writers introduce their readers in their travel accounts.

But anyone who picks up a nineteenth-century text by William Ellis, David Porter, C. S. Stewart, or any other text from the early 1800s by a missionary or sailor is likely to have a very different experience reading about Western encounters with South Sea Islanders from the one Melville offers. One does not find in the opening pages of most missionary accounts the kind of lavish or prurient detail that Melville records early in *Typee*. These examples of sexual-cultural contact do appear, but not in the early pages to frame the culture. Such accounts of first contact take some time for the expectant reader to find and usually are not afforded quite the same word count in which Melville indulges. The opening chapters of Stewart's journal, for instance, focus almost exclusively on the landscape. Some accounts will quote from others (as Ephraim Eveleth quotes from Stewart), but only because the writer believes something is better described by another—not to assemble an arsenal of examples that prove a particular point. Furthermore, in many such texts the first details we learn about the natives are not sexual at all. In some texts, one has to really search to find examples of the status of sexuality in the missionaries' accounts: they do not appear at the beginning as the sine qua non of colonial encounters, as Herbert's analysis seems to imply. To pull such details out from the middle of books and place them side by side as Melville does is thus already to distort—and alienate them from—their initial reading context in the service of a new one.

To the extent that missionary writing corresponds generally to the generic expectations produced by travel writing, Melville's own work of extracting, condensing, and accumulating pointed details about first contact creates within the pages of his text an intertextually scaffolded sense of both cultural and textual inevitability that never existed in those earlier texts. This is Melville's most conscious creation of a queer frame of reference, if we think of queer in non-normative sexual terms. We wait for Tommo's own perverse first encounter with the natives, knowing that it certainly must come soon because he has prepared us for it. To extract comparable details from missionary accounts that show similarity with Melville's own is therefore to miss the point about *Typee*'s innovation. It is through the accumulation and placement of similar details alongside each other at the opening of *Typee* that Melville creates the sense of a cultural archetype.

Melville's extractions and recirculations of these details thus also reframe their meaning. The orgy of capture on the *Dolly* and the old salt's encounter with the Nukuhevan Queen acquire comic status and seem to exist in the present tense for the reader in ways they never did for the missionaries. In his *History of the Sandwich Islands* (1829), for example, Ephraim Eveleth seems content to treat the matter of sexual vice only once it has been cured: the "facts," he says, are that once he learns of the existence of immortal life, "the drunkard becomes sober; the lewd person pure; the thief falls in love with honesty; and the idolater looks away from the creature to the Creator, and strives to raise his life to a heavenly standard."[37] Sins are cataloged in far fewer words than the glories of eternal life and treated merely as the condition for salvation. Even where missionaries' initial descriptions of natives do highlight differences in sexual behavior and mores, the mode of description is much more muted than Melville's. In his *Historical Sketch of the Hawaiian Mission,* the Reverend Samuel Colcord Bartlett matter-of-factly describes the Hawaiians as "a well formed, muscular race, with olive complexions and open countenances, in the lowest stages of barbarism, sensuality, and vice." We are told that "the most revolting forms of vice, as Captain Cook had occasion to know, were practiced in open sight," but Bartlett elects to let the statement stand at that.[38]

Although Bartlett refers to "barbarism, sensuality, and vice," comments on the natives' nudity, and dismisses the polygamy he sees, he does not linger on or revel in these details. Unlike Melville, he seems to see sex as something vicious not to be lingered on. He moves on in successive paragraphs to discuss questions of human sacrifice, science, and eating. The most revolting forms of vice "are practiced" in the passive voice, invoked only to be occluded. It is quite often the case that the islanders' sexual behavior will be conveyed obliquely through words like *vice* or *sensuality,* not through detailed descriptions or stories that elaborate or plot. Moreover, even these oblique details do not usually appear in the text's introduction, where they condition readers' expectations. Where they do appear, they are usually embedded within the text, often even a hundred pages or so into the narrative.

The fact that most missionary accounts of life in the South Seas do not offer elaborate descriptions of the natives' behavior can be explained by the very project in which they are engaged. The missionaries' evangelical goals are elaborated as a gift to the islanders. Several American agencies published instructions for the missionaries that outline their goals primarily in terms of what they needed to accomplish among themselves as a group. In 1823, the American Board of Commissioners for Foreign Missions published

Instructions to the Missionaries about to Embark for the Sandwich Islands; this document outlines the need for missionaries to be united and to make themselves "available for piety." It cites friendship with the natives as being one of the keys to success but never really offers much description of what the missionaries will encounter when they arrive.[39]

The fact that these missionary accounts do not erect elaborate descriptions of sexual life in the South Seas thus seems striking, or at least somewhat unexpected, given Melville's treatment of first contact in the opening pages of his book. In stipulating these generic expectations, Melville goes some distance toward showing us how the missionary accounts themselves are resignified and reframed through their reconstruction. Melville thus also puts both himself and his reader in a position to test the generic expectations that he assumes his reader to have, creating the effect of testing even his own account against those of the missionaries—a fact that is central to understanding the operation of the book's irony and the narrator's ambivalence toward the very authorities he invokes. Through this kind of ironic resignification of the missionary framework, Melville shows on the one hand how thoroughly intertwined the history of sexuality is with the religious frameworks of description, and on the other how central irony can be to the disarticulation of sexuality from religion, especially when each relies on the language of the other.

Virtuous Vices and the Problem of Audience

What becomes clear throughout the book are the ways that the stories Tommo claims to have heard and read chisel out a boundary between the narrative paradigms he has been given and the details he presents. Like so many travel writers, Tommo wants to show us things that "are seldom proclaimed at home" (37), and he struggles to present those details in something like their own terms while also translating them into terms his audience will understand. Where Melville strives most for language to describe the Typees' worldview is in those moments when he tries to conceptualize virtue, sexual behavior, and gender roles beyond the linguistic structures he knows, with only the language he has. These are the places in the text where Melville stretches the language he has available to him to describe what is unfamiliar—where analogy becomes both his ally and his enemy.

The problem of describing the Typees' sense of "virtue" demonstrates the case nicely. Tommo says he has been told that the Typees "had no word in their language to express the idea of virtue" (151). Although he dismisses this assertion, he avers that such a statement, were it to be taken seriously, "might be met by stating that their language was almost entirely destitute of terms to express the delightful ideas conveyed by our endless catalogue of civilized crimes" (151). Civilization, he suggests, is itself barbaric in many ways, and virtue is not the domain only of those "civilizations" that have a word for it. Virtue is connected not just to ideas of good breeding or civilization; it is connected also with standards of sexual behavior, its opposite, *vice,* being the operative term for all things sexual in accounts of South Sea life up to the middle of the nineteenth century. Following his comments about virtue, he continues that the Typees are most happy and, he implies, most virtuous because of the things that do not characterize their way of life. First among these is money: "That 'root of all evil' was not to be found in the valley" (151). But also among the virtuously missing, perhaps an effect of the absence of money, is the absence of unhappiness defined in terms of gender and sex roles: "In this secluded abode of happiness there were no cross old women, no cruel step-dames, no withered spinsters, no love-sick maidens, no sour old bachelors, no inattentive husbands, no melancholy young men, no blubbering youngsters, and no squalling brats" (151–52). In America, all these figures have in common their location outside the conventional structure of marriage, even if the terms of their exclusion (and therefore the terms of their virtue) are still derived from the Christian theology that Tommo ascribed to the Protestant missionaries. It is not that there are no "old women," "step-dames," "spinsters," "maidens," "bachelors," "husbands," "young men," or "youngsters" in *Typee*; Tommo has observed examples of them all. But in *Typee* they already have lost their pejorative adjectives. One might read this fact as evidence that Tommo's effort to distinguish virtue and even sociosexual states of being in Typee from their American counterparts collapses back into itself:

after all, his language is no less American English for its efforts to describe the Typee social world. Unlike those moments in the text when English simply is not up to the task and he must use words like *tappa* and *Ti* to describe irreducibly foreign objects, when Tommo wants to convey a yet-to-be-abstracted idea of virtue, English does supply him with the tools. But this collapse of the socially foreign and the linguistically familiar nonetheless indicates the possibility that virtue and sexuality themselves might have other forms in Typee, even if Tommo has no language to describe them other than the one he already knows. What we can see beginning to open up here is a space for nonpejorative sexual sociability outside of traditional marriage, but those details seem to have no recognizable shorthand for Melville's audience, so they exist only as details.

From the beginning of the book, Tommo sees himself as outside of any evangelical project, but the words he has available to describe what he sees throw him back into the frameworks from which he wants to distance himself. The fact that he regularly invokes a range of texts from the Bible to *Robinson Crusoe* to *Paradise Lost* (texts that also evoke a range of attachments to Christian belief) invites us to see where his translations break down—where, in other words, he struggles for language beyond the familiar texts and intertexts he has already cited. The words from the native culture that he does retain—*taboo, Ti,* and *tappa,* for instance—throw his other descriptions into sharp relief, suggesting the degree to which he strives for literary terms beyond known English referents. Translation reaches its limits when equivalent words in English do not exist, but these words nonetheless circulate as further evidence of Marquesan strangeness and perversion. By inhabiting both language worlds fully, Tommo can aim more precisely to designate their peculiarities and their antagonisms without having to abandon either until the end. In this way, Melville's language enacts what is "strange" and "incomprehensible" while also generating interest for readers to whom Tommo has promised a "stirring adventure." Thus Melville's efforts to demarcate the boundaries between his own descriptions and the worldviews he cites point to a space in his text that cannot be fully assimilated to Western points of view—even and perhaps especially where those boundaries fail to be maintained.

It may well be the fact that these details could not be assimilated within the missionary point of view that so angered reviewers like William Oland Bourne and thus worried Wiley. They wanted more of a simple moral story. In the absence of this formal simplicity, one of the biggest accusations Bourne could make against Melville was that these details could not possibly be accurate. What Bourne fails to realize is that Melville has perhaps done the missionary movement a service, having succeeded in both simplifying and complicating the story that the missionaries tell about their encounters with the natives of the South Seas. He simplifies it by augmenting the sexual nature of contact with the natives—collecting and assembling descriptions that amount to a textual pattern—even if he then complicates his own simplification by later relying on the same religious frameworks in whose name vice and sensuality are pitted against Christian conversion.

But those details that are already not assimilable to existing narrative frameworks of missionary aims—whether to affirm or question those frameworks—are allowed to stand and circulate freely in the text. It is precisely through these kinds of unassimilable details that *Typee* thus creates a descriptive space that pries open a nondominant way of thinking about civilization in the nineteenth century. Some of these same unassimilable details eventually produce and acquire queer meanings when they resonate with other details. We might even say that these are the same kinds of details that Melville recognizes as dispersed in the missionary accounts—details that come to be comprehensible to readers like Stoddard only after they are recognized for the resonance they have with the details dispersed in other texts.

The popularization of *Typee*'s plots about the naked natives that Melville's characters first encounter also made possible the circulation of those details seemingly unassimilable to that plot: details that were filtered through the murky and seemingly boundless secular Christian framework, as well as those details that did not quite fit the only officially identified romance on the island, between Tommo and Fayaway. Tommo would not claim the same attachment to Kory-Kory, the same terms of adoration for Marnoo, or the same dependence on Toby that he would claim for his avowed love object, Fayaway. Without a doubt, the most overt language of love in the novel is reserved for professions of Tommo's love for Fayaway. But precisely because these filtered details were important to advancing the plot of the text, they could never be left totally behind as *Typee*'s secrets were circulated to the ends of the earth. They lay in wait for readers who would perversely see something more appealing in Tommo's participation with Mehevi in the culture of the Bachelors' Ti, more tender in his descriptions of Marnoo, and something attractive even in his intimacy with Kory-Kory, notwithstanding Tommo's description of Kory-Kory as a "hideous object" (102). It is possible to read these details as part of the formation of another narrative type, however, only when enough parallel examples are accumulated to allow them to resonate as such.

Between Showing and Telling: *Typee*'s Ironic and Erotic Immanence

Because of the time lag between reading and writing about reading, but also because we know so little about queer reading practices in the nineteenth century, it is difficult to pinpoint with precision when *Typee*'s queerness became visible to its readers. The best information comes to us through writing that allows us to trace the gradual development of references to a web of writers (and texts), which seems to signal emergent efforts to identify or describe complex modes of same-sex sociability and world-making that have yet to be defined as identities. To the extent that writing and its circulation create public consciousness of such worlds and social encounters (and do not merely reflect them), it is possible that Stoddard had as much to do with producing Melville's queerness as Melville's own writing did—despite the fact that there was no widespread acknowledgment of what Stoddard took to be obvious until many years after *Typee* first appeared. (Recall that Stoddard's story was published twenty-seven years after Melville's book came into print.)

Even reviewers drawing comparisons between Melville's and Stoddard's writing (and relationships between men were more *consciously* central to Stoddard's prose than to Melville's) tended to skip over the seemingly bland fact that the *South-Sea Idyls* stories were all about love affairs between men;[40] they were far more interested in measuring the relationship between Stoddard's and Melville's faithfulness to the truth of South Seas living. One reviewer claimed that "Mr. Stoddard has seized the very spirit and tone of the life of which he tells."[41] If so, this spirit is at least in part derived from Melville. Furthermore, what seems hidden in plain sight from so many commentators is something very peculiar about this "spirit and tone of life" that Stoddard elsewhere describes in his letter to Walt Whitman: he is attracted to the South Seas because it is the place where love between men is free and he can escape "the frigid manners of the Christians."[42] This uneven history of the text's reception suggests, on the one hand, that there is a web of textual understanding unfolding among readers and writers at the end of the nineteenth century. On the other hand, it suggests that whatever *Typee* is showing us in the details it describes is not what it is telling us at the level of plot. This gap between what the text shows its readers and what it tells its readers—usually known as dramatic irony—is filled with lengthy passages of description that embed the homo-relationality central to Tommo's life in the South Seas. Embedded in passages of description—and yet also lost between what the story tells and what it shows—is the nascent sexuality of the text that can only be described in terms of its immanence, since it is not yet visible as such. How Stoddard and perhaps Whitman, too, came to recognize what Whitman termed "adhesiveness" in South Seas' lifeworlds and the writing about them turns on accumulated readings of such descriptive passages that amount to the creation of a frame of reference.

To restate the point slightly differently, it is precisely through descriptive details that had yet to become consonant with the simple abstraction of homosexuality that Melville's *Typee* has come to seem queerest to readers. *Typee* is not a drama of a love affair between men, as Stoddard's stories are. But it does feature quite intense attachments between men. These kinds of relationships first reach their fullest realization at the center of Stoddard's novels and stories, but the language for describing them has been a long time in the making. These features of the text are shown, but they are not described as types of sexual or intimate relationships. So by the end of the nineteenth century, Stoddard and others do to the writing of Melville and others what Melville has done with the texts of the missionaries. They cherry-pick texts and excerpts, assembling them alongside each other, and thus create a sense that through these sites of same-sexual sociability between (and world-making by) men, replete with their lush and elaborate place descriptions, queer worlds become visible as such. In an exquisite irony, Melville's acquired queerness is the result of a historical repetition of Melville's own model of recirculation in *Typee*: just as the missionaries' stories of sexual perversion were plucked from their hiding places and accumulated side by side, so too is *Typee* served up as a queer dish for which Melville himself composed the recipe. Its trace persists in Stoddard's writing, in Edward Carpenter's *Ioläus,* and even finds its way into Whitman's correspondence.

These collections of writing and traces of reading create the frames of reading and understanding that Martin suggested were lacking among many readers when *Typee* was first released. Take for example Tommo's descriptions of Marnoo, a character who appears only sporadically in *Typee* since he is "taboo," meaning he can move freely between even warring tribes without any harm coming to him. Among the natives, he is the figure of social circulation par excellence. And Tommo is at his homoerotic queerest when describing him: Marnoo is nothing less than a "Polynesian Apollo" with a "cheek . . . of a feminine softness" (162), "naked arms," "brilliant eyes," and "natural eloquence" (164). From our vantage point, it seems difficult not to see how intensely compelled Tommo is by Marnoo. We are even told outright that Marnoo "roused [Tommo's] desire" (163). Martin and Justin D. Edwards have cited textual antecedents to some of these encounters in other accounts of South Sea travels. Martin argues, for instance, that Marnoo's androgyny has a history in French Tahitian literature, while Edwards points to a passage from Stewart's description of a Marquesan prince as a forerunner to Melville's Marnoo: "Piaroro [is] a prince by nature as well as blood, one of the finest looking men I ever saw, tall and large, not very muscular, but of admirable proportions, with a general contour of figure . . . that would do grace to an Apollo."[43] But Melville does not call attention to this intertextuality as he did when he cited from Stewart's and Porter's writings. He does not, therefore, foreground

these encounters in terms of a narrative pattern as he did in the
opening chapters of his text when he was describing sexual contact
between Western men and South Seas women.

As incredible as it may seem that these passages could ever
have been hidden in plain sight, it is important to remember that
what mutes Melville's presentation of those male-male erotics is the
text's pronounced language of Tommo's love for Fayaway, his consciously avowed love object. So obvious does he take his state of
affairs to be that he declares—in the same chapter where he catalogs
the "Polynesian Apollo"—that "if the reader have not observed ere
this that I was the declared admirer of Miss Fayaway, all I can say is
that he is little conversant with affairs of the heart, and I certainly
shall not trouble myself to enlighten him any farther" (161). The
presumed straightforwardness of his attraction for her throws everything else into high relief. Only to later readers does this appear
to be a pattern—largely, I think, because not enough examples had
yet appeared that would lead Melville to see this particular pattern
of sexual sociability between men as both a cultural and a literary
conceit.

Which is not to say that *Typee* does not participate in queer
type development. Once it becomes possible to see the text's queerness at all, we can also see how *Typee* begins to create its own internal patterns by accumulating instances of Tommo's fascinated
descriptions of men. These begin to make visible a particular type of
sexualized sociability—but it is a beginning that can be recognized
as a beginning only once the type evolution it sets in place advances
further.

One place where *Typee* allows us to see its relatively unconscious participation in textual pattern development, or more specifically where Melville builds on existing type language to grasp
for language to describe what Tommo sees, is in the account of
the Bachelors' Ti. Scholars have recently commented on the significance and development of the bachelor type as a precursor to the
homosexual and as a site for reimagining cultural participation in
ideologies of reproduction.[44] Writers' consciousness of the significance of this type can be seen in texts ranging from Charles Lamb's
"A Bachelor's Complaint of the Behavior of Married People" and

James Fenimore Cooper's *Notions of the Americans: Picked Up by a Travelling Bachelor* through to Melville's own later "The Paradise of Bachelors and the Tartarus of Maids."[45] The fact that there was so much literary and social interest in the category of the bachelor makes it that much more interesting that Melville does not situate his treatment of bachelors in *Typee* within the same missionary intertextual frameworks that he does his moment of cultural contact. That he does not might suggest to us that however obvious the persistence of the bachelor type may have been in nineteenth-century American literary life, it does not signify easily as an exotic phenomenon or as part of the South Seas' sexual type pattern that he participates in producing.

Melville couches *Typee*'s bachelor life in terms of its similarity to world bachelor culture. But as he does throughout *Typee*, he also in turn opens up space for us to see his own participation in complicating the bachelor type. The Ti is a space where only the men gather and where the tribe's leader, Mehevi, holds court. Despite Tommo's accounts of the men's marriages, he insists on calling this place the "Bachelors' Ti." Tommo makes daily visits to the Ti and likens his eating experiences there to that of "bachelors, all the world over, [who] are famous for serving up unexceptionable repasts" (188). To measure the peculiarity of Typee bachelor culture, Melville translates it into the register of bachelor cultures from "the world over." The term seems to make a round peg out of a square hole, perhaps out of courtesy to Melville's readers, or perhaps because Melville had no other language to adequately describe what Tommo was seeing. In any event, the homosocial culture of the South Seas seems not to have emerged yet as singular on its own terms, and coming to those terms may well constitute Melville's first contribution to literary bachelorhood.[46]

Mehevi is one complicated "bachelor," to say the least. Tommo's descriptions convey a complexly gendered figure. His first encounter with Mehevi leads him to feel simultaneously mothered, emasculated, and manhandled: as an elder attempts to administer medical treatment to Tommo's injured leg, "Mehevi, upon the same principle which prompts an affectionate mother to hold a struggling child in a dentist's chair, restrained me in his powerful grasp, and actually encouraged the wretch in this infliction of torture" (99). As the authoritative representative of male social sexual roles, Mehevi's significance extends also to his embodiment of marital conventions in Typee. Tommo's initial sense of Mehevi as both maternally affectionate and paternally powerful is confirmed by the ways Mehevi makes intense social and sexual attachments across sex and gender.

It is again through descriptions of Mehevi, as Tommo conveys to us the marriage structure of the Typees, that we can begin to see how Melville's descriptions, rather than his plotting of story details, contribute to the prolonged latency of our recognition that Tommo himself has a "marriage life" similar to Mehevi. It is notable that only very late in his stay with the natives (and late in the text) does Tommo claim that he notices any kind of "matrimonial relations subsisting in Typee" (223). Up to this point, he has noticed a wide range of relationships. Among these were what he took to be "Platonic affection" between the sexes (223) and the "confirmed bachelor[hood]" of Mehevi and the members of the Ti or "Bachelor's Hall" (223–24). But Tommo suspects that the bachelors of the Ti might be "carrying on love intrigues with the maidens of the tribe" (224). He concludes: "A regular system of polygamy exists among the islanders; but of a most extraordinary nature,—a plurality of husbands, instead of wives; and this solitary fact speaks volumes for the gentle disposition of the male population" (225). (Tommo seems to presume that this system produces increased male femininity.) By introducing the sociosexual relationships among the Typees in terms of matrimony—prior to describing them in terms of "polygamy"— Tommo accomplishes yet another feat of narrative piggybacking: he folds the relationships between men into the marriage between a man and a woman. In the context of an otherwise familiar marriage story where the woman is the identified love object, the extra man becomes a kind of accessory. Even the description of how this "regular system" operates begins with the girls and seems not quite to explain the role of this second man:

> The girls are first wooed and won, at a very tender age, by
> some stripling in the household in which they reside. This,
> however, is a mere frolic of the affections, and no formal
> engagement is contracted. By the time the first love has a little

subsided, a second suitor presents himself, of graver years, and
carries both boy and girl away to his own habitation. This
disinterested and generous-hearted fellow now weds the young
couple—marrying damsel and lover at the same time—and all
three thenceforth live together as harmoniously as so many
turtles. (225–26)

The presence of the woman (and perhaps the comparison to turtles)
would seem to make the marriage recognizable to non-Polynesian
eyes. The language that describes this "regular system" does not
offer us any other alternatives for understanding how these relationships might work and does not in any way acknowledge that this
system also makes men and women equally viable lovers for other
men.

There are two key examples of how this polygamous marriage
works in the text, only one of which is flagged for us as such, although both demonstrate Tommo's more pronounced linguistic self-
consciousness of the love relationships between men and women
(compared with his descriptions of the relationships between men).
Both also demonstrate the extent to which invoking the marriage
narrative becomes one condition of possibility for showing (without telling about) relationships beyond the conventional two-person
marriage paradigm. The clearest example of the "regular system of
polygamy" is flagged for us when Tommo exemplifies this three-
person paradigm. He admits that he has observed one of these polygamous threesomes, seemingly initiated by Mehevi: "Mehevi . . . was
not the only person upon whom the damsel Moonoony smiled—the
young fellow of fifteen, who permanently resided in the house with
her, was decidedly in her good graces. I sometimes beheld both him
and the chief making love at the same time" (224). To whom they
are making love—Moonoony or each other—is never made clear
in the text. The "sometimes" indicates a kind of regularity beyond
coincidence, suggesting not only that the sexual acts are worthy of
notice, but also that they may subscribe to a different conception of
sexual privacy from what Tommo is used to. It is also notable that
as he describes Mehevi's lovemaking, Tommo seems particularly
detached, never placing himself in the context of immediate observation as he does when he describes other parts of Typee life, but

only commenting on a way of being he seemed regularly to inhabit in the past.

In this detached way, Tommo can claim to be describing Mehevi's marriage, but he never acknowledges that his own primary relationship web in Typee is the other obvious example of triangulated marriage—despite the fact that he everywhere *shows* us his own triadic intimate arrangement. Kory-Kory is as devoted to him as Fayaway is, and the three travel everywhere together. Tommo never says so, but his own relationship with Kory-Kory and Fayaway structurally resembles Mehevi's. Just before Tommo leaves the Typee valley, and long after the point at which he has described the marriage structure, we get a glimpse into the intensity of his attachments. Tommo is thinking wistfully of home and of leaving the valley. He fixates on the lonely old warrior who sits weaving cocoa-nut branches all day long and describes his act of looking: "Whenever my gentle Fayaway and Kory-Kory, laying themselves down beside me, would leave me awhile to uninterrupted repose, I took a strange interest in the slightest movements of the eccentric old warrior" (282). This particular detail is the closest he comes to describing his sleeping arrangements and subtly assumes that there are times when they both do not leave him so "uninterrupted." Our intrepid narrator seems somehow divided against himself: he cannot see himself as the same kind of man that Mehevi is, although he can make Mehevi the object of his own descriptions. The fact that this moment of autochthonous identification never materializes leaves it for the reader to recognize, which is why its recognition is dependent on its readers' developing frameworks for understanding it.

The second striking feature of the words that describe this social arrangement of sexual relationships is the utter absence of moralizing language. Christian moralism disappears at the moment when it seems most likely to appear: the moment when, as in the opening example of the missionary wife's encounter with the natives, Protestant ideas about sexuality clash with native ideas about sexual roles and sexual difference. Further, the absence of censorious language by default allows the "second suitor of graver years," whether it be Mehevi or Tommo himself, to have a relationship with both the damsel and the first lover on equal terms. Tommo perhaps reaches his own sense of limit in this regard, since the language he uses to distinguish Fayaway and Kory-Kory can never really refrain from elevating the status of his affection for Fayaway. She is clearly the avowed object of Tommo's desire. He can earnestly long for her and idealize her in the text in a way that he does not (perhaps cannot) recognize Kory-Kory. At the same time that Tommo openly desires only Fayaway, his social relationships in the Typee valley (the unit of three that he forms with Fayaway and Kory-Kory) closely mirror the matrimonial arrangement that Mehevi has. There is no clear evidence from Tommo's description of the chief and the young man "making love at the same time" that Mehevi takes the young man as his love object. The text does not confirm in any overt sense that the chief and the young man are lovers; nor does it treat the possibility of such a reading with disdain or refusal. Tommo's seeming neutrality on the matter seems to suggest the absence of a prohibition against homosexuality and already opens up possibilities for readers to see a glimmer of license for sexual relationships between men. Melville shows them, however, without actually telling them. We will eventually come to need more examples of such showing in order to recognize the emergence of a narrative type, but what already seems to be opening up through these descriptions is a sense that narrative objectification—where one speaker describes and therefore treats the world around him, including its people, as objects outside himself—can help to generate, in perhaps delayed ways, modes of understanding subjectivity. It is not just that Melville shows us homoerotic relationships here, but how (and when) his descriptions of these relationships factor into our ability to see and read them.

To say that Tommo conveys an intense, even sexual, appreciation for Toby, Kory-Kory, Marnoo, and even Mehevi is to say not just that he objectifies them, but also that they exist in somehow parallel structure to the rest of the world that Tommo likewise describes. After all, the Polynesians in particular are not only members of a society but features of a whole different island world. This is where we begin to see a paradox at the heart of sexual type accumulation and the "acquired queerness" that marks Melville's and *Typee*'s print circulation. To see Tommo and Kory-Kory as the queer figures they become risks reducing them to *themselves*: to a bounded identity category that abstracts them out of the very situatedness that defines them, out of the environments in which they are embedded, and out of the textual descriptions through which they are *shown,* not told or explained. The accumulation and placing of sexual details alongside each other are at once a mode of gathering and abstracting that obscures the embeddedness, the complexity, and the messiness that makes abstraction of sexuality possible to begin with.

This is why it is so important to hold on to the fact that throughout *Typee* all of the relationships Tommo describes are situated relationships. A very specific environment licenses them. From the very opening of the book, the landscape appears to us as exceptional, itself imbued with a kind sexual agency: the Typee valley's "green and sloping acclivities," "deep and romantic glens" convey a scene that "insensibly swells into lofty majestic heights," "all apparently radiating from a common centre, and the upper extremities of which are lost to the eye beneath the shadow of the mountains" (34). Tommo feels "a pang of regret that a scene so enchanting should be hidden from the world in these remote seas, and seldom meet the eyes of devoted lovers of nature" (34). Regularly he comments on the sights "that will ever be vividly impressed upon my mind" (60), claiming in conventional literary fashion that "had a glimpse of the gardens of Paradise been revealed to me I could scarcely have been more ravished with the sight" (64). Usually inspired by the way he reads the environment around him, Tommo's descriptions shift from extremes of alacrity to fear—the one often turned in on itself into the other—but they always have a kind of intense visceral quality to them.

Out of Tommo's captivation with his physical surroundings emerges his strongest statement that connects "the tranquillizing influences of beautiful scenery, and the exhibition of human life under so novel and charming an aspect" (134). This statement sums up the scene that has just preceded it, which suggests that particular sexual practices (exhibitions of human life) do indeed emerge out of the tranquility of the landscape: "Frequently in the afternoon [Kory-Kory] would carry me to a particular part of the stream, where the beauty of the scene produced a soothing influence upon my mind. At this place the waters flowed between grassy banks, planted with enormous bread-fruit trees, whose vast branches interlacing over-head, formed a leafy canopy; near the stream were several smooth black rocks." This location comes to be entextualized as the site of domestic bliss, a room, replete with "a delightful couch" made of a leaf-lined cavity (133). This is where, both soothed and inspired by the landscape and accompanied by his intimates, Tommo says, "I often lay for hours, covered with a gauze-like veil of tappa, while Fayaway, seated beside me, and holding in her hand a fan woven from the leaflets of a young cocoa-nut bough, brushed aside the insects that occasionally lighted on my face, and Kory-Kory, with a view of chasing away my melancholy, performed a thousand antics in the water before us" (134).

In comparing the trees to a canopy that transforms a rock into a couch, Tommo is already exceeding the primitivism he attributes to the landscape. But this is rather the point. The landscape, viewed through his eyes, is constantly imbued with social significance. In fact, it structures his entire imagination of the social world of Typee, by way of understated comparisons with the social world Tommo knows. (A similar comparison exists in Tommo's description of the breadfruit tree, which he first compares to the patriarchal elm in New England before describing its edges as a "lady's lace collar" [138].) But Tommo's sense is that the environment naturalizes par-ticular social relationships, even as his own comparisons call atten-tion to their constructedness.

The fact that Western travelers and observers objectify the people and lands they are writing about has come under consider-able fire in recent years for the ways in which these texts deny sub-jectivity and even humanity to the people so described. Bruce Har-vey critiques travel writing for the ways it projects non-Americans as features of the landscape, thus ultimately denying the possibility for a fully inhabitable textual subjectivity in the context of these narratives: "Human subjects (other than the narrator, that is) typi-cally fold into the scenery rather than becoming dramatic actors in their own right." Kory-Kory is one of the characters that Harvey de-scribes as "folded into the scenery." On the one hand, Kory-Kory's subjectivity may well be limited within the confines of the text. Harvey insists nonetheless that even Kory-Kory, "behind the prison-bars of his own culture," can be seen as more than a narrative prop: he displays a "resistant materiality" in propelling Tommo's gaze to begin with.[47] Problems no doubt emerge when a text that flattens figures like Kory-Kory into features of the landscape then becomes so authoritative that imagining their subjectivity becomes difficult. But it is also possible to imagine that the liberal ideal of self-possessed subjectivity is not the only ground on which characters can be recognized or exert literary influence.[48]

Melville might never have predicted that his *Typee* would be excerpted and included in Carpenter's *Ioläus: An Anthology of Friendship* (1908) and thus read as part of an emerging pattern of queer writing. How could he? He might more successfully have predicted the decimation of the populations of the Marquesas, given his critique of the "civilizing" influence of the missionaries and of Westerners more generally.[49] (Thus was Stoddard able to see how, in carrying a story of the Typee valley's secrets "to the ends of the earth," *Typee* "plucked out the heart of its mystery and beautiful and barbarous Typee lies naked and forsaken.") There is, however, an embedded sexuality that comes to be read only when the frameworks for reading it have been developed as such and acquired by readers. Out of even the flattest figures least endowed with subjectivity, like Kory-Kory, stories of complex sociability and lifeworlds can be told.

The circuits of literary circulation breed unpredictable literary and social products. But this is not to say that the texts themselves do not participate in producing their own unintended outcomes. The linguistic experiment that was *Typee* generated a range of responses that constantly shifted emphasis to and from different aspects of the text. To a large degree, the combination of religious and sexual controversy facilitated the textual reproductions of *Typee,* making it possible for readers to see how what Melville actually did write became queerer and queerer in its rereadings—and arguably perhaps more and more perverted in all kinds of ways. The stuff of both the explicitly identified sexual features of first contact accounts as well as the seemingly implied homoerotic descriptions could be more fully seen retroactively, once a full-fledged narrative type had developed—even though the type arguably could not have developed, in its American incarnation, without *Typee.*

Postscript: The New (Queer) Melville and the Death of *Typee*

If *Typee* and its circulation have been as instrumental to nineteenth-century queer type production as I'm suggesting, one question nonetheless remains: how and why has circulation been so unkind to *Typee*? Why has its status as queer text not reemerged along with that of other Melville staples like *Moby-Dick, Pierre,* and *Billy Budd*? Perhaps the most obvious answer is that it contains no tantalizing lines like those from *Moby-Dick,* in which Ishmael describes sleeping with Queequeg like a man and a wife, "in our hearts' honeymoon," "a cosy, loving pair."[50] As an index of intimacy, Tommo's depiction of Kory-Kory as a "hideous object" cannot really compete, especially given the desire of so many readers for "positive" queer images. But the abyss that lies between these two descriptions calls attention to another modality of circulation that transforms *Typee* over time: Melville's own return to, his intensification of, and thus his recirculation of many of those early themes that preoccupied him in his first novel. Showing, in other words, morphs into telling as *Typee*'s queerness bleeds into Melville's later work (as well as the work of others, like Stoddard), where it finds more conscious articulation. The later queer Melville is the one through which the earlier one disappeared.

But *Typee*'s queer disappearance and resurgence through the later Melville texts are also tied up with two other, overlapping modes of Melville circulation: the repopularization of Melville in the 1920s through literary criticism (especially the New Criticism) and the persistent presence of Melville as an intertextual force in the writings of twentieth-century queer writers like Hart Crane, Robert Duncan, and later, Tennessee Williams. It would be tempting to say that the queer Melville has been there all along, if only we'd known how to find him. But given the importance I am claiming for the literary circulation of *Typee,* I'd prefer to say that he's been there all along, if only we'd known how he found us.

2 THE STODDARD ARCHIVE AND ITS DISSED CONTENTS

ON APRIL 14, 1905, the front page of the San Francisco *Call* featured a large image of two authors, Henry James and Charles Warren Stoddard, drawn as if they were facing off against each other. The headline refers to only one of them, as it urges readers to "Welcome the Author of 'South Sea Idyls.'" The caption below the image reads: "Two distinguished Americans who were honored guests last night at a dinner given by the Bohemian Club as a tribute to one of its founders, who returns to California to live again among the friends and scenes of his early manhood." If either the *Call* or the Bohemian Club recognized Henry James as the superior writer, they were not letting on.[1]

Today it would be hard to imagine how James could be overshadowed by Stoddard in a newspaper headline. Few know the story of Stoddard's itinerant but prolific writing life: that he published poems, fiction, essays, and even editions, the most widely known concerning primarily his travels to the South Seas, his life in California, and his conversion to Catholicism; that he was among the nucleus of writers to produce California's first significant literary magazine, the *Overland Monthly* (widely credited with catapulting Bret Harte into local color fame); that he socialized and corresponded

WELCOME THE AUTHOR
OF "SOUTH SEA IDYLS"

The owl entertained illustrious company at the Bohemian Club last night. At a dinner given to hail the homecoming of Charles Warren Stoddard, Henry James, celebrated writer, Enrico Caruso, renowned singer, and Dr. Woodworth, eminent instructor, were among the distinguished guests.

HENRY JAMES.   CHARLES WARREN STODDARD.

Front page of San Francisco *Call*, April 14, 1905.

with virtually every major writer of his day; that he was a professor of English at Notre Dame and at Catholic University in Washington, D.C.; or that despite his connections, his widely regarded output, and his adventures, he died alone, unemployed, and penniless, having anxiously collected and sutured together every scrap of newsprint ever to bear his name. He may not have made much money through his writing, but it is fair to say that Charles Warren Stoddard enjoyed a fairly fabulous life in print in a wide range of genres and venues and was favorably reviewed by critics no less prominent than William Dean Howells.[2]

What people today do know of Stoddard, they likely know from anthologies. Examples of his fiction appear (often alongside James's) in just about every collection of gay or queer male writing published during the past one hundred years. Editors of these anthologies comment on the importance of whom he knew (basically everyone in the literary world of his time—and he was an avid autograph collector) and with whom he slept. They comment on his personal place in the cultural history of sexuality—as an early gay writer, cruising the South Seas and participating in (sometimes resisting, sometimes inhabiting fully) established colonial or medical narrative conventions for describing homosexuality.

But scholars since, even the most sympathetically nelly ones, have not been kind to Stoddard. Twentieth-century critics pretty much all agree that Stoddard's writing fails to pass aesthetic muster. Carl Stroven, whose 1939 PhD dissertation remains the most comprehensive account of Stoddard's work and life, declared that "he never acquired the knack of making fiction plausible, and when he wrote it . . . the result was always bad."[3] John W. Crowley describes Stoddard as "a writer whose prose was as purple as his ink: a product of 'The Genteel Tradition' at its stupefying worst."[4] Robert Gale thought that he ultimately "became a self-indulging old sybarite who neglected his great literary talent."[5] Even his most devoted champion, Roger Austen, could not help but admit that "most of Stoddard's books deserve to remain in the background."[6] These critics find Stoddard too sentimental, too verbose, and his fiction too implausible. The few more recent critics of Stoddard's work make no claims for its merits; they sidestep the business of his writing altogether. Like strangers passing a car wreck, promoters and critics alike display a distinctly horrified glee in dismissing his work. But no one can really explain why anyone should bother reading him or why he deserves to be in these anthologies at all.

Stoddard's persistent recovery and wholesale dismissal ironically index what is actually significant about the larger archive of his work: his prescient, meta-archival sense of the roles collation, circulation, and "archivation" play in producing queer life as such. He is, in short, Dayneford *avant la lettre*. The Stoddard archive showcases brilliantly the status of literature and literary circulation for producing queer social communities—and even vocabularies of self-reference—within Gilded Age America. In fact, it is precisely because of what critics see as the derivative and sentimental nature of his work that Stoddard exemplifies so perfectly the queer traffic in nineteenth-century American letters.

Like Dayneford, Stoddard was "companioned from youth up" by a collection of "literary sympathies." As a young poet, he even sought out the opinions of the authors whose books could be found on his shelf or whose taste he admired: Lord Alfred Tennyson, Ralph Waldo Emerson, Cardinal Newman, John Stuart Mill, Bayard Taylor, Bret Harte, Oliver Wendell Holmes, Thomas Wentworth Higginson, Oscar Wilde, Herman Melville, and Walt Whitman. (And these are only the ones who actually replied to Stoddard with assessments of his poems.)[7] He counted among his friends Mark Twain, who wrote that Stoddard was "the purest male I have known, in mind and speech."[8] Among the most oft-cited influences for Stoddard were Melville and Whitman. But seeing Stoddard's admiration of these writers merely as confirmation of their genius and his own inadequacy misses the very way Stoddard's reading and writing situate their work in relationship to each other as well as a host of other, more and less queer writers. It is, in fact, admiration that drives Stoddard's habit of literary collecting, an admiration that tends to make its presence felt as sentimentalism in his writing.

My project here is neither to reclaim nor condemn the sentimentalism, but to consider the effects of Stoddard's sentimental literary embraces and material textual accumulations as textual and cultural forces. The pages that follow begin by situating Stoddard within a dense network of literary and cultural contacts before then taking a closer look at his engagements with some of the many writers whose work he read and accumulated—beginning with Whitman and Melville. Doing so offers insight into the worlds Stoddard saw and built through the textual accumulation and anthological reading that preceded his own acts of writing. At the level of individually produced pieces of writing, Stoddard's engagement with the two writers is both mimetic and generative: through both social and literary experiments in following and imitating Whitman and Melville, Stoddard's sense of self as well as his literary sensibilities begin to take the form of lyricized stranger sociability in the prose form of travel writing. The model of influence at stake in Stoddard's writing plays itself out at the level of form as well as content and is central to understanding Stoddard's literary methodology: an anthological reading as a sentimental literary embrace, which in turn becomes the engine of queer literary production, culminating with novel writing at the end of his life.

As Stoddard embraces and recirculates the writing of others, he in turn develops a metacommentary on the origins of his texts' sentimental form. These metatextual features—his intertextuality and his discursive reframings of others' writing—allow us to see the ways that Stoddard's form archives the conditions of its own production and documents the generative force of the queer traffic in literature. The mawkish embrace that we see in Stoddard's writing, and which his critics decried as purplish sentimentalism, is not just a structure of feeling but a methodology of literary production central to the literary history of sexuality in nineteenth-century American fiction. This mode of reading anthologically produces a form of writing that we may well have forgotten how to read ourselves.

Through the lens of Stoddard's epistolary exchange with Whitman, we can see that what may appear to be the clearest example of singular literary influence is refracted through and supplemented by Stoddard's impulse to collect and engage with the writing of others. Tracing Stoddard's anthological reading as the queer traffic in his writing, we begin to see the generative, cumulative force of this model of reading not only as a mode of self-making-up, but a force of literary and discursive production. Anthological reading gives rise to anthological writing as a collection of literary antecedents, not unlike those in Dayneford's queerly social library, dances (sometimes awkwardly) across the pages of Stoddard's prose.

How to Grow a Queer Text, 1890s Style: Stoddard's Literary Network

Stoddard's repeated recovery as an early gay writer and his simultaneous critical dismissal on sentimental terms seem to work against each other, the one highlighting and the other dismissing the significance of his writing. But the editorial embrace and the critical dismissal of Stoddard have one thing in common: they both abstract him from the dense cultural context through which he came to understand his literature and himself. The recovery project confers on Stoddard a gay identity that he did not imagine for himself—and does not account for the embeddedness of Stoddard's gay literature in a broader literary context. Yet his dismissal obscures the conditions under which Stoddard's social and literary circulation contributed to his later recognition as an early gay writer.

The sentimentalism that critics dismiss at the level of content and aesthetics in Stoddard, first of all, was not always either highlighted or indicted. In his own historical moment, Stoddard enjoyed the esteem, company, and endorsement of some of the most important literary figures of his time and did so in terms that were not reducible, or even concerned with, his gay plots.[9] In the reviews of the range of work that Stoddard published,[10] he seems to have obtained at least a modicum of literary success. His most widely recognized work then and now is *South-Sea Idyls,* a collection of linked short stories first published separately in magazines and then as a single book in 1873. These stories chronicle the adventures of its unnamed, and loosely autobiographical, narrator as he travels through the islands of the Pacific and develops relationships, often sexual in nature, with men there.

What Stoddard's contemporary reviewers regularly noticed was the quality of description in his prose that conveyed life in the South Seas so vividly. The *Literary World* hailed the collection of stories for the peculiar type of realism this description produced. *South-Sea Idyls* attracted the reviewer's notice because "the queer stories have a substantial basis of fact" and because "all types of the purely sensuous life are represented in these highly-colored photographs."[11] The *Overland Monthly* also commented on the "idealized sketches" and remarked that "Stoddard was 'enthused' over the lovely islands of the Pacific—over their coral shores, their palmgroves, their water-falls, their deliciously tinted peaks, their remoteness, and their amiable, sensuous people, who treated him like a brother, because he fraternized with them in the mood of a poet and a humanitarian."[12] The reviewer continues: "If it is thought sometimes too exuberantly descriptive, or too florid and sensuous, these are qualities that will be corrected or tempered by experience."[13] If what the reviewers describe as the sensuous quality of Stoddard's prose is an effect of his enthusiasm, their sense of his sensuousness would seem to correspond also with the more pejorative sentimentalism that others claim marks his work.

As a description of Stoddard's work, *sensuous* is striking on a number of levels. It marks both the people of the South Seas and Stoddard's writing about them. What is sensuous about the people is, in Stoddard's depictions, their unabashed sexuality, especially the men's open willingness to be sensuous with him. But although *sensuous* describes something about Stoddard, in another sense it does not describe Stoddard at all: to the extent that *sensuous* locates sexuality, the adjective finds it not in Stoddard per se (as a property of his self) but outside of himself in exotic settings (primarily the South Sea Islands) and in his writing. The reviews suggest that Stoddard's crowning achievement as a writer emerges from his ability to bring an entire environment and its social life into view and to do so accurately. The purple-prosed sentimentalism that earns Stoddard a reputation for being a bad writer by more recent standards actually seems to be the ground for his success in his own time—even if sensuousness also had limitations that realism might have been presumed to temper (as the *Overland Monthly* reviewer intimates).

This sensuous idealism seems to have been the product of conscious formal innovation on Stoddard's part, the result, as he sees it, of combining poetry and prose. In one of his letters to Whitman, Stoddard described his story as a "proze idyl."[14] (The term stuck, as the whole collection of his stories became *South-Sea Idyls.*) As the reviewers see it, the "mood of the poet" infuses his description of the "sensuous people," combining the spirit of poetry with the form of prose. To understand Stoddard's project of literary fusion, we need to understand the significance he attributed to situating himself in a broad literary context of reading and writing, and thus recognize the literary sources that Stoddard recombined and recirculated in his own work.

Stoddard spent much of his life as something of a nineteenth-century literary groupie. He read widely and voraciously, and he sought to create and fix himself within the literary coteries of his time. From a young age, Stoddard sought out literary celebrities as vigorously as many of us follow rock bands or movie stars. He counted among his wide circle of friends Whitman and Melville of course, but also Mark Twain (Samuel Clemens), Rudyard Kipling, Ambrose Bierce, Ina Coolbrith, Joaquin Miller, Bret Harte, Henry Adams, Robert Louis Stevenson, and William Dean Howells. Howells was particularly ardent in his support of Stoddard and consistently encouraged his work. Stoddard went from literary groupie to South Seas traveler with little hesitation. Inspired by the examples of *Typee* and *Robinson Crusoe*, Stoddard took many excursions to the South Seas (his favorite places were Hawaii and Tahiti), where he worked as a newspaper correspondent and sought escape from those "frigid manners of the Christians" and found "the fullest joy of my life."[15] These travels provided him with fodder and inspiration for most of his writing well beyond the *South-Sea Idyls,* writing that was published in California (where Stoddard had moved with his family as a child), in book form as well as in newspapers and periodicals.

That sexuality was embedded within a larger range of important social and cultural concerns for Stoddard is also mirrored in the way he embedded himself within the broad literary culture of his time. One of the more peculiar artifacts in the Stoddard archive at the University of California, Berkeley stages perfectly Stoddard's sentimental embrace of his literary heroes. The Autograph Album of Charles Warren Stoddard contains verse, prose, and signatures from an impressive array of American and English authors. Stoddard used autograph collecting as a means of producing social and literary relationships—of reaching out to writers in embarrassingly craven ways and refusing to let them go, even when they'd imagined their polite responses were complete. The scraps of text within the autograph book reveal the degree to which Stoddard and his network of literary alliances—strangers and friends alike—communicated through annotated snippets of published text. A good indication of the texture of Stoddard's autograph book can be seen in the example of his autograph from Bayard Taylor. It is accompanied by an insert that contains, inscribed on the left, the poem "The Poet to His Readers" by Oliver Wendell Holmes:

> O sexton of the alcoved tomb
>> Where souls in Lacthern [?] cerements be,
> Tell me each living poet's doom!
>> How long before his book shall die?
>
> It matters little, soon or late,
>> A day, a month, a year, an age,—
> Tend [?] oblivion in its date
>> And Finis on its title-page.
>
> * * *
>
> Before we sighed, our griefs were Told;
>> Before we smiled, our joys were sung
> And all our passions shaped of old
>> In accents lost to mortal tongue.
>
> * * *
>
> Deal gently with us ye who read!
>> Our longest hope is unfulfilled,—
> The promise still outruns the deed,
>> The towns, but not the spies [?] we build.

On the right side of the page is a short letter to Stoddard from Taylor, itself the repetition of a poem Taylor had earlier recited to Stoddard:

> My dear Stoddard,
>
> Here is the last stanza of the poem I repeated to you:
>
> Thou no man resent his wrong,
> Still is free the Poet's song;

> Still, a stag, his thought may leap
> O'er the herded swine and sheep,
> And in pastures far away
> Lose the Burden of the Day.
>
> Always your friend,
> Bayard Taylor
>
> San Francisco
> June 11, 1870[16]

The sheet contains yet another work on the opposite side, Taylor's travel memoir *Eldorado,* which he published in 1850 but had written in 1849 in California, where he traveled to cover the Gold Rush for the *New York Tribune.* The page is obviously fragmented, its different poems framing each other, but it is also framed by the extratextual promise of enduring friendship between the two men that Taylor's closure understands to precede the writing of the letter itself. Neither generates any original prose to cement or further their bond. Taylor merely assembles poems, but his letter suggests that this act of assembly is nonetheless generative. At once quite private and yet evacuated of personal content, the album page seems to accumulate texts that sustain, if not produce, the friendly embrace that Taylor recognizes in his closure. This gesture to an enduring and unwavering friendship—"Always your friend"—may be the only original composition on the whole sheet. Convention would not have required such a grand flourish at the end of the letter. Its presence sustains the bond to which it gestures through a textuality marked by nothing more than circulation itself.

Stoddard's correspondence on its own would make for a fascinating study of the role letters play in consolidating the publishing culture of his time. Many letters in Stoddard's vast collection resemble the one Taylor writes to him, inserted with poems and textually scaffolded—a miniature, personal epistolary magazine. His own letters, and the letters to which others respond, frequently frame acts of literary production. Given that Stoddard engaged in detailed correspondence with virtually every major literary figure during his time—editors, writers, reviewers, and professors of literature—these letters, taken collectively, are also an astonishing reflection of the ways the American publishing industry at the end of the nineteenth century was both created and reflected through sexual relationships between men.

Within this circle of literary and social circulation, Stoddard was almost universally known as "Dad"—his "children" were frequently lovers he had metaphorically adopted.[17] In a letter to Howard Sutherland, dated January 14, 1903, Stoddard outlines this practice in a postscript. The body of the letter is typical of Stoddard's literary letters in that it advances his thoughts about his own novel and about other writers, notably Dante Gabriel Rossetti. It is also typical for the ways Stoddard fuses literary analysis with personal metacommentary. The postscript carries on a parallel conversation: "What you said about Christmas and children broke my heart. I am an old—very old Bachelor. All my life I have been adopting sons. I can't very well adopt daughters. The boys grow up and get married and I am left the same old Bachelor, but *older and more lonesome.*"[18] Whether all those who ultimately called Stoddard "Dad" were his lovers is unclear. Unmistakable, however, is the fact that the moniker originated to mark Stoddard's sexual relationships with younger men. Could one reassemble the collection of books and letters that Boston book dealer Charles E. Goodspeed auctioned off upon Stoddard's death, a fascinating cultural history could be written, detailing through his literary practices, missives, and reflections how very queer American publishing networks were at the end of the nineteenth century.

The Stoddard letters give us a limited sense of how central Stoddard was within this web of cultural alliances, especially toward the end of his life (and also how melancholy he had become in his exclusive reliance on his male friends—unlike many of them, Stoddard did not have a shadow married life). The collection includes folders of letters between Stoddard and various writers, ranging from Mark Twain (whom Stoddard served as a traveling secretary) and Joaquin Miller, to lesser-known writers of his day such as Howard Sutherland and Yone Noguchi, as well as important literary editors like William Dean Howells and Frank Putnam, longtime editor of the *National Magazine*. The interconnectedness of the various figures in Stoddard's life can be gleaned from looking at just a few examples from these letters. Many of these adopted children, like Putnam and Japanese American poet Noguchi, were or would become married with children, although marriage did not completely displace their attachments to him.[19] Noguchi was long a favorite lover of Stoddard's, even after he married Ethel Ames, who was a frequent editor and reviewer of Stoddard's work (and one of his intimate correspondents).[20] Putnam, who commissioned a year's worth of stories from Stoddard for the *National Magazine,* likewise retained and even facilitated his own attachment to the bachelor world that Stoddard headlined. In June 1904, Stoddard wrote to Noguchi that

> Frank Putnam wrote me a line saying that his wife and little ones are going away as soon as they are able to travel and then you will come to him and help keep Bachelors Hall. Won't that be jolly? O, then we shall see each other and be happy. . . . O, Yone, dear! If only I had my little Bungalow and money enough to run it how happy we might be! Well: we visit and make the most of what we have and thank God that we are not starving as so many poor people are.[21]

Stoddard's letters overall enact through circulation the relationships they aim to congeal through metaphor. Strangers interpolate themselves into Stoddard's queer family of friends and lovers through the language of familial intimacy.[22] The traffic through literature describes and also sutures an elaborate network of queer relationships within the system of American publishing circles—all operating through the sentimental embrace of epistolary form.[23]

While Stoddard's letters on their own terms reveal his yearning for literary and sexual connection to other men, this mode of making connection was generative for Stoddard in other ways. It helped him actually to produce fictional writing. The best example of how Stoddard's letters facilitate his literary production beyond letters themselves can be seen in his correspondence with Whitman.

Autography, Apostrophe: Stoddard's Poetic Embraces

Charles Warren Stoddard first wrote to Walt Whitman on February 8, 1867, sending him some of his poems and hoping to engage one of his literary heroes in a sustained correspondence—or at least get his autograph.

Whitman didn't respond.

But Stoddard was persistent. Undeterred, a couple of years later he tried again. This time he seemed to have thought more carefully about how to pitch himself to his favorite poet. He crafted his letter in such a way that Whitman's poetry might hail him into Whitman's sphere. Writing from Honolulu, Hawaii, in March 1869, Stoddard appealed to Whitman by recycling and reframing one of Whitman's brief lyric apostrophes in order to articulate, by analogy, the relationship he imagined between himself and Whitman. Aiming both to enact and personalize the kind of stranger sociability that Whitman articulates in "To You," Stoddard wrote:

> To Walt Whitman.
>
> May I quote you a couplet from your "Leaves of Grass"? "Stranger! If you, passing, meet me, and desire to speak to me, why should you not speak to me? And why should I not speak to you?"
>
> —I am the stranger who, passing, desires to speak to you. Once before I have done so, offering you a few feeble verses. I don't wonder you did not reply to them. Now my voice is stronger, I ask, *why will* you not speak to me?[24]

The letter continues with a description of the experiences and impressions Stoddard acquired as a traveler in the South Seas. By implication, he extends Whitman's metaphor of the stranger into the following description, worth quoting at length since it becomes the earliest incarnation of Stoddard's story "A South-Sea Idyl":

> So fortunate as to be traveling in these very interesting Islands I have done wonders in my intercourse with these natives. For the first time I act as my nature prompts me. It would not answer in America, as a general principle, not even in California where men are tolerably bold.
>
> This is my mode of life:
>
> —At dusk I reach some village, a few grass huts by the sea or in some valley. The native villagers gather

about me, for strangers are not common in these parts.
I observe them closely. Superb looking, many of them.
Fine heads, glorious eyes that question, observe and then
trust or distrust with an infallible instinct. Proud, defiant
lips, a matchless physique, grace and freedom in every
motion.
    I mark one, a lad of eighteen or twenty years who
is regarding me. I call him to me, ask his name giving
mine in return. He speaks it over and over, manipulating
my body unconsciously, as it were, with bountiful and
unconstrained love. I go to his grass-house, eat with
him his simple food, sleep with him upon his mats, and
at night sometimes waken to find him watching me
with earnest, patient looks, his arm over my breast and
around me. In the morning he hates to have me go. I
hate as much to leave him. Over and over I think of him
as I travel: he doubtless recalls me some times, perhaps wishes me back with him. We were known to one
another, perhaps twelve hours. Yet I cannot forget him.
Any thing that pertains to him now interests me.[25]

On first reading, it would seem that Stoddard continues to appropriate Whitman's textual strategies so as to reflect Whitman back to
himself. Stoddard adopts Whitman's tone of prosaic description in
Leaves of Grass (even repeating references to "grass huts" and the
"grass-house"). It could even be said that Stoddard at once assumes
the position of Whitman's lyric speaker (as he "mark[s] one, a lad of
eighteen or twenty years, who is regarding me").
    But this very act of appropriation also displaces Whitman—
and eventually the agency of the lyric "I" altogether—at precisely
the moment at which Stoddard embraces him so cravenly. Stoddard
may be the "I" who marks the lad, but the agency he attributes
to Whitman (as author and as lyric speaker) he does not claim for
himself: the lad plays the role of sexual subject, cruising Stoddard
and "manipulating [his] body unconsciously . . . with bountiful and
unconstrained love." And in adapting Whitman's poetic form to organize his own sexual experience in terms of a lyricized stranger
sociability, Stoddard also multiplies it. Both Whitman and the lad

are strangers to Stoddard, the one being the audience of the letter (whom Stoddard has never met), the other the represented stranger within the letter. What Whitman and the lad have in common is the sense that they are reading Stoddard. Like Dayneford, Stoddard himself is "made up" or hailed by the books and people he has read.

Stoddard's letter further displaces Whitman (under the guise of making him central) by adapting a skeletal poetic frame into a fleshed-out prose description. The letter to Whitman adds something that was never there in the poem: contextual detail and a narrative setting (replete with plot). "To a Stranger" is one of Whitman's simplest lyrics—a mere two lines long. Stoddard treats it as a frame on which he can hang his details and, eventually, grow his story as an event that unfolds across time and in a very specific space. Whitman's stranger could perhaps be anyone, but Stoddard's stranger could not. Whitman's "you" is abstract; Stoddard's "you" is, first, Whitman and, second, in the description of his encounter a specific "lad of eighteen or twenty years."

Reading Stoddard's writing anthologically allows us to see the ways in which other books and writers that he embraced inform the writing that fleshes out Whitman's skeleton. It can be argued, for instance, that he borrows the setting from Melville. Around the same time that Stoddard first wrote to Whitman, he also wrote to Melville for his autograph, claiming that he went to Hawaii and sought traces of Melville there (and enclosing a copy of his—Stoddard's—short poem "Cherries and Grapes"). Melville's response was brief but polite: "I have read with much pleasure the printed Verses you sent me, and, among others, was quite struck with the little effusion entitled 'Cherries and Grapes.' I do not wonder that you found no traces of me at the Hawaiian Islands."[26] As we saw in chapter 1, in another of Stoddard's *South-Sea Idyls,* his narrator is lamenting the decimation of South Seas native life as an effect of Melville's storytelling. The character, trying to apprehend the Typee valley from afar, observes, "I happened to know something about the place . . . for Herman Melville has plucked out the heart of its mystery, and beautiful and barbarous Typee lies naked and forsaken."[27] Given Stoddard's anxiousness to correspond with Melville as well as his later blaming of Melville's readers for leaving Typee "naked and forsaken," we begin to see a picture of how accustomed Stoddard had grown not only to writing and seeing the world through Melville's eyes,[28] but of assuming that other writers would imitate Melville's travels as he had. If we take seriously Stoddard's claim (articulated in a later story) that much of what his characters know about South Seas Island life is learned from Melville,[29] we begin to see that at the moment when Stoddard is most formally (apostrophically) Whitmanian, he is at least equal parts Melvillian.

As obvious as these influences might have been to Stoddard, neither Whitman nor Melville would likely have recognized their respective reflections in Stoddard's writing. After all, each only politely tolerated him. But taking only the complicating trace of Melville in Stoddard's writing, we begin to see how fleshing out the skeleton of Whitman's lyric apostrophe is ultimately not a straightforward project for Stoddard.

Melville and Whitman are but two of the tracks we can see in this short letter if we read Stoddard's writing (and his tendency to understand himself through other writing) anthologically. The traffic of reading that leaves its material trace on Stoddard's writing is denser. Stoddard showcases this traffic, sometimes quite diffusely, through, say, his use of pastoral conventions like the *locus amoenus* and the retreat from society, but at other times in ways that can be linked to specific texts. Through Stoddard's accounts of the importance of his own reading, even within this one short letter to Whitman we can see the tracks of Daniel Defoe's *Robinson Crusoe*, Richard Henry Dana's *Two Years before the Mast,* and Bayard Taylor's "To a Persian Boy: In the Bazaar at Smyrna."

On his first trip on a boat, as a young boy sailing with his family from the American East Coast around the horn to California, Stoddard carried two books with him. One of these was, he reports later, "a pocket copy of 'Robinson Crusoe,' upon the flyleaf of which was scrawled, in an untutored hand, 'Charley from Freddy,'—this Freddy was my juvenile chum." He explains: "Frequently I have thought that the reading of this charming book may have been the predominating influence in the development of my taste and temper; for it was while I was absorbed in the exquisitely pathetic story of Robinson Crusoe that the first island I ever saw dawned upon my enchanted vision."[30] Thereafter, he imagines his own island encounters as if he were Crusoe himself, even keeping his own kind of diary. In these descriptions of island relations to prospective chums, Stoddard imagines himself less a Whitman than a Crusoe. Later, as Stoddard was reading *Two Years before the Mast,* his avatar became Richard Henry Dana. (He eventually published an edition of Dana's book in 1899, with a scholarly introduction.)

And to add yet another item to the bookshelf refracted through Stoddard's description of his "lad" in the Whitman correspondence, we might turn to Bayard Taylor's "To a Persian Boy: In the Bazaar at Smyrna" (from *Poems of Place,* 1851). The poem's speaker recounts the force of the Persian boy's eyes and lashes, "from under which . . . shone on me / the rich voluptuous soul of Eastern land, / Impassioned, tender, calm, serenely sad."[31] A similar sense of being taken over indexes the located sensibility of Stoddard's work and marks the relationship between the narrator of the "South-Sea Idyl" and his lad who "is regarding me . . . manipulating my body unconsciously." In later incarnations, we will see that the lad comes to emerge from the landscape as if he himself were a feature of the land.

Whitman's lyric, socialized into prose, becomes the vessel through which an accumulation of Stoddard's reading comes to life in condensed form. But the tracks through this correspondence are not visible without an account of Stoddard's history of reading and his status as something of a literary hoarder. In light of the textual engagements that precede Stoddard's letter exchange with Whitman, we can also begin to understand what Whitman has made possible for Stoddard as well as the conditions of anthological reading that help make queer readings and adaptations of Whitman's work possible. Whitman's influence in this passage is as diffuse as it is central. "To You" has acquired a setting and specific details. It can be seen to resonate with Stoddard's history of experimental self-representation through the writing of others. The skeleton of stranger sociability is shrouded with descriptive language that idealizes the environment, all the while displaying (without consciously showcasing) the interconnectedness of social and literary circulation in Stoddard's writing. What we get is a glimpse of the effects, in writing, of the performative character of Stoddard's reading and collecting, and of the centrality of this reading and collecting to the emergence of queer social communities and vocabularies of self-understanding (or "making up") that Dayneford's library shelves showcase. Nor is that fact lost on Stoddard, who in continuing to evolve this practice further even develops a metacommentary on it. Later in his letter to Whitman, he claims that the spirit in which he reads Whitman ultimately makes his written description of the lad possible, as if Whitman's poem has been reading, even writing him as he is reading it:

> You will easily imagine, my dear sir, how delightful I find this life. I read your Poems with a new spirit, to understand them as few may be able to. And I wish more than ever that I might possess a few lines from your pen. I want your personal magnetism to quicken mine, how else shall I have it? Do write me a few lines for they will be of immense value to me.
>
> I wish it were possible to get your photograph. The small *Lithograph* I have of you is not wholly satisfactory. But I would not ask so much of you. Only a page with your name and mine as you write it. Is this too much?[32]

He counts himself among a select group of readers who can read Whitman's work with a knowing wink to a speaker who, they believe, acknowledges them. The "new spirit" with which Stoddard claims to read Whitman is (later) recognized in the writing of John Addington Symonds, Edward Carpenter, and even D. H. Lawrence—and has been well documented in the scholarly work of Eve Kosofsky Sedgwick, Michael Moon, Betsy Erkkila, Jerome Loving, Michael Robertson, and others. These writers and scholars point to the ways in which Whitman was something of an "English (far more than . . . an American) prophet of sexual politics for the nineteenth century," as Sedgwick puts it.[33]

There's no denying that, as Michael Warner points out, "the attention to the body and to sex that Whitman achieved . . . represents a watershed in modern culture,"[34] and that many continue to see themselves embodied in his work. But the cult of personality that continues to adhere to Whitman and other canonical queer writers has obscured the conditions of their own emergence *as* literary celebrities within already existing literary subcultures. In the context of the Whitmania that emerges in the latter part of the nineteenth century, Stoddard was an early adopter. The writers most often cited as evidence of the queer community that forms through reading Whitman write much later than Stoddard. (Symonds is the best example: although he first read and appreciated Whitman in 1865, he didn't write his famous letter to the poet until 1890.) Stoddard had long since completed his correspondence with Whitman by this point. In fact, as Jonathan Ned Katz points out, Stoddard was finished with his South Sea travel adventures by 1874 and had moved on to Italian lovers and locales.[35] So in one sense, Stoddard may be unique for the ways he produces some of the earliest documentation of the performative force of reading Whitman.

But if the Stoddard case creates an earlier example of a queer Whitman phenomenon that has already been diagnosed as emerging later, Stoddard's reading and writing practices do more than shore up an argument for Whitman's exceptionalism. There is a broader subcultural context of literary circulation at play here that creates the conditions in which Whitman's exceptionalism makes sense. Like Carpenter and Edward Prime-Stevenson after him, Stoddard reads Whitman alongside—and through—his own writing practice and refracts Whitman's influence, in turn, through the writing of others. In so doing, he both exemplifies and diffuses (perhaps even mutes, as a result) a seemingly straightforward model of influence that his correspondence with Whitman would on the surface suggest. To recognize Whitman's aesthetic exceptionalism is to see him, as Stoddard does, within a constellation of other writers (like Melville and Taylor), whose shared ghostly presence in Stoddard's writing amplifies and expands the literary effect of Whitman.

In the context of Stoddard's anthological reading and writing practices, the generative force of reading Whitman stems as much from his membership in a library of other representations as it does from Whitman's uniqueness or experimental poetics. It is not, after all, Whitman's trademark long lines or lyric catalogs that attract

Stoddard to his poetry but his adhesiveness. Stoddard is drawn to the content of Whitman's writing—a content that he has learned to detect through reading a history of pages passed from hand to hand. And it is through Whitman's content more than his form that Stoddard might be said to engage in a queerly formal literary experiment—one rendered practically invisible by the fact that Stoddard's anthological reading and writing practices are ultimately more important to the queerness of his own form than the influence of Whitman. As Stoddard develops what he would come to call his "proze idyls," collecting them as a series of linked stories (and later writing a novel that loosely follows the same formal principle), the books he produces come to resemble more the anthologies of Carpenter and Prime-Stevenson than the poetry of Whitman.

Fermenting the "Proze Idyl": From Stoddard to Whitman, the Sequel

In the ensuing correspondence between Whitman and Stoddard, the relationship between the environment of the South Seas' racialized sexual expression (attributed to Melville) and its formal tone begins to take further shape. Perhaps both flattered and intrigued, Whitman finally did reply to Stoddard, albeit briefly and with epistolary restraint: the letter, in other words, was short but sweet.[36] It would be another year before Whitman would hear from Stoddard again, but in the meantime the scene Stoddard described to Whitman in his letter—of meeting the eighteen-year-old boy in Hawaii—had flourished into Stoddard's "A South-Sea Idyl," first published in the *Overland Monthly* in September 1869 and later in the *South-Sea Idyls* collection. The encounter with the "lad" grew into the following description:

> Fate, or the Doctor, or something else, brought me first to this loveliest of valleys, so shut out from every thing but itself, that there were no temptations which might not be satisfied. Well! here, as I was looking about at the singular loveliness of the place—you know this was my first glimpse of it; its abrupt walls, hung with tapestries of fern and clambering convolvulus; at one end two exquisite water-falls, rivaling one another

in whiteness and airiness—at the other the sea, the real South
Sea, breaking and foaming over a genuine reef, even rippling
the placid current of the river, that slipped quietly down to
its embracing tide from the deep basins at these water-falls—
right in the midst of all this, before I had been ten minutes in
the valley, I saw a straw hat, bound with wreaths of fern and
maile; under it a snow-white garment, rather short all around,
low in the neck, and with no sleeves whatever.

There was no sex to that garment; it was the sponta-
neous offspring of a scant material and a large necessity. I'd
seen plenty of that sort of thing, but never upon a model like
this, so entirely tropical—almost Oriental. As this singular
phenomenon made directly for me, and having come within
reach, there stopped and stayed, I asked its name, using one of
my seven stock phrases for the purpose; I found it was called
Kána-aná. Down it went into my note-book; for I knew I was
to have an experience with this young scion of a race of chiefs.
Sure enough, I have had it. He continued to regard me steadily,
without embarrassment. He seated himself before me; I felt
myself at the mercy of one whose calm analysis was questioning every motive of my soul. This sage inquirer was, perhaps,
sixteen years old. His eye was so earnest and so honest, I could
return his look. I saw a round, full, rather girlish face; lips ripe
and expressive—not quite so sensual as those of most of his
race; not a bad nose, by any means; eyes perfectly glorious—
regular almonds—with the mythical lashes "that sweep," etc.,
etc. The smile which presently transfigured his face was of that
nature that flatters you into submission against your will.

Having weighed me in his balance—and you may be
sure his instincts didn't cheat him (they don't do that sort
of thing)—he placed his two hands on my two knees, and
declared, "I was his best friend, as he was mine; I must come
at once to his house, and there live always with him." What
could I do but go?[37]

This passage is remarkable for the ways it further mutes the "I"
and locates the agency of desire elsewhere. The narrator's sentences
regularly displace him from the position of grammatical subject as

he foregrounds the external origins of his own desire and actions. It is "Fate, or the Doctor, or something else" that has brought him here, and we find him hailed as much by the environment he is describing and apprehending. Consider as well the way the lad/lover is introduced. He is actually a feature of the landscape, presented to us through a structure of synecdoche as a series of parts framed by assumptions about the context in which those parts appear. The lad appears first as a set of clothes, "a straw hat, bound with wreaths of fern and *maile*; under it a snow-white garment, rather short all around, low in the neck, and with no sleeves whatever." And though the boy is marked by the purity associated with his "snow-white garment," the narrator understands his attraction not only as an attraction to purity but also as an attraction to temptation: after all, "this loveliest of valleys, [was] so shut out from every thing but itself, that there were no temptations which might not be satisfied."

The description and displacement that structure the sexual encounter further obfuscate the origins of agency at precisely the moment at which agency would appear to be foregrounded. Most of the wooing appears to be the boy's shameless work ("He continued to regard me steadily, without embarrassment"). But the lad's agency itself has been licensed by the landscape out of which he has appeared. And it is description itself, as it shifts almost imperceptibly from the landscape to the lad, that transforms him into an object of desire: "His eye was so earnest and so honest"; his "round, full, rather girlish face; lips ripe and expressive" with "not a bad nose," "eyes perfectly glorious—regular almonds—with the mythical lashes" and "the smile which presently transfigured his face." The power the boy has is very much like the power of landscape: it is "nature that flatters you into submission against your will." In the context of description, conscious decision seems to be lost in the verdure.

Nor is the scene without its recognition of the ways writing itself anticipates the encounter. Even before we get to the description of Kána-aná, we are told that the first thing the narrator does is write Kána-aná's name in his notebook—an action that precedes the smile and steady gaze from Kána-aná: "Down [the name] went into my note-book; for I knew I was to have an experience with this young scion of a race of chiefs. Sure enough, I have had it." Only after Kána-aná's name is written in the notebook does he pursue the narrator: the act of writing seems to have been a decisive move on his part, but the narrator cannot quite decide who makes the decisive moves here. At the sentence level, his own capacity for observation— the ostensible origins of description—are not completely within his power. The description of the erotic encounter blends so easily into the romanticized description of the environment that the sublimity of the natural world seems to dissolve the ownership of desire into a feature of the body and infuse into the writing itself.

This described setting that is the mise-en-scène for the characters therein is the site of an accumulated textual consciousness. To write about the mode of life Stoddard so cherishes in the South Seas is to put in play, with various degrees of authorial consciousness, the range of associations that have accrued to description within the South Seas. The mass of such literary accumulations allows Stoddard to condense what has been more sparsely sprinkled throughout texts of other writers into a single encounter. Through the concrete description of details it offers, the location paradoxically becomes generic. The environment of Stoddard's story is no longer specified as Hawaii (as it was in Stoddard's earlier letter to Whitman). It has become a generic South Sea Island environment, typifying the kind of sociability it showcases all the more for the ways its accumulation of detail amounts also to a condensation of detail where we no longer even need a specific place name. The resulting story is not (or not any longer) an imitation of Whitman but a departure, at least formally, from the poet whose epistolary embrace Stoddard sought—a seeking that gave rise (in part) to the text itself (a nicely counterintuitive example of what Stoddard's "sentimentalism" actually accomplishes).

If Stoddard recognized that contradiction, he didn't let on. Upon his return to San Francisco from his South Seas excursion early in 1870, he could not resist sending Whitman the *Overland Monthly* version of the "South-Sea Idyl." And it is in this letter to Whitman that he coins the term *proze idyl* to characterize the piece. The story arrived with the following enclosure, remarkable for the ways it misreads and distorts Whitman's influence:

To Walt Whitman,

In the name of Calamus listen to me! before me hangs
your beautiful photograph, twice precious, since it is
your gift to me. Near at hand lies your beloved volume
and with it the Notes of Mr. Burroughs.

May I not thank you for your picture and your letter? May I not tell you over and over that where I go you
go with me, in poem and picture and the little volume of
notes also, for I read and reread trying to see you in the
flesh as I so long to see you!

I wrote you last from the Sandwich Islands. I shall
before long be even further from you than ever, for
I think of sailing towards Tahiti in about five weeks.
I know there is but one hope for me. I must get in
amongst people who are not afraid of instincts and who
scorn hypocrisy. I am numbed with the frigid manners of
the Christians; barbarism has given me the fullest joy of
my life and I long to return to it and be satisfied. May I
not send you a proze idyl wherein I confess how dear it
is to me? There is much truth in it and I am praying that
you may like it a little. If I could only know that it has
pleased you I should bless my stars fervently . . . .

You say you "don't write many letters." O, if you
would only reply to this within the month! I could then
go into the South Seas feeling sure of your friendship
and I should try to live the real life there for your sake
as well as for my own. Forgive me if I have worried you:
I will be silent and thoughtful in future, but in any case
know, dear friend, that I am grateful for your indulgence.

Affectionately yours,
Charles Warren Stoddard.[38]

By hailing Whitman "in the name of Calamus," he unwittingly (and
thus ironically) marks his own divergence from Whitman. Stoddard's
Calamus is not Whitman's. For Stoddard, the "name of Calamus" is
peripatetic, whereas for Whitman it is precisely American. The gap
between Whitman's context and Stoddard's also plays itself out in

Stoddard's assumption that Whitman needs someone to live life for his sake because, he assumes, Whitman cannot live the life he might want in America. Whitman may indeed go wherever Stoddard goes in both spirit and text, but Stoddard is in part also rejecting something in Whitman in order to escape what is at the heart of Whitman's poetry: American life. In the South Seas, he finds people are less afraid of "instincts" and less prone to "hypocrisy." Stoddard's own sense of utopianism clouds his very reading of Whitman and leads him to construct a false homology. Whitman does not shrink from what Stoddard sees as the obsequiousness of American life; its contradictions and hypocrisies are a source of Whitman's creative energy and connection. For Stoddard, these contradictions and hypocrisies are an albatross.

Nor is this paradox lost on Whitman, who is quick to see Stoddard's limitations as a reader and the ways his preoccupations translate into particular forms of description. Stoddard's nature, according to Whitman, corresponds with a particular mode of expression— "simple," "direct," and "naïve"—itself,[39] we assume, connected to what Whitman would describe in his next response to Stoddard as the "extravagant sentimentalism" that America would prevent:

> I have just re-read the sweet story all over, & find it
> indeed soothing & nourishing after its kind, like the
> atmosphere. As to you, I do not of course object to your
> emotional & adhesive nature, & the outlet thereof, but
> warmly approve them—but do you know (perhaps you
> do,) how the hard, pungent, gritty, worldly experiences
> & qualities in American practical life, also serve? how
> they prevent extravagant sentimentalism? & how they
> are not without their own great value & even joy?
>
> It arises in my mind, as I write, to say something of
> that kind to you—
>
> I am not a little comforted when I learn that
> the young men dwell in thought upon me & my
> utterances—as you do—& I frankly send you my
> love—& I hope we shall one day meet—
>
> > —I wish to hear from you always,
> > Walt Whitman[40]

Whitman describes and acknowledges a mode of queer being and writing that is diametrically opposed to the more dominant forms of queer writing associated with writers like Oscar Wilde and Henry James at around the same time. And even here, the term *queer* operates as a fudgy adjective that none of these writers would likely have used to describe their work—although it comes closest to capturing the indeterminacy operating in the Stoddard–Whitman correspondence, especially compared with the more identitarian vocabularies we have at our disposal for describing such modes of sexual sociability today. Whitman makes a gentle but firm distinction between Stoddard's predilections and his own preference for the "pungent, gritty, worldly experiences & qualities in American practical life"— all the while encouraging Stoddard to continue reading his work in that "new spirit" to which Stoddard referred in the earlier letter. Whatever Whitman's qualms over Stoddard's sentimental, direct, or naïve expression might be, he nonetheless sees something worth encouraging in this new spirit of reading. (Neither Stoddard nor Whitman, one assumes, had read Friedrich Schiller's influential essay opposing the naïve and the sentimental.)[41]

Even if the tension Whitman identifies between Stoddard's sentimentalism and his own gritty practicality is somewhat lost on Stoddard, that tension no doubt fertilizes the growth of Stoddard's hybrid "proze idyl." That process of intersubjective literary production is not one we tend to associate with Whitman's sui generis status as self-made poet. This letter that began with the skeletal structure of the modest lyric "To You" reveals to us the germ of a process of literary circulation that gives rise to the structure that will define Stoddard's long prose works: a structure marked by exchange (of text objects like letters, poems, and stories, of images and autographs, and of worldviews).

From Reading to Writing Anthologically

The story that first took shape in Stoddard's letter to Whitman and then grew into "A South-Sea Idyl" would grow again later into Stoddard's novella-like, three-part story that came to be titled "Chumming with a Savage"—an episodic tale within a book that is itself a collection of episodic tales.[42] The excerpts discussed above partly comprise Part One; Part Two shows us Kána-aná's travels to America (which make him miserable); and the final Part Three is the narrator's return to Kána-aná's home island, only to find his beloved chum has died. The resulting episodic structure is significant not just because it multiplies the model of stranger sociability that Stoddard sees in Whitman and adapts to contexts represented in the travel writing of others, but also because it amplifies at a formal level the piecemeal, "fragmented," anthological nature of reading and literary accumulation that define Stoddard's long prose writing in both *South-Sea Idyls* and his novella, *For the Pleasure of His Company: An Affair of the Misty City.*

Like "Chumming with a Savage," *For the Pleasure of His Company* also follows this three-part structure that showcases the life of a struggling writer named Paul Clitheroe as if it were a series of only loosely linked episodes and relationships, not unlike the nameless main characters of the linked tales in *South-Sea Idyls.* Arguably the earliest queer novel to be set in San Francisco, the book charts Clitheroe's turns at writing, acting, and love in the Bay Area. Success at both love and writing ultimately eludes Paul, and the ending sees his escape from America into the arms of three naked South Sea Islanders, with whom he sails away. Considered autobiographical by both Stoddard and its readers, the text that finally emerged was reprinted in 1987 by the Gay Sunshine Press as *For the Pleasure of His Company,* "the first relatively open American novel with homosexual themes."[43]

Both *South-Sea Idyls* and *For the Pleasure of His Company* prefigure the anthological form of later collections and are the result of the kind of anthological reading that can be attributed to both Dayneford and Stoddard. Paul Clitheroe could just as easily be writing about the nameless narrators of Stoddard's proze idyls or Prime-Stevenson's Dayneford when he makes the metafictional claim that if he were to write a novel, he would "write a story without its pair of lovers; everybody shall be more or less spoony—but nobody shall be really in love." When his friend Miss Juno objects, saying, "It wouldn't be a story,"[44] he essentially elaborates a theory of queer fiction writing that interrupts the kind of novelistic love conventions to which Lauren Berlant claims even most queer theorists subscribe.[45] Clitheroe continues to elaborate his vision of a social landscape defined less by a traditional love plot and more by a series of episodic sociosexual encounters. Clitheroe's book

> would be a history, or a fragment of a history, a glimpse of a life at any rate, and that is as much as we ever get of the lives of those around us. Why can't I tell you the story of one fellow—of myself for example; how one day I met this person, and the next day I met that person, and next week some one else comes on to the stage, and struts his little hour and departs. I'm not trying to give my audience, my readers, any knowledge of that other fellow. My reader must see for himself how each of those fellows in his own way has influenced me.[46]

A collection of narrative pieces placed in succession, incomplete character development, plot motivation that is not ultimately driven by the goal of monogamous coupling: these are some of the ways Stoddard's own writing has more in common with anthologies than other novels. The "more or less spoony" aesthetic project of *For the Pleasure of His Company* operates at the intersection of sentimental style and a love plot structured by serial monogamy between men where "nobody shall be really in love." Spooniness allows Stoddard to stand to one side of a plot focused on a pair of lovers without using the novel to affirm the normative form of love that even queers have trouble troubling these days.

There is, obviously, a discernible route to be followed from Stoddard's correspondence with Whitman to the project of Stoddard's novel. But our existing ways of understanding influence and intertextuality don't really account for the unpredictable paths and distortions that queer circulation effects. To be sure, I have delved into only a small section of Stoddard's literary remains. Much more could be said, for instance, of Stoddard's scrapbooks—his assembly of his own life through the collection of everything printed by or about him—and of his encyclopedic correspondence with other writers and editors of his time (some of which I cite in the early sections of this chapter). But Stoddard's mawkish embrace of Whitman read through the prism of the anthological reading that foreshadows Stoddard's anthological prose style goes some distance already toward exemplifying what I think is at stake in Stoddard's oeuvre: that queer literary history may perhaps be as fruitfully (if radically differently) narrated through an account of the anthological impulses of a Dayneford or a Stoddard as they are through a Whitman or a Melville. Stoddard's strategies of entextualization and accumulation suggest to us a model for understanding the performative force of reading and writing queer life anthologically at the end of the nineteenth century.

This model focuses less on the love that cannot speak its name than on the multitude of voices that are made to do so—sometimes even in spite of themselves. Not all the books on Dayneford's shelves, after all, were written by queers or intended for a nineteenth-century queer audience. They depend on acts of rogue circulation and on being framed and reframed by—or socializing with—other texts. This model of collection operates less in the service of seeking a vocabulary of sexual identity or a conventionality than it does on world-making. It focuses on the narration and production of social worlds and frameworks that facilitate self-understanding. What Stoddard and Whitman, Dayneford and his books all seem to recognize is that strategies of seemingly derivative entextualization index an emerging consciousness of textual accumulation as a mode of a modern queer "making-up." The anthology, after all, persists as a dominant literary genre of gay and lesbian writing, no less so than the novel. If Stoddard and readers like him are any indication, the anthological impulse to collect and place side by side, within the pages of individual books, a diverse array of episodes that draw widely on both queer and mainstream literary antecedents makes the case for looking not just at but beyond the usual suspects (like Whitman) for a more robust (queer) literary history. The time is ripe for us to do the painstaking editorial work of excavating the queer traffic in literature, yes, but also to do the theoretical work of explaining why and how that traffic matters. Doing so in turn allows us to see the gay novel not as a genre hived off from other writing but, rather, as an effect of much broader literary networks and reading practices.

3 TYPE COMPLICATION AND LITERARY OLD MAIDS

IN 1922, when Edith Wharton published her serialized novella *The Old Maid: The 'Fifties,* it must have seemed logical for her to imagine Charlotte Lovell, the book's title character, as a quaint anachronism. Not only is she displaced historically in this text, she is displaced at the level of narrative voice: although the story is ostensibly about her, Charlotte's is not even the central consciousness of the novel that tells her story. We experience the events of the novella from the perspective of her conniving cousin, Delia Ralston. Wharton's choice of historical setting as well as protagonist seems both conscious and striking. The text's title makes this old maid—a woman of meager means, who bears a child out of wedlock and must rely on her cousin to keep the secret while helping raise her child—exemplary of the 1850s.[1]

It is no coincidence that the figure of the old maid enters Wharton's historical novel around the same time that the modern lesbian comes fully into view as such—or that Wharton needs to reach back as far as 1850 to situate her imagined old maid as merely a failed heterosexual, by marrying and child-rearing standards. (Charlotte can give birth, but she does not earn the right to raise her own child in the context of the novel: official mothering is the domain of the married Delia.) By the late nineteenth century and beginning of the twentieth, the literary old maid has come to inhabit the same fictional contexts as the literary lesbian. At the end of the nineteenth century, especially in fiction about women in New England such as Sarah Orne Jewett's Maine stories and Henry James's *The Bostonians,* the old maid and the lesbian overlap conceptually to such an extent that they become almost indistinguishable. This near-fusion by the end of the nineteenth century may help to explain why Wharton chose to set her story in the 1850s and not, say, the 1880s or 1890s. But what Wharton's choice also allows us to see quite clearly is the (at least imagined) historical specificity of a type—the old maid.

Although it has become commonplace to see the old maid as a socially queer literary figure and thus a historical analogue for the lesbian, I argue here that we might better understand the relationship between the two in terms of type complication: the process by which one textual version of a social type (in this case, the often abstractly depicted old maid) comes to be tested against a range of details that extend or complicate her social and textual boundaries so as to make possible the imagination of another type (the lesbian, marked by her sexual sociability with other women). As the old maid accrues to herself an increasing amount of detail, it also in turn becomes increasingly possible to envision her and the sociotextual space around her in extended fictional and eventually novelistic proportions. In this space, which opens up the possibility of old maids' primary social attachments existing within communities of other old maids, both the old maid and the lesbian whose sociability is sexual can become potential protagonists. But this type complication is possible only if we begin by recognizing the extent to which, however socially queer the old maid may be, she is nonetheless not necessarily lesbian in her queerness. Beginning with this distinction that Wharton implicitly makes is a necessary condition for investigating the processes of recirculation and type complication that make it possible for the lesbian to seem as if she emerges out of the paradigm of the old maid.

In its seeming anachronism, Wharton's *The Old Maid: The 'Fifties* highlights the unpredictable nature of literary type circulation that makes it possible for the old maid constantly to be resignified as she is tested against a range of literary contexts—such that she can seem parallel to, and then inextricably linked with, lesbianism. Only later (as in Wharton's version) is she disarticulated from that same entanglement. Part of what makes this possible is the very abstraction at the heart of types themselves: types can be translated into a range of specific examples. But a careful examination of the twinned (if overlapping) literary histories of the old maid and of the lesbian exposes the limits of such a range at any given moment in literary history. In other words, the old maid will not be any one thing the reader or writer wants her to be at any one point in history. As I shall show in the following pages, this is because the very processes of type complication are localized, connected to particular reading practices, to the textual histories embedded in the forms of texts themselves, and to modes of literary expression—all of which draw on the energy of striving beyond the boundaries of abstract types and also on the conventions of literary circulation.

One of the key ways we can see this process being played out is in those moments of description that articulate the old maid's but also the lesbian's relationship to the social and linguistic environments of the text. This process of type complication highlights, at the level of form, a kind of emotional and linguistic striving to create contexts and language worlds for modes of sexual sociability that seem to be at odds with their historical and social contexts. A striving to articulate the terms on which being an old maid has a place in both social and textual worlds facilitates the parallel, and ultimately overlapping, world-making that surrounds sexual sociability between women. But as I will suggest toward the end of this chapter, if the success of this project is the creation of a literary world in which characters like lesbians and old maids fit, this success comes at a cost, too. For at precisely the moment when these characters seem to fit so nicely, abandoning the textual striving toward world-creation also shifts the terms of self-reference for the characters within those worlds. Once the old maid and the lesbian can be imagined as belonging somewhere, the characters and the literature in which those characters appear also seem to lose the sense of striving beyond themselves that generated their world-making efforts to begin with.

A Surfeit of Old Maids

If we consider her appearance across a range of American literary magazines at the end of the eighteenth century, the old maid would seem to be something of a minor, stock character—abstracted from most contexts and often seen to be at odds with them. Thinly conceived but roundly renounced, she seemed to be everywhere and yet belonged nowhere. She appears in quite short snippets, letters, or poems—almost always as a nameless personage, referred to by others and even signing her name to letters simply as "Old Maid." She rarely has a name of her own or anything that looks like an individualized life. Old maids like those in Frances Brooke's weekly periodical (1755–56) and Arthur Murphy's play notwithstanding, we tend not to think of the eighteenth century as the golden age of the old maid: we are far more likely to recall her strong historical associations with New England at the end of the nineteenth century.[2] But as I've already suggested, by the end of the nineteenth century the old maid has acquired quite a series of lives for herself. If she was once transcendentally homeless, the old maid came to make her home in a range of particular literary places, none more prominently than New England. We can see this range in the following montage of textual moments: Basil Ransom's observation in *The Bostonians* that "Olive Chancellor was unmarried by every implication of her being. She was a spinster as Shelley was a lyric poet, or as the month of August is sultry";[3] Louisa Ellis's considerate refusal of Joe Dagget in favor of her embroidery and her dog in Mary Eleanor Wilkins Freeman's "A New England Nun"; Celia's culminating Thanksgiving Day feast for all the town's spinsters and her resolve to adopt two girls and bring them up as "dyed-in-the-wool old maids" in Rose Terry Cooke's "How Celia Changed Her Mind"; the custodial ways of Harriet Beecher Stowe's Aunts Roxy and Ruey on Orr's Island; Sarah Orne Jewett's Miss Harriet Pyne, whose "scheme of life was as faultless as the miniature landscape of a Japanese garden."[4] The 1850s do, of course, furnish us with some memorable old maids like Nathaniel Hawthorne's Hepzibah and Stowe's Miss Ophelia.[5] But old maids populate American literature to such an extent in the latter half of the nineteenth century that they become an oft-invoked type.

Literary criticism of the old maid has tended to revolve around the extent to which she is either repressed or subversive. The critical history of Freeman's "A New England Nun" (1887) is a nice barometer of these trends in the critical analysis of old maids in terms of gender and sexuality. For many years, the dominant reading of this story focused on Louisa Ellis's repressed sexuality. Larzer Ziff claims it as "an example of sexual sublimation."[6] Jay Martin comments on the story's "passive sterility," and Perry Westbrook accuses her of having "permit[ted] herself to become unfitted for life."[7] In his biography of Freeman, Edward Foster insists that "it is precisely the absence of desire and striving which is the story's grimly ironic point."[8] David Hirsch chimes in with the claim that she exemplifies the "suppression of the Dionysian."[9] Even feminist critics, who have otherwise tried to reclaim the significance of the spinster figure, have found in Louisa Ellis a model of frigidity and fear. Barbara Johns concludes that "the sexual fear is unmistakable" and argues that Louisa Ellis is the clearest example of a character marked by "a penchant for order, a preference for the indoors, and a solitude akin to a religious retreat that makes the spinsters who are more tolerated than respected in New England Society."[10] The most important feminist revision of this argument belongs to Marjorie Pryse who quieted the existing orthodoxy only to replace it with her own insistence on Louisa Ellis's subversiveness: "In analyzing 'A New England Nun' without bias against solitary women, the reader discovers that within the world Louisa inhabits, she becomes heroic, active, wise, ambitious, and even transcendent, hardly the woman Freeman's critics and biographers have depicted. In choosing solitude, Louisa creates an alternative pattern of living for a woman who possesses, like her, 'the enthusiasm of an artist.'"[11] Subversive, not servile, Louisa Ellis went from being a wallflower to a feminist heroine with the stroke of Pryse's pen. And she did it with gusto. Appropriating the implied psychoanalytic approach of the earlier critics and using it against them, Pryse read images of sexuality throughout the story: the three aprons she wears, for instance, suggest "symbolic if not actual defense of her own virginity."[12]

More recently, critics have extended the argument about the old maid's subversiveness to make of her a queer literary figure. Often described as a historical analogue for the modern lesbian and more properly the modern queer, the old maid has become something of a rallying point for recent feminist and queer scholarship. Dale Bauer, for instance, reads spinsters as inherently subversive: "Remaining outside the marriage market promises a way to subvert a rigidified nineteenth-century culture."[13] Increasingly, as scholarly attention has turned to the history of sexuality, many of these stories have come to be read and collected as part of a tradition of lesbian literature, with no less emphasis on their subversiveness. And in an act of criticism that amounts to subverting this subversive hypothesis about the old maid's incipient lesbianism, Benjamin Kahan has suggested that the figure's implicit celibacy creates the conditions under which the old maid becomes available for homoerotic sociability to begin with.[14]

By far, most of this attention has been paid to writers at the end of the nineteenth century, especially Sarah Orne Jewett, who is widely known to have been part of a Boston marriage with Annie Fields (after James T. Field's death in 1881) but who also wrote fiction set in Maine, often featuring spinsters or widows, some of whom developed intimate erotic attachments with each other.[15] In her documentation of types of spinsters, Barbara Johns does not really have a category for the type who was attracted to other women. Other critics have since read some of the stories she cites (such as Freeman's "A Moral Exigency") as examples of intimacy that is, in Susan Allen Toth's words, "uncomfortably excessive."[16] It is precisely the "uncomfortably excessive" that recent queer critics have delighted in uncovering. Of these, Susan Koppelman is responsible for claiming a veritable subgenre of lesbian writing in the nineteenth century with her collection of stories, *Two Friends and Other Nineteenth-Century Lesbian Stories by American Women Writers*.[17]

Scholars have identified in local color writing an abundance of women who either exist outside of traditional marriage structures (old maids and spinsters, for instance) or who, even if they are married, seem to have bad marriages or strive to create attachments beyond their marriages.[18] Judith Fetterley and Marjorie Pryse go so far as to claim that the sexual subversiveness that has been claimed on behalf of this body of fiction has been foundational for American regional writing. They argue that in their account of regional writing by women, "regionalism enters fiction by way of the queer": "the very form of regionalist fiction is queer and queer in a way that touches on issues of sexuality," and they "see it as a precursor to what could legitimately be called lesbian literature."[19] Most of the stories they offer to document their claims appear in the 1880s or later. Their analysis documents a wide range of texts, most of which also appear in their earlier coedited anthology, *American Women Regionalists:* Stowe's *The Pearl of Orr's Island* (1861–62), Freeman's "A New England Nun" (1887), Cooke's "How Celia Changed Her Mind" (1891), and Alice Cary's "My Grandfather" (1852), among others. Despite the mandate of queer theory to offer an alternative to identity politics, however, Fetterley and Pryse nonetheless identify queerness with identity and the interiority of characters. They focus on the production of regionalism by way of "queer consciousness"— which assumes a coherence of that consciousness on behalf of either the writers or the central characters. (This distinction is often elided as the argument shifts from biographical to narratological claims.) The individual's "sense of being queer" grammatically transforms *queer* into a kind of identity-state unintended by the contemporary queer theorists they cite: queerness, they assume, "shapes the consciousness" that produces our historically first set of regionalist texts (all of which are late-century texts).[20] Queer consciousness thus is presumed to precede not just regional writing but sociability itself.

None of these analyses, to my mind, accounts for the complexity of the literary type complication in American literature that makes the parallels and overlaps between the literary old maid and the modern lesbian seem so obvious to us. Nor are the political paradigms through which we read old maid figures like Louisa Ellis much help in understanding this historical problem—except insofar as we might say, for example, that Louisa Ellis can conceivably stand in opposition to heteronormativity and still be sexually repressed. In which case, we still have a problem in explaining how it is that what seems most subversive can also be, from another perspective, quite sexually conservative. To see the old maid as "queer" only in her resistance to heteronormativity obscures the precise status of the old maid in lesbian literary history. It masks what exactly makes it possible for us to identify the nub of her queerness and what, if anything, is sexual about it. No existing account resolves the contradictions in this history. On the one hand, the centrality of the old maid stimulates detailed consideration of the literary form that being unmarried takes. On the other hand, the old maid figure is resolutely assumed to be a sexual failure. She is imagined precisely (and paradoxically) as an asexual type: one who somehow fails at heterosexual love (for a multitude of reasons: being choosy, making the wrong choice, and so on) or someone who was never interested in it to begin with. It is easy to see why the old maid is a queer figure, but it is harder to see what makes her a historical forerunner to lesbian sexuality.[21] But the historical connection can, I think, be gleaned in its complexity if we compare not just the literary examples of old maids and lesbians but the overlapping processes of type complication that make them legible to begin with, and which in fact undo the fantasies of coherence that obtain when we think about types. It is therefore the nature of the worlds and descriptive details that coalesce around these types of nonheterosexual female sexualities that offers us some insight into the ways in which women's sexuality in nineteenth-century literature became visible.

What interests me here in the process of this literary evolution at play are the ways the literature about old maids incorporates moments of type complication into itself, and the effects of this evolution on the textual imagination of worlds where sexual sociability between women is central. On its own terms, this process of type complication is interesting for the social configurations that come to be described in response to received wisdoms and conventional narratives about what it means to be an old maid. A key mode of type complication is the testing of an existing type concept against other detailed representations of types-in-the-world through acts of reading. The effect is twofold: (1) an accumulation of textual detail (quite literally, more words) that rounds out the presumed flatness of the type; and (2) the situation of the type in the world, such that the boundary between the figure and its contexts becomes blurred. This circulatory energy complicates received textual wisdoms about old maids in a number of ways: through outright questioning of the narrow construction of old maids in print; through a multiplication of representations of old maids, first across periodicals quite broadly but eventually within the confines of single literary works; and ultimately through an expansion of details that create round characters of old maids, details describing unmarried women with more complicated sociosexual lives and rooting them more firmly in a particular cultural location. The terms of this cultural location arguably appear to us most concretely in texts where female characters are described in fully articulated contexts—in contradistinction to the existing terms of type.

Ladies' "Auxiliaries" Society

Consider, for instance, Catharine Maria Sedgwick's 1834 short story "Old Maids." Its title signals a shift from the singular to the plural; the plural form was rarely used in periodical literature only thirty years before. Indeed, what is remarkable about Sedgwick's story is its collection, across a mere six pages of the *Ladies Companion* magazine, of more individualized old maids than had appeared across the pages of many periodicals during the last decade of the eighteenth century. The plural form allows her to offer a collection of discrete examples under the umbrella of a type that otherwise seemed to be universal and abstract.

Sedgwick's story, a conversation between Mrs. Seton and Anne, is essentially an articulation of the conditions under which being an old maid is preferable to being married. An older woman they know has just married and Mrs. Seton is none too pleased. The problem, they decide at the outset, is in part one of terminology: "There are terrors in the name," one explains; the other responds, "Yes, I know there are; and women are daily scared by them into unequal and wretched connexions."[22] Mrs. Seton proceeds to summarize and then respond to the burdensome term *old maid*:

> "The name does not designate a condition but a species. It
> calls up the idea of a faded, bony, wrinkled, skinny, jaundiced

personage, whose mind has dwindled to a point—who has outlived her natural affections—survived every love but love of self, and self-guarded by that Cerberus suspicion—in whom the follies of youth are fresh when all its charms are gone—who has retained, in all their force, the silliest passions of the silliest women—love of dress, of pleasure, of admiration; who, in short, is in the condition of the spirits in the ancients' Tartarus, an impalpable essence tormented with the desires of humanity. Now turn, my dear Anne, from this hideous picture to some of our acquaintance who certainly have missed the *happiest* destiny of woman, but who dwell in light, the emanation of their own goodness. I shall refer you to actual living examples—no fictions."

"No fictions, indeed, for then you must return to the McTabs and Grizzles. Whatever your philanthropy may hope for that most neglected portion of our sex, no author has ventured so far from nature as to portray an attractive old maid. Even Mackenzie, with a spirit as gentle as my Uncle Toby's, and as tender as that of his own 'Man of Feeling,' has written an essay in ridicule of 'old maids.'" (99–100)

As Mrs. Seton goes on to describe a range of old maids she has known, she exemplifies (through argument by example itself) the process of a type's linguistic evolution in the context of widely circulated but narrow literary convention. In the passage above, Mrs. Seton responds to other writers' treatments of narrowly conceived sociosexual types and tests representations of that type against the world around her. The conversational structure of the story in turn dramatizes a mode of readerly (and writerly) response to existing linguistic structures: at once Mrs. Seton is a model of type revision and complication, even as she confirms the power of fictional types (like the McTabs and Grizzles) to organize matches beyond the world of the text.

The perceived negativity of the "old maid" stimulates Mrs. Seton to imagine the conditions under which being an old maid is preferable to being married. The only positive *textual* example she can come up with is that of the biblical Rebecca: "Perhaps not one of the fair young creatures who has dropped a tear over the beautiful sentence that closes the history of Minna, has been conscious that she was offering involuntary homage to the angelic virtues of an *old maid*" (101). But from this, she puzzles out a moral to her listener and expands her range of examples to include women in her immediate environment. While she ultimately maintains ipso facto that no woman ought to "*prefer* single life" (107), she very clearly insists, "I would have young ladies believe that all beautiful and loveable young women do not of course get married—that charms and virtues may exist, and find employment in single life—that a single woman, an old maid (I will not eschew the name), may love and be loved if she has not a husband, and children of her own" (101–2). Included in her list of those who might have good cause not to wed are women like Flora M'Ivor, who "has been surrounded by circumstances that have caused her thoughts and affections to flow in some other channel than love" and who "need not wed a chance Waverly" (102); Violet Flint, who mothers her widowed brother's children; Sarah Lee, who tends kindly to people and strawberry beds alike; and Lucy Ray, who "has lived in others and for others, with such an entire forgetfulness of self . . . has, through every discouragement and disability, reached a height but 'little lower than that angels'; and when now her flickering light disappears, she will be lamented almost as tenderly (alas! for that almost) as if she were a mother" (106–7). What unites all these examples is the self-abnegation— where women become supporting actors to the main drama of society, part of the landscape of domesticity itself—something that Mrs. Seton spells out in greater detail as she recounts the story of Lizzy Grey, a schoolteacher whose younger sister (the girl she essentially mothered) ultimately marries Lizzy's fiancé. As individualized as each example is, then, the brevity of each and its relative paucity of detail combined with the pattern of self-sacrifice offer us a limited account of the "attractive old maid."

Nonetheless, if we look at literary representations of old maids just before and shortly after the publication of "Old Maids," it becomes clear that Sedgwick's story registers a shift that does not necessarily amount to a clear transformation of the earlier type of "old maid." One of the most popular stories told by and about unmarried women at the end of the eighteenth century was that they became "old maids" because they were too choosy. "The Heron: A Tale for the Old Maids," a short allegorical poem, published first in 1744 in the *American Magazine and Historical Chronicle* and reprinted in 1785 in the *Boston Magazine,* concludes with a warning to the old maid reader, comparing her to the poem's central figure, the Heron:

> But he who scorn'd their Betters so,
> Scorns them—and lets the Gudgeons go;
> And now all gone, both good and bad;
> (A Finn on no Terms to be had)
> Poor Long-shanks seeing no great Choice,
> Knew 'twas a Folly to be nice;
> And so to make his Supper sure,
> Eat Snails like any Epicure.[23]

The old maid appears in this poem only indirectly—as represented by the Heron (gendered male)—a fact that emphasizes the paucity of detail in which old maids might be imagined in print, even as the poem assumes that the implicit comparison will resonate obviously because readers should know already what it means to be this particular type. The conventions through which old maids are understood may be thin, but they attend most of the appearances of the old maid in print at the end of the eighteenth century in American periodicals. The same conception of the old maid as one who had plenty of options in her youth, only to find herself unmarried at the ripe "old" age of about twenty-five, is sprinkled throughout magazines of the time, in short, curt snippets and in a range of genres: in poems like the "Epigram on an Old Maid Who Married Her Servant" (1776) and "The Old Maid's Soliloquy" (1785); in letters like that from "An Old Maid" to the Bachelor of the *Pennsylvania Magazine* (1776); and in literary personae like *Worcester Magazine*'s Tom Taciturn. All offer similar stories of women (some from first-person recorders) who describe, in retrospect, having received no shortage of marriage offers in their youth—only to remain single in their middle or older years. None paints the figure of the old maid in great detail; nor does any offer anything more than a few lines of reflection on the figure they clearly paint on the outside of society more generally. Paradoxically, the old maid is a staple, albeit abstracted, character in this periodical literature, but one who can be imagined only as a type and not as an individual. She thus bears out Anne's observation that "no author has ventured so far from nature as to portray an attractive old maid."

The proper place of old maids has in fact dogged the figure since her inception. From early in the eighteenth century, it was commonplace to see old maids and spinsters recognized in terms of an existential dislocation. Writing about her unmarried status in 1719, in England, J. Roberts says, "I write myself SPINSTER, because the laws of my country call me so." English law recognizes her, but a related text concludes, "As for us poor Spinsters, we must certainly go away to France also."[24] By the end of the century, the old maid's displacement would become so commonplace as to be joke-worthy. Oliver Goldsmith's Tony Lumpkin of *She Stoops to Conquer* hyperbolically invokes the rhetorical conventions of weddings in order to refuse marriage to Constantia Neville: "Witness all men by these presents, that I, Anthony Lumpkin, Esquire, of BLANK place, refuse you, Constantia Neville, spinster, of no place at all, for my true and lawful wife."[25] The dislocation here is paradoxical: the spinster belongs elsewhere (or nowhere), but this is effectively no less a way of placing the spinster in both English and American contexts. It is precisely the assumption that J. Roberts must go to France that makes her spinsterhood most English. Thus, the imagined dislocation of the spinster is its own form of location. The limitation of this awkward embrace is that the old maid rarely acquired a level of complexity—in terms of roundness of character or of plot detail surrounding her—where the spinster appears in literary contexts.

As Sedgwick's "Old Maids" suggests, however, this tradition—of situating the old maid in one literary context while proclaiming her to be at odds with that context or belonging more properly to another—generates its own counter-tradition in print. Readers (like Sedgwick) and characters (like Mrs. Seton) alike tested the givenness of literary types against the world around them—as if to read literature in utterly nonaesthetic ways. (The McTabs and Grizzles are not *just* literary characters; they exert influence on women's choices beyond the realm of the imaginary.) The extent to which even this counter-reading is mired in a tradition of textual conventions can be seen in the ways that Sedgwick, through Mrs. Seton, launches a defense of old maidenhood on religious and biblical grounds. Biblical exegesis, adapted to a fictional context, is marshaled in the service of creative and redemptive terms for the old maid.

Still, it is not as if Sedgwick's and Mrs. Seton's responses to other texts can be reduced to a way of reading that looks only backward—especially in light of the text's desire to exceed existing fictional portrayals of old maids. Sedgwick's experiment in type complication shows us the extent to which detailed descriptions of particular examples accumulate literary substance to existing types and conventions. The demand for descriptive particularity around individuals in turn opens up the possibility of imagining more than one type of life for the old maid. As a substantial body of mid-nineteenth-century literature suggests, the prominence of the old maid licensed a particular imagination of women's sexual sociability outside marriage—and indeed, sometimes inside marriage, too.

In 1845, for instance, Margaret Fuller described the rise of the class "contemptuously designated as old maids" and their broadening social roles: not only did there seem to be more old maids, but they were becoming more central to the social world itself. "The business of society has become so complex," she observes, "that it could now scarcely be carried on without the presence of these despised auxiliaries; and detachments from the army of aunts and uncles are wanted to stop gaps in every hedge. They rove about, mental and moral Ishmaelites, pitching their tents amid the fixed and ornamented homes of men." In explaining this sociological phenomenon, Fuller contrasts the old maid with married people, those marked by a "fulness of being" that leads her to ponder the extent to which old maids and bachelors have "tak[en] root on the earth" and in society. Once seen as averse to society, old maids, she points out, are no longer "auxiliaries": instead they are central to the workings of society itself.[26]

This is not to say that the tradition of existential dislocation has been left entirely behind. Stowe's Miss Ophelia and Hawthorne's Hepzibah Pyncheon strongly suggest otherwise. In fact, Miss Ophelia qualifies as precisely the kind of old-maid Ishmaelite

that Fuller had in mind: just as she appears in "the fixed and ornamented home" of Augustine St. Clare in New Orleans, she is also at
once fixed as a New Englander. The description we have of her and
of the place from which she hails depicts her as a doubly displaced
New Englander. First of all, Miss Ophelia has arrived in New Orleans in the face of her mother's wondering whether it "wasn't an
awful wicked place": "It seemed to [her mother] most equal to going
to the Sandwich Islands, or anywhere among the heathen."[27] But
Miss Feely has done so precisely because after forty-five years in
New England she hasn't seemed to fit there either. Nonetheless, in
the opening description of Miss Ophelia as both a product of her
northern environment and a cultivator of the southern environment
to which she has moved, the woman who is arguably the moral conscience of the novel finds herself strangely situated: both an extension of and an affront to the locations that would claim her as part
of them.

The example of Hepzibah Pyncheon is slightly different. Miss
Ophelia is essential to the world of New Orleans in the ways that
Fuller describes even if she does not really belong there. Hepzibah,
on the other hand, belongs so fully in the gloomy House of the Seven
Gables that her fate and demeanor are almost indistinguishable
from those of the house. This house is more than a mise-en-scène;
the house becomes a character itself: "like a human countenance"
the house once "impregnated the whole air" with the smell of fes-
tivity. Feminized, Seven Gables "presented the aspect of a whole
sisterhood of edifices, breathing through the spiracles of one chim-
ney."[28] Hepzibah's failure to marry is itself revisited upon the house,
which seems almost to mimic her being in the world. Despite being
intricately sutured to her domestic space, Hepzibah is also dramati-
cally alienated from the social world of the town. In chapter 2, after
we have been introduced to the house and its familial history, we
learn that "the Old Maid was alone in the house. Alone, except for
a certain respectable and orderly young man, an artist," who lives in
another gable—"quite a house by itself, indeed"; "for above a quarter of a century gone by, [she] has dwelt in strict seclusion, taking
no part in the business of life, and just as little in its intercourse and
pleasures." Even Hepzibah's pillow is "solitary."[29]

What the narrator says to us directly about Hepzibah is undoubtedly ironized by all the ways in which the novel dramatizes Hepzibah's interactions with the other characters in the book. However identified she may be with the crumbling Pyncheon house/heritage and however reluctant she is to form social attachments, she appears to us as intimately attached to a home—even if that home itself is so haunted by its troubled relationship to its owners, the town, and the very environs that all its inhabitants abandon it for Judge Pyncheon's house by the end.

What is significant about both these novels are the awkward terms in which they locate these supporting characters. Each character fits a particular location from which they are, in the larger context, displaced. The extent to which these characters are central to and in accord with the world that surrounds them in part defines their status as minor characters within these novels. The larger story of the novel embraces them, but only insofar as they earn subplots.[30] The old maid is constantly tested against her environment, even as she comes to be defined by it.

Nonetheless, there are some tests to which she is really never put. Whereas the old maid of the eighteenth-century periodicals was presumed to have been too choosy by rejecting husbands, Hepzibah and Miss Ophelia have had more limited suitors and presumably even less active sexual desire—past or present. The spinster has become a solitary figure, who is at odds both with the social and the sexual.[31] However queer a figure the old maid may cut, she is limited as a sexual type by her presumed asexuality. (Ironically, Edith Wharton imagines that Charlotte Lovell, the 1850s old maid, is an old maid because of, not despite, her active sexuality.)

Textual Self-Consciousness and the Spaces of Old Maids

However outside, and in some cases resistant to, heterosexual normality the 1850s old maid may appear to be—in other words, however queer she may seem to readers today—she is not yet widely connected, at the level of content, to the literary history of overtly acknowledged sexual love between women. Before the end of the nineteenth century, examples of sexual intimacy between, or sexual desire among, women rarely appear in old maid literature. In part, this is because spinsters appear to us so frequently as solitary figures. There is less sense of a spinster subculture than there would be by the end of the nineteenth century in, say, the suffrage and abolitionist movements or women's writing circles in New England. Suffice it to say that by and large midcentury lesbianism exists beyond old maid literature: often in pornographic texts and, as we will see presently, in gothic texts and texts about pastoral or exotic, often orientalist, locales.

Separate though these literary traditions may be, however, at the level of form there is a symbiotic relationship between them. The literary renderings of sexualized relationships between women do, I think, benefit from the type complication and modes of textual self-consciousness that allow the old maid to be imagined in a literary fullness not in evidence at the end of the eighteenth century. This is not only because this body of literature opens up possibilities for conceptualizing women's sexuality beyond the social institution of marriage. It is also because the literary old maid circulates more widely and more freely and thus can expand the world-imagining of the old maid figure at a more rapid rate. It thus becomes possible, even likely for the lesbian to logically become part of the widening world and life possibilities that are generated around the old maid.

Still, it is not as if the literary circulation of the old maid acquires such a level of complexity that the figure of lesbian can be so easily inserted. The emerging literature of lesbianism is subject to its own warp and woof of type complication. There is a twist, however. Unlike the lesbian, who has yet to coalesce as such, the *old maid*— as a figure and as a phrase—appears to be a known quantity at any one point in time, even if she is subject to change through processes of recirculation. Where the literature of the old maid tests the elasticity of the phrase *old maid* and highlights the shifting boundaries of its social meaning, literature that treats sexual desire between women does not work with the same abstractions of type. It works instead with already complex literary vignettes or thumbnail sketches. Nonetheless, a similar impulse toward type complication can be discerned in this literature. If we look at what happens in nineteenth-century texts that more overtly take up consideration of erotic love between women, we can see a similar preoccupation with describing and placing erotic attachments between women in these bookworlds. What also becomes clear is that there is no equivalent catchphrase like *old maid* to test against a series of contextualized examples. Instead, descriptions of places (at the level of both form and context) operate as strange (and textually elaborate) versions of types themselves. They operate through intertextual structures and by calling up existing ways of thinking and writing about the locations of sexuality. As we shall see in the examples below, the very evidence of this intertextuality and its attendant descriptions appears in literally more words.

One short story that overtly takes up the sexual love of one woman for another in this layered way, calling on conventions of the gothic and of British romanticism, is Rose Terry Cooke's "My Visitation" (1858).[32] Unlike literature about the old maid, this story does not directly complicate an abstract type. It invokes a series of texts that hover in and overlap throughout. The story begins with the following epigraph from Alfred, Lord Tennyson:

> Is not this she of whom,
> When first she came, all flushed you said to me,
>
> *   *   *   *   *   *   *
>
> Now could you share your thought; now should men see
> Two women faster welded in one love
> Than pairs of wedlock?
>
> —"The Princess"[33]

We then learn rather quickly that the first person narrator has been lying in bed reading Charlotte Brontë's *Shirley*; she sometimes tells her story by ventriloquizing William Wordsworth; at another point, when the narrator is at the beach in Maine, she is reading "some quaint German story, some incredibly exquisite bit of Tennyson, some sensitively musical passage of Kingsley, or, better and more apt, a song or a poem of Shelley's—vivid, spiritual, supernatural; the ideal of poetry; the leaping flame-tongue of lonely genius hanging

in mid-air, self-poised, self-containing, glorious, and unattainable"
(21). I will say more about the conditions under which the Roman-
tics are invoked in the mediation of the narrator's relationship to her
surroundings. For now, though, I'd like to consider the ways this
textual scaffolding connects to the kind of story the narrator seeks to
tell and her conceptualization of her emotional incoherence, which
she stages deftly through conventions of narrative incoherence.

The narrator's opening anxiety about her story's status as
story strikes an odd note. It seems at once overdetermined, banal,
and yet surprisingly genuine. Of all the texts that the narrator invokes throughout the story, that opening "exquisite bit of Tennyson" relates most closely to the story she tells—although a case can
be made that *Shirley* also fits within such a tradition. In what is
one of the more stunningly blunt declarations of nineteenth-century
lesbianism, she describes "falling passionately in love with Eleanore
Wyse" (16)—a phrasing that she consciously chooses, for, as she
says, "no other phrase expresses the blind, irrational, all-enduring
devotion I gave to her; no less vivid word belongs to that mad-
ness" (16). This opening epigraph creates the sense that the story
we are about to hear aims to supplement Tennyson's tale, sharing
the thought of "two women faster welded in one love / Than pairs
of wedlock." But the line of influence is not straightforward. Having created this intertext for herself, the speaker actually begins her
story with a pronounced statement of her worry that the story does
not hang together. Such a worry might be justified if the speaker
believed herself to be telling a kind of story that had not been told
before. But the worry itself takes the fairly conventional form—that
of a gothic convention that renders it almost banal:

> If this story is incoherent—arranged rather for the writer's
> thought than for the reader's eye—it is because the brain which
> dictated it reeled with the sharp assaults of memory, that living
> anguish that abides while earth passes away into silence; and
> because the hand that wrote it trembled with electric thrills
> from a past that can not die, forever fresh in the soul it tested
> and tortured—powerful after the flight of years as in its first
> agony, to fill the dim eye with tears, and throb the languid
> pulses with fresh fever and passion.

> Take, then, the record as it stands, and ask not from a cry
> of mortal pain the liquid cadence and accurate noting of an
> operatic bravura. (14)

The "languid pulses," "sharp assaults of memory," and "electric
thrills from [the] past" all explain why the few commentators on
Cooke's story remark on her formal and thematic affinities with
Poe.[34] Further, as Terry Castle has argued, a discernible literary tradition depicts lesbian desire through ghostly figures.[35] This tradition,
in fact, continues beyond Cooke in other nineteenth-century stories
like Elizabeth Stuart Phelps's "Since I Died" (1873) and Alice Brown's
"There and Here" (1897). All the stories in this tradition, it might be
said, frame sexual desire between women within a condition of impossibility. Stories like these affirm Valerie Rohy's contention, which
she makes about later nineteenth-century American writing, that
imagined impossibility is itself a way of representing lesbianism.[36]

But Cooke's narrator does not just make Eleanor's death the
condition under which she can articulate her desire; rather, Eleanor's death creates the conditions under which she can put her passion to rest. In other words, the story tries to articulate the conditions under which the narrator's consciously sexual love for Eleanor
is a live phenomenon. The gothic frame is indeed a convention, but
it may also mask a genuine sense of incoherence, if we consider the
absence of a literary tradition of sustained or detailed life narratives
about sexual love between women. Throughout the story, Cooke
assembles a montage of literary conventions as if to create a sense
of coherence for this story. Just as the story reaches for literary precursors, so too does the narrator reach outside herself for an understanding of her inside emotional life.

For this narrator, the sense of belonging and fitting in a particular setting structures both the way she understands her attachment
to Eleanor as well as the way she recovers from the heartbreak of
that attachment. She translates the story of her love for Eleanor into
a hieroglyphic legend, part of which reads:

> Nor did I like to see the goddess moved; expression did not
> become her; the soul that pierced those deep eyes was eager,
> unquiet, despotic; nothing divine, indeed, yet, in my eyes,

it was the unresting, hasting meteor that flashed and faded
through mists of earth toward its rest—where I knew not, but
its flickering seemed to me atmospheric. (17)

Later, she describes the way that Eleanor's presence affects her, "as
sunshine does, with a sense of warm life and delight" (17); she comments on Eleanor's "starry height above common people" (18). And
when she discovers that "I never could have loved any man as I did
her," and knows that this is an unrequited love, she tells us that she
"went from home to new scenes and fresh atmosphere" (19). At
Gloucester Beach in Maine, the speaker finds the scenery mediated by her emotional life. Here, she reads Wordsworth, finding that
"Nature never did betray the heart that loved her" (20), and her
sense of equilibrium is restored. She passes the time with a man who
will become her husband by the end of the story—one who also had
fallen for Eleanor. Gradually, she says, "I felt life stealing back to its
deserted and chilly conduits; I basked like a cactus or a lizard into
brighter tints and a gayer existence" (21). Herman knows that the
narrator's love for Eleanor is all that stands between him and marriage, and so he waits, sitting with her "under the old cedars that
shed aromatic scents upon the sun-thrilled air," reading Tennyson
and Shelley to her (21). Only after she hears that Eleanor has died,
and after she has returned from the beach, does the ghostly Eleanor
(whom she designates *It*) begin to pervade the narrator's immediate
surroundings. This haunting persists until Christmas, when after the
narrator responds to Eleanor's cry "Forgive! Forgive!" we learn that
"a gleam of rapture and rest relaxed the brow, the sad eyes; love in-
effable glowed along each lineament, and transfused to splendor the
frigid moulding of snow" (31).

   At every turn, we can see the ways in which the narrator appeals both to the world around her as well as to conventions of describing that world as a means of grasping for emotional coherence.
Eleanor's presence, whether real or imagined, sometimes interrupts
that easy coextensiveness. At other times she seems to anchor it.
Coherence for this narrator does not seem to be about establishing and maintaining a bounded self. Rather, the coherence of the
story seems to rest on establishing a credible relationship between
the plot (the description and resolution of the love story) and the

world in which that plot is set. The story thus showcases a narrator reaching beyond herself and reaching toward (and extending) pieces of well-known literature. The speaker's depiction of a story so consciously about sexual love amounts to more than an expression of desire or a sense of identity. It strives to create both a social world and a language world beyond the expression of individual desire.

Sexual Orientationalisms

To an extent, sexual desire between women has always had a worldliness about it, embodied usually in the ways that Western writers and travelers fetishized the places that seemed most exotic to them. Edward Said famously observed that "sexual experience unobtainable in Europe" and "a different type of sexuality" not only promoted Orientalist fantasies but helped fuel European imperialism from the early modern period onward.[37] As a range of recent respondents to the wave of thinking inspired by Said have begun to argue, however, the inverse is also true: imperialism itself promoted particular sexual fantasies, too.[38] As I argue elsewhere in this book, exotic locales were not the only sites of sexual desire between women (other likely sites are women's educational spaces, including convents, and pornographic parodies of those spaces). What we can see emerging, however, is the extent to which different kinds of places carry highly charged sapphic sexual connotations. In this sense, we might say that particular places, like the Turkish harem, circumscribe forms of exotic sexuality that can be invoked through the bundle of language that describes them without fully naming or reducing them as such.[39] In the context of a transatlantic literary marketplace, those sexual fantasies were obviously not the sole property of Europe. They circulate with the literature in American contexts and infuse the published writings of Americans, too. What we can see from literary locations of sexual desire between women is not just that places carry sexual connotations with them; these literary places also have a formal history that writers invoke and recirculate as they offer expanded narratives about place and sexuality.

A good example of a writer who uses the formal history of

place to expand on and test the language of love between women is Octave Thanet, the pen name of Alice French.[40] Thanet published a short story titled "My Lorelei" in *The Western* (1880). Its narrator and protagonist, Mrs. Louis Danton Lynde, develops an extramarital attachment to another woman, named Undine, while traveling in Germany. Heidelberg is the site of the tale—itself presumably drawn from the author's experience (recorded in her journal) of her European tour with her father.[41]

Not unlike Rose Terry Cooke, Thanet constructs the textuality through which one female character understands her passionate attachment to another out of references to other, famous literary examples—examples that also call attention to the place and setting of the relationship in question. Also like Cooke, Thanet engages a series of overt literary references in the telling of her story. The title makes the most obvious connection: "My Lorelei: A Heidelberg Romance." Nineteenth-century readers would have been well aware of the link between Heidelberg and German Romantic poet Heinrich Heine's famous poem about the Lorelei, a legendary Greek siren whose song lured sailors to their death.[42] This narrator, Constance, calls the other woman "my Lorelei," but this Lorelei figure's actual name is Undine. The Lorelei is a type that becomes complicated when used to describe a situation that is similar to Undine in only the most basic sense: they are both sirens. In a reversal of the Lorelei story, however, it is Undine who dies, not the sailor/narrator she has lured. The name *Undine* itself can be seen to interrupt the coherence of the Lorelei tale, drawing as it does on Friedrich de la Motte Fouqué's 1811 story of the water nymph of the same name. As in Hans Christian Andersen's later and now more familiar story "The Little Mermaid," Undine assumes human form to gain a soul through marriage in the La Motte Fouqué tale. At one point in "My Lorelei," the narrator is even reading the French *Undine* aloud to her companions. What distinguishes Thanet's Lorelei from the many references to Lorelei appearing in periodical writing at this time is the way Thanet does not just refer to the story but adopts it as a frame for her own tale.

The intertexts of the Lorelei and Undine not only layer but also exacerbate a temporal displacement, which the text highlights in its descriptions of place. The story—told through a series of journal entries—begins in Heidelberg:

> We have been here two weeks; we expect to be here two months. The town is a queer, quaint, many-gabled, abominably paved place, with the famous Heidelberger Schloss shouldering its red walls through the trees of the western hills, like the Middle Ages looking down on us. When the sun sets, its rugged towers are outlined against a golden background, such as Fra Angelico gives his Madonnas. Our hotel fronts the Anlage, a charming street, of which only one side is bordered with cream-colored brick, while the other rolls back in wooded hills, where the White Caps hold their Kneipen, and the band plays on summer nights.[43]

Heidelberg is marked by its sensuality, its pastoral quality, and its mythic proportions. The landscape has a kind of temporal agency and logic presented to us in the phrase "the Middle Ages [look] down on us." Later, Constance concludes, "I seem to have stepped out of the bustle and hurry and struggle of modern life. It is bliss, after Chicago" (84). What convinced her is the public sexual culture that she observes, proceeding to describe a pair of lovers who linger, absorbed in each other:

> Occasionally he would take her hand and hold it for a few moments, smiling. He had providently spread a gay handkerchief on the grass, for his clothes were new, beyond a doubt; and he looked tranquilly and unreservedly happy. They said little; but several times the *restauration* waiters brought them beer, and at noon, they ate a great deal of bread and cheese and a large sausage, which they appeared to have brought with them. When night fell, and we went homeward, we overtook them walking hand in hand among the trees. They looked supremely satisfied with life; possibly a trifle stolid, but innocent as Arcadia. Undine glanced up at them as they passed. "They are happy," she said; "probably they are very lately married; but fancy two Americans spending a day in such a way!"
> "I don't like American lovers," said I. (84)

Just as these German lovers appear as a feature of the environment, so too does Constance experience Heine's Lorelei quite literally as a feature of her surroundings—an aural accessory to a scene that begins as a visual panorama and ends in the words of Heine's poem:

> The sun had sunk below the horizon; only a few crimson streaks, like the careless strokes of an emptied brush, stained the yellow glow in the west. Far below us was spread the town, a huddle of pointed roofs and church spires; directly beneath, the Neckar ran noiselessly over its rocks; to the right and to the left stretched the hills. The near hills were green, and checkered with corn-fields and vineyards; but in the distance the dark purple outlines looked darker against the yellow sea of light. The shadows of the ruined towers lay long and heavy on the grass. Away to the right, a solitary nightingale was singing; and as we stood listening for a moment, vaguely awed by the beauty and the melancholy of the scene, some students, out of sight, began Heine's song:—
>
> > Du hast Diamanten und Perlen,
> >   Has Alles was Menchenbegehr,
> > Und hast dite schönsten Augen,—
> >   Men Liebchen, was willst du mehr? (86)[44]

The Lorelei emerges almost seamlessly out of its context to become a double frame—a feature of the landscape and a narrative that organizes the action. Constance's cousin Ted hums the refrain of the song with his arm around Undine, who is clearly the "Du" of the first line. (Ted is engaged to be married to Undine but is also flirting with another character, Grace Wilmott. A man who chased Grace eventually kills Undine inadvertently.) But more important, the song appears as a frame from the narrator's first person perspective. Undine becomes a Lorelei figure, not for Ted but for Constance, who hereafter refers to her as her Lorelei at least twice (85, 87). As we come to see, the one irreducible feature that Heine's Lorelei and Constance's Lorelei share are these beautiful eyes, the "schönsten Augen," which interrupt all of Constance's efforts to have us see her desire for Undine differently.

This song becomes so powerful a framing device for Constance's perception of Undine that it resists all of Constance's efforts to recast her love for Undine as, at one point, maternal, and at another, sisterly. Consider the following scene:

> That evening, passing Undine's door, it opened and she came
> out; by the lamp-light her face looked pale. For the first time,
> she seemed to me not the beautiful, cold lorelei about whom
> I was weaving a fanciful romance, but a girl who had no
> mother, and who was too rich to have many friends. Almost
> involuntarily, I drew her to me and kissed her. The faintest
> flush tinged her cheek. I can't describe how oddly she looked
> at me, saying, "Then, I don't chill you, Constance."
>   "Not to mention," said I, laughing. Then I kissed her
> again. It is possible she was pleased at something; it is possible
> she was hurt at something. I half believe she is as puzzled over
> the pleasure or the pain, as I am puzzled over that curious look
> in her eyes. (87)

Constance writes that she kisses Undine because Undine looks orphaned, like "a girl who had no mother." Yet this mother-daughter reframing of the more persistent Lorelei frame cannot undo the emotional puzzle that hangs over the scene at the end. Pleasure and pain seem indistinguishable for both in the wake of this apparently involuntary show of affection. In the last sentence of the description, the language of Lorelei once again emerges as Constance puzzles over "that curious look in her eyes." The maternalism that Constance invokes to explain her kissing Undine cannot quite do the job of containing her befuddlement. Heine's song, with its focus on Lorelei's bewitching eyes, creeps back as the more dominant textual mediator. One gets the sense in reading the story that Constance experiments with this language of motherhood and sisterhood, testing each language configuration against the relationship before her. Neither sticks. The Lorelei and its context persist as the best way to index the exotic erotic maternalism between the two women.

Later, as the subplot thickens, so too does Constance's jealousy on Undine's behalf. The party has had an unpleasant encounter with the "cretin" who, we learn retrospectively, eventually stabs Undine. Ted continues to flirt with Grace Wilmott; Constance frets.

She begins to hope that Undine does not care for Ted. In fact, she tells Undine that she is too good for him. Undine's reply, which Constance uses as the occasion to remind us of her attachment to her husband, Louis, exerts a force that organizes our way of thinking about all the love relationships in the story—and at the very moment when the plot seems to be reaching its apex:

> "I don't know about that," she said; "and besides, Constance, we don't love people because they are good, but because we can't help it."
>
> Nothing appropriate occurring to me to say, I said nothing; but I felt, with rush of thankfulness so intense that it was pain, how much I respected Louis. (93)

The evacuation of agency from desire articulated here by Undine is striking. "We can't help" loving some people. In this story, desire seems somehow to emerge out of the landscape like the Lorelei song itself. In fact, the pain of desire that strikes Constance seems always to be triggered by and filtered through her surroundings. The last time that Constance talked about emotional feeling as pain was just after she had kissed Undine. The diary writing turns from Undine's summary of love to a sentence-long summary of her fatigue—flagged again by the singing of the Lorelei siren song. The next day the party is scheduled to travel to Schwetzinger and as Constance withdraws to her room, we are told,

> A wretched old German, with a villainous voice, promenades beneath my window, singing over and over again the first two lines of the Lorelei:—
>
> > "Ich weiss nicht was solt es bedenten,[45]
> > Das ich so traurig bin!"
>
> I am tired; I am out of spirits; I wish I could sleep a long, long time. (93)

The Lorelei leitmotif—as soundtrack, as love object, as intertext, and as a marker of Germany being a place out of modern time—reaches its crescendo at this point in the text. It solidifies the pain of love and organizes the story of a love that seems to be structured by this place out of time.

But the relationship and the story organized by Heine's poem also generate another kind of story in the end: one that seems to offer a modern alternative to traditional structures of entailment and inheritance. The tale ends with a retrospective report of Undine/ Lorelei's death, which takes place the day after, when Constance and her party go off to Heidelberg Castle. There is a deathbed declaration of love and a parting kiss. One might be inclined to read Undine's death as the death of possibility. But Undine herself sees it as a strange opportunity. She is determined to lay out to whom she will bequeath her wealth. Undine's message primarily concerns entailment, but the event assumes the weight of the repeated references to the framing poem and its infusion of the two women's attachment to each other:

> I have left half my property to Ted; then I have left something to Aunt Eliza,—all she would take, you know she is rich; and I have left some fifty thousand in legacies to some poor people I have known; the rest I have given to you. You are my sister, Constance; you will take my money, won't you? It makes me happy to think of your having it."
> . . . What could I say to her? I sat silent, with a heavy heart, while one by one the street lights sprang out of the darkness, and by their gleam I took my last look of my darling's face.
> They were singing over among the hills the same little love-song of Heine's, which I heard, for the first time, the day we visited the castle . . . .
> She turned those "loveliest eyes" wistfully up to mine. "*You* will always love me, Con, won't you? Now call Ted. Kiss me first." Even as I kissed her, I felt her lips stir with a smile. "Connie, do you remember the day at the castle, when I wished? Well, the ring is a true fairy, for I wished Ted might love me as long as I lived,—and he will." (97)

Even as Undine is wishing that her fiancé will love her as long as she lives, she hopes that Constance will love her always. It is Constance, indeed, who gets the last kiss. Knowing this, even when Ted bursts in, proclaiming his love, Constance wryly remarks, "Yes, he might kiss her hands and her hair, show his useless remorse in any frantic way he would,—it did not matter what he did any more, for Undine lay there with her last smile forever fixed on her beautiful mouth; as if dead she smiled at his pain, as living she smiled at her own" (97–98).

Undine's death is thus the occasion for a curiously modern structure of inheritance: the deathbed parceling out of belongings amounts to an oral will for Undine, who chooses to leave her wealth to her friends and lovers, not to her family. This is excused because Undine's aunt is rich, but the story closes with a line that makes it clear that Constance was a very particular kind of friend to Undine. The experience and the inheritance have proven nourishing. In Constance's closing words, "As for me, Undine's legacy has prospered with us. I am more in love with my husband than ever. My dear mother is still with us. On the whole, I am a very happy woman,— but I have never made another friend" (98). Undine's death makes Constance more sure of her marriage, but just as sure of what Undine has meant to her.

What is notable in both "My Visitation" and "My Lorelei" is the fact that there is no existing type language against which to test the social belonging of sapphic sexuality in these texts. Instead, what Claude Lévi-Strauss would call *mythemes* (in this case, they are not always mythic in proportion) come to be recirculated and resignified. In appealing to what seem to be old (or older) stories, a tale like "My Visitation" gravitates toward what seems outside of modernity and in doing so generates quite a modern narrative. This process depends on the accumulation of the kinds of details we attribute to description. The fact that descriptions themselves have formal literary properties can be seen in the ways that at precisely those moments of textual description both Cooke and Thanet invoke literary conventions to create their textual worlds. Although Cooke describes a pristine rural American world while Thanet describes a history-laden German one, the strategies they employ are remarkably similar.[46]

It would seem that if old maid literature is engaged in type complication that tests an abstraction against detail, a way to think about what "My Visitation" and "My Lorelei" are doing is to look at them in terms of type accumulation. As I've been trying to suggest, although these different kinds of linguistic type treatments take place in what seem to be parallel literary traditions (in terms of current critical idioms), it may make sense to suggest that one kind of type testing makes possible another kind of type accumulation. This might seem a logical conclusion to draw in light of the fact that the lesbian type emerges at the end of the nineteenth century and she can be seen so often in the kind of local color literature that also features old maids. The process by which this movement takes place in language also interrupts what would appear on some counts to be a teleological assumption that the only logical end of this descriptive accumulation is type creation. One thing that the literature of the old maid shows us is the unpredictability of literary type testing. The very fact that the old maid and the lesbian separate again in twentieth-century literature—the old maid restored to her earlier status as failed heterosexual, as opposed to active lesbian—indicates the extent to which literature often works both toward and against the very phenomenon of literary types.

Seeing both the old maid literature and the emergent lesbian literature as involved in similar processes of world-making and type testing does not, however, fully account for what distinguishes these parallel processes. There does still seem to be a formal difference here that might be accounted for in the fact that neither the Cooke nor the Thanet story has the equivalent of a social type term like *old maid* to complicate.[47] But what if we were also to consider place descriptions and their attendant conventions as type carriers? In other words, that places themselves carry their own abstracted stories that persist not in type language but in details? This might be one way of distinguishing what we see in the Cooke and Thanet stories from what we see in the old maid literature, but also of accounting for similar preoccupations with types and places as they relate to modes of sociability for women outside of marriage. Cooke and Thanet would seem to be engaged in a project of type complication quite similar to those of writers about old maids, if less widely shared. They complicate sexual place types without necessarily complicating existing social types: the social type may not yet exist as such, but the place type does. The effect nonetheless is a literary reorganization of social life that accommodates and includes sexual sociability between women. This analysis does not assume the teleological movement toward sexuality as identity but instead highlights a paradoxically backward-looking energy. By invoking a textual tradition of location and description, both strains of literature effectively disperse individual characters into a context, undoing their sense of coherence so as to refashion and recast their terms of self-reference. Seen this way, both these bodies of literature would seem to be connected at the level of literary form to a larger effort to carve out in writing the relationship of individuals to their surroundings in terms of subject-object dynamics.

In the larger scheme of things, then, these bodies of literature are separate but also peculiar, sometimes overlapping, examples of literature increasingly concerned with its roots in places. Collectively, they enable us to explore the interrelation of two kinds of historical phenomena that might seem unrelated: (1) sexual love between women has been domesticated primarily as an exotic, ancient, or foreign phenomenon, or, in pornography, as immoral, if titillating;[48] and (2) the creation of stories rooted in place is perhaps also facilitated by an increasing desire in Anglo-American literary culture, from the beginning to the middle of the nineteenth century, to conceptualize the emergence of subjectivity out of engagements with nature and landscape.

One remaining question is, why now? What is so significant about these descriptive moments at this moment in literary history? By the middle of the nineteenth century, there is a good deal of critical discussion about the significance of descriptions of environment, and particularly nature, to self-understanding and representation. Two of the most important contributions to this conversation belong to John Ruskin and Ralph Waldo Emerson. In "The Poet," Emerson famously argues that "the Universe is the externisation of the soul. . . . Since everything in nature answers to a moral power, if any phenomenon remains brute and dark, it is that the corresponding faculty in the observer is not yet active."[49] In light of these comments, we might judge the landscape of the narrator of "My Visitation" to be an "externising" of a transcendental soul—not necessarily her own, if we follow Emerson—but the landscape does become anthropomorphized.

This is the very kind of project that Ruskin criticizes, however, when he discusses the "pathetic fallacy" in *Modern Painters*.[50] Conventionally understood, the pathetic fallacy is the attribution of human emotions to inanimate objects or things. In coining the term, Ruskin undertakes to distinguish the speaker's biased perception of nature looking back at him from the power of nature itself: "'Blue' does *not* mean the *sensation* caused by a gentian on the human eye; but it means the *power* of producing that sensation: and this power is always there, in the thing, whether we are there to experience it or not, and would remain there though there were not left a man on the face of the earth. Precisely in the same way gunpowder has a power of exploding."[51] What Ruskin is critical of is the tendency of poets and painters to assume that nature behaves like humans. But this does not mean he evacuates the external world of a power to transform human behavior and self-understanding. He wants, rather, to emphasize

> the difference between the ordinary, proper, and true appearances of things to us; and the extraordinary, or false appearances, when we are under the influence of emotion, or contemplative fancy; false appearances, I say, as being entirely unconnected with any real power or character in the object, and only imputed to it by us.
>
> For instance—
> "The spendthrift crocus, bursting through the mould
> Naked and shivering, with his cup of gold."[52]

Ruskin seeks precisely to distinguish the "real power or character in the object" from what is "only imputed to it by us." In his powerful reading of Ruskin, J. Hillis Miller points to the difficulty of making this distinction in language.[53] He argues that even where we attempt to account for the "real power or character in the object," in the language we choose to carry that power, the best we can do is veil the object. Even if we resist reading the object through the imputations of the speaker, we must at least read the object through the imputations of the writer. Either way, we seem to be trapped in a system of imputation, where setting acquires the personality and power of the perceiver who describes or writes. Emerson's description of the problem affords us a little more room to maneuver, in that he opens the possibility of unconscious projection: "If any phenomenon remains brute and dark, it is that the corresponding faculty in the observer is not yet active." Still, we are left with the sense that the power and faculty belong to a bounded self, however inactive the "corresponding faculty" may be. But Ruskin's original formulation of the subject-object relationship actually goes further in allowing for the possibility that an encounter with the external world allows for a transformation of the self-in-the-world—not just a projection of the self into the world. As he says, "'Blue' . . . means the *power* of producing that sensation: and this power is always there, in the thing, whether we are there to experience it or not, and would remain there though there were not left a man on the face of the earth." Ruskin's formulation allows us to hold on to both the sense that humans attribute power to nature that is really their own at the same time that he allows for nature to have its own particular power. The combination of humans' ability to attribute power to nature (whether Ruskin likes it or not) and nature's own perceived power highlights the overdetermined sense (highlighted perhaps nowhere less than in discussions of literary nationalism) that the particulars of place are themselves generative and disruptive.

Futures for Old Maids

What the literature I have been discussing here so far highlights are the ways that description, which by definition presents a scene by breaking it down into minute components, creates worlds even as it dismantles the boundaries of selves by locating them *in* descriptions. Description, we might even say, is the opposite of the kind of literary abstraction we associate with types—which is why each works well to prop up and undo the other. Types are perhaps discernible once enough detail has accumulated around them, and yet those same types are complicated when tested against new details. We might even go so far as to say that homosexuality, as a type of human behavior, can only become "the love that dare not speak its name" once enough details have accumulated around it that it can be invoked in a setting without being fully described. But is there something that makes this an especially sexualized problem beyond just a literary type problem?

Leo Bersani has argued that sexuality emerges precisely out of self-shattering into the social. In *A Future for Astyanax,* Bersani argues that social encounters dissolve the boundaries of individual types for Henry James's characters.[54] It is no coincidence, I think, that a large number of writers in the nineteenth century gravitate toward queer sexualities as a key means of testing abstract types against detailed contexts. Many of the most important texts of nineteenth-century American literature do precisely this. But there is also something distinct about the literature I've been describing in its treatment of female sexuality. The old maid literature, as well as Thanet's and Cooke's stories, all strive toward describing a world and finding a language for that world in which their characters' dramas make sense. This striving is essential. We get the sense in all of these texts that the lack of fit drives the search for a fit. Occasionally, a text reaches outside itself for other texts, for characters to try to find language that they don't fully have. The entire effort is disruptive, even self-shattering at moments. It may be painful for readers to identify with those characters who seem out of place and not fully comfortable. But there is an energy to this writing that is displaced when all the pieces do come together and the characters do fit their contexts quite well. We can see both the benefits and the shortcomings of literature that seems to move beyond this sense of striving for a world, and for linguistic conventions to describe that world, in a text like Sarah Orne Jewett's "Martha's Lady"—a text that displays the convergence of the old maid literature and literary representations of sexual love between women and that also attempts to expand the scope of the tales we have seen so far from short story into novella.

The long history of type complication I've been describing through this chapter lies beneath the surface of "Martha's Lady." This history infuses the text through a number of well-chosen words and images that coalesce in the effort to tell the story of the lifelong, passionate love of one woman, the maid, Martha, for Helena Vernon, the cousin of Martha's employer, Miss Harriet Pyne. The scene of the tale is tellingly facilitated by the old maid figure, Miss Pyne, in whose house the story unfolds (and whose main occupation in the story, it seems, is to witness its unfolding).[55] Harriet is always described to us in terms of the advantages of old maidenhood:

> She was the last of her family, and was by no means old; but being the last, and wonted to live with people much older than herself, she had formed all the habits of a serious elderly person. Ladies of her age, a little past thirty, often wore discreet caps in those days, especially if they were married, but being single, Miss Harriet clung to youth in this respect, making the one concession of keeping her waving chestnut hair as smooth and stiffly arranged as possible. (203)

And later, we learn of the "protest in her heart against the uncertainties of married life" (213). Helena, Harriet's Boston cousin, is defined from the outset by her exotic Indian clothing and "the good breeding of her city home" (204). When the story begins, we are told that everyone knew Miss Pyne "had company" because "one of the chairs had a crimson silk shawl thrown carelessly over its straight back, and a passer-by who looked in through the latticed gate between the tall gate-posts, with their white urns, might think that this piece of shining East Indian color was a huge red lily that had suddenly bloomed against the syringa bush" (202–3). The shawl is a feature of the environment into which an Orientalist seductiveness is condensed. We also learn that "there was something about the look of the crimson silk shawl in the front yard to make one suspect that the sober customs of the best house in a quiet New England village were all being set at defiance" (203). Later, the narrator describes Helena as a "siren in India muslin" (209).

By contrast, Martha, Harriet's maid, wears "heavy blue checked gingham" and could "climb the cherry-tree like a boy" (207). In fact, our first introduction to Martha is through Harriet's wondering "in agony if Martha were properly attired to go to the door" (204). Martha is defined from the opening of the story by dullness, indifference, and clumsiness, as Harriet frets regularly over Martha's domestic skills. It is through the alliance Martha forges with Helena that she actually learns best how to do the things central to setting up and running Harriet Pyne's house. They bond over the picking of cherries and through careful consideration of where flowers should be placed and how. Martha realizes that "she not only knew what love was like, but she knew love's dear ambitions" (208). Before she leaves, Helena says to her, "'I wish you would think of me sometimes after I go away. Won't you promise?' and the bright young face suddenly grew grave. 'I have hard times myself; I don't always learn things that I ought to learn, I don't always put things straight. I wish you wouldn't forget me ever, and would just believe in me'" (211). The ways Martha has of loving and remembering Helena in her absence all are mediated by and represented through elements of Martha's surroundings.

The ways in which the narrator characterizes key emotional states and memories into a language of environment or landscape are central to understanding the characters in this narrative. Toward the end of the story, and forty years after the first two chapters, both unmarried women—Harriet and Martha—are presented to us through descriptions of settings. Harriet, for instance, "had long ago made all her decisions, and settled all necessary questions; her scheme of life was as faultless as the miniature landscape of a Japanese garden, and as easily kept in order" (212). If Harriet's life was a landscape of sorts, then Martha was a feature of that landscape: "She was unconsciously beautiful like a saint, like the picturesqueness of a lonely tree which lives to shelter unnumbered lives and to stand quietly in its place" (215). In turn, Martha remembers her love by pulling out the handkerchief Helena sent her with a piece of wedding cake and "once in two or three years she sprinkled it as it if were a flower" (215). She also follows Helena around the globe in spirit on an atlas, in effect transforming Helena quite literally into a place on the map:

> A worn old geography often stood open at the map of Europe
> on the light-stand in her room, and a little old-fashioned gilt
> button, set with a piece of glass like a ruby, that had broken
> and fallen from the trimming one of Helena's dresses, was used
> to mark the city of her dwelling-place. In the changes of a dip-
> lomatic life Martha followed her lady all about the map. (216)

This passage is the only moment where Helena appears as "Martha's Lady." When Martha recalls bits of news that she has heard about Helena's life, the narrator tells us that

> these things seemed far away and vague, as if they belonged
> to a story and not to life itself; the true links with the past
> were quite different. There was the unvarying flock of ground-
> sparrows that Helena had begun to feed; every morning Mar-
> tha scattered crumbs for them from the side doorsteps while
> Miss Pyne watched from the dining-room window, and they
> were counted and cherished year by year. (216)

At the end of the story, Martha and Helena are in the room that Martha had restored to its state during Helena's first visit. Helena finally remarks, "'You have always remembered, haven't you, Martha dear?' she said. 'Won't you please kiss me good-night?'" (219).

It would be hard not to see Martha as a heartbreaking figure. We get the sense that she is so very tied to her milieu that she cannot do anything to further her own desire—except through the routines she has established in memory of Helena, themselves products of maintaining that milieu. We might be relieved or thrilled that Martha's affection is finally returned in the last lines of the story, but it is not hard to see that Martha's problem is, in some ways, that she has come to fit too well. In one sense, Martha's belonging is a mark of success if we think of the increasing tendency, in the fiction we have read through so far, for characters literally to find places for themselves in the world and for writers to find ways of describing those character-setting relationships. The type complications and literary testing we have seen in the old maid literature and in the two examples of texts about women's sexual sociability mobilize a kind of rhetorical energy precisely in their striving to establish a context in which these characters make sense. But when they finally do—when the old maid and the lesbian seem to come together in a story like "Martha's Lady"—the putative success is limited. If we see the represented discomfort and the ensuing disruption of a subject-world boundary as central to sexuality, then something of that energy-producing rupture has disappeared. In this sense,

Martha has something in common with Freeman's Louisa Ellis—even if Martha's story ends differently. Recall that "A New England Nun" charts Louisa Ellis's coming to the decision that she ultimately prefers the intimacy of her physical surroundings to the intimacy of marriage. The main action of the story appears to be the refusal of sexual desire, in favor of maintaining a seemingly static world. Louisa's attachment to surroundings *is,* I think, a way of making sense of her sexual desire (even if she is asexual). But Louisa fits so well into her context that the story depicts her as if she were in a textual vacuum. She has become so well sutured to her environment and her routine that she is not available for any form of sexual attachment.

The fit, in other words, can be too perfect. In his famous definition of local color from *Crumbling Idols* (1894), Hamlin Garland insists that local color fiction "has such quality of texture and back-ground that it could not have been written in any other place or by any one else than a native."[56] This sense of an utter fit with one's environment creates the illusion that the quirky types of local color fiction, old maids and lesbians included, have a place in the world. Recently the assumptions about the authenticity of such a smooth connection have been subject to trenchant analysis, and a lively critical discussion has emerged concerning how the regional and the local function, at the end of the century, in relationship to national and even global structures. Many critics have read local color writing as a site of resistance to normative nationality—a way of understanding the nation by way of its regional peculiarities. The most recent critical work to reprise this thesis is Judith Fetterley and Marjorie Pryse's book *Writing Out of Place,* which focuses primarily on gender and form in regional writing.[57] This argument, however, dates back at least as far as Garland himself and continues a long-standing tradition of seeing regionalism and local color writing as somehow subversive of a hegemonic national standard. Reacting strongly against this privileging of the rural life as a kind of subversive nationalism and the resulting idealization of that pristine connection, Amy Kaplan and Richard Brodhead have been dominant proponents of the view that these rurally set tales are the fantasy of the metropole and ultimately a commodity fetish.

Kaplan, for instance, describes regional writing as a kind of "literary tourism"—defined by the "perspective of the modern urban outsider who projects onto the native a pristine authentic space immune to historical changes shaping their own lives."[58] Brodhead similarly insists on the ways regionalism is bound up with "class privilege and cultural hierarchy," regarding the mode as a kind of "cultural elegy . . . memorializing a cultural order passing from life," a "record of a loved thing lost in reality."[59] The problem, we might say, rests in assuming that types who are so seamlessly sutured to their contexts are more realistic or more subversive than those who are more eccentric to their environments.

Seen this way, both the testing of the old maid against a detailed environment and the complication of place types seem to reach their greatest success as well as their point of exhaustion in local color fiction. With the advent of the new discourses of sexology and psychology to explain psychosexual and sociosexual behavior, however, there would come to be new linguistic laboratories for type complication. The old maid and the lesbian would come to occupy distinct categories—represented in works as diverse as Catherine Wells's *The Beautiful House,* Edith Wharton's *The Old Maid: The 'Fifties,* and Radclyffe Hall's *The Well of Loneliness.* This is not to say that context would cease to have any significance for representations of either lesbians or old maids. But the terms of that anxious striving for self-understanding would come to be more psychological than spatial. A good example of this internalization is Gertrude Stein's 1903 formulation in *Q.E.D.:* "It is one of the peculiarities of American womanhood that the body of a coquette often encloses the soul of a prude and the angular form of a spinster is possessed by a nature of the tropics."[60] Stein focuses less on the form of literary externizing (to adjust Emerson's term) and more on the ways that the external itself is internalized. Implicit in her statement is the assumption that the tropics are a sexual place type available to begin with to make sense of inner life. Already the lesbian and the spinster are on their way to further type complication—replete with all the ambivalence about fitting into the world that we see in "Martha's Lady." The path of stylistic testing that the old maid has traveled—across this period of roughly a hundred years and across an astonishing array of different texts, with all the baggage of her ambivalence—would make it possible for Henry James to condense and adumbrate a contained process of type complication, within the pages of a single novel, *The Bostonians*.

4

READING *THE BOSTONIANS'S* HISTORY OF SEXUALITY FROM THE OUTSIDE IN

AT THE BEGINNING of Henry James's *The Bostonians*, Olive Chancellor and Verena Tarrant are two women who happen to live in Boston. Only by the middle of the book do they become the eponymous "Bostonians." This evolution occurs through the novel's structure of oblique narration where what we know about them is conveyed by the narrator through the represented consciousness of other characters. (They first appear to us as "the Bostonians" in Book Second when the narrator describes the thoughts of Olive's sister, Mrs. Luna, whose "motive was spite, and not tenderness for the Bostonians.")[1] It is Basil Ransom, however, the Southern spoiler of the Bostonians' romance, for whom the phrase carries the most weight. We have regular, if indirect, access to Ransom's thoughts about the Bostonians as the narrator depicts him brooding over Verena and strategizing ways to win her away from Olive.[2] The book's title might initially suggest to us that all the characters collectively constitute the Bostonians (on the first page, Mrs. Luna calls our attention to the fact that "nobody tells fibs in Boston" [803]); however, only Olive and Verena together are called "the Bostonians" within the novel.[3] That the Bostonians effectively evolve into *themselves* throughout James's novel is masked by the title's deft assumption that they have *been* themselves from the very start.

Today, it might seem obvious to us, as it has been to a wide range of critics, that James's "Bostonians" can readily be categorized as lesbians and James's novel as a lesbian novel. From our twenty-first-century vantage point, it is easy to see what Olive and Verena anticipate. David Van Leer summarizes this critical perspective when he describes Olive as "certainly the first fully conceived lesbian protagonist in modern fiction."[4] *The Bostonians* by extension is widely considered to be among the first lesbian novels. Given its plot parallels with numerous later novels, like Catherine Wells's 1912 serial novel *The Beautiful House* and Radclyffe Hall's *The Well of Loneliness,* James might be said to have inaugurated the triangulated plot design wherein a relationship between women ends when one of them prefers the life and embrace of a man, a conventional marriage instead of a Boston marriage. (Whether this is a happy or a tragic ending may depend on whether your sympathies lie more with Olive Chancellor or Verena Tarrant.) The very term *the Bostonians* even conjures up the idea of the Boston marriage, which persists as a complicated euphemism for female homosexuality for fin de siècle lesbianism itself.[5] Peter Coviello and Benjamin Kahan have both recently registered compelling resistance to a reading of the novel's anticipatory lesbianism: Coviello focuses on the limits of the speakable to offer an "untimely" argument that understands Olive Chancellor's desire within the available political vocabulary of her scene: "For Olive," says Coviello, "reformist feminism is the closest approximation of a language in which her passion might find a kind of shelter."[6] Kahan meanwhile foregrounds the putative celibacy of the old maid as the ground of possibility for structure of desire at the heart of James's book, a structure of desire that is untethered to particular sexual acts while making sexuality itself palpable.[7] Inspired as I am by Coviello's and Kahan's insights about the untimely and the celibate, I nonetheless take a different approach to understanding *The Bostonians*: this approach is concerned more with place than time and with reading James's novel as the result of literary and social experiments that precede his book. In reading *The Bostonians* as the effect of literary circulation, to which a located mode of sociability is central, I am suggesting that *The Bostonians* constitutes an intertextual meditation on the extent to which civic affiliation names a mode of interior belonging without acceding to the status of autochthonous identity.

James's novel, to put it another way, does not just archive an early conceptualization of either lesbianism or desirous celibacy; its narration and description collectively archive and showcase the role that social and literary circulation plays in the making of *The Bostonians* in terms of exteriority and narration focalized from the outside in. Just as James's novel has a kind of afterlife in the genre of the lesbian novel, it also has its own prehistory that lingers in its pages. This prehistory makes presence felt, for example, where narrative form illustrates the social logic of typing, and where its very descriptions of places serve as repositories for modes of being. Place types and their descriptions operate, as I have argued from the beginning of this book, as an archive of historical assumptions about how place defines its characters from the outside in. For James, as we shall see, place is also a deftly concealed index of his intertextuality and his fascination with French naturalist fiction. One way to think about how James's Bostonians evolve is through a dialogic process of both testing his characters against and relying on the history of the discourse he will use to describe them.[8] Another is to think about how descriptions of particular places in Boston recall the long history of the erotics of female-female education that piggyback on the form James uses to convey them. *The Bostonians,* as both title and term, also calls attention to a paradox of the seeming continuity in our literary historical understanding of sexuality. *The Bostonians* focuses on characters but defines them by their setting, which by nature is external to them—in formal features that also are the novel but originate outside that novel, too.

At a basic level, Olive and Verena are defined by Boston, just as Boston is defined by them, a move that fuses them to the context in which they appear. The title fixes our attention on individuals at the same time that it siphons attention away from individuation and toward the environment that makes them legible. If *the Bostonians* as a term does index a sexual relationship, it does so in ways that exceed our conception of sexuality as a property of the individual.

Further, the evolution in the term's usage throughout the novel calls attention to the process of its own unfolding, offering us an understanding of the ways in which a language of sexual sociability ultimately evolves across space and time.

It is the task of this chapter to investigate these concomitant unfoldings of literary language and modes of sexual sociability through the language of place that defines them. In its attention to evolution and the workings of a language of types, *The Bostonians* consolidates in one literary work the ongoing processes of the literature about old maids in the shorter fiction I discussed in chapter 3. It internalizes, at the level of form, and dramatizes, at the level of content, the cumulative process of typification that has been at work in the circulation of magazine fiction, where fictional conventions of understanding characters by way of their contexts have been emerging. James never explicitly acknowledged any debt of influence to the likes of Alice French, who wrote under the pseudonym Octave Thanet, or Mary Eleanor Wilkins Freeman. But like them, he circulated his fiction in literary magazines and he was cognizant of the conventions and context of writing with which his own work resonates. James's notebooks reveal that he is fully aware that there is a particular type of New England woman in the making. And as we already have seen, the women in these stories, which accumulate at a rapid pace by the end of the nineteenth century, frequently hail literally from New England landscapes—defined by their place in ways not unlike "the Bostonians." By the time this type of New England woman finds her way into James's novel, she has moved from the country to the city. She has moved from being the central figure of discretely serialized stories to being the central figure of a serially circulated novel. Nonetheless, in the figures of Olive Chancellor and Verena Tarrant, this New England woman still lives in the pages of a magazine insofar as James's novel was published serially in the *Century Magazine*. In *The Bostonians,* however, her existence has expanded generically: to have acquired world enough and time to be at the heart of a novel. Broadly speaking, then, this chapter aims to understand how James makes "the Bostonians." This making can be seen in terms of a process of typification and in terms of the pressure that the resulting language of types exerts within the text.

Parsing the literary history of sexuality in terms of genre[9] and by way of *The Bostonians* responds to and attempts to work through the dilemma confronted by any scholar who investigates the history of sexuality more generally and the history of homosexuality specifically. Crudely speaking, this is a dilemma of difference versus similarity: Do we look to the past as a way of understanding the origins of contemporary sexuality, or do we see in the past very particular modes of sexual sociability that are distinct from our own? It seems to me that we can do both simultaneously. But the question has taken the form of a long-standing debate among scholars, many of whom situate themselves within the same critical tradition. Numerous scholars (Jonathan Ned Katz and David Halperin deserve particular mention) have argued that homosexuality, as most of us currently understand it, has a conceptual life span of only about one hundred years, extending back only as far as the late nineteenth century.[10] To impose modern terminologies of understanding sexuality back beyond this time would amount to anachronism. But it is by now well known that representations of same-sex sexuality have a much longer literary history in English, extending back, according to some accounts, at least as far as Chaucer and broadening to include traditions in languages beyond English. As we have already seen, the earliest anthologies of what we might now term *queer writing* are populated by writers not only from the French and German traditions but extending back to the Greeks and Romans. This longer (and wider) history sheds important light on our modern understandings of sexuality. Two things are worth pointing out within this critical history. One, whether scholars are interested in similarities to or differences from present forms of sexuality, the overwhelming tendency in this body of work is to focus on questions of individual identity and desire. Two, a mere glance at some of the titles of the books in this field would offer a cursory index of the ways in which this debate amounts to a problem of language.[11] How do we make sense of language that resembles or seems to describe familiar social structures but ultimately is not the language we continue to use? How do we talk about Renaissance lesbianism? Romantic friendship in the nineteenth century? Do terms like *proto-lesbian* or *queer* just fudge (not to say *queer*) the whole enterprise? The problem is not just one of terminology or of reconciling different language that describes the same thing; rather, it concerns the ways that language itself construes (or misconstrues), with varying degrees of historical accuracy, the very object it purports to describe.

The particular case of *The Bostonians* (and the ways it has been understood) can be seen as symptomatic of this problem generated by the historical nature of the language of sexuality. What enables later readers to see *The Bostonians* as a lesbian novel is the standardization of a language of sexuality that had not yet taken place by 1885–86 when it was first published. But it is close enough in time that many scholars have felt comfortable making the translation from terms that seem almost to describe sexuality into sexuality itself. James often does offer us a glimpse of Olive's peculiar sexual dissidence when his narrator points out that "there are women who are unmarried by accident, and others who are unmarried by option; but Olive Chancellor was unmarried by every implication of her being. She was a spinster as Shelley was a lyric poet, or as the month of August is sultry" (816). Olive is not just unmarried but existentially unmarried. Being unmarried is what she does and what she is. But even here, where James comes closest to making Olive's sexual status a property of her "being," he presents us with a description that holds being in tension with a social obligation. Her being is defined as much by a relationship (or lack of it) to the world outside her as it is by any desire that emanates from her. There is a residue in this comparison that cannot be rationalized by reducing Olive's existentially unmarried status to her being, tout court. And all of this is framed through Olive's status as a Bostonian (as well as Ransom's status as a Southerner—a tension that, in the wake of the Civil War, encodes within itself an allegory of national proportions, including, importantly, the debates about slavery, which hover in the background of this drama).

Indeed, much of the evidence we see for reading James's Bostonians as lesbians requires an act of translation, precisely because, as many scholars have noted, the novel never really trades in the language we now use to describe sexuality.[12] The closest James comes to characterizing his Bostonians in medical or psychological terms is in his depiction of Olive as "morbid."[13] John Stokes suggests that

morbidity was indeed a nineteenth-century euphemism for homosexuality.[14] But this reading of *morbidity* as euphemism also should
give us pause enough to consider the historical parameters of our
translating *euphemism* itself. Consider the following passage, often
cited by critics as evidence, even code, for Olive's euphemistic lesbianism, focalized through Ransom's perception of her:

> Basil Ransom was a young man of first-rate intelligence, but
> conscious of the narrow range, as yet, of his experience. He
> was on his guard against generalisations which might be hasty;
> but he had arrived at two or three that were of value to a gen-
> tleman lately admitted to the New York bar and looking out
> for clients. One of them was to the effect that the simplest divi-
> sion it is possible to make of the human race is into the people
> who take things hard and the people who take them easy.
> He perceived very quickly that Miss Chancellor belonged to
> the former class. This was written so intensely in her delicate
> face that he felt an unformulated pity for her before they had
> exchanged twenty words. He himself, by nature, took things
> easy; if he had put on the screw of late, it was after reflection,
> and because circumstances pressed him close. But this pale girl,
> with her light-green eyes, her pointed features and nervous
> manner, was visibly morbid; it was as plain as day that she
> was morbid. Poor Ransom announced this fact to himself as
> if he had made a great discovery; but in reality he had never
> been so "Boeotian" as at that moment. It proved nothing of
> any importance, with regard to Miss Chancellor, to say that
> she was morbid; any sufficient account of her would lie very
> much to the rear of that. Why was she morbid, and why was
> her morbidness typical? Ransom might have exulted if he had
> gone back far enough to explain that mystery. (809–10)

What is worth noting first is that this is Ransom's thinking reflected,
again, through the voice of the narrator. Ransom's first-rate intelli-
gence, we are told, cannot prevent him from observing what is moreover obvious, although his experience of the world is thin: Olive
is "visibly morbid." So obvious is Olive's morbidity that Ransom
is transfixed by it, and the narrator cannot avoid repeating it: the
word *morbid* is hammered into Ransom's consciousness (and ours)

five times in the last few sentences of this passage. The repetition is almost at odds with the distance that irony is supposed to create. Repetition seems to create the illusion of verification and statistical accumulation, however subjective, while ironic narration is supposed to distance us from those very conclusions. And yet, as both Judith Butler and Susan Sontag have emphasized, repetition itself is central to the disruptions enacted through queer subject formation and camp alike (sometimes all at once).[15] Although we are presumably supposed to see the distance between ourselves and the narrator, the narrator and Ransom, and finally, Ransom and Olive, the repetition of the word nonetheless has a cumulative and defining effect, even if that effect is distorted by the narrator's refracting this viewpoint through Ransom's point of view. Despite the refractions of repetitions and points of view, Olive's morbidity has calcified into evidence for her lesbianism ever since.

Nonetheless, the obviousness of Olive's morbidity is at odds with the mystery of its source. After all, we are also told: "It proved nothing of any importance, with regard to Miss Chancellor, to say that she was morbid; any sufficient account of her would lie very much to the rear of that." Why her morbidness was typical is much more uncertain: "Ransom might have exulted if he had gone back far enough to explain that mystery." Indeed, Olive's morbidness becomes both typical and mysterious in the same moment. What becomes increasingly clear as we confront not just the evidence but the form this evidence takes is that status as a sexual type is much more mysterious and complex than we have thus far understood—its coherence undone by the ironic distance through which we see Olive, as well as by the range of implied comparisons that make Olive legible to other characters in the novel. If Ransom's assessment is any indication, making sense of what is typical requires looking backward from Olive, to see what is "to the rear of that." Likewise, we might say that the first part of James's novel lays out what is "to the rear" of the Bostonians becoming "the Bostonians." This rhetoric of place might paradoxically be seen to look forward to the queer Olive in the ways in which Wendy Graham describes both Olive and James himself, but not necessarily in the ways we expect.[16]

James's (and Ransom's) preoccupation with what is "typical" in this passage presents itself throughout *The Bostonians* as characters attempt to judge, make sense of, and even prop up other characters. The terms they have for doing so predate the circumstances in which they appear to the characters. Typification in *The Bostonians* is more mysterious than critics have acknowledged thus far, in large part because of the novel's formal awareness of how much the language of type depends, weirdly, on its own evolution across time and space within the text. This chapter thus focuses on the myriad and necessarily converging ways that the text enables the Bostonians to become types: the narrative layers that place Olive at the center of a novelistic panopticon where types appear by way of perspective; the intertextual layers that bubble beneath the surface of James's text; James's intense interest in telling a story about *place*; and the ongoing sense, embodied not in Olive but in Basil and in the Tarrants, that sexual sociability is bound up with fantasies of civic order and the public face of social life. It may be time to relieve Olive of her symbolic responsibility as the foundational lesbian of the novel, so as to understand the ways in which its world—its social apparatus with its attendant perspectives and circulations—finds her, as well as Verena, and ultimately exceeds them both.

James not only creates a character but also enacts a world, already in the making before he imagines it, a world in which that character makes sense. Understanding how he does so requires understanding the importance of place to James's writing and how his sense of place makes legible the situatedness as well as the temporality of sexual typification. Much as "the Bostonians" masks the linked formal and social processes by which the novel generates the characters of its own title, so too does the modern language of sexuality, usually sexological and psychological, mask the formal and social processes by which sexuality itself came to be recognized as such. The pages that follow engage in a further investigation of these complex contexts and processes that James both invokes and creates for his Bostonians.

The History and Temporality of Type

It might be said that the business of the novel has since its inception been the business of typification: to explain how a person whose status is inconsistent becomes (or fails to become) a particular type (rake, gentleman, lady). Indeed, we have already seen the functioning of type complication within the pages of this book. But according to the *Oxford English Dictionary, typification* as a word that designates the process or action of typifying does not appear until the nineteenth century. The first recorded use is by Jeremy Bentham: "A distant and fanciful analogy," he says, "which there is between the event *typified* and the real event made use of for *typification*."[17] It is precisely in the abstruse quality of this statement that part of the mystery of typification lies. It is not by accident that the action of typification is described here in the passive voice; passivity is essential to the word. The very clumsiness of the word *typification* ensues from its grammatical use in the passive voice. But what it stumbles over is its own sense of process and the implied but absent agent of the process by which typification takes place. This sense of an actorless process persists in other recorded uses of the term in the nineteenth century as well, all of which seem to gesture to typification as an act of language, often the effect of metaphor, not of human agents exactly. An 1845 issue of *Blackwood's Magazine,* for instance, contains this sentence: "The four-paned rattling window of that clumsy typefication of slowness, misnamed a diligence."[18] Similarly in Arthur Baker's *A Plea for "Romanizers" in the Anglican Communion,* we read about "the typification, the earnest and the pledge by outward miracle, of the reality of the sacramental grace."[19] Even the definition of *typification* appears to confer activity on language: "Typification: the action of typifying; representation by a type or symbol; also, that which typifies, or serves as a type, symbol, or specimen of something: an exemplification." It is the type or symbol that represents. The *that* in the phrase "that which typifies" remains unclear. In the case of types represented in language, it is the very word *type* that typifies something.[20]

Theorists of typology in fact attest to the generative quality of types, the way in which they give rise, at later times, to variations of themselves.[21] Frank Kermode offers the following explanation:

> Strictly speaking, a type is distinguished from a symbol or allegory in that it is constituted by an historical event or person (as Christ makes Jonah the type of his resurrection, and

St. Paul the crossing of the Red Sea by the Israelites a type of baptism). A type can therefore be identified only when fulfilled by its antitype, a later event in a providentially structured history; the Old Covenant is a type of the New. . . .

Types are essentially what Auerbach has in mind when he speaks of *figurae*, events or persons that are themselves, but may presage others. Their purpose, to put it too simply, is to accommodate the events and persons of a superseded order of time to a new one. A writer conscious of standing on a watershed between past and present might well be interested in typology, though his use of the word "type" might not have the exactness required by scholars, and he might let it be con- taminated by other devices for accommodating an old veiled sense to a new order of time.[22]

What Kermode is insisting on here, with essential recourse to Eric Auerbach, is the way in which types come to be accommodated to later times and places, often in the service of innovation. (As his discussion continues, he argues that American writers like Nathaniel Hawthorne and Ralph Waldo Emerson "loosened up the concept.")[23]

In *The Bostonians,* Henry James trades consciously in the lan- guage of types. He seems fully aware that while the antitype marks its own distance in time and space from the initial type, the latter by necessity leaves a residue on the former. And vice versa: Olive's fulfillment of morbidity somehow makes the quality of morbid- ness recognizable—at least as Basil Ransom sees it. In this case, it may well be the type that makes the antitype legible as such. When Basil Ransom muses about Olive's "typical" morbidity, he realizes that the mystery of it goes well beyond the example of Olive, that something beyond Olive finds its residue in her, even though this something is beyond Ransom's ken. On the one hand, we might think about James as providing an innovation upon old types; an- other approach would be to suggest that the preexisting types are the lenses through which Ransom sees Olive, even if he is unaware of the types' origins.[24]

This dialectical relationship between type and antitype goes some distance toward helping us explain the paradox of typology at the heart of *The Bostonians,* for it allows James to authorize typological continuity and discontinuity all at once—without assuming a teleological relationship between them. Indeed, this sense of type as simultaneously innovative and conservative persists in James's treatment of types throughout *The Bostonians*. In other words, James demonstrates a keen awareness that typification is a process with its own temporality. James's ongoing effort to define and describe his main characters as Bostonians participates in two temporal movements. The history of the language of type suggests to us that types are future-oriented: they "presage" or prefigure. Corollary to this suggestion is the sense that antitypes are backward-looking.[25] And yet his version of antitype seems to be projecting something new (at least from our vantage point). On this score, James is working in both registers at once. In the first instance, James would seem to be an innovator; he builds up a type within the novel (the slow evolution of "the Bostonians"). At the same time, from the beginning of the novel, a wide range of characters trades liberally and consciously in the language of type—the effect of which practically collapses any possibility of temporality, shutting down the possibility of change for characters who are seen as types from the perspective of other characters.

For the types whose evolution he does not dramatize, James offers us a glimpse into the ways that the language of type glibly organizes characters' perceptions into categories that exist prior to those perceptions. In these cases, the language of type operates as an often dismissive shorthand, which gestures to a body of knowledge signified by but never fully unpacked through that language of type. The language of type is at once consciously backward-looking and future-oriented: "typing" brings bodies of past assumptions and received wisdoms to bear on immediate circumstances. There is almost no character in the novel that is not described as some sort of type. But it is almost never a compliment to be seen as a type in James's world.

The Rhetorical Space of Type

Throughout *The Bostonians*, the language of type requires physical space and expresses itself in terms of rhetorical space.[26] Typification in *The Bostonians* is complicated throughout the novel by the fact that the language of type appears through a process of invested but indirect observation; that is, one character will judge another as a type or as "typical," even as this point of view is offered to us through the free, indirect discourse of the narrator. But the description is always imposed by someone else, in the wake of an observation and often offered from the ironic perspective of the limitedly omniscient narrator. Basil Ransom is perhaps the character most likely to reduce those around him to types, the clearest example of which is his assessment of Olive Chancellor: "Nothing would induce [Basil] to make love to such a type as [Olive]" (816). Desire would seem to be negatively entangled with the problem of type here. But it seems also to be rendered more diffuse through the language of type. After all, Ransom also sees Doctor Prance as a type ("If his cousin could have been even of this type Basil would have felt himself more fortunate" [844]); he makes sense of the librarian at Harvard through her type ("He considered with attention the young lady's fair ringlets and refined, anxious expression, saying to himself that this was in the highest degree a New England type" [1023]); and he loathes Verena's father, Selah Tarrant, due to his type ("He was intensely familiar—that is, his type was; he was simply the detested carpet-bagger. He was false, cunning, vulgar, ignoble; the cheapest kind of human product" [853]). He even sees Verena herself through the lens of type. In a telling transposition, we are told that "he had read, of old, of the *improvisatrice* of Italy, and this was a chastened, modern, American version of the type, a New England Corinna, with a mission instead of a lyre" (1044). In all these cases, Ransom imports generalizations as types to make sense of a context whose details he does not know by experience. He can thus judge through a combination of first encounters and induction, where typing imports a kind of stock knowledge. The language of type would also seem to collapse its temporality in terms of *evolving* perceptions, creating the illusion that the *before* of conception is the same as the *after* of perception.

But Basil is not the only character to type so readily. Olive is just as quick to judge. She sees it as an intellectual failure to resort to understanding people as types. Still, she cannot escape her own thoughts. She exhibits disdain for the Tarrants: "As we know, she had forbidden herself this emotion as regards individuals; and she flattered herself that she considered the Tarrants as a type, a deplorable one, a class that, with the public at large, discredited the cause of the new truths" (902). She has just as little time for Henry Burrage and his "type," or for his mother: "She wished to heaven that conceited young men with time on their hands would leave Verena alone; but evidently they wouldn't, and her best safety was in seeing as many as should turn up. If the type should become frequent, she would very soon judge it. If Olive had not been so grim, she would have had a smile to spare for the frankness with which the girl herself adopted this theory" (938); "But how could Olive believe that, when she saw the type to which Mrs. Burrage belonged—a type into which nature herself had inserted a face turned in the very opposite way from all earnest and improving things?" (1083).

From this brief survey, it would appear that Olive reduces to a "type" anyone who might compete with her for Verena's attention. But notably, Olive never reduces Basil Ransom to a type (perhaps because she takes him so seriously as a threat); further, Olive is not exempt from appearing to Verena as a type either, albeit in positive not negative terms: from Verena's perspective, we're told that "Olive was the very type and model of the 'gifted being'; her qualities had not been bought and paid for; they were like some brilliant birthday-present, left at the door by an unknown messenger, to be delightful for ever as an inexhaustible legacy, and amusing for ever from the obscurity of its source" (908). Olive may be the novel's protagonist, but the narrator plays no favorites: Olive earns no more compliments as a type from the narrator than from Ransom.

These judgments—whether by Basil Ransom or the narrator—all amount to social exposure. The distance that the ironic narration creates is essential to the novel's panopticon quality. The form measures distance in space as much as allegiances. Contempt exudes from Olive's reduction of people to types, just as Ransom's understanding of people as types marks his desire to master them as unknown objects of his perception. Even when Verena more generously declares to Olive that she is sympathetic to Ransom because he is "the type of the reactionary" (1067) whose mind she wants to change, she is offering a well-intended, though ultimately lame, insult designed to appease Olive. In all of these examples, the very word *type* protrudes from its context, breaking ranks with the descriptive subtlety that is one of the hallmarks of James's writing.

Following Hannah Arendt, we might even say that the very language of type puts the typed person at odds with society itself. Type acquires a greater edge under conditions in which conformity is expected (however unrealistic that conformity might be). In *The Human Condition,* Arendt identifies modern society with this kind of "conformism, the assumption that men behave and do not act with respect to each other."[27] The modern science of economics, which coincides with the rise of the social, she argues, "could achieve a scientific character only when men had become social beings and unanimously followed certain patterns of behavior, so that those who did not keep the rules could be considered to be asocial or abnormal."[28] Not coincidentally, for Arendt the novel is "the only entirely social art form."[29] This claim makes a good deal of sense to me, as it explains why the novel can offer us a glimpse of sexuality as a mode of sociability. Few novelists are as complexly social as Henry James.

James's complex version of the social is a product not just of his shrewd observations of the world around him. (He famously advised that a writer should "try to be one of the people on whom nothing is lost!")[30] As we have seen, this complexity ensues from the forms James uses to create sociality itself. In spite of their range, the examples above collectively reveal the interconnectedness of the social and formal process of typing in the novel. Such judgments require the distance of physical space between observer and observed (a distance constantly both highlighted and collapsed by the narrator). The layers of distance in turn generate rhetorical space. In other words, their social complexity takes a quite specific form. We need the ironic distance that James creates in the instances where his characters "type" others. This provides us with a glimpse of what may happen when "the Bostonians" themselves become a type. Ultimately, we will see that the making of "the Bostonians" will require not just the exposure of distanced perspectives but the accumulation of perspectives and repeated exposures that make the typing convincing. This accumulation of perspectives, episodes, and, ultimately, competing types—all filtered through the panoptical irony created by the narrator—may well be what distinguishes James's novel from the magazine fiction I examined in the previous chapter. Where the central characters in those stories strove beyond themselves—looking to their environments (and the language that conveys them) for some way to make sense of their social relationships—James demonstrates the way that social relationships are always understood beyond individuals themselves, anyway. As we will see presently, James's marking of Olive and Verena as peculiar, indeed abnormal Bostonians emerges because we can see the ways *they are seen by others*. This is only possible because they are both ensconced within the Boston world. Through Basil Ransom, they come to be seen as eccentric to the Boston world in which they move—just as eccentric to it, paradoxically, as Ransom himself is from the start. Indeed, being ensconced within the world of Boston becomes the condition of possibility for others, like Ransom, Mrs. Luna, and even the narrator, to comment on Olive and Verena's peculiarity.

What the various meditations on type thus far should make clear is the extent to which types, in their social locutions, are not terms of self-reference. Further, at the level of form, typification as a process requires publicity, the distance of perspective and judgment, as well as repetition to be meaningful. If James is doing something new, its newness has been mistakenly associated with the rise of identitarian social categories that come into being after *The Bostonians* is published and seem far more focused on individual self-reference. Whatever newness exists is made possible by the contexts of literary and social circulation that converge in James's writing. *The Bostonians* obviously stands precisely at a watershed in the literary history of sexuality in that it has been understood as a first type of novel. But this understanding alone overlooks the essence of James's project, which was never to write a lesbian novel. As he says in a notebook entry that we will examine in detail later in this chapter, his goal is to prove he can write an American novel. This frame already indicates that James understands his characters not in the register of sexuality in which they have come to be most widely known but as characters defined by place. This is not to say, however, that there is no connection between place and sexuality; on the contrary, it is to insist on this historical connection. As I've been trying to suggest, it is possible to see the various idioms of place operating collectively as a language of sexuality before the fact, operating through a kind of global, ethnographic imaginary. James positions his writing within the context of a global imaginary, implicitly universalizing the very local modes of sociability that he sees operating through the drama of his characters. James's work threads this association between character types and their places through his writing even as the novel evinces symptoms of his era's increasing tendency to shift the burden of sexual dissidence from place to person. What *The Bostonians* shows us is the extent to which the last place we will find the sexual subjectivity of "the Bostonians" is within the Bostonians themselves. The following sections will explain just how large a role social and textual circulation plays in creating the conditions under which "the Bostonians" come to be imagined as types, and how the form of James's writing is tied up with these modes of circulation that create types from the outside in.

The Making of "the Bostonians" I: The Form of Their Place in the Text

From the opening lines of *The Bostonians,* James establishes his focus on the dimensions and idiom of place to make sense of his characters. He calls attention to the space between characters within the very places that ultimately seem to read them as much as they read each other. What ensues, with every mention of Boston or what is Bostonian about Olive's house or even Olive herself, is a gradual process of accumulation and of seeing the characters through a slightly shifting prism of linguistic expectations and sociological assumptions. The novel opens with the following scene: Olive's sister, Mrs. Luna, announces to the waiting Basil Ransom that

> Olive will come down in about ten minutes; she told me to
> tell you that. About ten; that is exactly like Olive. Neither five
> nor fifteen, and yet not ten exactly, but either nine or eleven.

> She didn't tell me to say she was glad to see you, because she
> doesn't know whether she is or not, and she wouldn't for the
> world expose herself to telling a fib. She is very honest, is Olive
> Chancellor; she is full of rectitude. Nobody tells fibs in Boston;
> I don't know what to make of them all. Well, I am very glad to
> see you, at any rate. (803)

Whether Mrs. Luna is right when she says that "nobody tells fibs in
Boston" or when, a couple of sentences later, she describes Boston as
an "unprevaricating city" (803), her opening lines set the tone—at
once earnest and ironic—with respect to the novel. Mrs. Luna wants
to be believed, of course (and at this point, we have no choice but
to believe her; she is our only source of information), but she undermines herself by accusing everyone else in Boston of wanting the
same thing. She invites Ransom to think about Bostonians in particular casts of truth and irony. Though he finds Mrs. Luna rather too
familiar, he is happy to play her game:

> He threw [the book] down at the approach of Mrs. Luna,
> laughed, shook hands with her, and said in answer to her last
> remark, "You imply that you do tell fibs. Perhaps that is one."
> "Oh no; there is nothing wonderful in my being glad to see
> you," Mrs. Luna rejoined, "when I tell you that I have been
> three long weeks in this unprevaricating city."
> "That has an unflattering sound for me," said the young
> man. "I pretend not to prevaricate."
> "Dear me, what's the good of being a Southerner?" the
> lady asked. (803)

In "pretend[ing] not to prevaricate," Ransom appears to claim his
status as an outsider, a non-Bostonian—even though he is also quick
to point out that earnestness is no guarantee of one's honesty when
he says, "You imply that you do tell fibs." Pretending not to prevaricate under such circumstances may well be indistinguishable from
being unprevaricating. For Mrs. Luna, being a Southerner entitles
one to prevarication in precisely the flirtatious way that Basil engages her here. Her status as a comic figure might well lead us to
dismiss the ways in which she reads the characters around her were
it not for the fact that everyone else in the text, the narrator included, reads in this way, too. We are encouraged to see Basil Ransom's

Southernness as a marker of his speech and his character. Just sentences later, James's narrator explains to us that the imprint of that Southernness has been stamped into his speech:

> He came, in fact, from Mississippi, and he spoke very perceptibly with the accent of that country. It is not in my power to reproduce by any combination of characters this charming dialect; but the initiated reader will have no difficulty in evoking the sound, which is to be associated in the present instance with nothing vulgar or vain . . . . the reader . . . who desires to read with the senses as well as with the reason, is entreated not to forget that he prolonged his consonants and swallowed his vowels, that he was guilty of elisions and interpolations which were equally unexpected, and that his discourse was pervaded by something sultry and vast, something almost African in its rich, basking tone, something that suggested the teeming expanse of the cotton-field. (804)

Ransom's speech, like Mrs. Luna's assumptions, is teeming with an unspoken racialized history that speaks through him.[31] The narrator's description of Ransom's voice as "almost African" cannot help but associate his Southernness with the ideology of slavery and the fact that slaves too were often understood, in the white imagination, as "almost African." It must be said, of course, that such an imagination of Ransom as a metonymy for slavery is also a stock feature of Northern (Yankee) fantasy. It is thus in this context of tapping into an existing archive of information that the making of "the Bostonians" begins. It establishes, first of all, a comparative base by which people in Boston and people from the South are defined and pits them against each other. As Mrs. Luna and Basil Ransom encircle each other rhetorically, Mrs. Luna's attempts to close the unfamiliar space between them exposes the rhetorical shape of racialization by proximity, as if Ransom's "almost African" speech coded his relationship to racism, too.

This physical and rhetorical dance does not just create from the beginning the voyeuristic narrative distance that James will need for his irony to work. It also allows him to circulate descriptions about Olive through other characters before we get to meet her. At the beginning of the novel Ransom doesn't know that he will eventually be engaged in (and win) a battle over Olive's soon-to-be protégé, Verena Tarrant. He doesn't know much about Olive at all. But he does have a framework for understanding Olive that he imports to make sense of her before he even meets her. Even without Mrs. Luna's help, he knows and assumes a good deal about Boston and its inhabitants. He is disappointed but not surprised, therefore, when Mrs. Luna informs him that Olive is a "female Jacobin," a "roaring radical":

> "Well, I suppose I might have known that," he continued, at last.
> "You might have known what?" [Mrs. Luna asks.]
> "Well, that Miss Chancellor would be all that you say. She was brought up in the city of reform."
> "Oh, it isn't the city; it's just Olive Chancellor. She would reform the solar system if she could get hold of it." (805–6).

In this exchange, we already see a tension emerging between two competing ways of explaining Olive Chancellor before either Ransom or the reader has met her in person. Ransom sees Olive as a symbol of the city itself, part of the dominant reforming ways he associates with Boston as a whole; Mrs. Luna sees her as an extremist and attributes Olive's reforming nature to her peculiarity. Mrs. Luna, though, is hardly a source of authority. In the economy of the novel, it becomes clear that Ransom's opinion should be taken more seriously than Mrs. Luna's.

This circulation of language about Olive is essential to the ways the novel allows us to make sense of her. Throughout Book First, Ransom relies on what he has already heard about Boston to organize his perceptions—not unlike James himself, whose novel depends on what his readers have already heard and read. In this sense, type actively offers Ransom a way of reading that takes place through him, one that is not exactly generated by him. Consider the way that the narrator describes Ransom's reading of Olive's house and the agency that accrues to things in this passage:

> Nevertheless it seemed to him he had never seen an interior that was so much an interior as this queer corridor-shaped drawing-room of his new-found kinswoman; he had never

felt himself in the presence of so much organized privacy or of
so many objects that spoke of habits and tastes. Most of the
people he had hitherto known had no tastes; they had a few
habits, but these were not of a sort that required much uphol-
stery. He had not as yet been in many houses in New York,
and he had never before seen so many accessories. The general
character of the place struck him as Bostonian; this was, in
fact, very much what he had supposed Boston to be. He had
always heard Boston was a city of culture, and now there was
culture in Miss Chancellor's tables and sofas, in the books that
were everywhere, on little shelves like brackets (as if a book
were a statuette), in the photographs and water-colours that
covered the walls, in the curtains that were festooned rather
stiffly in the doorways. (814–15)

It is the "general character of the place," literally the interior of
Olive's home but also exterior to Olive's self, which is Bostonian; the
culture of the city and of Olive persists in its things. The very objects
in Olive's house are said to "speak"; but they don't tell Ransom
anything he doesn't already know. This is not a process of discovery
but one of confirmation. In an act of circular reading, Ransom sees
"very much what he had supposed Boston to be"; that is, he attaches
a story to the environment he observes that precedes his encounter with it. This encounter leads him to conclude that although "he
had for a moment a whimsical vision of becoming a partner in so
flourishing a firm" (by marrying Olive), "it was very easy for him
to remark to himself that nothing would induce him to make love
to such a type as that" (816). In this moment, we observe Ransom
distancing himself from Olive, at the same time that the narrator
distances Ransom from us. His snide thought exposes just as much
about him as about Olive but reveals how indebted we are to the
space surrounding both characters for our understanding of them.
(Nor is Olive any more generous than Ransom in her regard of him.
She writes to Basil because he is her cousin and because it is "what
her mother would have done." Olive's sense of duty is hereditary,
and her sense of the South is about as reductive as her assessment of
Ransom as "too simple—too Mississippian" [812–13].)
Rarely does James steer us away from any understanding of

either Olive or Ransom created by dint of the environment of their upbringing—Olive by the city of Boston, and Basil by the plantation of Mississippi. The significance of these places never really fades from view. At precisely the moment in which we get a glimpse of Olive's interior, the language that describes that interiority, like that of her house, exceeds her person and locates itself in the strange subjectivity afforded to the speaking things. Likewise, we are reminded of Ransom's service to the Confederacy in the Civil War, just as we are reminded that Olive has a fabulous view of Back Bay.

There is only one occasion on which Olive Chancellor is described to us as a Bostonian in the singular, and it is through the eyes of the narrator, who is the one describing Olive's refusal of courtship and marriage. (The "new woman" is, of course, a northerner, not a southerner.) The narrator is explaining Olive's tolerance for Verena's entertainment of male suitors:

> Olive could enter, to a certain extent, into that; she herself had had a phase (some time after her father's death—her mother's had preceded his—when she bought the little house in Charles Street and began to live alone), during which she accompanied gentlemen to respectable places of amusement. She was accordingly not shocked at the idea of such adventures on Verena's part; than which, indeed, judging from her own experience, nothing could well have been less adventurous. Her recollections of these expeditions were as of something solemn and edifying—of the earnest interest in her welfare exhibited by her companion (there were few occasions on which the young Bostonian appeared to more advantage), of the comfort of other friends sitting near, who were sure to know whom she was with, of serious discussion between the acts in regard to the behaviour of the characters in the piece, and of the speech at the end with which, as the young man quitted her at her door, she rewarded his civility—"I must thank you for a very pleasant evening." She always felt that she made that too prim; her lips stiffened themselves as she spoke. But the whole affair had always a primness; this was discernible even to Olive's very limited sense of humour. It was not so religious as going to evening-service at King's Chapel; but it was the next thing

> to it. Of course all girls didn't do it; there were families that
> viewed such a custom with disfavour. But this was where the
> girls were of the romping sort; there had to be some things
> they were known not to do. (909)

In observing in a parenthetical note that "there were few occasions
on which the young Bostonian appeared to more advantage," the
narrator highlights the advantage that Olive is refusing. For her, it is
a matter of "custom" to entertain young men, but when she speaks,
her lips reflexively "stiffened themselves," much like the curtains
that Basil Ransom described in her drawing room.

This is one of only a few uses of the word *Bostonian* before
the middle of Book Second, when Olive and Verena are referred
to collectively as "the Bostonians" for the first time. The first, as
we have already seen, appears in Ransom's assessment of Olive's
drawing room. The second appears very close to it, when Olive re-
luctantly invites Ransom to her meeting after dinner. At this point,
Ransom has already heard from Mrs. Luna about the meeting and
thus feels comfortable in asking, "Is it something very Bostonian?
I should like to see that" (818). Olive does not really respond to his
question, but later in the conversation, when Ransom has again emphasized that he sees the evening as "such a chance to see Boston,"
Olive says, "It isn't Boston—it's humanity!" (819). By this point in
the text, however, Basil's association of Olive and her activities has
been repeated so many times that Olive's effort to universalize her
activities is futile. To Ransom, Olive is already a particular kind
of Bostonian, about whom he may want to know more, but only
just to confirm his prejudices. His viewpoint, an effect of his own
displacement, is that much more emplaced, despite his belief that it
is Boston's provincialism that both narrows his view of Olive and
universalizes Olive's view of her own perspective.

This gradual accumulation of detail and repetition that solidifies Olive's status as a Bostonian through the eyes of Basil Ransom reaches its apotheosis in the last chapter of Book First. This is
when Verena moves into Olive's house on Charles Street: "Verena
was completely under the charm" (956); "[Olive] had never known
a greater pleasure" (956); "Nothing happened to dissipate the
good omens with which her partnership with Verena Tarrant was

at present surrounded. They threw themselves into study" (960); and Olive remarks on "the way her companion rose with the level of the civilisation that surrounded her, the way she assimilated all delicacies and absorbed all traditions" (962). We are told that "they admired the sunsets, they rejoiced in the ruddy spots projected upon the parlour-wall, they followed the darkening perspective in fanciful excursions. They watched the stellar points come out at last in a colder heaven, and then, shuddering a little, arm in arm, they turned away, with a sense that the winter night was even more cruel than the tyranny of men" (963).

This lengthy record of the intimate and educative life on Charles Street leads up to the following observation by the narrator:

> All this doubtless sounds rather dry, and I hasten to add that our friends were not always shut up in Miss Chancellor's strenuous parlour. In spite of Olive's desire to keep her precious inmate to herself and to bend her attention upon their common studies, in spite of her constantly reminding Verena that this winter was to be purely educative and that the platitudes of the satisfied and unregenerate would have little to teach her, in spite, in short, of the severe and constant duality of our young women, it must not be supposed that their life had not many personal confluents and tributaries. Individual and original as Miss Chancellor was universally acknowledged to be, she was yet a typical Bostonian, and as a typical Bostonian she could not fail to belong in some degree to a "set." It had been said of her that she was in it but not of it; but she was of it enough to go occasionally into other houses and to receive their occupants in her own. It was her belief that she filled her tea-pot with the spoon of hospitality, and made a good many select spirits feel that they were welcome under her roof at convenient hours. (964–65)

Up to this point, our sense of Olive as a type has been defined through a combination of her agitation on behalf of women and Boston's general reputation for reform. Here, Olive comes to be understood in the context of a slightly different social network. Her relationship to Verena now defines her as part of a particular "set"—"in it but not of it" and yet circulating through it and having the "occupants" of "other houses" move through her own. The phrase "in it but not of it" is similar to Basil Ransom's earlier sense of the objects speaking their Bostonian culture to him. The category of "Bostonian" lays claim to those it names and thrusts them into a web of sociability. Whereas the novel had earlier described Olive going to meetings outside her home and hosting individual official visits, the narrator stresses here the practice of one house's occupants visiting another's.

This social circulation seems instrumental to Olive and Verena's becoming "the Bostonians." Even Basil Ransom, until the moment he whisks Verena away from her debut at the Music Hall, refers to them as such, however ironically, as if "the Bostonians" were their collective name. Throughout Books Second and Third, the narrator's represented speech and thought about a range of characters consolidate this collective status. We are told at one point that "[Mrs. Luna's] motive was spite, and not tenderness for the Bostonians" (1061); that "there would not be half an hour in the day during which Basil Ransom, complacently calling, would find the Bostonians in the house" (1062); and later that "[Basil] knew that the Bostonians had been drawn thither [to the Cape], for the hot weeks, by its sedative influence, by the conviction that its toneless air would minister to perfect rest" (1120). It is almost as if Ransom is inspired by the consolidation of "the Bostonians" as such (as much as he is also encouraged by Verena), for "he [even] reflected that it would hardly do to begin his attack that night; he ought to give the Bostonians a certain amount of notice of his appearance on the scene" (1123).

Each time that Basil reflects on "the Bostonians," one gets the distinct sense that he does so very deliberately, as if he is thinking about his own act of perception, or that the narrator offers us Ransom's observations very deliberately. Ransom's last visit to the Cape, three chapters from the end, is punctuated by two scenes in which he apperceives Olive and Verena: "Like his friends the Bostonians he was very nervous; there were days when he felt that he must rush back to the margin of that mild inlet; the voices of the air whispered to him that in his absence he was being outwitted" (1175). By this point in the novel, we have long known that "the Bostonians" are not Ransom's friends. He remarks moments later:

> It was the afternoon-train that had brought him back from Provincetown, and in the evening he ascertained that the Bostonians had not deserted the field. There were lights in the windows of the house under the elms, and he stood where he had stood that evening with Doctor Prance and listened to the waves of Verena's voice, as she rehearsed her lecture. There were no waves this time, no sounds, and no sign of life but the lamps; the place had apparently not ceased to be given over to the conscious silence described by Doctor Prance. (1176)

The "conscious silence" attributed to Doctor Prance's description ensues from Miss Birdseye's death and marks the mourning that hovers in the air. But Ransom's concern with the lack of life he observes is not really a preoccupation with the absent Miss Birdseye but with the absent voice of Verena Tarrant. As confident as Ransom is, he is also never entirely sure that the Bostonians as a unit might not prove indivisible. For each time the narrator conveys Ransom's thoughts about the Bostonians, these thoughts continually enact the unity that Ransom's actions aim to undo. At each turn, whether it is in singular or plural form, the word *Bostonian* conjures up an image that exists in excess of both the individual Bostonian as well as the individual circumstances and actions attributed to her. Within the text, James's attention to cumulative language, repetition, and ironic distance thus produces a plenitude of language, tinged with ambivalence, to buttress his Bostonians. Although Olive and Verena are ostensibly the primary objects of interest in this novel, everywhere the novel tries to sharpen its focus on them, its language generates a field around them that ultimately directs us away. This double movement, formulated through the perspective of Basil Ransom, which threatens to fragment the Bostonians even as they are coming together, is what generates the heaping dose of ambivalence that attends their consolidation as types. Even when the Bostonians have been divided, as we shall see, this ambivalence persists in the closing tones of the novel. What becomes apparent is the sheer quantity of language that goes into creating and describing the Bostonians as we come to know them, which focuses our attention on a very different kind of evidence in the literary history of sexuality. This plenitude of language thus calls for different ways to conceptualize the literary history of homosexuality, broadly construed, whose critical traditions have tended to focus on reading for what is missing, untold, or unspeakable, except through euphemism.

The Making of "the Bostonians" II: Forms of Publicity and Their Hidden Histories of Sexuality

We have just observed some of the ways in which form dramatizes the significance of space and location to the making of "the Bostonians" by way of narrative perspective within the social relationships of the novel. For James, description is tied not just to narrative complexity but to the aesthetics of world-making more generally, which generates a plenitude of language. Nowhere do novels generate this plenitude of language more than in those places where they describe their milieu. It would be no exaggeration to suggest that James was obsessed with the details of milieu in producing *The Bostonians*. Importantly, James does not just focus on place as a way of figuring and exfoliating the social relationships among the characters in his novel. In fact, it is more the other way around: his Bostonians give him a way of writing about a particular place, America. From the very germ of James's novel, outlined in his notebooks, we get a strong sense of how he imagines the connections among the key constellation of issues we have been examining thus far: place, types, publicity, the relationship between two women in Boston, and the literary forms that organize them:

> The subject is strong and good, with a large rich interest. The relation of the two girls should be a study of one of those friendships between women which are so common in New England. The whole thing as local, as American, as possible, and as full of Boston: an attempt to show that I *can* write an American story. There must, indispensably, be a type of newspaper man—the man whose ideal is the energetic reporter. I should like to *bafouer* [trample] the vulgarity and hideousness of this—the impudent invasion of privacy—the extinction of all conception of privacy, etc. Daudet's *Évangéliste* has given

me the idea of this thing. If only I could do something with that *pictorial* quality! At any rate, the subject is very national, very typical. I wished to write a very *American* tale, a tale very characteristic of our social conditions, and I asked myself what was the most salient and peculiar point in our social life. The answer was: the situation of women, the decline of the sentiment of sex, the agitation on their behalf.[32]

James's concern with types defined by place is so prominent here as to be almost overdetermined. Above all, he is attempting to write a quintessentially American novel—"very national, very typical," "characteristic of our social conditions." But to get there, James takes both an allegorical and an intertextual route. The "local" is elevated to the national by virtue of parallel structure: "the whole thing as local, as American, as possible, and as full of Boston." It may seem obvious that for years Boston had been an elevated representative of American life. But the Boston that James describes is not a Boston hungover from Puritan life (though it cannot shed this tradition, whose seriousness lends credence to the symbolic status of Boston as the site of James's American novel). It is the Boston of the suffrage movement. His interest in "the Bostonians" is an interest not just in them for their own sake but for their symbolic national status. While James may be drawing on Boston's (and New England's) traditional national significance, he does so to mark a shift in national character, calling attention to a new "salient and peculiar point in our social life." The novel's focus on the "relation of the two girls" is both central and incidental to the project: central in that James sees this relation as an irreducible signifier of American life; incidental in that it is a vehicle for a commentary on American life, not in itself James's primary object of interest. This is important because James is pointing to the centrality of these relationships to national life, not to their marginality or their locality. That James sees himself participating in the writing not of niche literature but of national literature is first of all important to establish, given that his text may be considered as part of a niche literature.

In his thinking about these friendships between women as typically American, two things preoccupy James: one is the invasive rise of publicity, or what he terms the "impudent invasion of privacy";

the other is "that *pictorial* quality" that he would like to import from Alphonse Daudet. Nowhere in *The Bostonians* does James explicitly acknowledge Daudet. And only in the minor figure of the newspaper man, Matthias Pardon, whom he ridicules, does he provide us with a figure who intrudes on the characters' privacy. Rather, as we have observed, the more effective way that James attempts to *bafouer* and expose the impudent invasions of privacy is through his use of irony. Both James's meditations on privacy and Daudet's "pictorial quality" thus can be seen to persist in the form of James's text, the first through the distancing effect of ironic narration and the second through the descriptive quality of environment that has led many commentators to regard the period during which James wrote *The Bostonians* as his "naturalist" period.[33] Each of these formal elements conceals a history connected to the literary and social expression of nonnormative sexuality, as James would have known it. It is worth elaborating here on the ways this secret history persists, not so much in the gaps of the novel but in those moments where the text offers us the most language.

In his notebook description of *The Bostonians*, the history of James's contempt for "the impudent invasion of privacy" owes itself to his disdain for newspapermen. That disdain for the press is itself tied to the James family's odd connection to the history of the Oneida community founded by John Noyes in upstate New York. As a young man, Henry James Sr. had been a temporary supporter of the religious commune, whose unorthodox sexual customs included male continence (a form of birth control based on preventing ejaculation), mutual criticism (a method of public censure for moral wrongs), and perhaps most controversially, the system of complex marriage, a form of polyamory whereby every man was married to every woman and vice versa. In order for any couple to cohabitate, they had to gain the permission of a third person or group of persons and stipulate that they would not be exclusive sexual partners. A system of "ascending fellowship" was used to introduce virgins into the system of "complex marriage."[34] Although he later changed his mind, James Sr. was recorded as having said of the male leaders at Oneida that "they were fathers, and husbands, and brothers, like myself."[35]

Some twenty-two years (and a changed mind) later, this statement would come back to haunt him. In a series of letters, Henry James Sr. waded into a debate about suffrage and "Woman's Rights." In this context, James Sr. wrote a letter on marriage that was excerpted and published much later in *Woodhull and Claflin's Weekly*. The best account of this whole affair can be found in Alfred Habegger's book *Henry James and the "Woman Business."*[36] The salient parts for our purposes here are that a piece of this letter was excerpted and circulated so as to make it appear that James Sr. was a supporter of free love. The argument of his letter essentially was that the exclusive nature of marriage actually stimulated spiritual growth in a man. But in the letter he wrote, rhetorically, that

> I marry my wife under the impression that she is literally perfect, and is going to exhaust my capacity of desire ever after. Ere long I discover my mistake. . . . My good habits, my good breeding, my hearty respect for my wife . . . prevent my ever letting her suspect the conflict going on in my bosom; but there it is, nevertheless, a ceaseless conflict between law and liberty, between conscience and inclination. . . . I see very well that the bond ought to be loosened in the case of other people. . . . But as for me, I will abide in my chains.[37]

The letter set off a storm of controversy and sensational public debate and seriously tarnished the reputation of James Sr., who was now taken to be a bad father and husband. He was widely seen as a defender of Henry Ward Beecher, who had been accused in print of adultery. Scrutiny by the press was relentless. Henry James Jr. returned from Europe in September 1874 right on the heels of the whole affair and was disgusted by the press's prurient interest in his family's personal life. Later, James Jr. would come to associate the intrusiveness of the nineteenth-century paparazzi with the very topic of Oneida. In a bristling review of Charles Nordhoff's book *The Communistic Societies of the United States*, James insists that "the whole scene [at Oneida] is an attempt to organize and glorify the detestable tendency toward the complete effacement of privacy in life and thought everywhere so rampant with us nowadays."[38] Uncharacteristically for James, he seems unable (or unwilling) to distinguish the journalists' exposure of his family's private life from the issue that so concerned the press about his father. Thus the demise of privacy that interests James so much in the writing of *The Bostonians* emerges out of ideas about the possibilities for elaborating alternative sexual cultures in America.

This secret place-history of the origins of James's disgust with the effacement of privacy is not completely obscured in *The Bostonians*. It attaches directly to the Tarrant family as evidence of their oddness and in turn attaches to Verena. The notebook entry seems to suggest that it is the treatment of the suffrage plot that would expose the demise of privacy. The clearer tie to Oneida in the text, however, is Verena's father, Selah Tarrant, who was once himself a member of the community. Although we get a strong sense of Olive's oddness and morbidity throughout the text, Verena too has inherited a legacy of perversity. We learn early in the novel that Verena's father had been "for a while a member of the celebrated Cayuga community, where there were no wives, or no husbands, or something of that sort (Mrs. Tarrant could never remember)" (865). Mrs. Tarrant, we are told, had

> incurred the displeasure of her family, who gave her husband
> to understand that, much as they desired to remove the shack-
> les from the slave, there were kinds of behaviour which struck
> them as too unfettered. These had prevailed, to their thinking,
> at Cayuga, and they naturally felt it was no use for him to say
> that his residence there had been (for him—the community
> still existed) but a momentary episode, inasmuch as there was
> little more to be urged for the spiritual picnics and vegetarian
> camp-meetings in which the discountenanced pair now sought
> consolation. (865)

The widespread contempt for Selah Tarrant takes on a particular relish in the text, from the perspectives of both Olive Chancellor and Basil Ransom. Whereas, as we have already seen, Olive resents the taint the Tarrants lend to the cause of "new truth," Ransom's assessment is more scathing for its own sake:

> Ransom simply loathed him, from the moment he opened his
> mouth; he was intensely familiar—that is, his type was; he

> was simply the detested carpet-bagger. He was false, cunning,
> vulgar, ignoble; the cheapest kind of human product. That he
> should be the father of a delicate, pretty girl, who was ap-
> parently clever too, whether she had a gift or no, this was an
> annoying, disconcerting fact. (853)

Although James substitutes his association of the demise of privacy
with the Oneida community for an association of the demise of privacy with the Bostonian community he depicts, the world of Boston
and the world of the Cayugas are markedly different in the way
they are presented to us in James's novel. The difference can be seen
again in the way James situates one in a climate of complex description but not the other. The language of type that defines "the
Bostonians" appears alongside scrupulously narrated detail that in
fact often works against the reductive language of type. There is no
such detail to provide texture for the Cayuga/Oneida community in
the novel. Stripped from any context that might lend depth to his
experience there (as the context of Boston deepens the complexity
of Olive Chancellor's representation, for instance), Selah Tarrant, in
dogged pursuit of publicity from the newspapermen, has no source
of complexity. He is thus rendered practically synonymous with the
obsequious Matthias Pardon, just as Oneida and the demise of privacy have become synonymous for Henry James.

This stark difference in the level of detail afforded his Bostonians and the Oneida community is a direct result of the other
formal preoccupation apparent in his notebook entry: James's interest in "pictorial quality," which as promised carries with it another secret history that extends far back in French literature. As
in any novel, some characters—usually those central to the text—
are shrouded in details; others are not and are therefore allowed
to stand as more flat types. In his longing to imitate the "pictorial
quality" of Daudet's *L'évangéliste,* James establishes both his appreciation of and resistance to Daudet's form of description. But he
also worries that at the level of content his text may seem derivative.
Much as James might like to see form as distinct from content, he
realizes the extent to which his admiration of Daudet's form cannot
fully leave Daudet's content behind. No doubt he fears that the title
character in *L'évangéliste,* Mme Autheman, might resemble Olive

Chancellor too much. A rich Protestant proselytizer in France, she controls the entire town and eventually wins the soul of a young Catholic girl, who leaves her family and would-be husband to join the missionary cause.

Earlier in the same notebook entry, James exclaims that "Daudet's *Évangéliste* has given me the idea of this thing."[39] What appeals to James about Daudet is the manner of description that brings the environment itself to life. Unlike Émile Zola and Gustave Flaubert, Daudet, in James's estimation, wrote by "quick, instantaneous vision," not relying so much on "the taking of notes."[40] Like James, Daudet defines his novel as a novel about place: its subtitle is *Roman parisien*. *L'évangéliste* is published in 1883, *The Bostonians* in 1886, and later, in 1896, Daudet supplies what might be read as a rejoinder, *Sappho: Parisian Manners,* the last piece that would make the three novels a kind of dialogic trilogy.[41] In a subsequent notebook entry, James also insists that his novel resembles another French text, Honoré de Balzac's *La fille aux yeux d'or.* This novella features a battle between an estranged brother and sister for the title character, a young Creole woman who has been lover to both. In all these cases, the form James admires so much is in how these French writers craft stories about sexual or intense love between women. James thus imports into his work both the triangulated lesbian plots as well as a particular quality of description, which establishes a symbiotic textual relationship between the description of place and the ethnographic quality of that description as it relates to women's sexual sociability. As James argues in "The Art of Fiction," description itself is a way of telling a story; the distinction between description and narration is false: "I cannot imagine composition existing in a series of blocks, not conceive, in any novel worth discussing at all, of a passage of description that is not in its intention narrative."[42] It is not just that the descriptive, pictorial quality is associated with French naturalism; indeed, it is associated with representations of same-sex sexuality between women.

This tradition is associated not only with French realist texts but with texts, usually in the history of pornography, in which one woman educates another in the ways of sexuality. At least since Samuel Pepys's famous effort to read *L'école des filles* with one hand, English readers and writers have looked to French literature for sexually illicit educational exchanges between women. In *The Invention of Pornography*, Lynn Hunt points to two key texts in the rise of the pornographic tradition in France that locate the origins of pornography in satires of Catholicism and debates about education for women: *L'école des filles: La philosophie des dames* and *L'académie des dames*.[43] In fact, there is a substantial body of literature in both French and English, often satiric, set first in convents or nunneries where women could be educated, but later, with the secularization of women's education, extended to places concerned with the subcultural context devoted to the education of women (including brothels). Janet Todd has suggested that "lesbianism had always been a voyeuristic topic in pornographic or semi-pornographic works for men, especially those deriving from France, where the convent was synonymous with titillating forms of female sexuality."[44] The texts within this tradition of the titillating convent all bear out the extent to which this culture of place is understood in terms of a culture of sexuality. Even though the dialogues between women usually concerned the passing on of heterosexual knowledge (women talking about how to have sex with men), it was not uncommon, as in *L'école des filles*, for the women to be turned on by their own sexual language. By the end of the nineteenth century, the dialogue form of these texts in English (and their accommodations to English, such as *The Whore's Rhetorick* [1683]) has gradually expanded into modes of description and more detailed plots (as we see in *Venus in the Cloister*, Denis Diderot's *Memoirs of a Nun*, and even *Letters from a Portuguese Nun*). What persists, however, across the range of formal innovations is the stubborn association of female-only spaces for education with a shared language of sexuality between women. This long-standing association of illicit sexual sociability with sites of women's education persists into the America that James is describing.

In 1899, Denslow Lewis delivered a lecture to the American Medical Association in which he warned against the dangers of young women forming close female friendships, something arguably facilitated by women's colleges:

> The young girls, thus thrown together, manifest an increasing affection by the usual tokens. They kiss each other fondly on

every occasion. They embrace each other with mutual satisfaction. It is most natural, in the interchange of visits, for them to sleep together. They learn the pleasure of direct contact, and in the course of their fondling they resort to cunni-linguistic practices . . . . after this the normal sex act fails to satisfy her.[45]

Implied in some of these texts, and overtly stated in others, is the overwhelming (even overdetermined) sense that educating women together will lead to lesbianism—all because the environment facilitates both physical closeness and the pleasures of "direct contact" in a context of intense intellectual engagement. The female body is stimulated both by learning and by the proximity of other bodies, even if they are female.[46] It seems to be no coincidence that the French writers to whom James looked for formal inspiration, like Daudet, also seem tied to a complex tradition in France that associates sexual sociability between women with educational environments.

Of course, it would be a stretch to suggest that all forms of description in French naturalism bear the trace of what we now recognize as lesbianism. However, two things are clear: first, there is a persistent and long-standing imagination of sexual sociability developing between women in women-only spaces; second, the most identifiably naturalist French texts that James cites offer accounts of female same-sex love. The "pictorial quality" of Daudet's writing attaches itself to the very particular depiction of one woman, Mme Autheman (who has affixed multiple bolts on her bedroom door so that her husband cannot enter), in pursuit of a young protégé who will enter the female community of Protestants in France.

It is not mere coincidence, therefore, that James infuses his own descriptions of Boston with a narrative quality that reflects the social relationships being formulated in the text. We have seen this tendency to code descriptions with character exposition already in many of the examples cited thus far (Basil's perception of Olive's drawing room; Olive and Verena reading books intensely and then walking arm in arm outside). Another good example can be seen in the narrator's description of the view from Olive's drawing room just after Verena moves in with Olive:

The western windows of Olive's drawing-room, looking over the water, took in the red sunsets of winter; the long, low

bridge that crawled, on its staggering posts, across the Charles;
the casual patches of ice and snow; the desolate suburban
horizons, peeled and made bald by the rigour of the season;
the general hard, cold void of the prospect; the extrusion,
at Charlestown, at Cambridge, of a few chimneys and stee-
ples, straight, sordid tubes of factories and engine-shops, or
spare, heavenward finger of the New England meeting-house.
There was something inexorable in the poverty of the scene,
shameful in the meanness of its details, which gave a collective impression of boards and tin and frozen earth, sheds and
rotting piles, railway-lines striding flat across a thoroughfare
of puddles, and tracks of the humbler, the universal horse-car,
traversing obliquely this path of danger; loose fences, vacant
lots, mounds of refuse, yards bestrewn with iron pipes, telegraph poles, and bare wooden backs of places. Verena thought
such a view lovely, and she was by no means without excuse
when, as the afternoon closed, the ugly picture was tinted
with a clear, cold rosiness. The air, in its windless chill, seemed
to tinkle like a crystal, the faintest gradations of tone were
perceptible in the sky, the west became deep and delicate, everything grew doubly distinct before taking on the dimness of
evening. There were pink flushes on snow, "tender" reflections
in patches of stiffened marsh, sounds of car-bells, no longer
vulgar, but almost silvery, on the long bridge, lonely outlines
of distant dusky undulations against the fading glow. These
agreeable effects used to light up that end of the drawing-
room, and Olive often sat at the window with her companion
before it was time for the lamp. (963)

From the beginning of this passage, our apprehension of the scene
is organized by the fact that it is the windows themselves that "look
out." The meetinghouse rises to view. Although there is something
"shameful in the meanness of its details" (perhaps akin to the way
Olive has paid the Tarrants to let Verena stay with her), once Verena
appears in the paragraph, she lends a "clear, cold rosiness" to the
scene and the air "tinkle[s]." And in spite of the professed ugliness
and vulgarity that the narrator attributes to the scene, the effect on
Olive is nonetheless "agreeable" and "light[s] up that end of the

drawing-room." The scene itself is thus imbued with all the complications of the relationship itself: the foreboding sense of the scene's "inexorable poverty," the "path of danger," and yet also a certain loveliness and pleasant affect. Through the "pictorial quality" a scene of intimacy emerges.

The drawing room, we should remember, is also the scene of Verena's education.

The Bostonians and the Art of Fictional Sexuality

As I pointed out earlier, in my introduction, Mikhail Bakhtin argues that utterances connect the history of society to the history of language, and "not a single new language phenomenon (phonetic, lexical, or grammatical) . . . can enter the system of language without having traversed the long and complicated path of generic-stylistic testing and modification."[47] In the spirit of Bakhtin, therefore, we might see *The Bostonians* not just as part of a newly emerging genre (the lesbian novel) but also as the effect of a "long and complicated path of generic-stylistic testing and modification." Several histories of sexuality as an idiom of place speak through both the form and content of the text. Other stories and histories that we have not explored here also persist in the traces of influence that organized James's thinking about both novel writing and relationships between women (the influence of Hawthorne, for instance, especially *The Blithedale Romance,* and certainly James's experience of his sister Alice's relationship to Katherine Loring).[48] Types are not invented but reconfigured, perhaps even diffused, through James's text such that the genres read their way into James's novel. As a result, we may need to think of James's novel not just as the antitype it has been all along but as a type carrier, threading through a history of other types condensed into the figure of Olive as Bostonian.

Except this does not fully accord with the persistent critical sense that something is beginning to change around the time that James is writing, and not merely with the shift to identitarian forms of sexuality defined in the burgeoning fields of sexology and psychoanalysis. The novel is not just the story of an individual; it is a world-making project. James was a conscious theoretician of the novel and perceived the novel in English to be undergoing a period of reanimation, at least in its critical apprehension. In "The Art of Fiction," which he wrote just before *The Bostonians*, he observes:

> Only a short time ago it might have been supposed that the English novel was not what the French call *discutable*. It had no air of having a theory, a conviction, a consciousness of itself behind it—of being the expression of an artistic faith, the result of choice and comparison. . . . It was, however, *naïf*; . . . and, evidently, if it be destined to suffer in any way for having lost its *naïveté*, it has now an idea of making sure of the corresponding advantages. During the period I have alluded to there was a comfortable good-humored feeling abroad that a novel is a novel, as a pudding is a pudding, and that this was the end of it. But within a year or two, for some reason or other, there have been signs of returning animation—the era of discussion would appear to have been to a certain extent opened.[49]

Whether it is historically true that the English novel suffered through a period of critical complacency is beside the point here. In his own reflections on form, James clearly considered himself an innovator.

But at this moment in history, what might it mean to open an "era of discussion" within the novel in terms of sexuality? The stories we have available to us thus far suggest that James is an innovator because he began to formulate a version of an identity-based social group. And yet in light of the analysis above, to cast James as a pioneer storyteller about identitarian forms of sexuality would seem to flatten all of the formal and social complexity that attends his efforts to convey how those Bostonians ultimately evolve into themselves, not to mention the ways that evolution is thwarted and undermined along the way. We would suddenly miss what distinguishes the novel from the literature that comes both before and after it.

How, then, do we think about James's contribution to the emergence of the lesbian novel? His contribution is, I believe, tied to his fastidious attention to the "pictorial quality" he so admired in Daudet's writing. Although the genealogies and analogues of James's novel are extensive, varied, and sometimes even invisible in the actual text, he engages them to productive ends. The result is a different sense of scope. James simultaneously offers us a narrowing focus on his Bostonians and expands the level of detail with which he paints their world. The cumulative effect of this pictorial quality lends complexity to characters and worlds that, for a long time, featured in episodes or subplots and persisted as minor literary characters. That James traces the process of typification (and perhaps even its demise) across the time and space of a novel may constitute his best contribution to the rise of the lesbian novel. The contribution may well have been an unwitting one, considering his disdain for the demise of privacy, which he associated with the increasing public debate about sexual cultures. There is no evidence, for instance, that James likes his Bostonians any more than he likes any other characters in the novel. The ending of the text, after all, leaves everyone punished: Ransom may have won the girl, but as he leaves Olive preparing to address the abandoned crowd at the Music Hall, we see a crying Verena Tarrant and close with this final observation from the narrator: "It is to be feared that with the union, so far from brilliant, into which she was about to enter, these were not the last [tears] she was destined to shed" (1219). It would be fair to say, though, that the narrator's persistent ambivalence toward these Bostonians will continue to speak through the details of many more lesbian novels. Indeed, it may well be that the ambivalence James generates toward social sexual types—through his ironically distanced, though detailed and repeated attention to the process of typification—will be his greatest contribution to the genre he helped found. Who is to say how that ambivalence will continue to circulate?

5

WORLDS INSIDE
Afterlives of Nineteenth-Century Types

Act as though, for instance, you were a traveller sitting next to the window of a railway carriage and describing to someone inside the carriage the changing views which you see outside.

Sigmund Freud, "On Beginning the Treatment"

Minds inhabit environments which act on them and on which they in turn react.

William James, *The Principles of Psychology*

WHEN WE SAY THAT LITERATURE makes worlds or that queer life is a world-making project, such a statement gestures to a process that is productive, even cumulative. One of the stories I have been telling in this book is that the circulation and collection of short-form writing—stories, poems, magazine ads, letters—create the conditions under which texts accumulate alongside each other, thereby framing, amplifying, and even standing against each other. The anthology, the story collection, the novella all feature narrative units that stand alongside each other, adding up and existing relationally, like the books in Dayneford's library. These literary works all present nineteenth-century place types that prefigure without anticipating the forms of twentieth-century sexuality that have become naturalized for us. These accumulations of writing make possible larger-scale writing, which tracks characters across time and place and ultimately facilitates the emergence of the queer novel. They also make it possible for us to read the circulation of other nineteenth-century novels—like Herman Melville's *Typee* and Henry James's *The Bostonians*—for the ways they participate in generating the very frames of reference by which they come to be read. The worlds represented within all these books require imaginative force that increases the scale of queer life from minor figure to protagonist, from episode to lengthy narrative arc. Fictions of queer life (environmentally, temporally, romantically, and psychically) come more fully into view as a life narrative, subject to change over time, as fictional episodes are positioned alongside each other and in sequence, if not in series—all while the homosexual as a sexological and psychological type is becoming a species.

In this period of transition (the late nineteenth and early twentieth centuries) from shorter to longer fictions, from isolated episodes to collated texts, from place types to psychological types, what happens between the covers of books both expands and contracts. It expands in the sense that fictions about social relations structured specifically around historically queer types have become longer, more complex, and more focalized around the world of homosexuality. It contracts in the sense that the amorphous shape of queerness whose boundaries bleed into the landscapes around them comes into sharper focus, as if the shape of a queer life were a matter of individuation. Neither of these points refutes Eve Kosofsky Sedgwick's long-established argument for a universalizing approach to the ways in which homosocial, even homoerotic, attachments have been central to the organization of social life as such. It is simply to observe that as queer life also takes minoritized forms within this otherwise universalizing logic, attending to the narrative rhythms and forms that render intelligible subcultural forms of queer life requires understanding the modes of sexual sociability that circulation also leaves behind.

As literary circulation and the circulation of discourses about literature together make it possible to imagine a queer novel, our sense of the history of the form brings into view a world hitherto both assembled in pieces and circulating in plain sight. Long-form fiction—including stories, story collections, novellas, and novels— focalizes attention on queer protagonists whose dramas position us to view through them the shape of a narrative world. Owing in large part to the psychological and psychoanalytic categories of homosexuality, inversion, and perversion that emerge around the same time, we have tended to emphasize the inner processes of identity formation, identification, desire, pain, and loss in our assessments of queer historical fiction. Early queer novels such as *The Well of Loneliness* and *The Picture of Dorian Gray* have generally been read as portraits of queer affect and tragedies of narcissism and/or inversion.[1]

Much has been written on modernist fiction's cross-pollination with the emerging fields of psychology and psychoanalysis in the late nineteenth and early twentieth centuries and on psychoanalysis as a site of origin for the modern homosexual. But few scholars take up the transition between modes of narrating queer life as these modes, too, shift from the outside in. In one way, this book so far has documented a counter-narrative to that origin story by tracking the circulation of texts, characters, and authors through located sites of sociability that do not rely on the emergent language of psychology to organize meaning and desire in their narrative worlds. What remains underemphasized by this body of work is the persistence of the logic of place types within emerging discourses of interiority.

As I show in this chapter, in the shift toward narrating queer types according to their inner lives and desires as emergent psychological types, the language of place and race types does not disappear so much as it shifts inside. This inward shift creates a narrative challenge that centers on the problem of narrating the inner life of queer desire as a force within a fictional world. I offer three case studies that take up this problem, two novellas and a novel: Sarah Orne Jewett's "Martha's Lady" (1898), Gertrude Stein's *Q.E.D.* (1903/1950), and Henry Blake Fuller's *Bertram Cope's Year* (1919). Each of these texts has garnered for itself a reputation for anticipating a later form of modern queer life. "Martha's Lady," a novella with five short chapters, is widely understood to anticipate the figure of the melancholic lesbian captured most famously in *The Well of Loneliness*, as Heather Love discusses it; *Q.E.D.* stands, despite its lack of circulation, among the first modern lesbian novellas; and *Bertram Cope's Year* is understood as closet fiction that revolves around the withheld interior life of its eponymous protagonist. Each of these texts also redeploys the vocabulary of place and race types precisely to define (or in the case of Fuller, to refuse to define) the inner life and desires of its characters. Each in its own way also nicely exemplifies arguments that have been made much more recently about modern sexuality from the vantage point of queer theory. "Martha's Lady" reads easily as an illustration of Judith Butler's theory of melancholic incorporation of a lost love object; *Q.E.D.* remains firmly within the logic of queering the color line that Siobhan Somerville has outlined; and *Bertram Cope's Year,* meanwhile, seems like just the kind of world that Eve Sedgwick longed for at the end of "How to Bring Your Kids Up Gay," where a gay man is central to the social world around him, the object of desire for men and women alike, in different ways.[2] Such otherwise compelling readings of these texts from the vantage point of contemporary orthodoxies, however, overlook the ways these textual avatars of modern queer life also rely on residual terms in the course of narrating the interior lives of the characters at the heart of their narrative worlds. If worlds have been made through the rogue circulation and complication of sexual types—inside and outside of fiction—throughout the nineteenth century, those world-shaping types move fully inward in the service of texts whose narrative drama centers on characterizing the inner life of consciously queer desires. The history of sexual types has been well documented as being entrenched within the system of racial typology. Disarticulating the two is nigh impossible in this period, despite the overwhelming whiteness of the characters themselves. These stories all bear the discursive traces of race, then, while simultaneously operating within almost exclusively white worlds. Racial exoticism persists in small details that do the essential work of carrying this history forward—as if somehow the characters' class status positions their status as sexual types to rise above that racialized history.

Tracking Jewett's, Stein's, and Fuller's mobilizations of type language thus allows us to see the vestigial pasts of sexuality that cannot perhaps be fully rationalized within our current thinking about it. The accumulation of detail that has created these queer worlds, I argue, at once helps to make homosexuality possible as an abstraction—and erases the visibility of its own history and creativity, allowing that history to persist as mere traces of earlier forms. The very fact that these writers seem to assume the possibility of writing novels with queer protagonists registers a shift away from the world-making parameters foregrounded within earlier fiction and toward greater fictional self-consciousness of plot and interiority. But in focusing less on the problem of world-making, they assume the scope of writing that these earlier texts made possible— all while seeming to conceal the very conditions under which their own concerns with interiority and plot came to be filled with ironic possibility. These texts archive, almost imperceptibly, the history of types and literary circulation that give them shape to begin with.

Martha's Exotic Lady, Redux

As we have already seen, by the time the New England spinster sallies forth toward her twentieth-century dalliance with lesbianism, she finds herself at a typological intersection that has been at least a century in the making. The quintessential figure of the American old maid has gone, in the words of Margaret Fuller, from reviled "moral Ishmaelite"[3] to James's not-so-cryptic "Bostonian"—arguably because New England local color fiction has served as a formal holding environment for its emergence. I return here to "Martha's Lady" to further explore its status as a text that straddles the shift from type complication to interiority in the narration of queer lives. While my earlier reading of this text positioned it within the context of the old maid's diachronic unfolding across the nineteenth century, my reading of the text here foregrounds its resonance with literary texts written around the same time for the ways they collectively mark a transition in the narration of sexuality from outer to inner life. More than a decade after *The Bostonians* was published, Jewett's text fills its otherwise flatly defined character with longing for her employer's

cousin, a worldly lady named Helena, whose appeal is marked by
the racially tinged exoticisms of type.

First published in the October 1897 issue of *Atlantic Monthly,* "Martha's Lady" participates in the well-established tradition
of circulating tales of New England spinsters in serial publications,
which I discussed earlier.[4] The text has been read widely through the
prism of its main character's melancholy as a code for the unsayable.
In discussions of the text's reception, critics frequently cite a letter
that Jewett wrote to Sarah Whitman:

> It is impossible to say how your letter has heartened me. I send
> you love and thanks,—it is one more unbreakable bond that
> holds fast between me and you. You bring something to the
> reading of a story that the story would go very lame without;
> but it is those unwritable things that the story holds in its
> heart, if it has any, that make the true soul of it, and these
> must be understood, and yet how many a story goes lame for
> lack of that understanding. In France there is such a code, such
> recognitions, such richness of allusions; but here we con-
> fuse our scaffoldings with our buildings, and—and *so*! . . . I
> thought that most of us had begun to grow in just such a way
> as she did, and so could read joyfully between the lines.[5]

Whitman's letter and critics' repeated citation of it cue us to read
the story's "unwritable things" and to read "between the lines"—
reproducing, in effect, a textual version of sexuality as the form of
the unspoken, where texts themselves produce epistemologies of the
closet. Heather Love proceeds to identify in this mode of representation a "spinster aesthetic": "In 'Martha's Lady,' Jewett imagines
what it would mean to have one's entire identity defined by absence,
longing, and lack."[6] This clustering of closeted readings of the text's
queerness through which lack indexes melancholic affect overlooks
the richly textured ways that location, travel, and the condensed
traces of racialized exoticism do anything but record absence. In
fact, from the opening lines of the story, they register themselves
quite openly as a vocabulary for glimpsing inner life.

"Martha's Lady" opens by making location and movement
within the story central to the machinations of longing and desire.

A description of old Judge Pyne's house, which "many years ago," we are told, "wore an unwonted look of gayety and youthfulness," establishes the scene of "pleasure-making."[7] This scene features a chair on which a "crimson silk shawl [had been] thrown carelessly": a "piece of shining East Indian color" that a passerby might read as a "huge red lily that had suddenly bloomed against the syringa bush" (202–3). Miss Harriet Pyne appears, conspicuously single, but refusing to wear the "discreet caps" typical of unmarried women of her age (older than thirty). She "had company" (203). The house is, in effect, a spinster house, marked as much by the culture of unmarried women as that culture would seem to be marked by its colorful association with exotic locales. The "company" is Harriet's cousin, Helena Vernon, who adds to the otherwise "ascetic" house a sense of liveliness. It is Helena who "set herself to the difficult task of gayety" over against the "dull interior," whose "former activities seemed to have fallen sound asleep" and that "typified these larger conditions" of postwar decline and ennui (204).

The main drama of Jewett's novella, however, concerns not Harriet Pyne and her lively and charming yet mischievous cousin, but Miss Pyne's seemingly hapless handmaiden, Martha. A young woman in service to the old maid, Martha is described early in the text as "dull," "indifferent to everyone else," "clumsy" (206), "simple," and "slow" (208)—yet completely captivated by Helena, the "siren in India muslin" (209). Nowhere in the early pages of the story does the narrator offer us anything more than an outside view of Martha's conclusions. What we learn of her desire is written on her body and rendered visible through her actions. Her "eyes were as affectionate as a dog's, and there was a new look of hopefulness on her face" (206). When Helena wants cherries picked from the tree, Miss Pyne volunteers that Martha will do it. When Miss Pyne worries that Martha is not learning quickly enough, it is Helena who represents Martha's emotional investment in her job to her cousin: "Martha will learn fast enough because she cares so much" (207). The shape of Martha's inner life comes to us only in short statements that the narrator discloses about her budding love for Helena. When she overhears Helena pleading on her behalf, for instance, we learn that "from that moment, she not only knew what love was like, but she knew love's dear ambitions" (208). This coming to love in turn is understood through architectural language: "To have come from a stony hill-farm and a bare small wooden house was like a cave-dweller's coming to make a permanent home in an art museum" (208). Martha's affection is externalized through the vocabulary of outer life.

It is not surprising, then, that the structure of Martha's desire continues to be sketched in action rather than in interior monologue. Taking advantage of her status as "the siren in muslin," Helena makes it her mission not only to represent Martha's "care" to her employer but also to inspire and instruct Martha in the ways of doing a good job, effectively mobilizing Martha's desire in the service of her servitude. Without telling Miss Pyne, for instance, Helena instructs Martha to arrange the picked cherries on a fancy white dish and send them to the minister. When Harriet receives surprise thanks for the gift in the form of a book of sermons, she is taken pleasantly aback by the fact that the initiative taken on her behalf has made her look good. Helena describes the action as evidence of Martha's progress. The closest we come to learning how Martha thinks about Helena is the narrator's statement, "all for love's sake she had been learning to do many things, and to do them exactly right" (210).

Doing things "exactly right," as Helena has shown her, becomes in turn a way for Martha to sustain her love even after Helena leaves. On her last morning in the house, Helena even instructs her in this art of desire, asking her, "Won't you keep the flowers fresh and pretty in the house until I come back? It's so much pleasanter for Miss Pyne, and you'll feed my little sparrows, won't you?" (210). In response to Helena's wish that Martha will "think of me sometimes after I go away," Martha, we are told, devotes herself to the "higher joy of pleasing the ideal" (211): for the forty years between Helena's visits, Martha maintains her routine, including, notably, the picking of the cherries. Miss Pyne is "often congratulated upon the good fortune of having such a helper and friend as Martha," and Martha believes, as she says half aloud to herself, "I owe everything to Miss Helena" (215). So fully has she internalized her lost love that when she looks in the mirror, she "hoped to see some faint reflection of Helena Vernon, but there was only her own brown old New England face to look back at her wonderingly" (215). Martha would thus seem to be the very picture of modern sexuality, anticipating the model of Freudian melancholic incorporation as Judith Butler would come to describe it: sustaining her loss by internalizing her lost love object. But the story exceeds that narrative about Martha in its depiction of Helena, Martha's object of desire, through the vestiges of nineteenth-century vocabulary frames.

Helena, her clothing already marked by exotic foreign locales, remains a figure of global circulation. She has proceeded to marry and live a "brilliant much-varied foreign life" (214). And Martha follows her avidly in textual form—through letters and maps. One letter from Helena to Miss Pyne is notable for its bittersweet message to Martha, "Tell Martha all that I say about my dear Jack [her husband]," and asks that Harriet tell Martha she is coming back to visit the following summer: "I shall come home next summer and bring the handsomest and best man in the world to Ashford. I have told him all about the dear house and the dear garden; there never was such a lad to reach for cherries with his six foot two" (213). Realizing that her own cherry-picking prowess has been replaced by Jack's (in perhaps more ways than one), "Martha cried over it, and felt a strange sense of loss and pain" (213). This pain does not, however, prevent her from continuing to follow Helena's movements through the world on "a worn old geography [that] often stood open at the map of Europe":

> A little old-fashioned gilt button, set with a piece of glass like a ruby, that had broken and fallen from the trimming of one of Helena's dresses, was used to mark the city of her dwelling-place. In the changes of a diplomatic life Martha followed her lady all about the map. Sometimes the button was at Paris, and sometimes at Madrid; once, to her great anxiety, it remained long at St. Petersburg. For such a slow scholar Martha was not unlearned at last, since everything about life in these foreign towns was of interest to her faithful heart. She satisfied her own mind as she threw crumbs to the tame sparrows; it was all part of the same thing and for the same affectionate reasons. (216–17)

Martha thus structures her life as an act of desire where affection itself is condensed into the symbolic representations of her absent love object.

When Helena finally comes back as a widow, she immediately recognizes that Martha has not forgotten anything—the space of the house has become a holding environment for her attachment to Helena. It is at this point that we see, finally, what has perhaps been true all along: that Helena, too, loves Martha:

> That night Martha waited in her lady's room just as she used, humble and silent, and went through with the old unforgotten loving services. The long years seemed like days. At last she lingered a moment trying to think of something else that might be done, then she was going silently away, but Helena called her back.
>
> "You have always remembered, haven't you, Martha dear?" she said. "Won't you please kiss me good-night?" (219)

There is no doubt throughout the story that Martha's desire has been subsumed into her labor and that Helena has been instrumental to that process. But it seems just as true that Martha's labor has also given life to her desire. In these twinned habits of work and love, we also get a glimpse of the fact that Martha's work has had a habitual place in her lady's bedroom. She waits for her there "just as she used." It is merely a trick of narration that allows us to see the consummation of this desire in a kiss as the only climax to the story.

What begins to come into view in this story is not just the emergent glimpse of a sexuality constituted and sustained through loss or the residual persistence of an exotic form of sexual types from elsewhere. Rather, it is precisely the problem of narrating the inner life of queer desire against the backdrop of the worlds that have made it possible. Desire itself is focalized through Martha, but only rarely glimpsed from her perspective. Her inner life is represented to us, but the narrator withholds so much of it. Helena's status as an exotic place type (marked by putatively "India" colors and world travel) meets Martha's New England–fixed but contentedly melancholic attachment. The narrator's limits here are themselves curious: the narrator can see and describe Martha's love but has not been able to show us the habitual bedroom life of Martha and Helena's relationship. Nor can the narrator offer us more than occasional glimpses of the inner life of either Martha's or Helena's desire, except to suggest the constancy of Martha's love and the whirlwind nature of Helena's lively attachments. Both women remain reflections of their locations in the world, even as the story reaches toward understanding the ways in which desire might bridge the space between them.

Triangulated Types and Tropical Interiors in *Q.E.D.*

Their reputations tell us that Sarah Orne Jewett's prose style could not be more different from Gertrude Stein's. And yet Jewett's Martha—that tender of ground sparrows—nonetheless shares a transitional narrative moment with *Q.E.D.*'s Mabel Neathe: each of their stories relies on tropes of emplaced desire to generate a narrative topography of its characters' inner life. This type language for Stein remains fully indebted to the logic of racism—a point made forcefully by Jaime Hovey in her reading of the novel.[8] Written in 1903 but not published until 1950, four years after Stein's death, the text stands as a case of publication withheld (along the lines of E. M. Forster's *Maurice*).[9] Like *Maurice*, *Q.E.D.* is loosely autobiographical, known to be the story of the love triangle that existed among Stein herself, May Bookstaver, and Mabel Haynes while Stein was living in Baltimore and studying with William James. And like *Maurice*, *Q.E.D.* was published posthumously, under the title *Things as They Are*. It would be twenty more years before the text was published as *Q.E.D.*, a classic mathematical signature for a triangular geometric proof. The text continues to have a reputation as an unexceptional forerunner to Stein's landmark works, one that shows us Stein's characteristic style as still very much a work in progress. Carolyn Copeland has described the book as "the most conventional work that Gertrude Stein ever wrote. It has a plot, characters, a narrator, a beginning, a middle, and an end."[10] *Q.E.D.* has been read primarily as the precursor to Stein's more acclaimed work *Three Lives*, a forerunner in particular to the "Melanctha" section of that book, which reworks much of the material from the earlier text. *Q.E.D.*, as Hovey has argued, aligns its characters' sexual proclivities with locations in a way that affirms a racializing and racist logic of types, inherited from nineteenth-century thought, that comes to be fully revealed in "Melanctha." Because of its relatively conventional style, its status as audition for a more fully realized version of itself, its reliance on racist tropes, and its seeming disavowal by Stein herself, *Q.E.D.* stands as one of Stein's lesser works.

A nineteenth-century worldview persists in the text, not only through the afterlife of racial typology but in its own narrative mapping of the inner life through its associations of type with location. The narrative triangulation in this book bears the imprint of a previous era, replete with a reliance on place types and weblike social relationships. If *Q.E.D.* is "conventional," it is not only because it offers us "a plot, characters, a narrator, a beginning, a middle, and an end"; it also owes a debt to nineteenth-century conventions—something that few associate with the work of Gertrude Stein. For the characters who constitute the lesbian love triangle at the heart of *Q.E.D.*, type language serves to characterize their interiority even as it recalls the type embodiments of racism.

Stein's narrator is engaged in an experiment in describing interiority, which is arguably indebted to her teacher William James. Her stylistic deployment of atomatism as a path to stream-of-consciousness writing would come to define her work. But it is useful to remember another relevant Jamesian insight, quoted above as the second epigraph, that might help explain the pre-repetitive Stein's investment in the tendency of the outer world to shape the ways we view inner life: "Minds inhabit environments which act on them and on which they in turn react."[11] Turn-of-the-century James, like his contemporary Sigmund Freud, is at this point engaged with how to describe the shape of the mind. While James and Freud would each develop substantially different methods for approaching this problem, both operate from the vantage point of associating the shape of the mind with its environment. *Q.E.D.* makes a fictional world through an exploration of this narrative problem. The residues of type language are put into play stylistically through the characters' navigation of the space of relationality they share with each other. Types are seen always from the vantage point of others—theirs is not a vocabulary of self-reference. And despite scholarly complaints that the novel fundamentally reasserts the couple form, *Q.E.D.* builds its perspectival world in the form of a queer love triangle.

Q.E.D. opens with its three main characters on a steamer ship bound for Europe, a fact we learn from the vantage point of a Steinesque Adele who foregrounds the text's investment in the language of type as an index of location:

> She rather regretted that she was not to have the steamer all to herself. It was very easy to think of the rest of the passengers as mere wooden objects; they were all sure to be of some abjectly familiar type that one knew so well that there would be no need of recognising their existence, but these two people who would be equally familiar if they were equally little known would as the acquaintance progressed, undoubtedly expose large tracts of unexplored and unknown qualities, filled with new and strange excitements.[12]

Familiar "types" appear as "wooden objects" even as the particular women in question—Mabel and Helen—stand firmly in contrast with "the rest of the passengers." The three main characters are "college bred American women of the wealthier class" different in "their appearance, their attitudes and their talk," even if they were nonetheless "distinctly American," despite each bearing "the stamp of one of the older civilisations" (178–79). Helen Thomas is "the American version of the English handsome girl . . . a woman of passions but not of emotions" (179), while Adele herself admits, "I always did thank God I wasn't born a woman" (181). But it is the figure of Mabel who stands as arguably the best example of the diverse type traditions that bring the modern lesbian into view, narrated from the outside in:

> As Mabel Neathe lay on the deck with her head in Helen's lap, her attitude of awkward discomfort and the tension of her long angular body sufficiently betrayed her New England origin. It is one of the peculiarities of American womanhood that the body of a coquette often encloses the soul of a prude

and the angular form of a spinster is possessed by a nature of
the tropics. Mabel Neathe had the angular body of a spinster
but the face told a different story. It was pale yellow brown in
complexion and thin in the temples and forehead; heavy about
the mouth, not with the weight of flesh but with the drag of
unidealised passion, continually sated and continually craving.
The long formless chin accentuated the lack of moral significance. . . . It was a face that in its ideal completeness would
have belonged to the decadent days of Italian greatness. It
would never now express completely a nature that could hate
subtly and poison deftly. (179)

Here Stein makes explicit her investment in type logic that simultaneously affirms its location in the exterior world (New England,
Italy); writes it on the body (in "angular form," "heavy about the
mouth," and "yellow brown in complexion"); and yet shifts the
focus inward. "The soul of a prude" meets the "nature of the tropics." The afterlives of place- and race-based types that have been at
least a century in the making persist here in Stein's description of
Mabel. But if *Q.E.D.* recirculates the racist typology that she inher-
its here, as it surely does, it is doing so not only to avow a genealogy of racial types. It does so as well in the service of narrating the
inner life of Stein's character. If American women find their bodies
at odds with their natures, Mabel's face may indeed "tell a different story." But that story is one in which the portrait of desire is
given shape through its relationship to "the decadent days of Italian
greatness"—even in its failure to completely express such a nature.
Q.E.D. effectively concedes that the representation of the inner life
is shaped through the language of outer life.

While Adele goes on to insist that Mabel ultimately is defined
not by the "tropics" but by the "drag of unidealised passion," she
later expands her description by characterizing Mabel as one whose
"room" has the "perfect quality" and who is herself "a perfect hostess." The quality of the room merges with the quality of the personality: "The important element in the success of the room as atmosphere," she explains, "consisted in Mabel's personality." We are
told that "it is true of rooms as of human beings that they are bound
to have one good feature. . . . Mabel Neathe had arranged her room

so that one enjoyed one's companions and observed consciously only the pleasant fire-place" (188). We learn furthermore that

> such an Italian type frustrated by its setting in an unimpassioned and moral community was of necessity misinterpreted although its charm was valued. Mabel's ancestry did not supply any explanation of her character. Her kinship with decadent Italy was purely spiritual.
>
> The capacity for composing herself with her room in unaccented and perfect values was the most complete attribute of that kinship that her modern environment had developed. (188)

The narrator deftly collapses the description of Mabel's room with the description of Mabel's mind. She composes herself "with her room," and her "capacity" for so doing is "the most complete attribute of that kinship [with the place/race type of the Italian] that her modern environment had developed."

The material arrangement of the world organizing the very structures of thought also adheres to Adele, who finds herself embroiled in a conversation in which the shape of her understanding of passion emerges as an effect of describing constraints in the world outside. Her meditation on the paradoxical boundedness of being on the expanse of ocean gives way to commentary on the ways in which class status and passions organize the self:

> "One hears so much of the immensity of the ocean but that isn't at all the feeling that it gives me," she began. "My quarrel with it is that it is the most confined space in the world. A room just big enough to turn around in is immensely bigger. Being on the ocean is like being placed under a nice clean white inverted saucer. All the boundaries are so clear and hard. There is no escape from the knowledge of the limits of your prison. Doesn't it give you too a sensation of intolerable confinement?" (181)

Helen replies to Adele's description of this structure of feeling with further probing questions about the logics of class and desire that she sees at play here for Adele: "What do you really mean by calling yourself middle-class?" she asks first. Adele replies: "I simply contend that the middle-class ideal which demands that people be affectionate, respectable, honest and content, that they avoid excitements and cultivate serenity is the ideal that appeals to me, it is in short the ideal of affectionate family life, of honorable business methods." No less than a room in the ocean, the feeling of class for Adele is a convenient container for social life, where she can "avoid excitements and cultivate serenity." Helen's rejoinder is that such a way of thinking is, in effect, its own tolerable confinement: it "means cutting passion quite out of your scheme of things" (181). The intersubjective exchanges here point to the ways the passions themselves take shape as effects of political arrangements. If, as James argues, "minds inhabit environments which act on them and on which they in turn react," then Stein seems quite willing to follow this logic in making the environment itself a proper barometer for the matters of the mind. Moral sensibility, to continue with the nautical theme of the book, is itself less a matter of right and wrong than one of navigating bodies of water. Helen observes that Adele hasn't "a nature much above passionettes. You are so afraid of losing your moral sense that you are not willing to take it through anything more dangerous than a mud-puddle" (184). "Yes there is something in what you say," Adele replies, "but after all if one has a moral sense there is no necessity in being foolhardy with it. I grant you it ought to be good for a swim of a mile or two, but surely it would be certain death to let it loose mid-ocean" (184).

Nor is Adele herself exempt from this recourse to external action and atmosphere as a portal to her own soul. Later, when the women are back in New York, Adele and Helen have had a series of meetings in public places, and, finally, after sharing a "passionate embrace" (193) while waiting in a friend's private room, they agree to meet at Helen's house, presumably to resume their affections. Tension arises when Adele elects not to keep their date in a timely fashion and after some time passes, we are told that "there was between them now a consciousness of strain" (194). In an effort to explain the straining, Adele begins by proclaiming, "How completely we exemplify entirely different types" and proceeds to diagnose Helen as a "blooming Anglo-Saxon" with a "double personality"

(194–95). Not surprisingly, Adele refrains from diagnosing herself
except to display her structure of feeling through her description of
the person facing her. It is left to Helen to characterize Adele's particular display of emotion as surgical and exposing—in effect, as an
experiment in flaying a body: "You were not content until you had
dissected out every nerve in my body and left it quite exposed and it
was too much, too much. You should give your subjects occasional
respite even in the ardor of research" (195). Exposure is, according
to Helen, Adele's narrative approach, even as Adele's own motives
can only be described in terms that exteriorize them.

Narrative exposure ultimately becomes the central organizing
and world-making problem for the main characters in *Q.E.D.*, as
their points of view on each other's desire and relationality come to
define their positions in the text. The exterior world again serves to
provide the shape of emplotted desire. In the wake of their disinte-
grating affair, for instance, Helen and Adele continue to see each
other in the intervals they spend at Mabel Neathe's. The shape of the
relations among them becomes increasingly clear and yet unspoken
within this space: "All through the winter Helen at intervals spent a
few days with Mabel Neathe in Baltimore. Adele was always more
or less with them on these occasions. On the surface they preserved
the same relations as had existed on the steamer." And yet Mabel, if
she could avoid it, never left them alone together: "It was tacitly understood between them that on these rare occasions they should give
each other no sign." Helen and Mabel are having an affair—and
have had an affair—but Adele only begins to realize it just before she
is to leave for Europe again. When she talks with Mabel and learns
that Helen and Mabel "used to be together a great deal at College"
(196), Adele stops short of asking the questions she really wants
answered. And after this point, Adele's anxiety (filtered through the
narrator) about that information takes the form of the following
sentence: "Mabel's room was now for Adele always filled with the
atmosphere of the unasked question" (197). Anxiety is atmosphere
and the room again provides the shape of the mind. The next time
Adele comes to Mabel's room, she finds she cannot dismiss the unasked question: "Mabel was clothed with it as with a garment," and
when Adele brings the matter to a point, it is the shape of the room

that changes. "Dismayed by Adele's hot directness" and demand to "tell," Mabel finds that "the room grew large and portentous and to Mabel's eyes Adele's figure grew almost dreadful in its concentrated repulsion" (197–98).

The shape of the triangle now abundantly clear and the change in perspective reflected in the growth of the room, Adele oscillates between self-pity and sympathy for Mabel (since she is aware that she has put Mabel in the position of disclosing what Helen "won't like" [198]). Adele's triangulated consciousness appears clearly to Helen, who proceeds to write her a letter in which she likens her to "an ignorant mob": "You trample everything ruthlessly under your feet without considering whether or not you kill something precious and without being changed or influenced by what you so brutally destroy. I am like Diogenes in quest of an honest man" (199). Adele replies to Helen, confessing that she can make no defense of her behavior, but that she finds, in the face of the knowledge about Helen and Mabel's affair, "grown within me steadily an increasing respect and devotion to you" (199). Since there is no time for a letter reply before Helen comes to town again, Adele finds herself seeing Helen next as part of the trio for a prearranged date at the opera. Afterward, the shape of the world they occupy together through the shape of their competing desires begins to be spoken. Helen makes clear that she continues to care for Adele, and Adele makes clear that Mabel has told her of "the relations existing between you" (201). Helen's conviction, however, is that such knowledge should not have been confessed. Against the "sombre silence" of Adele's disclosure, Helen coolly responds: "If you were not wholly selfish, you would have exercised self-restraint enough to spare me this" (201). The two sit in "unyielding silence," Helen persuaded of Adele's narcissism and Adele of her right to know. Stein's description of this impasse relies again on the terms of spatial arrangement: "When an irresistible force meets an immovable body what happens? Nothing. The shadow of a long struggle inevitable as their different natures lay drearily upon them. This incident however decided was only the beginning. All that had gone before was only a preliminary. They had just gotten into position" (201).

If we read this passage as the language itself directs us—the drama of the irresistible force and the immovable body having been moved into position as the effect of a preliminary long struggle—we cannot help but recall the clues the text has given us all along about the origin story of this love affair. Adele would have us believe that the basis of attraction between herself and Helen has been the tension between two opposing viewpoints: a classic case of opposites attracting. But the opposition itself requires a world that has made it. Adele explains: "As for my instincts they have always been opposed to the indulgence of any feeling of passion. I suppose that is due to the Calvinistic influence that dominates American training and has interfered with my natural temperament" (208). Adele's own type background helps her explain her resistance not only to Mabel but to herself. Meanwhile, we must also consider that the condition of Adele and Helen's intimacy has always been Mabel. From early on, Mabel served as the invested witness to their affair: "Mabel would listen always with immense enjoyment as if it were a play and enacted for her benefit and queerly enough although the disputants were much in earnest in their talk and in their oppositions, it was a play and enacted for her benefit" (182).

Even when Adele and Helen are first alone, on the steamer, Adele conjures up a series of spatial relations to make sense of her relationship to Helen. She is looking "observingly at the stars" when "she felt herself intensely kissed on the eyes and on the lips." When Helen asks her if she ever stops thinking long enough to feel, Adele replies that she finds thinking "a pretty continuous process." And in reply to Helen's suggestion that she then leave Adele with her thoughts, Adele asks her not to go because she "[doesn't] want to stir": "I suppose," Adele confesses, "it's simply inertia." Left alone, Adele interprets her consultation with the stars and her inertia as "a bit of mathematics"—as if the spatial arrangement of the stars and of bodies in space could offer her a sufficient account of her own desire (186). These spatial arrangements all amount to a physical emplotment that derives its force from the drama of narrating the inner lives of these characters.

Throughout Q.E.D., the text recirculates and mobilizes place and race types to locate and demarcate forms of gendered and sexual intimacy. The drama of the text is in effect a drama of circulation:

a drama, that is, of social circulation made possible through an earlier history of textual circulation. It is also a drama of circulation that moves the outside in, at the level of content, while focalizing at the formal level on the very problem of reading and accessing the inner life of an intimate. This is a problem of both narrative and desire, where at every turn the characters of *Q.E.D.* seek to create topographies of each other's minds.

Little wonder, then, that Stein concludes the novella by putting her characters in motion again, making use this time of the device of *dis*location. Adele seeks solace in the "green earth on a sunny English hillside," only to discover how fully mismatched her melancholy is with its location (203). The narrative then displaces Adele's passion into nationalism so that she can emphasize to Helen how diminished her passion is. As if to put things back in their place, Adele insists on returning to America because "there is no passion more dominant and instinctive in the human spirit than the need of the country to which one belongs. . . . It is simply a vital need for the particular air that is native" (205–6). This "native," "instinctive" passion turns out, fittingly enough, to be a fantasy of pure whiteness. Adele returns to the "clean-cut cold of America," to the "clean sky and the white snow . . . all in a cold and brilliant air without spot or stain" (206). It is against this phantasmatic white landscape that Adele also distinguishes her desire for Helen: she came back not "to see you much as I wanted you . . . it was just plain America" (206). Here, as elsewhere in the text, the racialization of types continues to haunt the description and narration of queer desire.

Although the text ends, as it began, with the three women together in Europe where Helen and Adele find themselves kissing under a streetlight and stating their love for each other, the mise-en-scène fails to keep them in sync. Having met with Helen as "equals," Adele nonetheless endeavors to "lose her melancholy and perplexity by endless tramping over the Luccan hills but had succeeded only in becoming more lonely sick and feverish" (221). She is out of place—but only, it seems, because of the implication that she could be *in* place. Another condition of Adele and Helen's attraction to each other thus becomes physical distance itself. Despite their confessions of love, textual circulation ultimately maintains and sustains desire only in the face of its seeming impossibility. The last section of the tale offers an account of their correspondence after a period of no communication. After fighting it out "with her conscience her pain and her desire," Adele finally writes to Helen without knowing fully what to say. Helen replies that she wants Adele never "to deny that you care for me. The thought of your doing it again takes all the sunshine out of the sky for me" (226). The final line of the story has Adele responding to Helen's description of the emotional landscape between them in equally spatial terms: "I am afraid it comes very near being a dead-lock" (227). An irresistible force meets an immovable body—but in letters.

Q.E.D. is organized around the problem of discerning and representing the shape of others' interiority and desire. In this way, Stein follows William James in terms of positioning the mind within its environment: locating perception and/of inner worlds as a narrative problem for characters who are trying to express and address their desires with others. Such worlds, steeped in the social norms of their environments even when they emerge to depict queer life, are hardly free from the constraints of racist history and class aspirations. Recall here Kobena Mercer and Isaac Julien's observation that "the prevailing Western concept of sexuality . . . *already contains racism.*"[13] It would be surprising, indeed, for a queer world-making project at this or another point in history *not* to be so constrained. The prologue for the text, taken from *As You Like It,* includes the following key lines delivered by Silvius. In response to the question "What is love?" he replies:

> It is to be all made of fantasy,
> All made of passion, and all made of wishes;
> All adoration, duty, and observance,
> All humbleness, all patience, and impatience,
> All purity, all trial, all deservings. (177)

There is no language of fantasy, however, in this novella, at least not as the later Freud would have us understand it. No one articulates a wish in this text, but that doesn't mean there are no wishes, passions, or fantasies here. They appear instead through the filtration apparatus of narrative, as if, to adapt Freud, the narrator were sitting in a carriage describing the changing views that someone else sees outside.

A Cope-Shaped Hole in the Narrative Universe: The Case of Bertram Cope's Missing Interiority

If Stein's characters are narrated as though their inner lives were topographically describable, Henry Blake Fuller's Bertram Cope leaves the characters around him—almost all of whom share a desire for him—wondering precisely what it is that Cope thinks and wants. As Joseph Dimuro points out, the central theme of *Bertram Cope's Year* "has to do with the extent to which those around the passive figure of Cope project their desires onto him, or try to invest the sheer blankness of his character with aptitudes and romantic tendencies that he either does not possess or fails fully to comprehend."[14] Just as fully as Stein and Jewett define their characters' inner worlds through features of external environments, Fuller by contrast withholds his main character's internal topography. More than once the novel invokes characters (including Cope himself) who wonder, "Did the fellow not know his own mind?"[15] Since the moment of the book's publication, critics have commented on the ways that Bertram Cope constitutes a narrative enigma when it comes to the representation of who or what he actually wants. Cope has been read as "flat," "weakly drawn," passive, and indecisive.[16] In a veiled suggestion that the book invites closeted readings, Carl Van Vechten observes that "the story, apparently slow moving, really thrusts forward its emphatic moments on almost every page, but it would probably prove unreadable to one who had no key to its meaning."[17] Close to a century later, Dimuro would seem to confirm this reading when he suggests that *Bertram Cope's Year* "involves the necessity of double reading—a close attention to the relationship between surfaces and depths"—despite his acknowledgment that "all of the main male characters in Fuller's novel might be said to fit the category of the homosexual, or even the contemporary concept of the gay man."[18] As Edmund Wilson puts it, "Bertram's admirers all look to find in him a version of a semi-divine ideal that he makes no attempt to live up to; that he is quite unconscious that his beauty and charm, together with a hard, self-sufficient core of character, have caused them to endow him with qualities which he does not at all possess."[19] The text's opaque treatment of Cope has in turn been read as evidence of the text's formal structure, a comment on the satirical treatment of its main character that has itself been interpreted as evidence of Fuller's "fine realist" style.[20] Dimuro argues that to understand Cope's status as a screen for others' desires is to "capture [the book's] satirical tone."[21]

The case of Cope's missing desire also suggests Fuller's refusal to embrace young romantic love as the proper subject and end of fiction. *Bertram Cope's Year* thus enacts a contradiction in form: a novel that announces itself as a study in one character but that withholds so much of that character from us. This Cope-shaped hole in the narrative world of the novel becomes the central organizing principle for the text's formal investments in both realism and satire, since it is from this vantage point (the missing representation of Cope's desire and his inner life more generally) that its critics observe Fuller's refusal of the marriage plots that he saw in so many fictions of his day. The novel would seem to dissolve Cope as a queer type by making him unavailable to anyone in any depth, while nonetheless reconstituting him as something like the pond into which Narcissus looks, only to fall in love with himself as if he were another. What readers see in Cope is the reflection of their own desires—so much so that this feature of the text dominates even those moments where the narrator does provide us with glimpses of Cope's thoughts, wishes, and expectations (particularly in his letters to Arthur Lemoyne and in flashes of narrative monologue in the middle of the book).

What, then, might we make of Fuller's overall reluctance to define his protagonist either by his inner life and desires or by his embrace of the couple form? Fuller is, after all, essentially eschewing the dominant intellectual trends of his time. His resistance to young, romantic, monogamous love is well documented. And records show that Fuller read avidly in the emerging field of psychoanalysis, which would have furnished him with a strongly developed vocabulary about homosexuality that is absent from this book.[22] Fuller prefers instead to characterize the relationship between Bertram Cope and Arthur Lemoyne in terms that hark back to the late nineteenth century. Like Charles Warren Stoddard, Fuller calls Cope's male lovers "chums" upon whose household, in a gesture to Karl Heinrich

Ulrichs, "Urania, through the whole width of her starry firmament, looked down kindly" (175). Even these references are fleeting, the first appearing only a couple of times in the book, and the second only once. So averse is Fuller to the now-dominant terms of homosexuality and inversion that Edmund Wilson goes so far as to conclude that *Bertram Cope's Year* is essentially a homosexual novel without homosexuality at all: "Though it involves homosexual situations, [it] is not really a book about homosexuality. It has a kind of philosophic theme."[23]

To take seriously the prospect that *Bertram Cope's Year* advances a "philosophic theme" would be to investigate its status as a book about queer life without being a book solely about queer character per se. Cope might thus be seen as a type device who dissolves and comes into view in a rather peculiar rhythm that ultimately showcases the world around him. Fuller places his protagonist at the heart of a narrative world where he is desired by all (with the exception of Joseph Foster), whose love he ultimately both cultivates and spurns. If the novel creates and sustains the illusion that it is somehow *about* Bertram Cope, it ultimately gives us a *world* that is obsessed with Bertram Cope more than it gives us Cope himself. This world reproduces Cope as its unavailable object of desire over and over again—thus making of him a utopian object of desire in a queer world defined as much by its genderphobic and racist disappointments as it is buoyed by its society scene and its hoped-for matches.

Fuller masterfully directs our attention toward Cope through focalized narration that ultimately shows us more about those who watch and want Cope than it does about Cope himself. From the very first pages of the novel, the first-person narrator describes the constellation of want arranged around Bertram Cope:

> Wanted, in fact, a young male who shall seem fully adult to those who are younger still, and who may even appear the accomplished flower of virility to an idealizing maid or so, yet who shall elicit from the middle-aged the kindly indulgence due a boy. . . . We must find for them an age which may evoke their friendly interest, and yet be likely to call forth, besides that, their sympathy and their longing admiration, and later their tolerance, their patience, and even their forgiveness. (43)

The shape of desire from this point on belongs not to Cope but explicitly to the motley group of characters including "those who are younger still," "an idealizing maid," and the "middle-aged." We come to know them by name as the bachelor professor Basil Randolph (who wants to "cultivate" Cope); the wealthy widow socialite Medora Phillips (who first wants him to entertain her and later wants him for herself); three young women (Amy, Hortense, and Carolyn), all of whom at one point or another make a play for Cope (only Amy finagles a misguided but momentary engagement); Joseph Foster, Mrs. Phillips's disabled brother-in-law (a bitchy queen who keeps an eye and an ear on Cope from his perch in Mrs. Phillips's room upstairs and kvetches about him with Randolph); and his "chum," Arthur Lemoyne, who lives first at a distance and then comes to set up house with Cope, thus establishing himself as the chief rival to all other characters. Of all these, it is Arthur alone for whom Cope discloses actual longing (in his letters and in his confessions about the misbegotten engagement with Amy), although even this relationship falters as an effect of the ultimately limited openness to queer life that characterizes the world that is otherwise dazzled by Bertram Cope.

For his part, from the limited access we have to his thoughts, Cope is flummoxed from the get-go by all the attention, most of which he experiences as an imposition. When he comes to the house of Medora Phillips, the town's resident hostess with an eye for the queer guy, Cope reveals himself to be susceptible to the demands of others and to the force of obligation within his social context. We learn that

> he was no squire of dames, no frequenter of afternoon receptions. Why the deuce had he come to this one? Why had he yielded so readily to the urgings of the professor of mathematics? . . . Why must he now expose himself to the boundless aplomb and momentum of this woman of forty-odd who was finding amusement in treating him as a "college boy"? "Boy" indeed she had actually called him: well, perhaps his present position made all this possible. He was not yet out in the world on his own. In the background of "down state" was a father with a purse in his pocket and a hand to open the

purse. Though the purse was small and the hand reluctant, he
must partly depend on both for another year. If he were only
in business—if he were only a broker or even a salesman—he
should not find himself treated with such blunt informality and
condescension as a youth. If, within the University itself, he
were but a real member of the faculty, with an assured position
and an assured salary, he should not have to lie open to the unceremonious hectorings of the socially confident, the "placed."
(45)

This passage establishes early in the book some key dynamics of
the world of Churchton: as a lower-middle-class young man from
"down state," Cope is a class outsider whose "position" at the university is as yet insecure, though he does aspire to be a faculty member. Young yet upwardly mobile, Cope lacks the confidence of "an
assured position and an assured salary" and so finds himself subject
to what he calls "the unceremonious hectorings of the socially confident." Unsure of his own position, then, and yearning more for
status perhaps than love, Cope can't even decide how much sugar
he likes. When Mrs. Phillips asks him, "One lump or two?" we are
told his thought is, "The dickens! How do *I* know?" even as he
coolly replies, "An extra one on the saucer, please" (45–46). The
narrator's deft exposure of Cope's thought here, by way of narrated
monologue, undermines any assertion that Cope is a complete ci-
pher, while subtly and simultaneously creating the effect that if we
can't see what Cope is thinking, it is less the narrator's responsibility
(since the narrator can indeed see inside the heads of his characters)
than an effect of Cope's withholding and perhaps calculating nature
to be as opaque as others experience him to be.

In the face of what the other characters take to be Cope's
coolness but that the narrator reveals to be his absence of desire
for them, the fires of intrigue are stoked. Mrs. Phillips immediately gravitates toward him, inviting him to sit beside her, all while
telling herself, "Who would want him anything but slender?" (46).
Meanwhile, Basil Randolph, described as a "scholar *manqué*" who
would have "enjoyed knowing, and knowing intimately," some
young fellow at the college, appears alongside Medora Phillips as
"a rival, a competitor" (46–47). Basil Randolph uses his position

at the college to seek out more information about Cope; Mrs. Phillips's boarder, Amy Leffingwell, takes every opportunity to pursue an attachment with Cope at Mrs. Phillips's events, including singing with Cope and sitting with him at every chance she gets. Joe (Joseph Foster) will meanwhile eventually declare Cope to be a charlatan, but this doesn't stop him from chattering on about him nonetheless. In effect, Cope's uncertainty, reluctance, and even recalcitrance only highlight by contrast the density of desire that comes his way from others. Thus does the narrator telegraph the plot of the twenty-four-year-old Cope's year as he finds himself, an aspiring English professor tasked with lecturing and writing his thesis in the small midwestern university town of Churchton, the object of everyone's fascination, if not of their desire. The world around Bertram Cope appears to us primarily as a panoply of viewpoints from characters whose eyes and thoughts are oriented toward him.

The primary exception to Fuller's decision to avoid representing Cope's inner thoughts comes in the form of Cope's letters, written early in the novel, to Arthur Lemoyne. "With things as he wanted them," the narrator tells us, "his correspondent would be sitting there and letter-writing would be unnecessary" (72), thus creating a sense that in the letters we will finally see what Cope actually wants. And to some extent we do read here the frankest representations of his thoughts as he confesses to Lemoyne, "I miss you all the time" (73). He also describes (unflatteringly) all the characters at Mrs. Phillips's house: of Medora Phillips, he writes bitingly, "She pushes you pretty hard. A little of it goes a good way" (54). At another point he writes to Arthur of one of his afternoon's with Mrs. Phillips's company: "It was an afternoon in Lesbos—with Sappho and her band of appreciative maidens. Phaon, a poor lad of nineteen, swept some pamphlets and paper-cutters off the center-table, and we all plunged into the ocean of Oolong—the best thing we do on this island" (57). The letters constitute the only portal into Cope's soul, exposing his exacting dissection of those who project themselves onto his seeming placidity. The letters also engage in their own forms of withholding and misdirection. Cope, for instance, recalls for Arthur their intimate times together and his memory of Arthur's body, wondering if he is "holding [his] summer gains and weigh[s] twelve pounds more than [he] did at the end of June" (73), only later to pique his chum's jealousy when he reports on Basil Randolph's walking him home. "He stopped for a moment in front of my diggings, taking my hand to say good night and taking his own time in dropping it" (78). Cope uses this occasion once more to entreat Lemoyne, "You must come down here, and you must bring your hands with you" (78). Not surprisingly, Lemoyne's reply arrives replete with details from his own road trip with "one of our fellows in the choir" on which "a pleasant time was had by all—or, rather, by both" (105). The narrator tells us that "Cope dwelt darkly on this passage" (105), despite the more important, even "comforting" information about Lemoyne's plans to move to Churchton and his request that Cope find them suitable living quarters.

A close reading of these letters on their own undermines the dominant critical position, which suggests that Fuller's novel withholds Cope's interiority and his desire from us. Likewise we can find evidence, particularly during Cope's brief engagement with Amy Leffingwell and during the early days of Lemoyne and Cope's cohabitation, that the narrator has greater access to Cope's interior monologue than he has hitherto let on. And yet the position of the letters within the overall narrative framework would suggest that they exist in tension with the experiment in perspective that dominates the rest of the novel, where Cope is knitted and unraveled through the language of type in a rhythm that continually disrupts our sense of the boundaries around his inner life and his public performance.

Consider, for instance, the scene of writing itself. Cope begins writing his first letter to Arthur (or at least the first we see in the novel) while he is visiting Mrs. Phillips for tea. And despite his close proximity to her—he is sitting with Mrs. Phillips "side by side on the sofa"—the letter excoriates her: "Both were cross-kneed, and the tip of her russet boot almost grazed that of his Oxford tie. He did not notice: he was already arranging the first paragraph of a letter to a friend in Winnebago, Wisconsin. 'Dear Arthur: I called,—as I said I was going to. She is a scrapper. She goes at you hammer and tongs—pretending to quarrel as a means of entertaining you . . .'" (53). The writing of the letter would thus seem to have two audiences (in addition to the narrator and the novel's readers): Arthur Lemoyne and Medora Phillips. Cope later admits that writing the letter in a social space might well be rude. While "he was lingering in a smiling abstractedness on his fancy," Mrs. Phillips finally rebukes him by shouting, "Bertram Cope! . . . Do you do nothing—nothing?" (57). The meaning of Cope's letter writing for the social world around him (as evidence of social withdrawal), then, exists in strong tension with the access those letters offer us to Cope's desire. The letters don't dramatize a secret, however, so much as they measure the surfeit of desire for Cope himself. The novel creates the sense that Cope is less closeted in a homophobic world than he is positioned as the sublime object of everyone's desire. His inaccessibility only feeds that desire.

In this world that creates and dissolves Bertram Cope primarily through the eyes of others, the language of type becomes a barometer of impressions that, as they adhere to Cope, at least indexes the ineluctable attraction to type categories for arranging relationships to strangers. This act of creation and dissolution that takes place through point of view and type categories sustains a compelling rhythm throughout the novel. This rhythm begins with Basil Randolph and Medora Phillips speculating on Cope as a character type and ends with them speculating on the type of life that is about to unfold for him. Medora, among her grilles and lambrequins, was only too willing to talk about young Cope. Their early musings include the following:

> "A charming fellow—in a way," she said judicially. "Frank, but a little too self-assured and self-centered. Exuberant, but possibly a bit cold. Yet—charming."
>
> "Oh," thought Randolph, "one of the cool boys, and one of the self-sufficing. Probably a bit of an ascetic at bottom, with good capacity for self-control and self-direction. Not at all an uninteresting type," he summed it up. "An ebullient Puritan?" he asked aloud. (63–64)

By the end of the novel, Randolph is predicting that Cope and Lemoyne will be "keeping house together" (220), while Mrs. Phillips jealously frets that Cope will marry Carolyn. Although both fantasies/fears are fundamentally versions of the same coupled script, their argument over the future of Bertram Cope suggests that even after knowing him for a year, they still don't have a bead on him. Their speculations about his character type have merely led to even greater speculations about the type of life he will continue to lead—even if, in truth, both Randolph's and Phillips's predictions really amount to the same kind of coupled life. We have already had clues from Cope himself, however, in the wake of his escape from the Amy Leffingwell engagement, that "for a while, at least, and perhaps for always—he wanted to live in quite a different mode" (150).

But whatever we might think of the conclusions that characters draw about him at the end, what seems clear is that the inhabitants of Churchton remain fascinated by Bertram Cope. The novel creates a world whose queer protagonist stands at once as an index of nineteenth-century sexual types and, through its style of narration, as a refusal of sexology and psychology's equation of social behavior with particular kinds of interior life. He stands as an object of everyone's desire. Fuller, in short, writes a world where his queer protagonist is central to social relations, without being defined by his own desire. Cope's relative opacity puts us in the position of tracking the central drama of desire in the text as it circulates around him and about him without fully landing on him. In so doing, the text seems to build the kind of world that Eve Kosofsky Sedgwick once worried did not exist: a world where gay men were actively desired.[24] One might argue that Bertram Cope lives in such a world, even and especially because, as Basil Randolph observes, "liking is the great mystery" (219). To focus on the world that *Bertram Cope's Year* makes around Bertram Cope as others focus on his character—rather than focusing on the withheld character himself—thus allows us to see the emergence of a narrative world mobilized by fascination with queer life and narrated through distributed attention to him.

But to take stock of a world that makes space for a welcome queerness is also to account for what that world holds in place precisely through its opening up. Fuller's experiment with the rhythms of knitting and unraveling the forms of queer type that adhere to and release themselves from Bertram Cope does not find the same realization when it comes to other modes of social belonging. For instance, Arthur Lemoyne is established as a fool for taking his cross-dressing role too seriously in his drama club. The same characters who are fascinated by Bertram Cope and his queer desires— Mrs. Phillips, Basil Randolph, Amy Leffingwell, and Joe Foster—are repelled by Arthur's "overfeminine" performance (209). Explicitly genderphobic without being overtly homophobic, the characters all agree with the narrator's assessment that "the right sort of fellow, even if he had to sing his solo in the lightest of light tenors, would still, on lapsing into dialogue, reinstate himself apologetically by using as rough and gruff a voice as he could summon. Not so Lemoyne" (209). Basil Randolph is even secretly pleased that Lemoyne has disgraced himself so that Cope might "take heed" (209). The characters' aversion to Lemoyne's femininity aligns with other moments in the text that confirm its unease with women, such as Cope's description early on of Mrs. Phillips as a "scrapper" who "goes at you hammer and tongs" (53) and of Hortense as "dark and a bit tonguey . . . . I believe she would be sarcastic and witty if she weren't held down pretty well. I think she's a niece: the relationship leaves her free, as I suppose she feels, to express herself. If you like the type you may have it; but wit in a woman, or even humor, always makes me uncomfortable" (74–75).

Bertram Cope's world also proves to be just as committed to holding other social derogations as firmly in place as it holds its gender types. When Basil Randolph imagines his new bachelor pad, he imagines—and later installs—"an alert, intelligent Jap, who, in some miraculous way, could 'do for him' between his studies" (108). Nor are any of the characters much moved from such attitudes by the end of the book, when we are presented, first, at Mrs. Phillips's beach home with an escaped convict who (of course) breaks into the home, and later, at the university convocation where we are told that "there was recognition for a Chinaman, for a negro law-student, for a pair of Filipinos" (214). The remainder of the auspicious list includes unmarked, presumably white characters who require more detailed descriptions of their bodies. The last among them is Cope, for whom there is a "spatter of applause" (214). Whereas Cope, as barometer of a world that is relatively open to him, shifts in and out of focus as a "type," the text in its treatment of femininity and of bodies explicitly marked by race falters in unfortunately predictable ways.

Like *Q.E.D.,* the world that *Bertram Cope's Year* sketches makes the matter of its queer protagonist's inner life a narrative problem that gives shape to the web of relations surrounding him. This is a world that orients its desire toward Cope without his reciprocation—just as the novel's mise-en-scène is around the university without being of the university exactly. The world is populated by queer outsiders of one kind or another: bachelors, widows, the unmarried, the nonreproductive. Even young women find themselves queered in their heterosexual captivation with Bertram Cope, as they question the nature of their own desire in the face of his failure to return their interest. This is also notably a suburban rather than an urban world. At a time when, as George Chauncey has argued, queer subcultures increasingly converged on cities like New York and San Francisco, Fuller, like many of his nineteenth-century predecessors, positions his fictional world outside the city.[25] This desiring world remains mired in the racial logic of types, the class privilege of money, and, despite its homophilia, quite intense gender phobia. To the extent that Fuller depicts a version of queer desire that emerges as an effect of social encounters rather than originating within the consciousness of its central queer protagonist, we cannot help but recognize not its separation from the forces of oppression and inequality within the world around it but the fact that it is enmeshed within them.

Conclusion: Or, the Afterlives of Afterlives

As narrative worlds emerge and expand into matters of novelistic scale, the problem for the queer novel at the beginning of the twentieth century is, in one sense, the problem of novels more generally in this historical moment: How do we narrate the inner lives of characters? This is also the question that drives the emerging fields of psychology and psychoanalysis at the same time. Literature and psychoanalysis at the beginning of the twentieth century bequeath to us different stories about the formation of homosexuality in terms of narrative content. But strangely enough, although it is hard to imagine psychoanalysis before the structural model of Ego–Id–Superego and Freud's later description of the Oedipus complex, Freud too actually began his work on dreams as a pursuit of the landscape of the mind. The earliest edition of *The Interpretation of Dreams* includes a chapter on "Topography of the Mind" that would eventually evolve into Freud's structural model. Freud would transform his investment in the language of topology as his work developed, mostly leaving it behind. As we have seen, William James, with whom Gertrude Stein studied in Baltimore, likewise insists on the mutually constituting relation of mind and environment. Both psychoanalysis and psychology depend in this transitional moment on narrative techniques that display the shape of the mind as reflected through its descriptions of the world outside the mind.[26] Freud, for instance, relied on his patients' providing maps of their inner lives through the technique of free association: "Act," he said, in defining free association, "as though, for instance, you were a traveller sitting next to the window of a railway carriage and describing to someone inside the carriage the changing views which you see outside."[27] It was the challenge of the analyst to interpret the mind that was being revealed to him: to narrate, in effect, the story of another's mind. Psychoanalysis's reliance on literary tropes and tales has long been documented: Oedipus, Narcissus, and the Marquis de Sade, for example, furnished Freud with much of the material he metabolized in his work to interpret his patients' inner lives. But what we see here is that psychoanalysis and literature share a methodological challenge as both address themselves to the problem of narrating and describing the consciousness of sexual types. Both come up squarely against the spaces that have made those types legible as such, even (perhaps especially) when the interpretive apparatus of location, however metaphorically, defines the shape of inner life.

What does it mean to read the history of located modes of being back into the history of sexuality in a way that both informs and unsettles the very concepts of sexuality as a property of the self, and of writing about sexuality as emerging only in the wake of sexual identities as we now know them? The place types that circulate in and through nineteenth-century American literature are not indebted to the rise of sexuality as identity. In fact, the opposite may well be true: that sexuality can be narrated as such only when worlds have been made for it. It may be hard for us to imagine a time when the story we told about sexuality was less that it was a property of the self and more that it was a practice of sociability associated with particular locations and races of humans. Even to grasp this history requires starting with what now seems to be obvious about sexuality in the present: namely, that everyone has one. But once we displace that truism, we can see anew that desire is an achievement unlocked through worldly conditions, and that even the psychic life of desire comes burdened with the political shape that organizes it from the outside in.

By tracking the conditions under which worlds and protagonists come to be realized in the queer novel as such, we also begin to see what has exceeded, or failed to be rationalized within, novel-shaped space as we know it. The novel has furnished us with a narrative life of homosexuality that has traditionally relied on the codex form to create the boundaries around a life story, in effect creating a break with previous shorter fictions, poems, and case studies that may have foregrounded episodes rather than the *longue durée* of a life or a relationship. Because the period of the novel's emergence is also the period of the psychologization of homosexuality, these twinned processes have seemed successive, or at least mutually constitutive, but are not necessarily causal. The emergence of psychology also creates vestigial forms of literary sexuality. The circulation history of these forms is not one of mass distribution but of sites of intensity where coteries share texts or facilitate exchange among strangers. Such semipublic literary cultures in turn create insider networks that have generated many relatively inaccessible and thus unreadable works. This discontinuous genre of literature includes titles such as *The Intersexes* and "Sebastian au Plus Bel Age" by Edward Prime-Stevenson; *House of the Vampire* by George Sylvester Viereck; and *The Valley of Shadows* by Francis Grierson. The novel-shaped space of homosexuality is more diverse, in effect, than we have ever known. What seems at once to congeal in terms of genre (the queer novel) and identity (homosexuality) has therefore been more and less than we have yet to acknowledge.

CODA
Short Circuits and Untrodden Paths

I HAVE SOUGHT IN THIS BOOK to track the force that nineteenth-century networks of queer sociability and textual circulation exerted on the form that queer life took in literary fiction as fictional works expanded from short stories (or short episodes in longer works) into novel-length worlds that feature queer protagonists. Taking the emergence of the queer novel as my scene of inquiry, I used that scene to explore literary world-making in an effort to chart the space around and through which queer types came alive in fiction and moved around those fictional worlds in ways that seem only in retrospect to have been totally predictable as they settled into the world-making form of the novel. In one sense, this book confirms Peter Coviello's insight that queer sexual life in the nineteenth century has always been "untimely": full of unrealized futures, "unspeakable pasts," and "messy misalignments" with the emerging regime of sexuality as such.[1] This book emphasizes as well, however, that in this untimely historical moment, this thing we now call sexuality (whose obviousness distorts its own historicity) has also been out of place—both situated and elsewhere, a fact made clear through the now-obsolete vocabularies of place and race types that also have helped to organize the socio-fictional history of sexuality.

Literary circulation creates the conditions of possibility for texts to amplify each other over time and across space, an effect of the recursive nature of reading itself. Writers read and cite each other, framing each other's works, responding to them, and understanding themselves hailed by those works without reducing that hail to another author's specific intention. Yet to read the works in this study as part of a single, seamless archive, moment in time, or tradition would be to smooth out the jagged edges of a body of texts that only *seem* to anticipate something that now seems inevitable to us. In our inescapable commitment to our own frames of reading references that writers like Melville, James, Jewett, and Stein helped produce, it becomes difficult to see what has been lost to us as an effect of our own clear vision. I've tried in the course of this book to approximate something in that backward rather than anticipatory glance.

One conclusion we can draw, in terms of content, is that queer worlds existed before queer subjects as such. What seem so clearly to us to be sexualized and gendered character types were understood as place types who often were seen to bear the exotic traces of those locations on their bodies. Although it seems true that the queer protagonist is possible only after the emergence of the queer subject, it is nonetheless also true that the queer subject's narration owes its conditions of possibility to a world whose frames of reference persist as mere traces with the emergence of sexuality in the ways that Michel Foucault, David Halperin, Jonathan Ned Katz, and others have illustrated. As the early twentieth century shifts us more fully into an epistemology of sexuality grounded in interiority, these earlier ways of thinking sexuality as exterior to the self do not disappear fully: their historic materiality transmutes to metaphors as writers across fictional, scientific, and psychological genres reach to describe and understand the inner life of the mind as itself a landscape, a geography, a worldly nature.

As much as this book makes a hero of the productive force of circulation, the writing of it has also confronted me with its clear and sometimes regressive limits. At a time when we remain deeply invested in the concept of the circuit, the power of the network, and the need for coteries, these cultural forms regularly crystallize for us sites of alienation and exclusion from those very dominant forms.

That is no less true for the scene of queer theory than it is for any other scene for which there is an inner circle.

Through the course of completing this project, at the heart of which essentially are two large case studies, I have come up over and over again against the limits of its shape—that is, of the shape of a document that aims to understand the shape of a cultural form at a particular time. I've insisted that textual accretion has been one way to understand the emerging density of texts that make queer life narratable as such by the late nineteenth and early twentieth centuries. One form this accretion took, in its own time, was the careful collection and thus the rogue circulation of texts. The most famous example of such circulation may well have been the one that David Leavitt and Mark Mitchell describe in their introduction to *Pages Passed from Hand to Hand,* in which they present an excerpt from *Teleny; or, The Reverse of the Medal* (authored anonymously but suspected to be the work of Oscar Wilde); it was wrapped in brown paper and circulated among young men by way of a London bookstore, the Librairie Parisienne.[2] But Edward Prime-Stevenson's contemporaneous characterization of Dayneford's library—books collected and oriented toward each other as if they were members of a subculture—suggests that the practice of curating such titles was no isolated affair; nor was it a nationalist literary project. Personal libraries and networks were global and often multilingual in scope, consolidating and thus reproducing a wide-reaching humanities approach to texts that was also often implicitly the legacy of imperialist and even racist thinking. Emergent, explicitly identitarian queer textualities were keyed as well to narrative patterns that focused attention on repetitions of types and settings. Herman Melville and Charles Warren Stoddard made it their project to write back to the density of writing about South Seas sexual types while also recognizing the sexual appeal of those types and perpetuating a homophilic but racist fetish for them. So, too, do Sarah Orne Jewett and Henry James (albeit from almost opposing vantage points) take up the figure of the New England spinster as a site of narrative condensation and flourishing, replete with their own echoes and exoticizations of race and place types. As these writers and others grasped for vocabularies, settings, and plot patterns to make sense of the interiority of sexuality, they were aided by the late nineteenth-century expansion of print distribution and by the advent of new transportation methods for books and humans alike. These technologies made movement out of place possible, facilitated new human and textual encounters, and opened up to nostalgia for those left behind—all while creating the conditions for others to stage and reproduce encounters that they had previously only read about (as Stoddard and others did).

This book has focused a great deal of its energy on the matter of circulation: on books, characters, and people moving through and producing worlds. In so doing, it also enacts a methodology for reading the making and unmaking of sexual types as they take shape through literary form. Reading texts as imbricated within systems of circulation is not only a matter of reading content; it is also a matter of understanding how the processes of textual circulation give meaning to that content and transform that meaning. Through this work of tracking what is made visible through attention to the literary and social processes by which queer narrative worlds find print realization, assemble themselves together, frame and reframe each other in dialectical relation to their audiences, expand and contract in the face of this relation—I am also advocating for a practice of reading and an approach to genre that includes but exceeds the close reading of a single text.

Owing largely to its narrative scale, its multivocality, and its attention to describing the worlds in which characters live and move through space and time, the queer novel and the conditions for its emergence have been my main focus in this book. In focusing my study in this way, I have sought to understand fictional form as a space-making gesture for queer life. Along the way, I have in essence treated shorter selections of fiction (including short stories, novellas, and even episodes within longer works) as holding environments for the incubation and complication of sexual types. I made this choice in order to understand not just the evolution and emergence of sexual types per se but to offer a concomitantly more robust history of the conditions of possibility for narrating those types and for assessing the ways they could be narrated so as to exceed their seeming flatness.

One of the reasons I turned to fictional worlds of queer types has been to bring minoritization back into the ongoing conversations that queer theory has staged about literature at least since the earliest work of Eve Kosofsky Sedgwick. In *Epistemology of the Closet,* Sedgwick urges us to adopt a universalizing rather than a minoritizing approach to sexuality. In its moment, this approach was a necessary game-changer: it positioned us to see past the stark divide between homosexuality and heterosexuality and to regard homosocial attachments as central to the history of our social fabric. It has also opened up queerness as a way of understanding the perverse reach of desire and its unpredictable paths of realization in the world. But this shift from a minitorizing model of homosexuality to a universalizing queer model largely left behind the work of generations of writers and scholars devoted to inhabiting the space of marginalized minorities and articulating worldviews from that vantage point. I count myself among the generation of students inspired by queer theory's critiques of identitarian essentialism in the field of gay and lesbian studies and by its embrace of public sexual culture, especially in the early work of Judith Butler, Lee Edelman, Michael Warner, Lauren Berlant, and Leo Bersani. But in retrospect, it's hard not to see that the recovery work that was overlooked as gay and lesbian studies, as a field, was overcome in that moment.

Few queer theorists today speak much, for instance, of Jeannette Foster, Roger Austen, or Ian Young—some of the many scholarly minded queers who scoured libraries, tracked down letters, and assembled bibliographies of queer writing long before it was fashionable to do so. The works of Robert K. Martin, Catharine R. Stimpson, and many others likewise appear more as quaint footnotes to the main events of queer theory. Even more recent efforts to continue in this vein of scholarship by James Gifford, Christopher Looby, and others sometimes seem adjacent to the ongoing hermeneutics of queer theory. Such, perhaps, is the temporality through which we come to the history of sexuality: even our scholarship is organized by what Coviello has called the "untimeliness" of sex, best understood through the queerness of "erotohistoriography" that Elizabeth Freeman has described.[3] The point, however, is not to replace our universalizing approach to the history of sexuality with a return to minoritization but to understand the dialectical relationship between them, something to which Sedgwick remained sensitive throughout her work.

One key thing we miss in overcoming this early mode of scholarship (which tends to be understood as the recovery work of gay and lesbian studies) is its attentiveness to a version of what we now call intersectionality. In the 1970s, scholarship on gay and lesbian literature from the late nineteenth and early twentieth centuries was in some ways alive to the persistent overlap between discourses of homosexuality and discourses of race. Even a white gay man like Roger Austen, whose work was not especially focused on the politics of race, could not help but position his own study of homosexual literature alongside those of "the more respectable minorities: Jewish, black, Chicano, Oriental-American, and native American," whose literatures had attracted greater scholarly attention before any study of the gay novel had been undertaken.[4] Austen also cites Edward Prime-Stevenson at length for pointing out America's "racial uranianism," so prominent by the beginning of the twentieth century:

> The North-American (by such term indicating particularly
> the United States) with his nervosity, his impressionability, his
> complex fusion of bloods and of racial traits, even when of di-
> rectly British stocks, is usually far more "temperamental" than
> the English. He has offered interesting excursions at least to-
> wards, if not always into, the homosexual library. His novels,
> verses and essays have pointed out a racial uranianism.[5]

Nor is the long-standing tendency both to racialize sexuality and to see it as a foreign behavior lost on Austen either. When he receives news, in 1977, that Georges-Michel Sarotte is publishing a book in France about male homosexuality in American theater and novels from Herman Melville to James Baldwin, he says, "Given the combination of xenophobia-homophobia that has characterized our attitude toward gay literature, it is entirely appropriate that the first person to recognize in print what Americans have always preferred not to recognize is a foreigner."[6] As Jasbir Puar and others have pointed out more recently, American culture has suddenly flipped that script, in effectively pinkwashing its own racist and colonial histories, pro-jecting its homophobia onto nations, cultures, and races that seem politically perverse from a new vantage point focused on terrorism.[7] Such is the move from exotic others to respectable queers, as prim-itivism (already masked as homophilic racism) ghosts itself in the service of queer legibility. The very practice of recognizing sexuality as a mode of located and racialized sociability remains fully intact even in this inversion. Meanwhile the circuits of global capital, as Arnaldo Cruz-Malavé and Martin F. Manalansan, among others, have argued, have made American queer life (and even American queer theory) commodities for widespread consumption.[8] The queer, once the site of refusal for identity politics, has come to circulate as a cooler form of identity politics—ultimately undermining its own radical potential, much to the chagrin of its earliest theorists.

All of this is to say that we remain haunted by the historical alignments of race, place, sexual, and class types—even as the type vocabularies we have at our disposal for describing sexuality seem obviously discontinuous with the history I have sketched out here, and constantly in flux as they themselves circulate, reach their lim-its, and inspire us to reach for newer terms of self-reference. Ray-mond Williams taught us a long time ago that such emergences and crystallizations of focus come replete with residual cultural forms.[9] Just as queer theory took its point of departure from a body of texts assembled more eagerly under the sign of the gay and lesbian, so too did homosexuality; tracking the emergence of the queer novel is thus a process of tracking the residues of earlier worldviews.

Circulation itself, no less than sexuality, has a history of dis-placement and of overwriting one system of human circulation with another. The building of the railway saw government appropria-tion of Indigenous territory, for instance, in the name of inventing a mode of transportation for a nation when this "invention" served also as an act of violent destruction.

I'm under no illusion that the account this book offers of a genre history is complete. There are many paths not taken, or not taken up fully, and the panoply of texts that constitute the prehisto-ry of the queer novel, particularly in the nineteenth-century archive of American literature, is vast. Another version of this book might have attended to a different collection of texts that have already been hailed as nineteenth-century examples of queer novels, such as Theodore Winthrop's *Cecil Dreeme,* Julia Ward Howe's *The Hermaphrodite,* or Nathaniel Hawthorne's *Blithedale Romance.*

It might have included as well chapters tracking the circulation of sexual and racial types and their modes of relationality in African American and Indigenous writing: through attention to the cluster of queer writers that were central to the Harlem Renaissance; through a consideration of texts written during Reconstruction—or even during slavery—that foreground the radically diffuse social organization of kinship, sexuality, and intimacy tenaciously cultivated by black people in America; through the circulation of writing by and about Indigenous people that discusses, for instance, the berdache and nonmonogamous kinship forms. It remains inescapably true that even our understanding of the deviations from normative kinship forms and queer minoritarian life are steeped in the logic of whiteness, even as scholarship begins to reshape that dominant narrative.[10]

The texts that I have examined in this book foreground relationship webs rather than the monogamous couple form, and although the earliest examples we have of queer novels come from white writers, the dominant models we have for these social arrangements arguably come to us from African American and Indigenous cultural traditions. Both furnish us with diffuse kinship networks not based in monogamous property ownership. In her article "The Fourth Dimension," for example, Nancy Bentley points to the ways that African Americans under slavery were essentially excluded from normative genealogical modes of thought, explaining that they were in effect "kinless" because their lives were not organized by white familial and property norms. She argues that this was an effect of "natal transmission" and that such relations of nonwhite inheritance were predicated on "a bare genealogy."[11] Jordan Stein goes so far as to point out that even "anti-slavery media falls among the not explicitly sexual agents of normalization which made heterosexuality hegemonic."[12] Stein's point is not to reject the politics of antislavery but to focus on the very ways it upholds a hegemonic view of kinship in order to support its aims. Likewise, Mark Rifkin charts the hitherto untraced genealogies of Native American culture and its representations of berdache and nonmonogamous kinship structures that stand in opposition to settler heteronormativity in the nineteenth-century American history of sexuality.[13] As Elizabeth Povinelli has argued, "If you want to locate the hegemonic home of liberal logics and aspirations, look to love in the settler colonies." In her view, "liberal adult love depends on instantiating its opposite, a particular kind of illiberal, tribal, customary, and ancestral love."[14] The heteronormative world is, historically, composed precisely through (and in its reliance on) the illiberal others it invokes as bad examples. In this way, the history of minority or nonnormative sexuality is indivisible from the history of race and settler colonialism in America.

What we begin to see in late nineteenth- and early twentieth-century fiction is both a reliance on this logic of interlocking but extraliberal perversions and a strong desire to overcome them. As sexuality comes to be imagined and narrated as a property of the self, it represses its own historical solidarity with other located modes of sociability, even as it remains haunted by the traces of them. Its fictional settings shift from island paradises and regional locales to larger cities; its protagonists become white and relatively monied. Our readings of a queer African American novel or a two-spirit novel emerge more than a century later. Only recently has queer literary criticism come to foreground queer black and Indigenous worlds. The whitewashing of sexual types that takes place in late nineteenth- and early twentieth-century queer fiction becomes obvious in retrospect.

Once it has become possible to imagine same-sexual sociability at the heart of an entire narrative world, the terms of queer literary experimentation begin to shift: they move inside the sentence and inside the character. The accumulation of detail and the circulation of texts that created these queer worlds help to make homosexuality possible as an abstraction, erasing, at the level of content, the visibility of its own history and creativity, while treating the form itself as the repository of this creative history of circulation. The very fact that writers like Gertrude Stein, Henry Blake Fuller, Edward Prime-Stevenson, and other early twentieth-century gay and lesbian novelists seem to assume the possibility of writing novels with queer protagonists registers a shift away from the world-making parameters foregrounded within earlier fiction and toward greater fictional self-consciousness of plot and interiority. But in focusing less on the problem of world-making per se, they assume the scope of writing that these earlier texts made possible—all while seeming to conceal the very conditions under which their own concerns with interiority and plot came to be filled with ironic possibility to begin with.

In addition to providing us with a sedimented history of the queer worlds that give rise to queer subjectivity, the body of writing at the heart of this study also offers us a glimpse of a phenomenon that remains understudied in the history of sexuality: the political economy of queer publishing. From the universalizing standpoint, the history of queer publishing in America might be seen as the history of publishing more generally. There is a robust mainstream literature from the American nineteenth century that features homosocial and homosexual relations. Recall again Eve Kosofsky Sedgwick's advocacy for a universalizing approach to reading queer life and Robert K. Martin's suggestion that the best anthology of the history of gay writing was *The Norton Anthology of American Literature*. In the introduction to *The Literature of Lesbianism,* Terry Castle similarly identifies her anthological approach as defined by the history of ideas: she thus includes mostly canonical works of literature that identify the role of lesbianism "as rhetorical and cultural topos."[15] But if we zoom out from the scene of representation to account for the textual production and circulation of queer literature, we see the ways in which the publishing apparatus both facilitates and constrains the production of what becomes minoritarian and identitarian literature.

Many of the short stories we now find anthologized in collections of American gay and lesbian short stories began life through distribution in magazines such as the *Atlantic Monthly, Harper's,* and the *Overland Monthly.* A significant number of important books in the history of gay and lesbian literature of this period— particularly those that were not written by established writers like Nathaniel Hawthorne, Henry David Thoreau, or Walt Whitman— also relied on the wealth and means of their authors for realization (even these now-mainstream authors often had to contribute financially to their own success). Like John Addington Symonds, who privately printed *A Problem in Greek Ethics* (1901), Edward Prime-Stevenson famously printed *Imre* privately, in a batch of 125, in Rome in 1908. Gertrude Stein's and Natalie Barney's Paris salons were hubs of literary and cultural production—made possible because they could afford to establish them. Bachelor halls of the kind mentioned in Stoddard's letters and in Fuller's novel took place to connect writers to wealthy socialites and the well-connected tastemakers of the publishing world. Axel Nissen reports that "without friendship, specifically Winthrop's close friendship with the established writer and editor George William Curtis, it is unlikely that [Theodore Winthrop's *Cecil Dreeme*] would ever have seen the dark of print."[16] Stoddard too lived an itinerant life, moving between teaching gigs and cobbling together a writer's life that required extensive correspondence with editors and other writers. His elaborate scrapbooks, in which he collected all of his published work as well as his autographs from other writers, attest to the perceived ephemerality of writing and the need for collection.

The semipublic worlds of private distribution (like Stoddard's and Prime-Stevenson's) were a fixture among women writers as well. Here we find that the production of repeated narratives that coalesce into the motifs of the queer spinsters in New England local color writing collectively attend to a different world of queer textuality from that perhaps conveyed by a mainstream anthology of historical writing. We also see a rich correspondence about writing itself between writers such as Sarah Orne Jewett and Willa Cather. What many scholars have referred to variously as romantic friendships, Boston marriages, and chum relationships, but that also took the form of cluster relationships and triangles, appeared in texts that were both printed in plain sight and carefully curated in private by way of networks cultivated through a combination of money and letters. The boundary between what was publishable (and in turn marketable) at the end of the century and what required private printing or collection remains decidedly unclear. The circulation networks themselves and the queer worlds they made possible within and beyond books emerge into only partial view in this study.

The economics facilitating and underpinning these networks remain opaque to view in their totality.

Some parts of this history can be gleaned from the economic circuits that are now obvious to us: the circulation of texts and bodies around and beyond America was possible because of the technologies of print production and distribution as well as engines of economic development. Resource economies like whaling and mining made it possible for authors like Melville and Bret Harte to participate in the industries that gave rise to works ranging from *Typee* to "The Luck of Roaring Camp." We know that whatever else Boston marriages were, they were also economic units. Simultaneously, we begin to get portraits of the worlds that class circulation itself seemed to leave behind, such as those described by Jewett, whose rural Maine comes to us as a quaint anachronism that fuels the melancholy of Martha after her lady leaves to travel the world with her diplomat husband. Meanwhile, as Comstock laws took effect, clamping down on what could be distributed by post, representations of sex of all kinds came to be constrained. Portraits of the political economy of queer life more generally have come to us through the work of John D'Emilio, George Chauncey, Lisa Duggan, Jeffrey Escoffier, Amy Villarejo, Kevin Floyd, and others. We have a more developed understanding of the ways in which sexual subjects are shaped by capitalist forces and increasingly commodified. But aside from attention to the lesbian pulp novels of the mid-twentieth century and the body of work concerning erotica and pornography,[17] there has been scant attention to the history of queer books, or even to queering the history of the book as such—unless we include accounts of the life in print of now-canonical authors like Melville, Whitman, and Henry James, whose print circulations have been carefully tracked.

An inquiry into the history of queer literature, its genres, and its circulation is no mere antiquarian affair. At a time when gay and lesbian bookstores have come and gone, the status of LGBTQ literature, its writers, and its circuits today remains open to question. *GLQ* recently issued a call for papers that opens by asking, "Is there such a thing as LGBT Literature anymore?"[18] The editors proceed to acknowledge that the Lambda Literary Awards sure think so through their annual recognition of LGBTQ works of literature and even scholarship. But despite decades of scholarship that follows the universalizing approach of Sedgwick and others, well-established queer writers like Sarah Schulman observe that the mainstream cultural deck is stacked against them,[19] even as other writers insist that they are not queer writers at all—just writers who happen to be queer.

Attending to the world-making project of the queer novel invites us to read beyond the covers of any given novel to consider the conditions of possibility for the genre's emergence and recognition as such. These conditions are contradictory and unpredictable, despite feeling inevitable. Genre, as E. D. Hirsch once described it, is an invitation to form, a coming together of form and content.[20] But the formation of a genre is more than that: it is also an invitation to chart the shape of the world that makes it possible, to ask after the worlds it leaves out, and to address the ways in which those worlds are condensed and erased, infused and vestigial, dead and alive within it.

ACKNOWLEDGMENTS

THE STORY OF THIS BOOK is itself a story of circulation: an academic journey that has taken me from my hometown in North River, Newfoundland, to Halifax (Nova Scotia), London (Ontario), New Brunswick (New Jersey), Ithaca (New York), Minneapolis (Minnesota), and Edmonton (Alberta). To tell that story in the way it deserves requires more space than I can take here. Suffice it to say that the kind of book I have written here may be far removed from the place I grew up, but it holds close the spirit of creative transmission that defines how I grew up. I am grateful to my parents, Nick and Sylvia Hurley, for making words and books central to that *how*; to my siblings—Andrea, Paul, and Kenneth—for creating and sustaining language worlds with me; and to my extended family, chosen and biological, for the endless array of laughs, tunes, meals, and games.

Moving to Halifax to attend Mount St. Vincent University enabled me to understand the displacements and innovations that circulation enacts. Making new meant leaving old while holding both together as Halifax became a long-term home. Since our days in Halifax, Adèle Poirier has been a constant friend and support, always willing to kick the shins of anyone who wrongs me and waiting in the wings with firm embraces. Steven Bruhm and Peter Schwenger helped make me the person and the scholar I am today; they believed I could and should go to graduate school, and they never failed to pick me up along the way, even when I didn't deserve it. During my lowest moments, they, along with Chris Ferns, Rhoda Zuk, Maurice Michaud, Karen McFarlane, Goran Stanivukovic, Shawn Miner, Rosanne Balsom, and the late Emily Givner, gave me the gift of friendship when I most needed it and could offer the least in return. Barbara Markovits helped me to restore my inner resources. (Many hours spent dancing at Club NRG didn't hurt either.)

The *how* of writing this book began long before I wrote a word of the book itself, but the actual words started taking shape on the page as I wrote my dissertation. Completing my PhD at Rutgers was one of the most challenging and gratifying experiences of my life. This book began its life in that program, specifically in the office of my supervisor, Michael Warner, whose intellectual charisma was an inspiring force for my project's realization. I also relied on patience, generosity, and openness from a range of other advisors, including Michael McKeon, Meredith McGill, Ed Cohen, and Myra Jehlen. And without Cheryl Robinson, an entire generation of Rutgers graduate students would have been much less cheered and probably less cheerful.

Behind the scenes of my doctoral work stood several silent stars who have been guiding forces through the course of my writing, during and beyond the dissertation stage. Chief among them is my partner, Susanne Luhmann, whom I met at a conference mere weeks before I was set to return to Rutgers after a break from my studies. She has been a constant source of encouragement from near and far; years later, this relationship is the best one-night stand ever. For four years, it was lived across borders, on telephones, and online as I moved from Halifax to Highland Park and then to Minneapolis before we both ended up living in Edmonton. She has somehow managed to coexist with this project, as its life unfolded from dissertation to book, with only love for it and for me. Living with such an emotionally intelligent human being gives me joy every day. Our living room couch may need to be replaced after all this writing and sitting, but Ceilidh (our beloved doodle) and I promise to make up for it with extra affection and tail wagging.

My life in Edmonton, where I finally finished this book, has been enriched by an amazing collection of friends and colleagues with whom we share the love of cocktails, dinner parties, collective travels, late-night dancing, dog walks in the river valley, trips to the mountains, tarp runs, experiments with food, psychoanalysis, farmers' marketing, art, activism, and kettlebells. My friends and colleagues at the University of Alberta and its Department of English and Film Studies have helped to make me feel more and more at home. My graduate students continue to inspire and amaze me with the scope and depth of their work. Together they constitute the best part of my job.

While life may seem to have taken me from New Jersey to Edmonton and from dissertation to book in one fell swoop, there was another short but important stop along the way that has been essential to my finishing both. During the last year of my PhD, I took a one-year visiting assistant professorship at Macalester College in St. Paul, Minnesota. At Macalester I met three amazing friends on whom I relied to close the dissertation deal: Amy DiGennaro, Chris Willcox, and Diane Brown. Diane and I spent our Sundays that year writing together while Amy and Chris made me part of their family life. These three friends threw dinner parties and even a defense party for me. Having since changed careers to become a genius editor, Diane has been an undying supporter of my work and my biggest cheerleader. In addition to providing detailed editorial advice, she also introduced me to the incomparable Vanessa Doriott Anderson, freelance copy editor extraordinaire. Diane and Vanessa together sprinkled so much editorial pixie dust on this manuscript that the work of actually completing this book has felt like an airy victory lap.

This victory lap is only possible, finally, because of the tireless and yet cheerful work of so many amazing people at the University of Minnesota Press. I thank Richard Morrison first for believing in this project. It has been Doug Armato, however, who has really seen it through. With the help of Erin Warholm-Wohlenhaus, Gabriel Levin, and the rest of the transmittal team, Doug did the heavy lifting of shepherding this manuscript to print. Two anonymous reviewers provided essential guidance that has made this book better in ways I hadn't imagined. One in particular provided specific references and a detailed accounting of various flaws, and to that reader I owe a debt of gratitude for inspiring me to be a better scholar. I am grateful, as well, to Louisa Castner, whose shrewd editorial eye made my writing better as I was bringing this project to a close.

Finally, I acknowledge the material and financial supports for the work that has gone into this book. Writing this book has been supported by the Social Sciences and Humanities Research Council of Canada; the Mellon Foundation; Rutgers University; the American Antiquarian Society; the Department of English and Film Studies, the Faculty of Arts, the Office of the Vice-President (Research), and the Support for the Advancement of Scholarship Fund at the University of Alberta; the Killam Trust Foundation; Macalester College; and the Graduate Program of Literatures in English at Rutgers University. I have benefited from the research work of Priel Buzny, Laura Sydora, Matt Tétrault, Kaitlyn Purcell, Ayantika Mukherjee, and Adela Burke.

In my more flippant modes, I like to quantify the journey toward this book's publication in terms of space rather than time or pages: seven cities inhabited and seven moves made (all increasingly westward); three universities graduated; eight universities employed as instructor; countless relationships made, unmade, and sustained. The following is a list of people to whom I am individually and personally grateful. Each is dear to me for a different reason, and I hope you'll recognize your reason. If you have any doubt, I will happily tell you my story of what you mean to me in person: Jennifer Alabiso, Mohammed Al-Ghamdi, Judith Anderson, Karyn Ball, Lauren Berlant, Katherine Binhammer, Danielle Bobker, Ned Brown, Priel Buzny, Mary Chapman, Juliet Cherbuliez, Dianne Chisholm, Michael Cobb, Ed Cohen, Beau Coleman, Peter Coviello, Wendy Chun, Judy Davidson, Cecily Devereux, Mo Engel, Megan Farnel, Beth Freeman, Becky Hardie, Luis Iglesias, David Kahane, Catherine Kellogg, Leslea Kroll, Chris Looby, Dana Luciano, Carla MacDougall, Karen MacFarlane, Derrit Mason, Donia Mounsef, Nicola Nixon, Danielle O'Connor, Mike O'Driscoll, Kip Pegley, Natasha Pinterics, Sina Queyras, Lars Richter, Taylor Scanlon, Mark Simpson, Stephen Slemon, Edie Snook, Nicole Snow, Meredith Snyder, Jordan Stein, Kathryn Bond Stockton, Imre Szeman, Kyla Wazana Tompkins, Jo-Ann Wallace, Sara Warner, Mary Jo Watts, Brianna Wells, Jenny Worley, Rachel Zukiwski-Pezim, and Heather Zwicker.

In that clichéd act of closing by return, allow me to circle round one more time to my family: that web of relations determined as much by choice as it has been by genetics, people who have made so much possible for me over the years and across the many places I have lived. One of the things I point to in this book is the way that located modes of sociability have been central to understanding what we now take to be forms of inner life or properties of the self. My own inner life is likewise a product of the paths I have taken and the locations of my sociability, all of which have reinforced for me my sense of clannishness. Susanne and Ceilidh stand at the center of my hurley-burley, borgish clan, though this clan has included many others over the years: parents, siblings, aunts, uncles, cousins, lovers, and partners. The list specifically of Hurleys has expanded to include Gwen Hurley, John/Joanie Sadek, Andrea Dawe Hurley, Patricia MacLeod, Liam Sadek, Nick Sadek, and Briar Hurley—all of whom have provided with me with love and care, as they enrich my relationships to my parents and my siblings. I carry with me especially the influence, love, and aphorisms of my late grandmothers, Rose Hurley and Mary Hall. Having learned the art of family with them, I have also learned to make family with my extended network of queer kin, all of whom are mentioned in the paragraphs above. It seems fitting, then, to dedicate *Circulating Queerness* to the many people I have loved as family along the way to its realization. This book wouldn't have made it without the lot of you.

NOTES

Prologue

1. Edward Irenaeus Prime-Stevenson [Xavier Mayne], "Out of the Sun," in *Pages Passed from Hand to Hand: The Hidden Tradition of Homosexual Literature in English from 1748 to 1914,* ed. Mark Mitchell and David Leavitt (New York: Houghton Mifflin, 1997), 396.

2. Ibid.

3. That queer subcultures developed bodies of shared texts has long been known. As George Chauncey put it in his study of the history of queer communities in New York City, one effect of the impulse to collect and invent a tradition of writing was to create the ground for modern gay identity itself: "Having no access to a formal body of scholarship, gay men needed to invent—and constantly reinvent—a tradition on the basis of innumerable individual and idiosyncratic readings of texts. . . . By constructing historical traditions of their own, gay men defined themselves as a distinct community. By imagining they had collective roots in the past, they asserted a collective identity in the present." Chauncey, *Gay New York: Gender, Urban Culture, and the Making of the Gay Male World, 1890–1940* (New York: Basic Books, 1994), 283, 286.

4. Mitchell and Leavitt, introduction to their *Pages Passed from Hand to Hand,* xiii–xix; and James J. Gifford, introduction to *Glances Backward: An Anthology of American Homosexual Writing, 1830–1920,* ed. James J. Gifford (Peterborough, Ontario: Broadview Press, 2007), xv–xxvi.

5. See James Gifford, *Dayneford's Library: American Homosexual Writing, 1900–1913* (Amherst: University of Massachusetts Press, 1995).

6. Karla Jay, introduction to *A Perilous Advantage: The Best of Natalie Clifford Barney,* ed. and trans. Anna Livia (Norwich, Vt.: New Victoria Publishers, 1992), viii.

7. Djuna Barnes offers us ample examples from within this circle of literary production. Comparing Barnes's relationship to Thelma Wood with her relationship to the Dada artist Baroness Elsa von Freytag-Loringhoven, the latter's biographer, Irene Gammel, observes that "Where Wood gave Barnes a doll as a gift to represent their symbolic love child, the Baroness proposed an erotic marriage whose love-child would be their book." Gammel, *Baroness Elsa: Gender, Dada, and Everyday Modernity; A Cultural Biography* (Cambridge, Mass.: MIT Press, 2002), 349.

Phillip Herring tells us that *Ladies Almanack* was published in a small, privately printed edition under the pseudonym "A Lady of Fashion." Copies were sold on the streets of Paris by Barnes and her friends, and Barnes managed to smuggle a few into the United States to sell. A bookseller, Edward Titus, offered to carry *Ladies Almanack* in his store in exchange for being mentioned on the title page, but when he demanded a share of the royalties on the entire print run, Barnes was furious. She later gave the name Titus to the abusive father in *The Antiphon*. See Phillip Herring, *Djuna: The Life and Work of Djuna Barnes* (New York: Viking, 1995), 152–53.

For a discussion of Djuna Barnes's *Ladies Almanack* and the culture of lesbian textual reproduction, see also Kathryn R. Kent, *Making Girls into Women: American Women's Writing and the Rise of Lesbian Identity* (Durham, N.C.: Duke University Press, 2003), 125–37.

8. Louie Crew and Rictor Norton, "The Homophobic Imagination: An Editorial," *College English* 36, no. 3 (November 1974): 274.

9. Ibid. See also Roger Austen, *Genteel Pagan: The Double Life of Charles Warren Stoddard*, ed. John W. Crowley (Amherst: University of Massachusetts Press, 1991).

10. See Kevin Ohi, *Henry James and the Queerness of Style* (Minneapolis: University of Minnesota Press, 2011); and Jordan Alexander Stein, "*The Blithedale Romance*'s Queer Style," *ESQ: A Journal of the American Renaissance* 55, nos. 3–4 (2009): 211–36.

11. Stein, "*Blithedale Romance*'s Queer Style," 214, 211.

12. See Edward Carpenter, ed., *Ioläus: An Anthology of Friendship* (London: Swan Sonnenschein, 1902); and Edward Irenaeus Prime-Stevenson, *The Intersexes: A History of Similisexualism as a Problem in Social Life* (privately printed in 1908).

13. Michel Foucault, *The History of Sexuality*, vol. 1, *An Introduction*, trans. Robert Hurley (New York: Vintage, 1990), 43. The *Oxford English Dictionary* cites the first appearance of *homosexuality* as 1892, in Richard von Krafft-Ebing's *Psychopathia Sexualis*. In *The History of Sexuality*, Michel Foucault points to 1862 as the year of the term's first use, an assertion

confirmed by Jonathan Ned Katz in *The Invention of Heterosexuality*. Although *heterosexuality* was coined at around the same time, the latter is widely understood to have emerged as a necessary alternative to *homosexuality*. For more on this, see Diana Fuss, introduction to *Inside/Out: Lesbian Theories, Gay Theories* (New York: Routledge, 1991), 1–10; and Katz, *The Invention of Heterosexuality* (Chicago: University of Chicago Press, 2007).

14. Foucault, *History of Sexuality,* 18.

15. David M. Halperin, *How to Do the History of Homosexuality* (Chicago: University of Chicago Press, 2002), 88.

16. Eve Kosofsky Sedgwick, *Epistemology of the Closet* (Berkeley: University of California Press, 1990).

17. See Michael Warner, introduction to *Fear of a Queer Planet: Queer Politics and Social Theory,* ed. Michael Warner (Minneapolis: University of Minnesota Press, 1993), xxi–xxv.

18. Recent work within the field of queer literary study has sought to circumnavigate this before/after question by attending to queer time. Elizabeth Freeman has coined the term *erotohistoriography* to characterize the drags, delays, pauses, and asynchronicity of queer history. See Freeman, *Time Binds: Queer Temporalities, Queer Histories* (Durham, N.C.: Duke University Press, 2010). Dana Luciano likewise unsettles our normative attachments to time by focusing on what she calls "chronobiopolitics." See Luciano, *Arranging Grief: Sacred Time and the Body in Nineteenth-Century America* (New York: New York University Press, 2007). Peter Coviello meanwhile describes his approach to reading sex in the nineteenth century as "untimely" and "counterhistorical." I share his interest in "the emergence of modern sexuality [as a] slowly unfolding *process*" rather than an "event," as well as his interest in the ways that Foucault's sense of discourse has been both over- and underread. "The larger aim of *Tomorrow's Parties,* in its departures from practices of discursive contextualization," he argues, "is less to make clear the routes by which presexological forms of intimate relation came to arrive at what we now recognize as modern habitations of sexuality than to trace, in as much detail as we can, the outlines of any number of broken-off, uncreated futures, futures that would not come to be." While I see (and find compelling) the evidence of historical break that Coviello describes in his attention to the "broken-off" futures of sexuality, I would argue that these forms of sexuality are not as discarded as Coviello suggests. To consider the vestigial history of sexual types as place types, for instance, asks that we not just consider history's discards but assess the ways in which seemingly discarded histories have been partially metabolized

by the concept of sexuality itself, even when they seem to be disowned. See Coviello, *Tomorrow's Parties: Sex and the Untimely in Nineteenth-Century America* (New York: New York University Press, 2013), 20.

19. Such challenges to the whiteness of queer studies emerged especially in the late 1990s and early 2000s from the vantage point of queer-of-color scholarship. See David L. Eng, Judith [Jack] Halberstam, and José Esteban Muñoz, eds., "What's Queer about Queer Studies Now?" special issue, *Social Text* 84–85 (Fall/Winter 2005). Other work that expanded the terrain of queer scholarship includes David L. Eng, *Racial Castration: Managing Masculinity in Asian America* (Durham, N.C.: Duke University Press, 2001); Robert F. Reid-Pharr, *Black Gay Man: Essays* (New York: New York University Press, 2001); and Siobhan B. Somerville, *Queering the Color Line: Race and the Invention of Homosexuality in American Culture* (Durham, N.C.: Duke University Press, 2000).

20. Stephen Best and Sharon Marcus, "Surface Reading: An Introduction," *Representations* 108, no. 1 (Fall 2009): 3, 11, 10.

21. Franco Moretti's concept of "distant reading" depends on creating visual representations of large data sets of print culture in an effort to understand, for instance, the peaks and valleys of genre proliferation over time. See Moretti, *Graphs, Maps, Trees: Abstract Models for a Literary Theory* (New York: Verso, 2005). Bruno Latour meanwhile calls for a "sociology of associations." Latour critiques both structural approaches to the social ("Structure is very powerful and yet much too weak and remote to have any efficacy") and purely small-scale interpretive sites of the social ("But an 'interpretative' sociology is just as much a sociology of the social than any of the 'objectivist' or 'positivist' versions it wishes to replace. It believes that certain types of agencies—persons, intention, feeling, work, face-to-face interaction—will *automatically* bring life, richness, and 'humanity'"). Latour thus embraces an empiricist approach to sociology that "traces a network" but that, in effect, requires tracking the social oscillations between structure and epiphenomenon to understand the force of each on the other. Latour, *Reassembling the Social: An Introduction to Actor-Network-Theory* (Oxford: Oxford University Press, 2005), 9, 168, 61, 128.

22. Lauren Berlant, *Cruel Optimism* (Durham, N.C.: Duke University Press, 2011), 12.

23. I see this work as a companion approach to Kevin Ohi's discussion of the queerness of transmission. Ohi is concerned with the ways in which queer culture "move[s] from generation to generation" and asks "what is queer about the transmission of literary and cultural knowledge, and what conclusions might be drawn about the effects of that queerness on the

literary 'objects.'" Kevin Ohi, *Dead Letters Sent: Queer Literary Transmission* (Minneapolis: University of Minnesota Press, 2015): 1. My approach to circulation is less concerned with tracking the failures and possibilities of queer transmission than with seeing circulation as a means of understanding the conditions under which queerness becomes legible as such even prior to its transmittability.

24. See Emily Apter, *Against World Literature: On the Politics of Untranslatability* (New York: Verso, 2013); Wai Chee Dimock, "Deep Time: American Literature and World History," *American Literary History* 13, no. 4 (Winter 2001): 755–75; David Damrosch, *What Is World Literature?* (Princeton, N.J.: Princeton University Press, 2003); and Gayatri Chakravorty Spivak, *Death of a Discipline* (New York: Columbia University Press, 2003).

25. Michael Warner, *The Trouble with Normal: Sex, Politics, and the Ethics of Queer Life* (New York: Free Press, 1999), 139, 115–16.

Introduction

1. Roger Austen, *Playing the Game: The Homosexual Novel in America* (Indianapolis: Bobbs-Merrill, 1977), xiii.

2. Ibid., 1, xi.

3. Ibid., xiii. See also Jeannette H. Foster, *Sex Variant Women in Literature: A Historical and Quantitative Survey* (New York: Vantage, 1956).

4. Cited on the back cover of Eve Kosofsky Sedgwick, *Tendencies* (Durham, N.C.: Duke University Press, 1993).

5. Fiction equates almost exclusively with the novel here. This too-easy equation has been critiqued by a range of scholars, not just by theorists of narrative such as Northrop Frye, who long ago pointed to the "novel-centered view of prose fiction," but by scholars of LGBT writing such as Julie Abraham, who bemoans the novel's hegemonic status in lesbian writing. See Frye, *Anatomy of Criticism: Four Essays* (Princeton, N.J.: Princeton University Press, 1957), 304; and Abraham, *Are Girls Necessary? Lesbian Writing and Modern Histories* (Minneapolis: University of Minnesota Press, 2008).

6. Judith Butler has observed, "I'm not at ease with 'lesbian theories, gay theories,' for as I've argued elsewhere, identity categories tend to be instruments of regulatory regimes, whether as the normalizing categories of oppressive structures or as the rallying points for a liberatory contestation of that very oppression. This is not to say that I will not appear at political occasions under the sign of lesbian, but that I would like to have it permanently unclear what precisely that sign signifies." Butler, "Imitation

and Gender Insubordination," in *Inside/Out: Lesbian Theories, Gay Theories,* ed. Diana Fuss (New York: Routledge, 1991), 13–14. In a similar vein, Lee Edelman's *Homographesis: Essays in Gay Literary and Cultural Theory* (New York: Routledge, 1994) zeroes in on the instability of language to secure the meanings it announces for itself. Teresa de Lauretis, who coined the term *queer theory* in a special issue of *differences* in 1991, saw the term as a way to "recast or reinvent the terms of our sexualities, to construct another discursive horizon, another way of thinking the sexual." Teresa de Lauretis, "Queer Theory: Lesbian and Gay Sexualities," *differences: A Journal of Feminist Cultural Studies* 3, no. 3 (1991): iv. Disappointed by the ways in which she thought queer theory disarticulated itself from its roots in feminism, from theories of language, and specifically from the sexual, de Lauretis would soon distance herself from it, though she has recently written again in response to trends in current queer studies to offer her thoughts on the relationship of the sexual to the queerness of language in a discussion of "bad habits." She returns to her early commitments in queer theory when she says, "I call queer a text of fiction—be it literary or audiovisual—that not only works against narrativity, the generic pressure of all narrative toward closure and the fulfillment of meaning, but also pointedly disrupts the referentiality of language and the referentiality of images, what Pier Paolo Pasolini, speaking of cinema, called 'the language of reality.'" In her analysis of *Nightwood,* for instance, she reads "sexuality as enigma without solution and trauma without resolution—sexuality as an unmanageable excess of affect that can find textual expression only in a figural, oracular language, in hybrid images and elaborate conceits, or in the stream of allusions, parables, and prophesies with which the doctor attempts to fill the chasm between language and the real." Teresa de Lauretis, "Queer Texts, Bad Habits, and the Issue of a Future," *GLQ: A Journal of Lesbian and Gay Studies* 17, nos. 2–3 (2011): 244–45. What all of these thinkers display is a commitment to understanding *queer* not just as the umbrella term for all possible sexualities, but as a disruptive term, resistant to the norms of both sexuality and meaning-making, a site of specifically sexual resistance to identitarian norms.

7. Christopher Looby, "The Literariness of Sexuality: Or, How to Do the (Literary) History of (American) Sexuality," *American Literary History* 25, no. 4 (Winter 2013): 841–42.

8. Ian Hacking, *Historical Ontology* (Cambridge, Mass.: Harvard University Press, 2002), 100, 106.

9. See, for instance, Lisa L. Moore, *Dangerous Intimacies: Toward a Sapphic History of the British Novel* (Durham, N.C.: Duke University Press,

1997); Randolph Trumbach, "Sodomy Transformed: Aristocratic Libertinage, Public Reputation, and the Gender Revolution of the Eighteenth Century," *Journal of Homosexuality* 19, no. 2 (1990): 105–24; Valerie Traub, *The Renaissance of Lesbianism in Early Modern England* (Cambridge: Cambridge University Press, 2002); Jonathan Goldberg, ed., *Queering the Renaissance* (Durham, N.C.: Duke University Press, 1994); and Bruce Smith, *Homosexual Desire in Shakespeare's England: A Cultural Poetics* (Chicago: University of Chicago Press, 1991).

10. Alex Woloch, *The One vs. the Many: Minor Characters and the Space of the Protagonist in the Novel* (Princeton, N.J.: Princeton University Press, 2003), 14.

11. Matthew Garrett, *Episodic Poetics: Politics and Literary Form after the Constitution* (New York: Oxford University Press, 2014), 6.

12. Mitchell and Leavitt, introduction to *Pages Passed from Hand to Hand,* xvii.

13. Lord Alfred Douglas, "Two Loves," *Chameleon* 1, no. 1 (1894): 28. Douglas was Oscar Wilde's lover.

14. See Eve Kosofsky Sedgwick, "The Beast in the Closet: James and the Writing of Homosexual Panic," in *Epistemology of the Closet* (Berkeley: University of California Press, 1990), 182–212.

15. See Andrew Marvell, "To His Coy Mistress," in *The Norton Anthology of English Literature,* 8th ed., ed. Stephen Greenblatt et al., vol. B, *The Sixteenth Century and the Early Seventeenth Century* (New York: Norton, 2006), 1703.

16. See, for instance, Jonathan Culler, "Toward a Theory of Non-Genre Literature," in *The Theory of the Novel,* ed. Michael McKeon (Baltimore: Johns Hopkins University Press, 2000), 51–56.

17. See Ludwig Wittgenstein, *On Certainty,* ed. G. E. M. Anscombe and G. H. von Wright, trans. Denis Paul and G. E. M. Anscombe (New York: Harper, 1972 [1969]); and *Philosophical Investigations,* 4th ed., ed. P. M. S. Hacker and Joachim Schulte, trans. G. E. M. Anscombe, P. M. S. Hacker, and Joachim Schulte (Hoboken, N.J.: Wiley-Blackwell, 2010) for more on the difference between making philosophical or theoretical distinctions on behalf of conceptual categories and the meanings commonly understood to attend those categories in everyday language worlds. It is precisely the extent to which the circulation of literary language in the material world produces new or revised categories of understanding like "sexuality" or "the gay and lesbian novel." I will also have more to say shortly about genre theory and novel theory as well as the utility of both for understanding the relationship between circulation and generic/conceptual change.

18. See Jacques Derrida's *Rogues: Two Essays on Reason,* trans. Pascale-Anne Brault and Michael Naas (Stanford, Calif.: Stanford University Press, 2005). Although Derrida is primarily concerned in this book with theorizing rogue states and discussing the problem of sovereignty, he grounds his concept of the rogue initially within urban space: "Rogues or degenerates [*les voyous ou les roués*] are sometimes brothers, citizens, compeers" (63). In asking "What makes them separate beings, excluded or wayward, outcast or displaced . . . ?" he points out that the rogue "is defined always in relation to some street . . . [*rue*] in a city, in the urbanity and good conduct of urban life: the voyou and the roué introduce disorder into the street; they are picked out, denounced, judged, and condemned, pointed out as actual or virtual delinquents, as those accused and pursued by the civilized citizen, by the state or civil society, by decent, law-abiding citizens, by their police, sometimes by international law and its armed police who watch . . . over all the paths [*voies*] of circulation—all the pedestrian zones, highways, sea and air routes, information highways, e-mail, the Web, and so on. Between the democrat and the asocial voyou, the proximity [*voisinage*] remains ambiguous, the inseparability troubling, despite some essential differences" (63–64). Of further note is Derrida's assessment of the term *voyou,* which he reads as an "interpellation" (64) and thus a positing within the law precisely through the designation of being putatively outside the law: "The voyou is always a second or third person, always designated in the second or third person. . . . The word not only has a popular origin and use but is intended to designate someone who, by social pedigree or by manners, belongs to what is most common or popular in the people" (64). To historicize the ways in which the rogue or *voyou* might be positioned vis-à-vis democracy, Derrida reaches back to Gustave Flaubert's 1865 concept of *voyoucratie*: a way of designating "marginal power, the delinquent counterpower of a secret society" (65).

19. See Butler, "Imitation and Gender Insubordination."

20. Michael Warner, *Publics and Counterpublics* (New York: Zone Books, 2002), 55–56.

21. Benjamin Lee and Edward LiPuma, "Cultures of Circulation: The Imaginations of Modernity," *Public Culture* 14, no. 1 (Winter 2002): 192, 210. See also Dilip Parameshwar Gaonkar and Elizabeth A. Povinelli, "Technologies of Public Forms: Circulation, Transfiguration, Recognition," *Public Culture* 15, no. 3 (Fall 2003): 385–97.

22. Karl Marx, *Capital: A Critique of Political Economy,* vol. 1, trans. Ben Fowkes (New York: Penguin, 1976), 268.

23. See Michael Warner, *The Letters of the Republic: Publication and the Public Sphere in Eighteenth-Century America* (Cambridge, Mass.: Harvard University Press, 1990); Mark Simpson, *Trafficking Subjects: The Politics of Mobility in Nineteenth-Century America* (Minneapolis: University of Minnesota Press, 2005); Meredith L. McGill, *American Literature and the Culture of Reprinting, 1834–1853* (Philadelphia: University of Pennsylvania Press, 2003); and Meredith L. McGill, *The Traffic in Poems: Nineteenth-Century Poetry and Transatlantic Exchange* (New Brunswick, N.J.: Rutgers University Press, 2008).

24. Robert Darnton, "What Is the History of Books?" *Daedalus* 111, no. 3 (Summer 1982): 67.

25. Roger Chartier, *The Order of Books: Readers, Authors, and Libraries in Europe between the Fourteenth and Eighteenth Centuries*, trans. Lydia G. Cochrane (Stanford, Calif.: Stanford University Press, 1994), x.

26. See, for example, Adriaan van der Weel, "The Communication Circuit Revisited." http://www.let.leidenuniv.nl/English/B&P/Eltext/CCRev.html.

27. See Robert A. Gross and Mary Kelley, eds., *A History of the Book in America*, vol. 2, *An Extensive Republic: Print, Culture, and Society in the New Nation, 1790–1840* (Chapel Hill: University of North Carolina Press, 2010); Scott E. Casper et al., eds., *A History of the Book in America*, vol. 3, *The Industrial Book, 1840–1880* (Chapel Hill: University of North Carolina Press, 2007); Carl F. Kaestle and Janice A. Radway, eds., *A History of the Book in America*, vol. 4, *Print in Motion: The Expansion of Publishing and Reading in the United States, 1880–1940* (Chapel Hill: University of North Carolina Press, 2009).

28. For a more detailed history of the book and its distribution in America during the nineteenth century, see ibid. Volumes 2–4 outline the steady proliferation of publishers in nineteenth-century America, particularly in the Northeast, while also insisting on the local networks of print and reading, demonstrating, as Kaestle and Radway argue in volume 4, that there was no single nucleus of print culture.

29. Mark Simpson, *Trafficking Subjects*, xiii–xiv.

30. In his notebook James wrote of *The Bostonians*: "The subject is strong and good, with a large rich interest. The relation of the two girls should be a study of one of those friendships between women which are so common in New England. The whole thing as local, as American, as possible, and as full of Boston: an attempt to show that I *can* write an American story." James, *The Notebooks of Henry James,* ed. F. O. Matthiessen and Kenneth B. Murdock (Chicago: University of Chicago Press, 1974), 47.

31. Melville wrote this in a letter to *Typee's* first publisher, John Murray. Melville, *The Writings of Herman Melville,* vol. 14, *Correspondence,* ed. Lynn Horth (Evanston, Ill.: Northwestern University Press; 1993), 56.

32. An impressive body of literary criticism develops this claim. See, for instance, Richard Poirier, *A World Elsewhere: The Place of Style in American Literature* (Oxford: Oxford University Press, 1966); and Lawrence Buell, *The Environmental Imagination: Thoreau, Nature Writing, and the Formation of American Culture* (Cambridge, Mass.: Harvard University Press, 1995).

33. Jonathan Goldberg and Madhavi Menon argue that queering "requires what we might term 'unhistoricism'" and even "homohistory": "Instead of being the history of homos, this history would be invested in suspending determinate sexual and chronological differences while expanding the possibilities of the nonhetero, with all its connotations of sameness, similarity, proximity, and anachronism." While I see the political appeal of rejecting historical determinacy, I suggest that in its circulation, queer history cannot be deterministic in any case. We cannot predict in advance how history may circulate, in what form, and with what other contexts/texts of circulation it may resonate. Abandoning a commitment to careful empirical historical methods that would go along with creative queer readings seems to run the risk of producing a lot of inaccurate or bad queer history in the name of the mistaken virtue we might call "suspending determinacy" for its own sake. Goldberg and Menon, "Queering History," *PMLA* 120, no. 5 (October 2005): 1609.

34. Siobhan B. Somerville, *Queering the Color Line: Race and the Invention of Homosexuality in American Culture* (Durham, N.C.: Duke University Press, 2000), 3.

35. Sander L. Gilman, "Black Bodies, White Bodies: Toward an Iconography of Female Sexuality in Late Nineteenth-Century Art, Medicine, and Literature," *Critical Inquiry* 12, no. 1 (Autumn 1985): 218.

36. Jaime Hovey, "Sapphic Primitivism in Gertrude Stein's *Q.E.D.,*" *MFS* 42, no. 3 (Fall 1996): 549.

37. Lisa Duggan, *Sapphic Slashers: Sex, Violence, and American Modernity* (Durham, N.C.: Duke University Press, 2000), 27, 26.

38. Mark Rifkin, *When Did Indians Become Straight? Kinship, the History of Sexuality, and Native Sovereignty* (Oxford: Oxford University Press, 2011).

39. Kobena Mercer and Isaac Julien, "Race, Sexual Politics, and Black Masculinity: A Dossier," in *Male Order: Unwrapping Masculinity,* ed. Rowena Chapman and Jonathan Rutherford (London: Lawrence and Wishart, 1988), 106 (emphasis in the original).

40. Edward Prime-Stevenson, "From *The Intersexes*," in James Gifford, ed., *Glances Backward*, 4.

41. Vincent Woodard, *The Delectable Negro: Human Consumption and Homoeroticism within U.S. Slave Culture*, ed. Justin A. Joyce and Dwight A. McBride (New York: New York University Press, 2014), 24.

42. In a similar vein, Kyla Wazana Tompkins coins the term *queer alimentarity* to describe the phenomenon of the edible black body in late nineteenth-century American culture. See Tompkins, *Racial Indigestion: Eating Bodies in the 19th Century* (New York: New York University Press, 2012).

43. In light of Toni Morrison's argument that Africanism is central to the predominantly white literary imaginary of American literature, it is actually quite strange that so few of the fictional texts recovered from this period as gay and lesbian literature feature black characters. This exclusion seems so peculiar as to warrant a return to the archives to see what may well have been overlooked. See Morrison, *Playing in the Dark: Whiteness and the Literary Imagination* (Cambridge, Mass.: Harvard University Press, 1992).

44. M[ikhail] M. Bakhtin, "The Problem of Speech Genres," in *Speech Genres and Other Late Essays*, trans. Vern W. McGee, ed. Caryl Emerson and Michael Holquist (Austin: University of Texas Press, 1986), 65.

45. I have been using the words *homosexual, gay, lesbian*, and *queer* largely because these are the terms that seem to have persisted in usage. At the end of the nineteenth century, however, a much broader range of terms operated, including *sodomites, pederasts, urnings, Uranians, similisexualists, inverts, queers*, and, perhaps the strangest of all, *philarrhenic*. Derived from the Greek, this last word was Prime-Stevenson's adjective of choice in coining the category "American Philarrhenic literature." See Prime-Stevenson, "From *The Intersexes*," 4.

46. Michael N. Stanton, "The Novel: Gay Male," in *The Gay and Lesbian Literary Heritage: A Reader's Companion to the Writers and Their Works, from Antiquity to the Present*, ed. Claude J. Summers, rev. ed. (New York: Routledge, 2002), 486.

47. Sherrie Innes, "The Novel: Lesbian," in *The Gay and Lesbian Literary Heritage*, 491.

48. The identity politics of queer authorship have undergone a shift in recent years. Terry Castle takes on this position directly, arguing for the inclusion of a much broader range of texts, many written by men and by heterosexual women. See Castle, introduction to *The Literature of Lesbianism: A Historical Anthology from Ariosto to Stonewall*, ed. Terry Castle (New York: Columbia University Press, 2003), 1–56.

49. This argument is an important echo of Catharine Stimpson's claim that the lesbian—"as writer, as character, and as reader"—is "conservative

and severely literal. She is a woman who finds other women erotically attractive and gratifying. Of course a lesbian is more than her body, more than her flesh, but lesbianism partakes of the body, partakes of the flesh." Stimpson, "Zero Degree Deviancy: The Lesbian Novel in English," *Critical Inquiry* 8, no. 2 (Winter 1981): 364.

50. Bibliographies and field narratives of literary history—all of which have been central to the development of this project—began to be undertaken by feminists and scholars of what was then known as gay and lesbian studies. Jeannette H. Foster's 1956 *Sex Variant Women in Literature* sought to narrate the historical breadth and depth of literature featuring masculine women, women-loving women, asexual women, and women who might today be recognized as variously as lesbian, bisexual, transgender, or genderqueer. Barbara Grier's *The Lesbian in Literature* continued Foster's work by compiling a bibliography of books featuring lesbianism. Grier even coded the bibliography according to the degree of lesbianism featured: "A" for "major Lesbian characters and/or action"; "B" for minor characters/ action; "C" for latent, repressed, or "variant" lesbianism; and "T" for "poor quality" or, as she puts it, "trash." Grier's bibliography exists in three separate editions, published in 1967, 1975, and 1981. By 1981, Lillian Faderman, building in part on historical scholarship by Carroll Smith-Rosenberg, would update the narrative representation of lesbian literary history in *Surpassing the Love of Men*. Literature was Faderman's central archive, but in her introduction she suggests that the letters women writers exchanged with other women were just as important to her work. The project began with Faderman's interest in the letters and love poems between Emily Dickinson and her sister-in-law, Sue Gilbert, but in broadening the scope of her research, Faderman found that "it was virtually impossible to study the correspondence of any nineteenth-century woman, not only of America but also of England, France, and Germany, and not uncover a passionate commitment to another woman at some time in her life." The meta-cultural texts that framed these writers' lives were thus important evidence for Faderman's arguments. Her later work *Odd Girls and Twilight Lovers* expanded the contemporary frame of analysis that she had only begun to develop in *Surpassing the Love of Men*. See Foster, *Sex Variant Women in Literature*; Grier, *The Lesbian in Literature: A Bibliography*, 3rd ed. (Tallahassee, Fla.: Naiad, 1981), xix–xx; Faderman, *Surpassing the Love of Men: Romantic Friendship and Love between Women from the Renaissance to the Present* (New York: Morrow, 1981), 15–16; and Faderman, *Odd Girls and Twilight Lovers: A History of Lesbian Life in Twentieth-Century America* (New York: Columbia University Press, 1991).

Similarly, but separately, historians and literary critics compiled parallel accounts of writing by and about men, featuring romantic friendships, cross-dressing, and molly houses. Ian Young's *The Male Homosexual in Literature: A Bibliography* (Metuchen, N.J.: Scarecrow Press, 1975) was one of the earliest to document this literature. But Roger Austen argued, rightly, that no male equivalent to Jeannette Foster's 1956 book existed. He understood his later effort to track the "homosexual novel" in *Playing the Game* as a rejoinder to her earlier project. Indeed, the 1970s furnished us with important contributions to this emergent narrative about gay literary history, including Robert K. Martin, *The Homosexual Tradition in American Poetry*, rev. ed. (Iowa City: University of Iowa Press, 1998 [1979]), and *Hero, Captain, and Stranger: Male Friendship, Social Critique, and Literary Form in the Sea Novels of Herman Melville* (Chapel Hill: University of North Carolina Press, 1986); several books by Rictor Norton, including *The Homosexual Literary Tradition: An Interpretation* (New York: Revisionist Press, 1974), *Mother Clap's Molly House: The Gay Subculture in England, 1700–1830* (London: GMP, 1992), and *The Myth of the Modern Homosexual: Queer History and the Search for Cultural Unity* (London: Cassell, 1997).

51. In *Epistemology of the Closet*, Sedgwick argued for a "universalizing" rather than "minoritizing" approach to what she termed "antihomophobic" cultural analysis. One key virtue of this approach has been to regard social bonds ranging from the homosocial to the homosexual as central to culture more generally and not to be relegated to minor status.

52. Martin is quoted in Eric Savoy, "Arvin's Melville, Martin's Arvin," *GLQ: A Journal of Lesbian and Gay Studies* 14, no. 4 (2008): 609.

53. Austen, *Playing the Game*, xii.

54. Fiedler is famous for his description of "innocent homosexuality" as the central theme of American literature. Here he explains "why middle-class readers were not appalled at the implications of the homoerotic fable": "How could Antinoüs come to preside over the literature of the nineteenth-century United States, which is to say, at a time and in a place where homosexuality was regarded with a horror perhaps unmatched elsewhere and ever? Certainly, in the popular literature of the period, the 'sissy,' the effeminate boy, nearest thing to a fairy mentionable in polite books, was a target upon which the fury of a self-conscious masculinity vented itself with especial venom. In the long run, however, so violent a disavowal of male inversion fostered an ignorance of its true nature . . . 'evil love' could only be conceived of in connection with 'evil women,' and the relations of

males seemed therefore healthy by definition." Fiedler, *Love and Death in the American Novel* (New York: Criterion Books, 1960), 345–46.

For a reconsideration of Fiedler's infamous statement, see Christopher Looby, "'Innocent Homosexuality': The Fiedler Thesis in Retrospect," in *"Adventures of Huckleberry Finn": A Case Study in Critical Controversy,* ed. Gerald Graff and James Phelan (Boston: Bedford/St. Martin's, 1995), 535–51.

55. Austen, *Playing the Game,* xii. Louie Crew and Rictor Norton record a similar point of view: "One can, of course, simply refrain from writing on the subject that is nearest one's heart, and continue to accumulate notes for the work-in-progress for when the time is ripe. . . . One can do just about everything except utter the truth." Crew and Norton, "The Homophobic Imagination," 274. Like Stanton, Crew and Norton see truth or frankness as a sign of literary progress. But even in their analysis, "to accumulate notes for the work-in-progress" is an essential part of the process they record.

Austen comments on the specificity of the American context: "Compared with homosexual novelists abroad, early writers of gay fiction in this country were inhibited for several reasons—puritanism had a more terrifying effect on our writers, publishers, and readers, and in general America lacked an aristocracy of gentlemen loftily above the cares and concerns of the homophobic 'lower classes.' And as opposed to their compatriots who were writing poetry, the novelists suffered from having to specify who was doing what to whom, a problem that writers of gay verse were often able to circumvent. But in contrast to later American novelists faced with know-it-all Freudians who prided themselves on being able to recognize a 'fairy' when they saw one, our earlier gay writers were in a position to get away with a great deal—and some of them did." Austen, *Playing the Game,* 7.

56. Stimpson, "Zero Degree Deviancy," 364; ellipses original.

57. Abraham, *Are Girls Necessary?* xiii.

58. See Eve Kosofsky Sedgwick, *Between Men: English Literature and Male Homosocial Desire* (New York: Columbia University Press, 1985); Sedgwick, "Beast in the Closet"; D. A. Miller, "Anal Rope," *Representations* 32 (Fall 1990): 114–33; and Edelman, *Homographesis.*

59. Sedgwick, *Between Men,* 1.

60. D. A. Miller, *The Novel and the Police* (Berkeley: University of California Press, 1988), x.

61. See Valerie Rohy, *Impossible Women: Lesbian Figures and American Literature* (Ithaca, N.Y.: Cornell University Press, 2000); Kathryn R. Kent, *Making Girls into Women: American Women's Writing and the Rise*

of Lesbian Identity (Durham, N.C.: Duke University Press, 2003); Moore, *Dangerous Intimacies*; and Eve Kosofsky Sedgwick, ed., *Novel Gazing: Queer Readings in Fiction* (Durham, N.C.: Duke University Press, 1997).

62. Christopher Looby, "The Gay Novel in the United States, 1900–1950," in *A Companion to the Modern American Novel,* ed. John T. Matthews (Malden, Mass.: Wiley-Blackwell, 2009), 419–22.

63. Ibid.

64. Jordan Alexander Stein, "*The Blithedale Romance*'s Queer Style" *ESQ: A Journal of the American Renaissance* 55, nos. 3–4 (2009): 214.

65. It is interesting, for instance, that *queer,* long synonymous with unconventional or nonnormative, is, in some semantic contexts, a synonym for homosexuality, while in others it is a term preferred to (distinct from, even if it overlaps with) *homosexual, gay,* and *lesbian.* For accounts of the parameters of *queer,* see Michael Warner, introduction to *Fear of a Queer Planet: Queer Politics and Social Theory,* ed. Michael Warner (Minneapolis: University of Minnesota Press, 1993), vii–xxi; Judith Butler, "Critically Queer," in *Bodies That Matter: On the Discursive Limits of "Sex"* (New York: Routledge, 1993), 223–42; Eve Kosofsky Sedgwick, "Axiomatic," in *Epistemology of the Closet,* 1–63; Eve Kosofsky Sedgwick, "Queer and Now," in *Tendencies,* 1–19; and Eric Savoy, "You Can't Go Homo Again: Queer Theory and the Foreclosure of Gay Studies," *English Studies in Canada* 20, no. 2 (1994): 129–52. Despite the promise of *queer* to operate as an umbrella term for a wide range of sexual dissidence, scholars of transgender and transsexual studies have recently begun to question its limits based on the ways the term circulates. For instance, Jean Bobby Noble remarks on the extent to which in common parlance *queer* nonetheless continues to be a moniker of politically hip gay and lesbian (usually white) people than the more capaciously nonnormative upstart term it often purports to be. See Noble, *Sons of the Movement: FtMs Risking Incoherence on a Postqueer Cultural Landscape* (Toronto: Women's Press, 2006); and also Susan Stryker and Stephen Whittle, "(De)Subjugated Knowledges: An Introduction to Transgender Studies," in *The Transgender Studies Reader,* ed. Susan Stryker and Stephen Whittle (New York: Routledge, 2006), 1–17.

66. Claudio Guillén, *Literature as System: Essays Toward the Theory of Literary History* (Princeton, N.J.: Princeton University Press, 1971), 120, 111, 110. While I do not agree that form necessarily "matches" content (I think that often form conveys meaning that does not make itself manifest at the level of content), I do take seriously here Guillén's point that form can become content itself.

67. Bakhtin, "Problem of Speech Genres," 65.

68. See Michael McKeon, *The Origins of the English Novel, 1660–1740* (Baltimore: Johns Hopkins University Press, 1987).

69. See Marthe Robert, *Origins of the Novel*, trans. Sacha Rabinovitch (Bloomington: Indiana University Press, 1980).

70. See Northrop Frye, *The Secular Scripture: A Study of the Structure of Romance* (Cambridge, Mass.: Harvard University Press, 1976), 35–43.

71. Walter Benjamin, "The Storyteller: Reflections on the Work of Nikolai Leskov," in his *Illuminations,* trans. Harry Zohn, ed. Hannah Arendt (New York: Schocken Books, 1969), 87.

72. Sigmund Freud, *The Standard Edition of the Complete Psychological Works of Sigmund Freud,* vol. 4, *The Interpretation of Dreams (First Part),* ed. and trans. James Strachey (London: Hogarth Press and Institute of Psycho-Analysis, 1953), 279.

73. For other considerations of the novel's subgenres, see Georg Lukács, *The Historical Novel,* trans. Hannah Mitchell and Stanley Mitchell (London: Merlin, 1962); Nancy Armstrong, *Desire and Domestic Fiction: A Political History of the Novel* (Oxford: Oxford University Press, 1987); Kwame Anthony Appiah, "Is the Post- in Postmodernism the Post- in Postcolonial?" in *The Theory of the Novel,* ed. Michael McKeon (Baltimore: Johns Hopkins University Press, 2000), 882–99; and Michael McKeon, *The Secret History of Domesticity: Public, Private, and the Division of Knowledge* (Baltimore: Johns Hopkins University Press, 2005).

74. Gilles Deleuze and Félix Guattari, *Kafka: Toward a Minor Literature,* trans. Dana Polan (Minneapolis: University of Minnesota Press, 1986), 16, 18–20.

75. See Didier Eribon, *Insult and the Making of the Gay Self,* trans. Michael Lucey (Durham, N.C.: Duke University Press, 2004).

76. Michel Foucault, *History of Sexuality*, vol. 1, 18.

77. Ibid.

78. See Benjamin Lee, *Talking Heads: Language, Metalanguage, and the Semiotics of Subjectivity* (Durham, N.C.: Duke University Press, 1997); Michael Silverstein and Greg Urban, eds., *Natural Histories of Discourse* (Chicago: University of Chicago Press, 1996); Greg Urban, *Metaphysical Community: The Interplay of the Senses and the Intellect* (Austin: University of Texas Press, 1996); and Greg Urban, *Metaculture: How Culture Moves through the World* (Minneapolis: University of Minnesota Press, 2001).

79. Greg Urban, *Metaphysical Community,* 250.

80. Ibid., 256.

81. Gérard Genette, *Paratexts: Thresholds of Interpretation,* trans. Jane E. Lewin (Cambridge: Cambridge University Press, 1997 [1987]), 1–3.

82. Charles Sanders Peirce, *Collected Papers of Charles Sanders Peirce,* vols. 3–4, ed. Charles Hartshorne and Paul Weiss (Cambridge, Mass.: Harvard University Press, 1961), 423.

83. Hans Ulrich Gumbrecht, *Production of Presence: What Meaning Cannot Convey* (Stanford, Calif.: Stanford University Press, 2004), 2.

84. See Gumbrecht, *The Powers of Philology: Dynamics of Textual Scholarship* (Urbana: University of Illinois Press, 2003); and Lee, *Talking Heads,* 277–320.

85. For more on the agency of objects themselves, see Bill Brown, *A Sense of Things: The Object Matter of American Literature* (Chicago: University of Chicago Press, 2003); Bill Brown, ed., *Things* (Chicago: University of Chicago Press, 2004); and Peter Schwenger, *The Tears of Things: Melancholy and Physical Objects* (Minneapolis: University of Minnesota Press, 2006).

86. Warner, *Letters of the Republic,* xi.

1. Acquired Queerness

1. Charles Warren Stoddard, "In a Transport," in *South-Sea Idyls* (Boston: James R. Osgood, 1873), 302, 314.

2. There is some debate about what to call the narrator of *Typee.* Geoffrey Sanborn makes the case for referring to him as Herman Melville. Because his name appears as the author, he encourages readers to see his account as a true story. I have chosen here to refer to the narrator as Tommo because this is the only name by which he is known in the book. See Sanborn, introduction to *Typee,* ed. Geoffrey Sanborn (Boston: Houghton Mifflin, 2004), 1–14.

3. Initially the book was titled *A Narrative of Four Months' Residence among the Natives of a Valley of the Marquesas Island; Or, a Peep at Polynesian Life.* The title became more and more truncated over time, shifting first to *Typee: A Peep at Polynesian Life,* and eventually to the simpler *Typee.*

4. The extent to which Melville's *Typee* was an absolute best seller in the nineteenth century has been much debated by critics. Leon Howard states emphatically that "*Typee* was never a best-seller, even by the standards of the 1840s." Howard, historical note to the Northwestern-Newberry Edition of *The Writings of Herman Melville,* vol. 1, *Typee,* ed. Harrison Hayford, Herschel Parker, and G. Thomas Tanselle (Evanston, Ill.: Northwestern University Press; Chicago: Newberry Library, 1968), 298. Scholars have since modified this claim, focusing on reconsiderations of what counted as popularity and widespread circulation of the text. Sheila

Post-Lauria, for instance, documents *Typee*'s rise to the top of the best-seller list, situating it within the same literary culture that propelled Melville's literary compatriots to the same list—a list that, according to Post-Lauria, included George Borrow, Charles Briggs, Caroline Chesebro, James Fenimore Cooper, Fanny Forrester (Emily Chubbuck Judson), J. T. Headley, Caroline Kirkland, George Lippard, Catharine Maria Sedgwick, Anna Sophia Stephens, Harriet Beecher Stowe, and Bayard Taylor. See Post-Lauria, *Correspondent Colorings: Melville in the Marketplace* (Amherst: University of Massachusetts Press, 1996), 3. What we know about sales statistics gives us only part of the picture. Whatever we may want to say about *Typee*'s status as a best seller, one thing is clear: during Melville's lifetime, this book sold more than any other that he wrote, an estimated 9,598 copies in the United States and 6,722 in England. Today, *Typee* is arguably eclipsed by *Moby-Dick* as Melville's most read work. For sales statistics, see G. Thomas Tanselle, "The Sales of Melville's Books," *Harvard Library Bulletin* 17, no. 2 (April 1969): 195–215. We know much less about the extent to which the text circulated through pirated editions, though the culture of reprinting in the period of *Typee*'s initial publication would suggest that the text's circulation might be even more widespread than its print runs would indicate. On piracy and circulation during that time, see Meredith L. McGill, *American Literature and the Culture of Reprinting, 1834–1853* (Philadelphia: University of Pennsylvania Press, 2003).

5. Robert K. Martin, "Melville, Herman," in *The Gay and Lesbian Literary Heritage: A Reader's Companion to the Writers and Their Works, from Antiquity to the Present,* ed. Claude J. Summers, rev. ed. (New York: Routledge, 2002), 440.

6. Michael D. Snediker, "Melville and Queerness without Character," *Cambridge Companion to Herman Melville,* ed. Robert S. Levine (New York: Cambridge, 2014), 157, 159.

7. Ian Hacking argues that new social types, particularly homosexuality, only come into being and seem to multiply instances of social phenomena that have always been there when they are subject to scientific study. See Hacking, *Historical Ontology* (Cambridge, Mass.: Harvard University Press, 2002), especially the chapter "Making Up People," 99–114.

8. See Leslie Fiedler, *Love and Death in the American Novel* (New York: Criterion Books, 1960), 348. For a more recent treatment of non-innocent homosexuality in Melville, see Caleb Crain, "Lovers of Human Flesh: Homosexuality and Cannibalism in Melville's Novels," *American Literature* 66, no. 1 (March 1994): 25–53. See also Justin D. Edwards, "Melville's Peep Show; or, Sexual and Textual Cruises in *Typee*," in *Exotic*

Journeys: Exploring the Erotics of U.S. Travel Literature, 1840–1930 (Hanover, N.H.: University Press of New England, 2001), 20–32; Marc Maufort, "Exoticism in Melville's Early Sea Novels," *ALW-Cahier* 11 (1991): 65–75; Robert K. Martin, "'Enviable Isles': Melville's South Seas," *Modern Language Studies* 12, no. 1 (Winter 1982): 68–76; Robert K. Martin, *Hero, Captain, and Stranger: Male Friendship, Social Critique, and Literary Form in the Sea Novels of Herman Melville* (Chapel Hill: University of North Carolina Press, 1986).

9. Bryant argues that "in his revisions to his narrative—that is, his rethinking *now* of what he experienced *then*—we find his growing awareness of the relation of his evolving sexuality and his complicity in Western intervention." John L. Bryant, *Melville Unfolding: Sexuality, Politics, and the Versions of* Typee (Ann Arbor: University of Michigan Press, 2008), 73.

10. I do mean to evoke Stanley Fish's concept here, first presented in the essay "Interpreting the *Variorum*" but elaborated more fully in *Is There a Text in This Class?* Often taken to be a model for relativistic reading, Fish's concept highlights the way meaning is produced through the interpretive interaction between a text and its readers. The force of strong readers is part of what enables *Typee*'s emergence as a queer text, but its reputation as such depends on the multiplication not just of interpretive communities but of metatextual frameworks that develop and circulate independently of readers per se, as I will argue. In other words, I suggest that discursive circulation itself accrues agency that is not reducible to the agency of readers so central to Fish's model. See Fish, "Interpreting the *Variorum*," *Critical Inquiry* 2, no. 3 (Spring 1976): 465–85; and *Is There a Text in This Class? The Authority of Interpretive Communities* (Cambridge, Mass.: Harvard University Press, 1980).

11. Cindy Patton, *Globalizing AIDS* (Minneapolis: University of Minnesota Press, 2002), 7.

12. Foucault, *History of Sexuality,* vol. 1, 18.

13. The missionaries' focus is spelled out less as a cure for others' vices and more as a gift being presented to the islanders. Several American agencies published instructions for the missionaries, which outline their goals primarily in terms of what they need to accomplish among themselves as a group. See, for instance, the American Board of Commissioners for Foreign Missions, *Instructions to the missionaries about to embark for the Sandwich Islands; and to the Rev. Messrs. William Goodell, & Isaac Bird, attached to the Palestine Mission: delivered by the corresponding secretary of the American Board of Commissioners for Foreign Missions* (Boston: Crocker and Brewster, 1823). This document outlines the need for missionaries to

be united and to make themselves "available for piety." It cites friendship with the natives as being one of the keys to success but never really offers much description of what the missionaries will encounter when they arrive. I will have more to say about this and other missionary accounts later in this chapter.

14. Foucault, *History of Sexuality,* 18.

15. Editors have drawn this conclusion because they observe that Melville did not make these editions voluntarily and because the same kinds of sexual content and political critiques of missionary investments appear in later works like *Omoo* and *Mardi,* published by different presses. See Harrison Hayford, Herschel Parker, and G. Thomas Tanselle, "Note on the Texts," in *Typee, Omoo, Mardi,* ed. G. Thomas Tanselle (New York: Library of America, 1982), 1322–25. More recently, Geoffrey Sanborn endorsed the editorial decision, suggesting that it is the best compromise that could be brokered. His own edition is therefore also based on the Northwestern-Newberry Edition of *The Writings of Herman Melville,* originally published in 1968. Ironically, the Library of America editions are distributed by Penguin Putnam, a latter-day descendant of the same Wiley and Putnam that first published the revised American edition of *Typee.*

16. See the first nine pages of the 1846 Wiley and Putnam edition of *Typee.*

17. Nathaniel Hawthorne, *Salem Advertiser,* March 25, 1846.

18. Ibid.

19. William Oland Bourne, "*Typee:* The Traducers of Missions," *New York Christian Parlor Magazine* (July 1846): 75–76.

20. Melville, *The Writings of Herman Melville,* vol. 14, *Correspondence,* ed. Lynn Horth (Evanston, Ill.: Northwestern University Press; Chicago: Newberry Library, 1993), 56.

21. Perhaps the most ironically negative reviews of the revised edition of *Typee* are those that appear in the Hawaiian periodicals the *Friend* and the *Polynesian,* both published out of Honolulu. Daniel Aaron recounts the "antagonism which Melville's *Typee* and *Omoo* provoked among the so-called respectable element of the islands of the South Seas." Those who wrote these reviews tended to side with the missionary point of view, not with what Aaron describes as the "minority," who believed that the natives were not depraved until after the arrival of the white man. Melville was thus vilified for some time in the pages of both papers. As his marriage for instance was lampooned, the writers wondered whether Fayaway might not be offended. Aaron ends his article in sympathy with the sincerity of the papers' editors, if not in agreement with them. He cites a passage from the *Friend* dated April 1, 1853, that recounts, he claims "with almost naïf glee,"

"the story of a man so enamored with the spirit of *Typee*" that he "ordered fifty copies for circulation, but to complete the joke, his agent sent out the '2nd' instead of the '1st' edition, which, by the way, was expurgated of nearly every paragraph that breathed an anti-missionary spirit. The books lay for a long time unsold on the shelves of the auctioneer's store." Aaron, "Melville and the Missionaries," *New England Quarterly* 8, no. 3 (September 1935): 405, 408.

22. These included the anonymously published *The Modern Crusoe; or, King of the Cannibals of the Marquesas Islands* (London: James Henderson, 1869; first published in *Weekly Budget,* May–August), which actually plagiarizes Melville; Benjamin Barker, *Coriila; or, The Indian Enchantress: A Romance of the Pacific and Its Islands* (Boston: Flag of Our Union Office, 1847); Dora Hort, *Hena; or, Life in Tahiti,* 2 vols. (London: Saunders and Otley, 1866), in which the wife of a merchant in Pape'ete engages in an interracial romance; William Torrey, *Torrey's Narrative; or, The Life and Adventures of William Torrey* (Boston: A. J. Wright, 1848); James Bowman, *The Island Home; or, The Young Cast-Aways,* ed. Christopher Romaunt (Boston, 1851). Melville was translated into German by Friedrich Wilhelm Gerstäcker, who also penned *Tahiti: Roman aus der Südsee* (Leipzig: Costenoble, 1854); *Blau Wasser* (Leipzig, 1858); *Der kleine Wallfischfänger* [*The Young Whaler*] (Leipzig: Costenoble, 1856, 1858, 1876); *Inselwelt* (Leipzig: Arnold, 1860); and *Die Missionäre: Roman aus der Südsee,* 3 vols. (Iena: Costenoble, 1868).

23. Bill Pearson suggests that some "twenty-odd novels [were] set in the Pacific," mostly as propaganda for the missionary cause. Among these was a group of novels by William H. G. Kingston, including *Mary Liddiard; or, The Missionary's Daughter: A Tale of the Pacific* (London: Gall and Inglis, 1873). See Bill Pearson, *Rifled Sanctuaries: Some Views of the Pacific Islands in Western Literature* (Auckland: Aukland University Press, 1984), 56.

24. R. M. Ballantyne developed an entire series of travel books including *The Cannibal Islands; or, Captain Cook's Adventures in the South Seas* (London: James Nisbet, 1874); *Gascoyne the Sandal-Wood Trader: A Tale of the Pacific* (London: James Nisbet, 1864); *The Island Queen; or, Dethroned by Fire and Water: A Tale of the Southern Hemisphere* (London: James Nisbet, 1885); *The Lonely Island; or, The Refuge of the Mutineers* (London: James Nisbet, 1880); and *Philosopher Jack: A Tale of the Southern Seas* (London: James Nisbet, 1879).

25. *Robert Merry's Museum* (a nineteenth-century literary journal devoted to publishing children's literature) published what it claimed to be excerpts from *Typee*. (They were, however, more properly paraphrases of

some of the adventures in *Typee*—not taken directly from the text.) To a large extent, this budding genre of literature might be attributed to the success of *Swiss Family Robinson,* but there is clearly a Melvillian twist in the texts generated after 1846. See Mary C. Austin and Esther C. Jenkins, *Literature for Children and Young Adults about Oceania: Analysis and Annotated Bibliography with Additional Readings for Adults* (Westport, Conn.: Greenwood Press, 1996).

26. Quotations are taken from the Library of America edition of the text, based on the Northwestern–Newberry Edition of the writings of Herman Melville, which treats the 1846 first edition (not the first American edition) as authoritative. See Herman Melville, *Typee: A Peep at Polynesian Life,* ed. G. Thomas Tanselle, in *Herman Melville: Typee, Omoo, Mardi* (New York: Library of America, 1982), 13. Subsequent references to this edition will be parenthetical.

27. For an analysis of tattooing in *Typee* see Juniper Ellis, "Locating the Sign: Visible Culture," in *Tattooing the World: Pacific Designs in Print and Skin* (New York: Columbia University Press, 2008), 133–61.

28. As Melville would remark in his preface to *Omoo* (1847), the sequel to *Typee* (1846), "Nowhere, perhaps, are the proverbial characteristics of sailors shown under wilder aspects, than in the South Seas. . . . The Sperm Whale Fishery . . . is not only peculiarly fitted to attract the most reckless seamen of all nations, but in various ways, is calculated to foster in them a spirit of the utmost license." Melville, *Omoo: A Narrative of Adventures in the South Seas,* ed. G. Thomas Tanselle, in *Herman Melville: Typee, Omoo, Mardi* (New York: Library of America, 1982), 325.

29. In "Melville's Peep Show," Justin Edwards argues that the first writer to record this welcome by the Marquesan women is Nicholas Dorr, although sources would suggest that account is by Ebenezer (rather than Nicholas) Dorr and also that this account is much more muted than the account Melville would eventually provide. For more details, see Ebenezer Dorr, journal entry, April 17, 1791, "A Journal of a Voyage from Boston round the World," John Carter Brown Library, Providence, R.I.; quoted in *Joseph Ingraham's Journal of the Brigantine "Hope" on a Voyage to the Northwest Coast of North America, 1790–92,* ed. Mark D. Kaplanoff (Barre, Mass.: Imprint Society, 1971), 47, note 1. Captain David Porter, *Journal of a Cruise Made to the Pacific Ocean,* vol. 1 (Philadelphia: Bradford and Inskeep, 1815), 13. For a more detailed reading of the colonial dynamic at play in Melville's text, see Christopher McBride, *The Colonizer Abroad: Island Representations in American Prose from Herman Melville to Jack London* (New York: Routledge, 2004).

30. T. Walter Herbert Jr., *Marquesan Encounters: Melville and the Meaning of Civilization* (Cambridge, Mass.: Harvard University Press, 1980), 8.

31. Western accounts genuinely puzzle over why the native women would swim to foreign boats so seemingly seductively. In his *History of the Sandwich Islands,* the Princeton-born Baptist Ephraim Eveleth explains the behavior by way of the islanders' mythology. See Eveleth, *History of the Sandwich Islands: With an Account of the American Mission Established There in 1820* (Philadelphia: American Sunday-School Union, 1829), 25–26.

32. Porter, *Journal of a Cruise Made to the Pacific Ocean,* 1:13.

33. Ibid.

34. Ibid.

35. C. S. Stewart, *A Visit to the South Seas, in the United States' Ship 'Vincennes,' during the Years 1829 and 1830,* vol. 1 (London: Henry Colburn and Richard Bentley, 1832), 206.

36. Ibid.

37. Eveleth, *History of the Sandwich Islands,* 167.

38. S. C. Bartlett, *Historical Sketch of the Hawaiian Mission, and the Missions to Micronesia and the Marquesas Islands* (Boston: American Board of Commissioners for Foreign Missions, 1869), 5–6.

39. Another statement of the missionaries' goals appears in a three-page broadside in 1836, which responds to criticisms of the American missions in newspapers of the Hawaiian Islands. The *Sandwich Islands Gazette* had cataloged a series of abuses by the missionaries, to which the Sandwich Islands Mission responded: "To the friends of civilization and Christianity: Whereas differences of opinion have arisen, respecting the objects and operations of this *mission,* we feel it incumbent on us to state publicly the ends at which we aim. . . . The general object of the American Board of Commissioners for Foreign Missions . . ." (emphasis in original). Their most explicit statement of the project quotes directly from an earlier document outlining their directions: "The instructions and charge given to the members of this mission, were given in public, and have been widely circulated for the inspection of the world. In these we are commanded 'to aim at nothing short of covering these islands with fruitful fields and pleasant dwellings, and school and churches, and raising up the whole people to an elevated state of Christian civilization.' And to effect this, we are instructed to use our exertions, 'to introduce and get into extended operation and influence among them the arts, institutions, and usages of civilized life and society: above all to convert them from their idolatries, superstitions, and vices, to the living God.'" The official story of the missionaries is that they are more interested

in their own "exertions" than in cataloging the behaviors they are trying to alter. *The Sandwich Islands Mission,* broadside, 1836.

40. In the *Atlantic Monthly,* one reviewer blithely observed, without further comment, that the plot of Stoddard's "Chumming with a Savage" concerned "the history of the author's romantic friendship with a Tahitan [*sic*] boy." *Atlantic Monthly* 32, no. 194 (December 1873): 743.

41. One review of Stoddard's *South-Sea Idyls* makes it clear that *Typee* has settled into its status as novel and as narrative, and that in the ongoing publication of material the readings of *Typee* have begun to shift, as it resonated within the textual legacy it helped to generate. See "Literary Notes," *Appletons' Journal: A Magazine of General Literature,* November 1, 1873, 573–74.

Remarkable here, as in many reviews of Stoddard's book, are the terms of the reviewer's praise. Stoddard is credited with exceeding Melville because his offering seems more "true" and because he "has seized the very spirit and tone of life of which he tells."

Arthur Herman Wilson also comments on the similarities among the works of Stoddard, Melville, Stevenson, and other writers in terms of their representations of the South Seas. See Arthur Herman Wilson, "Escape Southward," *North American Review* 248, no. 2 (Winter 1939–40): 265.

42. Horace Traubel, *With Walt Whitman in Camden,* vol. 3 (New York: Mitchell Kennerley, 1914), 445.

43. Stewart, *Visit to the South Seas,* 1:204. See also Martin, *Hero, Captain, and Stranger*; and Edwards, "Melville's Peep Show."

44. For examinations of the significance and emergence of the bachelor type, see for instance Vincent J. Bertolini, "Fireside Chastity: The Erotics of Sentimental Bachelorhood in the 1850s," *American Literature* 68, no. 4 (December 1996): 707–37; Howard P. Chudacoff, *The Age of the Bachelor: Creating an American Subculture* (Princeton, N.J.: Princeton University Press, 1999); and Bryce Traister, "The Wandering Bachelor: Irving, Masculinity, and Authorship," *American Literature* 74, no. 1 (2002): 111–37. For extended explorations of the political and ideological ramifications of the bachelor figure for imaging the nation-state and reproductive time, see Michael Warner, "Irving's Posterity," *ELH* 67, no. 3 (2000): 773–99; and John Guillory, "The Bachelor State: Philosophy and Sovereignty in Bacon's *New Atlantis,*" in *Politics and the Passions, 1500–1850,* ed. Victoria Kahn, Neil Saccamano, and Daniela Coli (Princeton, N.J.: Princeton University Press, 2006), 49–74.

45. See Charles Lamb, "A Bachelor's Complaint of the Behavior of Married People," in *Essays of Elia* (Philadelphia: Henry Altemus, 1893),

225–34, originally published in 1823; James Fenimore Cooper, *Notions of the Americans: Picked Up by a Travelling Bachelor,* 2 vols. (London: Henry Colburn, 1828); and Herman Melville, "The Paradise of Bachelors and the Tartarus of Maids," *Harper's New Monthly Magazine,* April 1855.

46. For more fulsome discussions of the matter of queerness and literary bachelorhood in nineteenth-century America, see Christopher Looby, "Republican Bachelorhood: Sex and Citizenship in the Early United States," in *Homosexuality in the Eighteenth Century,* ed. Bryant T. Ragan Jr., a special issue of *Historical Reflections/Reflexions Historiques* (2007): 1–12; Katherine Snyder, *Bachelors, Manhood, and the Novel, 1850–1925* (Cambridge Cambridge University Press, 1999); and Michael Warner, "Irving's Posterity," *ELH* 67 (2009): 773–99.

47. Bruce A. Harvey, *American Geographics: U.S. National Narratives and the Representation of the Non-European World, 1830–1865* (Stanford, Calif.: Stanford University Press, 2001), 248, 247.

48. Rather than see Kory-Kory as a paragon of subjective complexity denied, Larzer Ziff sees his "resistant materiality" as a source of conflict for Tommo. The following passage from *Typee* exemplifies the matter for Ziff: "[Kory-Kory] rubs . . . slowly up and down . . . quite leisurely, but gradually quickens his pace, and waxing warm in the employment . . . approaches the climax of his effort, he pants and gasps for breath, and his eyes almost start from their sockets with the violence of his exertions" (*Typee,* 135). Ziff argues that "the author is here in touch with his own culturally created complexities, and their pressure upon him fuses an image of honest labor as sexual act in contrast with exploited labor as guilt-ridden sexuality." In Ziff's estimate, "The placing of physical love behind the curtain in America is an indication of the blockages between the body politic and the human body, of which, in a persistent, classical image, it is the enlargement." Ziff is more interested than I am in assigning meaning to Kory-Kory in terms of a symbol "of the psychic wound visited upon him by civilization and of wholeness that can be reclaimed by submission to the natural." While he reads this scene as symptomatic of a nineteenth-century American worldview that cloaks its desire for sexual expressiveness in a language of disavowal, I am interested in how Kory-Kory came to seem like such a logical embodiment of that problem to begin with. Ziff, *Literary Democracy: The Declaration of Cultural Independence in America* (New York: Viking, 1981), 7–9.

49. By the time Stoddard is writing, at the end of the nineteenth century, we know that the populations of the Polynesian islands have been decimated. Paul Gauguin famously went to the South Seas to paint its primitive cultures but arrived unable to find much of them left. Henry Brooks Adams

also saw in Tahiti a place for experimenting with the writing of history at its limits. He assembled/wrote *Memoirs of Marau Taaroa, the Last Queen of Tahiti* (privately printed in 1893). Marau Taaroa presumably responded, and her corrections were incorporated into the enlarged *Memoirs of Arii Taimai* (Paris, 1901). The fact that she claimed (or he did on her behalf) to have been the "last" queen of Tahiti is striking, but perhaps not surprising given that Europeans had been coming to the South Seas for almost two centuries. For information about Adams's text, I'm grateful to Virginia Gilmartin.

50. Melville, *The Writings of Herman Melville,* vol. 6, *Moby-Dick; or, The Whale,* ed. Harrison Hayford, Herschel Parker, and G. Thomas Tanselle (Evanston, Ill.: Northwestern University Press; Chicago: Newberry Library, 1988), 52.

2. The Stoddard Archive and Its Dissed Contents

1. Nor, it seems, did James much mind: Leon Edel records that James claimed he "enjoyed being feted by the Bohemian Club, where he talked with Charles Warren Stoddard, author of books and sketches about Hawaii and Tahiti." Edel, *Henry James: The Master, 1901–1916* (Philadelphia: Lippincott, 1972), 286.

2. Critics of his time generally liked his work—especially his travel writing—and there was a lot of it: in Howells's estimation, the stories in Stoddard's first collection, *South-Sea Idyls,* were "the lightest, sweetest, wildest, freshest things that were ever written about the life of that summer ocean." William Dean Howells, "Introductory Letter," in Charles Warren Stoddard, *South-Sea Idyls,* 2nd ed. (New York: Scribner's, 1892), v.

3. Carl Stroven, "A Life of Charles Warren Stoddard" (PhD diss., Duke University, 1939), 320.

4. John W. Crowley, editor's preface to Roger Austen, *Genteel Pagan: The Double Life of Charles Warren Stoddard,* ed. John W. Crowley (Amherst: University of Massachusetts Press, 1991), vii–viii.

5. Robert Gale, *Charles Warren Stoddard* (Boise, Idaho: Boise State University, 1977), 5.

6. Austen, *Genteel Pagan,* xliv.

7. Austen's *Genteel Pagan* sums up these reviews as follows: "Many of the replies were . . . faintly praising. Tennyson 'liked' the verses; Longfellow found 'a deal of beauty and freshness'; Emerson judged them 'good and interesting'; while Fr. John Henry Newman thought them 'elegant and touching.' Other responses were tactfully critical. William Cullen Bryant detected a 'certain unpruned luxuriance'; Henry Ward Beecher looked forward

to 'other maturer works'; . . . Bayard Taylor hesitated to prophesy whether Stoddard would 'become a part of our literature,' and Thomas Wentworth Higginson said it was too early to tell if 'verse is to be your appointed means of expression'—a view seconded by Thomas Hughes, who wrote that he did not think 'poetry will prove to be your vocation after a few years.'" Ibid., 33.

8. Mark Twain, *Autobiography of Mark Twain: The Complete and Authoritative Edition,* ed. Harriet E. Smith et al. (Berkeley: University of California Press, 2010), 1:161. Twain is also widely cited in scholarship on Stoddard to have characterized Stoddard as a "nice girl." In *Genteel Pagan,* Roger Austen cites a biography of Ambrose Bierce, but Bierce's biographer provides no documentation for the "nice girl" quip. I can find no original source for it and so I can only conclude that the quotation is apocryphal. This volume of Twain's letters addresses the quotation's dubious origin: *Mark Twain's Letters,* vol. 5, *1872–1873,* ed. Lin Salamo and Harriet Elinor Smith (Berkeley: University of California, 1997), 456, note 1.

9. William Dean Howells was a lifelong patron of Stoddard and even wrote a preface, in the form of an "introductory letter," to the 1892 edition of *South-Sea Idyls.* Howells deferred to the collection's "rare quality" and expressed his hope that "the whole English-reading world will recognize in your work the classic it should have known before." The 1873 and 1874 editions did not succeed as they should have, according to Howells, because in the first instance the book had been published on the "eve of the great panic of '73," and in the second instance the "London publisher defamed your delicate and charming text with illustrations so vulgar and repulsive." Howells, "Introductory Letter," in Stoddard, *South-Sea Idyls,* 2nd ed. (New York: Scribner's, 1892), v–vi. Howells seems to suggest that the illustrations done by an English artist are almost pornographic. The London edition that Howells mentions was published with the title *Summer Cruising in the South Seas,* illustrated by Wallis Mackay (London: Chatto and Windus, [1874]). Rudyard Kipling also saw some genius in Stoddard's novel, originally titled *So Pleased to Have Met You,* which he described as a "rummy, queer, original, fascinating" story and urged Stoddard to publish. It was Kipling who also suggested the definitive title, *For the Pleasure of His Company.* Kipling, "Rudyard Kipling at Naulakha," *National Magazine,* June 1905.

10. In addition to a book of poetry, his collection of short stories (which was released in at least nine separate editions in America and Britain), and his novel, Stoddard also was amazingly prolific as an essayist and a scholar. Some of his sketches of California life, *In the Footprints of the Padres* (San

Francisco: A. M. Robertson, 1902), continue to have a minor following. "A Bit of Old China," one of the earliest descriptions of San Francisco's Chinatown, is available through Project Gutenberg and earns Stoddard recognition as one of the earliest California writers. He also wrote about Henry Wadsworth Longfellow, whose poetry he loved from the time he was a teenager, and produced an edition of Richard Henry Dana's *Two Years Before the Mast.*

11. Review of *South-Sea Idyls, Literary World: A Monthly Review of Current Literature* (November 1873): 81.

12. Review of *South-Sea Idyls, Overland Monthly* (December 1873): 577.

13. Ibid. The nonmoralistic nature of these reviews arguably gives us some insight into the racial construction of sexuality at this point in history, since the "sensuous people" the reviewers see in Stoddard's work can be so blithely described as foreign brown people. (In fact, Stoddard calls attention to the dimensions of such a cross-cultural encounter as well as its ironic reversals in his novella "Chumming with a Savage.") Stoddard's work makes sense in light of recent developments in queer theory that seek to understand how Western assumptions about the intersections between race and sexuality locate racial and exotic communities as sites of queer cultural production. See, for instance, Gayatri Gopinath, *Impossible Desires: Queer Diasporas and South Asian Public Cultures* (Durham, N.C.: Duke University Press, 2005); and David L. Eng, Judith [Jack] Halberstam, and José Esteban Muñoz, eds., "What's Queer about Queer Studies Now?" special issue, *Social Text* 84–85 (Fall/Winter 2005).

That most reviewers overlooked both the racial and the sexual dimensions of Stoddard's writing may seem all the more striking to us today given that Stoddard was a contemporary of Oscar Wilde and Walt Whitman, both of whom were excoriated on moral grounds in the American press. The absence of pejorative adjectives within reviews of Stoddard's work can be seen, for instance, in the *Atlantic Monthly* where one unnamed reviewer observes, without further comment, that the plot of Stoddard's "Chumming with a Savage" concerned "the history of the author's romantic friendship with a Tahitan [sic] boy" ("Recent Literature," *Atlantic Monthly* 32, no. 194 [December 1873]: 743). The setting itself seemed to license both a social sexual practice and an idealized and accepted mode of description for that practice. In fact, for the reviewers Stoddard's plot seems to be incidental to his accomplishment at the level of style or form. Stoddard never caused the moral stir that Whitman did when he wrote and circulated *Leaves of Grass.* This is perhaps because the world Stoddard described, in all its "barbaric" sexuality, was a world that was not American, even though it flourished, at least in Stoddard's incarnation of it, as a product of American observation and imagination. The reviewers were essentially participating in a long history of tolerating the sexual proclivities of a cultural and racial elsewhere. As central as this aspect was to the fabric of the sketches and to the plots of Stoddard's stories, and as plainly presented as homosexuality was in the language of those stories, it never did raise ire or moral hackles.

14. Stoddard to Walt Whitman, April 2, 1870, *Walt Whitman Archive*, ed. Ed Folsom and Kenneth M. Price. http://whitmanarchive.org/biography/correspondence/tei/loc.01944.html.

15. Ibid.

16. Stoddard, Autograph Album of Charles Warren Stoddard, Collection of Charles Warren Stoddard Papers, Bancroft Library, University of California, Berkeley.

17. See Stoddard, "Rudyard Kipling at Naulakha." A letter to Stoddard from Herbert B. Turner, a Boston publisher, refers to this article on Kipling (July 7, 1905, Boston): "Last month I read with delight Dad's Visit to Kipling. I have read some of the others. They are all interesting and I have heard them spoken about. After the Christmas number is issued, how would you like a collection of these in book form adding a few more—something on Stevenson, Mark Twain, and Bret Harte would be relished keenly. Howells would probably allow you to write something about him. Why can't you do it?

"Dad, did I tell you I had ordered a copy of the new edition of 'Idyls'? I'm going to send it to you to autograph when I get it as it has been my custom with you." These materials appear in Stoddard's papers currently housed at the Bancroft Library, University of California Berkeley, box 1 (Letters), file 129.

18. Stoddard to Howard Sutherland, July 14, 1903, box 1, folder 5, Collection of Charles Warren Stoddard Papers, Bancroft Library, University of California, Berkeley (emphasis in original). What Howard said about children and Christmas was not clear from this letter; I have not been able to locate the letter to which this one is responding.

19. Stoddard was introduced to Noguchi through Joaquin Miller. Noguchi lived first with Miller and later with Stoddard for a while. Stoddard's role in supporting and facilitating Noguchi's rise as one of the earliest Japanese American writers would make for a fascinating study, especially given the multiple love triangles in which Stoddard and Noguchi were involved.

20. Stoddard's letters reveal elaborate, parallel correspondences with Noguchi and Ames during their period of courtship, during which Stoddard

was obviously also Noguchi's lover. Ames did review Stoddard's work, but it was also clear from Stoddard's correspondence with editors, including Frank Putnam, that he resented Ames's work and would often point out her grammatical and factual errors. On several occasions, he asked others if they would allow him to edit Ames's work.

21. Stoddard to Yone Noguchi, June 1904, Yone Noguchi Papers: Additions, 1896–1894, 1971 BANC MSS 71/39, Bancroft Library, University of California, Berkeley.

22. Arthur MacKay, one of Stoddard's admirers, wrote several letters to him, enclosing poems or referring to magazines he'd received in the mail. All his letters were signed "Your Kid"; MacKay even signed one on behalf of all the "Kids": "All the clan send their love—as does your Kid—Arthur L. MacKay." Arthur L. MacKay to Stoddard, August 20, 1905, Collection of Charles Warren Stoddard Papers, Bancroft Library, University of California, Berkeley.

23. See the letter to Stoddard from Herbert B. Turner, dated July 7, 1905, which also addresses Stoddard's status at the heart of the late nineteenth-century publishing world (note 17 above).

24. Stoddard to Walt Whitman, March 2, 1869 (emphasis in original), *Walt Whitman Archive*. http://whitmanarchive.org/biography/correspondence/tei/loc.01943.html.

25. Ibid.

26. Herman Melville, *The Writings of Herman Melville*, vol. 14, *Correspondence*, ed. Lynn Horth (Evanston, Ill.: Northwestern University Press; Chicago: Newberry Library, 1993), 399. Austen points to a doctor's diagnosis as the reason that Stoddard first went to Hawaii: having become a "nervous wreck," Stoddard was advised to take a long sea voyage and he chose Hawaii. (He had been living in San Francisco at the time.) Even a cursory reading of the available biographical material on Stoddard would generate a complex rationale for his first trip to the South Seas: he was suffering from a psychological malaise, struggling with his studies and, according to Austen, suffering from the homophobia that surrounded him. Austen, *Genteel Pagan*, 26.

27. Charles Warren Stoddard, "In a Transport," in *South-Sea Idyls* (Boston: James R. Osgood, 1873), 314.

28. There is some evidence that Stoddard may have written again to Melville. Melville's edited correspondence indicates that among his letters appeared a leaf to which, at one time, Melville had attached the copy of a second letter "To Charles Warren Stoddard." This letter has been lost, however, so its contents remain unknown. See Melville, *Correspondence*, 399.

29. Stoddard, "In a Transport," 314. I discuss Stoddard's reference to Melville in this story at the beginning of chapter 1.

30. Stoddard, *In the Footprints of the Padres*, 2–3.

31. Bayard Taylor, "To a Persian Boy: In the Bazaar at Smyrna," in *Poems of the Orient* (Boston: Ticknor and Fields, 1855), 124.

32. Stoddard to Whitman, March 2, 1869, *Walt Whitman Archive*. http://whitmanarchive.org/biography/correspondence/tei/loc.01943.html.

33. Eve Kosofsky Sedgwick, *Between Men*, 204.

34. Michael Warner, introduction to *The Portable Walt Whitman*, ed. Michael Warner (New York: Penguin, 2004), xxxi.

35. Jonathan Ned Katz, *Love Stories: Sex between Men before Homosexuality* (Chicago: University of Chicago Press, 2001), 203.

36. Whitman admitted that "those tender & primitive personal relations away off there in the Pacific Islands, as described by you, touched me deeply." Walt Whitman to Charles Warren Stoddard, June 12, 1869, *Walt Whitman Archive*. http://whitmanarchive.org/biography/correspondence/tei/loc.01685.html.

37. Stoddard, "A South-Sea Idyl," *Overland Monthly* (September 1869): 258.

38. Stoddard to Walt Whitman, April 2, 1870, *Walt Whitman Archive*. http://whitmanarchive.org/biography/correspondence/tei/loc.01944.html.

39. Horace Traubel, Whitman's friend and secretary, reports that when he and Whitman read through this letter in Camden, Whitman described Stoddard as follows: "He is of a simple direct naïve nature—never seemed to fit in very well with things here: many of the finest spirits don't—seem to be born for another planet—seem to have got here by mistake: they are not too bad—no: they are too good: they take their stand on a plane higher than the average practice. You would think they would be respected for that, but they are not: they are almost universally agreed to be fools—they are derided rather than reverenced." Traubel, *With Walt Whitman in Camden*, vol. 3 (New York: Mitchell Kennerley, 1914), 445.

40. Walt Whitman to Charles Warren Stoddard, April 23, 1870, *Walt Whitman Archive*. http://whitmanarchive.org/biography/correspondence/tei/loc.01686.html.

41. See Friedrich Schiller, "On Naïve and Sentimental Poetry," trans. William F. Wertz Jr., in *Friedrich Schiller: Poet of Freedom*, vol. 3 (Washington, D.C.: Schiller Institute, 1990), 307–98.

42. Stoddard, "Chumming with a Savage," in *South-Sea Idyls*, 25–79.

43. Stoddard, *For the Pleasure of His Company* (San Francisco: Gay Sunshine Press, 1987), back cover.

44. Stoddard, *For the Pleasure of His Company: An Affair of the Misty City* (San Francisco: A. M. Robertson, 1903), 135.

45. Lauren Berlant, "Love (A Queer Feeling)," in *Psychoanalysis and Homosexuality,* ed. Tim Dean and Christopher Lane (Chicago: University of Chicago Press, 2001), 432–51.

46. Stoddard, *For the Pleasure of His Company* [1905], 135.

3. Type Complication and Literary Old Maids

1. It has often been said that the old maid seems to disappear from literature in the twentieth century. For some time the view was so widespread that several recent books take as their starting point a reclamation of the figure, arguing that she is still alive and kicking, living in a striking array of novels for so seemingly obsolete a figure. See Laura L. Doan, ed., *Old Maids to Radical Spinsters: Unmarried Women in the Twentieth-Century Novel* (Urbana: University of Illinois Press, 1991); Naomi Braun Rosenthal, *Spinster Tales and Womanly Possibilities* (Albany: State University of New York Press, 2002); Sheila Jeffreys, *The Spinster and Her Enemies: Feminism and Sexuality, 1880–1930* (London: Pandora Press, 1985); and Heather Love, "Gyn/Apology: Sarah Orne Jewett's Spinster Aesthetics," *ESQ* 55, no. 3–4 (2009): 305–34.

2. Brooke's *The Old Maid* ran as a weekly publication written under the pseudonym "Mary Singleton, Spinster." It may well count as one of the earliest and most sustained instances of type complication for the "old maid." The periodical ran for twenty-two issues from November 1755 until July 1756, and was later collated as a single volume in 1764. Throughout the series, Brooke disputes prejudice against unmarried women through the persona of the spiritedly independent Mary. Topics include experiences of courtship and marriage, often in an ironic tone.

What is also striking about Brooke's Mary is how in signing her name "Mary Singleton, Spinster" she highlights the extent to which *spinster* and *old maid* have come to be synonymous. By the middle of the nineteenth century, at least in most American writing, *old maid* becomes the preferred term—although, generally speaking, where *spinster* does appear (even in Brooke's periodical), it seems to have shed its originary association with the occupation of spinning. For more basic information on Brooke and her writing, see Rebecca Garwood's biographical sketch under the heading "Biographies of Women Writers" (www.chawtonhouse.org). For scholarly treatment of this periodical, see for instance K. J. H. Berland, "A Tax on Old Maids and Bachelors: Frances Brooke's *Old Maid,*" in *Eighteenth-Century Women and the Arts,* ed. Frederick M. Keener and Susan E. Lorsch

(New York: Greenwood Press, 1988), 29–35; Lorraine McMullen, "Frances Brooke's *Old Maid:* New Ideas in Entertaining Form," *Studies on Voltaire and the Eighteenth Century* (1989): 669–70; Elizabeth Larsen, "A Text of Identity: Frances Brooke and the Rhetoric of the Aging Spinster," *Journal of Aging and Identity* 4, no. 4 (December 1999): 255–68; and Min Wild, "'Prodigious Wisdom': Civic Humanism in Frances Brooke's *Old Maid,*" *Women's Writing* 5, no. 3 (1998): 421–35.

3. Henry James, *The Bostonians,* in *Novels, 1881–1886,* ed. William T. Stafford (New York: Library of America, 1985), 816.

4. Sarah Orne Jewett, "Martha's Lady," in *Two Friends and Other Nineteenth-Century Lesbian Stories by American Women Writers,* ed. Susan Koppelman (New York: Meridian, 1994), 212; subsequent references to this edition will be parenthetical. See also Henry James, *The Bostonians*; Mary Eleanor Wilkins Freeman, "A New England Nun," in *A New England Nun and Other Stories* (New York: Harper and Brothers, 1891), 1–17; Rose Terry Cooke, "How Celia Changed Her Mind," in *How Celia Changed Her Mind and Selected Stories,* ed. Elizabeth Ammons (New Brunswick, N.J.: Rutgers University Press, 1986), 131–50; and Harriet Beecher Stowe, *The Pearl of Orr's Island: A Story of the Coast of Maine* (London: Sampson Low, 1862).

5. See Nathaniel Hawthorne, *The House of the Seven Gables* (Boston: Ticknor, Reed, and Fields, 1851); and Harriet Beecher Stowe, *Uncle Tom's Cabin* (London: John Cassell, 1852).

6. Larzer Ziff, *The American 1890s: Life and Times of a Lost Generation* (New York: Viking, 1966), 293.

7. Jay Martin, *Harvests of Change: American Literature, 1865–1914* (Englewood Cliffs, N.J.: Prentice-Hall, 1967), 150; and Perry Westbrook, *Mary Wilkins Freeman,* rev. ed. (Boston: Twayne, 1988), 58–59.

8. Edward Foster, *Mary E. Wilkins Freeman* (New York: Hendricks House, 1956), 106.

9. David H. Hirsch, "Subdued Meaning in 'A New England Nun,'" *Studies in Short Fiction* 2, no. 2 (Winter 1965): 133.

10. Barbara Johns, "Some Reflections on the Spinster in New England Literature," in *Regionalism and the Female Imagination,* ed. Emily Toth (New York: Human Sciences Press, 1985), 44, 43.

11. Marjorie Pryse, "An Uncloistered 'New England Nun,'" *Studies in Short Fiction* 20, no. 4 (Fall 1983): 289–90.

12. Ibid., 293.

13. Dale M. Bauer, "The Politics of Collaboration in *The Whole Family,*" in Laura Doan, ed., *Old Maids to Radical Spinsters,* 108.

14. Benjamin Kahan, *Celibacies: American Modernism and Sexual Life* (Durham, N.C.: Duke University Press, 2013), 39–41.

15. Although Jewett's most famous text is *Country of the Pointed Firs,* there is a reasonable level of agreement among critics that her representations of sexual love between women appear in *Deephaven,* "The Queen's Twin," and "Martha's Lady."

16. Susan Allen Toth, "'The Rarest and Most Peculiar Grape': Versions of the New England Woman in Nineteenth-Century Local Color Literature," in *Regionalism and the Female Imagination,* ed. Emily Toth (New York: Human Sciences Press, 1985), 20.

17. See Susan Koppelman, ed., *Two Friends and Other Nineteenth-Century Lesbian Stories by American Women Writers.*

18. It is often argued that this explosion of fiction that imagines the lives of women beyond marriage (even from within the boundaries of married life) was propelled by the simple fact that in the post–Civil War United States, particularly in the Northeast, there was an unprecedented number of unmarried women, women who, furthermore, would have no prospect of marriage. Alice Kessler-Harris points out that after the Civil War, more women than ever before remained unmarried in the United States: "The *New York Times* estimated in 1869 that about a quarter of a million young women in the eastern seaboard states could never look forward to any matrimonial alliance, because they outnumbered men by that much." Kessler-Harris, *Out to Work: A History of Wage-Earning Women in the United States* (Oxford: Oxford University Press, 2003), 98. It is not surprising, therefore, that writers would begin to imagine lives for those women who would never be married by either choice or circumstance. Indeed, spinsters are ubiquitous in nineteenth-century American literature. Spinster characters were obviously not all imagined as perverse or as erotically attracted to other women. For more on the types of spinsters and nineteenth-century women, see Johns, "Some Reflections on the Spinster in New England Literature"; Toth, "'The Rarest and Most Peculiar Grape'"; and Kathryn R. Kent, *Making Girls into Women: American Women's Writing and the Rise of Lesbian Identity* (Durham, N.C.: Duke University Press, 2003).

19. Judith Fetterley and Marjorie Pryse, *Writing Out of Place: Regionalism, Women, and American Literary Culture* (Urbana: University of Illinois Press, 2003), 315, 316, 319.

20. Ibid., 321.

21. Such an argument would hold only in the context of claims such as Adrienne Rich's. Rich includes in her lesbian continuum all women who have significant relationships to other women. See Rich, "Compulsory

Heterosexuality and Lesbian Existence," *Signs* 5, no. 4 (Summer 1980): 631–60.

22. Catharine Maria Sedgwick, "Old Maids," in *Tales and Sketches* (Philadelphia: Carey, Lea, and Blanchard, 1835), 98; subsequent references to this edition will be parenthetical.

23. "The Heron: A Tale for Old Maids," *American Magazine and Historical Chronicle,* November 1744.

24. J. Roberts, "The Spinster: In Defence of the Woollen Manufactures," in *The Town Talk, the Fish Pool, the Plebian, the Old Whig, the Spinster, etc.,* by the authors of the *Tatler, Spectator, and Guardian* (London: John Nichols, 1789), 416; "The Female Manufacturers Complaint," in *The Town Talk, the Fish Pool, the Plebian, the Old Whig, the Spinster, etc.,* by the authors of the *Tatler, Spectator, and Guardian* (London: John Nichols, 1789), 436.

25. Oliver Goldsmith, *She Stoops to Conquer; or, The Mistakes of a Night* (London: F. Newbery, 1773), 113–14.

26. Margaret Fuller, *Woman in the Nineteenth Century* (New York: Greeley and McElrath, 1845), 84–85.

27. Stowe, *Uncle Tom's Cabin,* 134.

28. Hawthorne, *House of the Seven Gables,* 9, 15, 16.

29. Ibid., 36–37.

30. Sexual love between women often appears in fleeting literary moments and rarely finds itself the central focus of extended narratives. See Lisa L. Moore, *Dangerous Intimacies: Toward a Sapphic History of the British Novel* (Durham, N.C.: Duke University Press, 1997).

31. We can see this also in Herman Melville, "The Paradise of Bachelors and the Tartarus of Maids," *Harper's New Monthly Magazine* (April 1855). Much more could be said about this text, but it is significant that the bachelors are described in terms that convey a certain sensuality and a sense of belonging evidenced by their aristocratic names, while the anonymous maids seem stripped of any sensual life by their toil as mill workers.

32. Cooke did not marry until later in life. When she published this story, she did so as Rose Terry. Today's readers would probably recognize her as Rose Terry Cooke. Although Cooke has been recognized—especially by commentators on nineteenth-century American women's writing—this particular story has received scant attention. It was not included in any of the collections of Cooke's work published in her lifetime and resurfaced recently only in Susan Koppelman's collection *Two Friends.* Apart from passing references in broadly sketched introductions, the only critical attention paid to this story has been Ralph J. Poole's "Body/Rituals: The (Homo)

Erotics of Death in Elizabeth Stuart Phelps, Rose Terry Cooke, and Edgar Allan Poe," in *Soft Canons: American Women Writers and Masculine Tradition*, ed. Karen L. Kilcup (Iowa City: University of Iowa Press, 1999), 239–61.

Cooke's most well-known story is arguably "How Celia Changed Her Mind," which was included in *Huckleberries* (1891). The title character begins and ends the story as an old maid, with a brief excursion into a harsh marriage in between. By the end, she resolves to bring up children as "dyed-in-the-wool old maids." The elements we most readily identify with the local color tradition are more pronounced here: strong dialect writing and a clear sense of the peculiarities of place. This story was also included in Judith Fetterley and Marjorie Pryse's *American Women Regionalists* (New York: Norton, 1992), 137–53, as well as Elizabeth Ammons's collection of Cooke's work, *How Celia Changed Her Mind and Selected Stories*, 131–50. Other commentators on Cooke include Van Wyck Brooks (briefly) in *New England: Indian Summer, 1865–1915* (New York: Dutton, 1940), 85–88.

33. Rose Terry Cooke, "My Visitation," in *How Celia Changed Her Mind and Selected Stories*, ed. Elizabeth Ammons, 14; subsequent references to this edition will be parenthetical. Cooke does not provide the specific reference for this poem, beyond the title, assuming no doubt that the poem and its author would be well known to her audience. These lines are extracted from canto VI of Tennyson's long poem "The Princess: A Medley" (1847). Cooke's version includes asterisks that the original poem does not. She has not excluded any lines from the excerpt.

34. Elizabeth Ammons suggests that Cooke took up "the short story technique, as Poe had set it forth"; Ralph J. Poole also details parallels between Cooke's story and Poe's works (he points to "Ligeia," "Berenice," "Morella," and "Eleonora" in particular). See Poole, "Body/Rituals." Indeed, the story first appears in *Putnams*, a magazine that published some of Poe's work.

35. Terry Castle looks back as far as the eighteenth century to diagnose what she sees as a pattern of ghostly lesbianism in history: "Once the lesbian has been defined as ghostly—the better to drain her of any sensual or moral authority—she can then be exorcized." Castle, *The Apparitional Lesbian: Female Homosexuality and Modern Culture* (New York: Columbia University Press, 1993), 6. Among the pre-1858 texts that Castle uses to bolster her claims are Daniel Defoe's *The Apparition of Mrs. Veal*, Denis Diderot's *La religieuse*, Théophile Gautier's *Mademoiselle de Maupin*, and Charles Baudelaire's poem, "Femmes damnées," from *Les fleurs du mal*. She argues that this pattern extends up into twentieth-century literature as well.

36. See Valerie Rohy, *Impossible Women: Lesbian Figures and American Literature* (Ithaca, N.Y.: Cornell University Press, 2000).

37. Edward W. Said, *Orientalism* (New York: Vintage, 1979), 190.

38. With respect specifically to homosexuality, this can be seen particularly in the body of literary criticism that brings together postcolonial studies and queer theory. See, for instance, Robert Aldrich, *Colonialism and Homosexuality* (New York: Routledge, 2003); Philip Holden and Richard J. Ruppel, eds., *Imperial Desire: Dissident Sexualities and Colonial Literature* (Minneapolis: University of Minnesota Press, 2003); Christopher Lane, *The Ruling Passion: British Colonial Allegory and the Paradox of Homosexual Desire* (Durham, N.C.: Duke University Press, 1995); and Kate Chedgzoy, Emma Francis, and Murray Pratt, eds., *In a Queer Place: Sexuality and Belonging in British and European Contexts* (Aldershot: Ashgate, 2002).

A great deal of this work has focused on male desire. Joseph A. Boone has found "the sexual politics of colonial narrative" nowhere so explicitly thematized "as in those voyages to the Near East recorded or imagined by Western men," for whom "the geopolitical realities of the Arabic Orient become a psychic screen on which to project fantasies of illicit sexuality and unbridled excess." Boone, "Vacation Cruises; or, The Homoerotics of Orientalism," *PMLA* 110, no. 1 (January 1995): 89. See also Donald H. Mengay, "Arabian Rites: T. E. Lawrence's *Seven Pillars of Wisdom* and the Erotics of Empire," *Genre* 27, no. 4 (Winter 1994): 395–416; Ronald Hyam, *Empire and Sexuality: The British Experience* (Manchester: Manchester University Press, 1990), 46–47; and Joseph Bristow, *Empire Boys: Adventures in a Man's World* (New York: HarperCollins Academic, 1991), 226.

But a large body of literature has also focused on the peculiar status of women as both agents and objects of desire. See, for instance, Felicity Nussbaum's exploration of feminotopias in *Torrid Zones: Maternity, Sexuality, and Empire in Eighteenth-Century English Narratives* (Baltimore: Johns Hopkins University Press, 1995), 135–66; and Ruth Bernard Yeazell's treatment of women travelers in *Harems of the Mind: Passages of Western Art and Literature* (New Haven, Conn.: Yale University Press, 2000), 84–93. Christopher Lane highlights the difficulties that female agency and sexual desire pose for scholars of empire and sexuality who consider writing by and about female travelers. Often seen as either complicit with imperialism or as radically other to it, women travelers seem to be misunderstood by critics who overlook the ambiguity of eroticization that attends women travelers and their conceptualization of and attraction to the sexuality of the women they meet or see. Lane looks specifically at the writing of Mary Kingsley and in effect contextualizes the more well-known literature of sapphism and orientalism that emerges around the writing of Lady Mary Wortley Montagu. See Christopher Lane, "Fantasies of 'Lady Pioneers,' between Narrative and Theory," in *Imperial Desire*, ed. Philip Holden and Richard J. Ruppel, 90–114. For more on sapphism and orientalism in Lady Mary Wortley Montagu, see Nussbaum, *Torrid Zones*; and John C. Benyon, "Lady Mary Wortley Montagu's Sapphic Vision," in *Imperial Desire*, 21–43.

See also Susan S. Lanser's consideration of anonymity and lesbianism in "The Author's Queer Clothes: Anonymity, Sex(uality), and *The Travels and Adventures of Mademoiselle de Richelieu*," in *The Faces of Anonymity: Anonymous and Pseudonymous Publications from the Sixteenth to the Twentieth Century*, ed. Robert J. Griffin (New York: Palgrave Macmillan, 2003), 81–102; and Sally O'Driscoll, "'Lesbian' Literary History in the Eighteenth Century," in *Women and Literary History: "For There She Was,"* ed. Katherine Binhammer and Jeanne Wood (Newark: University of Delaware Press, 2003), 64–73.

39. In her survey of early twentieth-century lesbian magazine fiction, Lillian Faderman makes the influential, if disputed, argument that "before the 1920's women were permitted a broader spectrum of expressions of love for their own sex, primarily for two reasons: (1) love relationships between women were not threatening, since it was understood that women would marry if they could, for economic and social reasons, despite such affectional ties; (2) it was generally believed that women, being for the most part non-sexual outside of procreative activity, were entirely unlikely to engage in 'improper . . . intimate relations' with other females, and that those few who did transgress were easily identifiable through external characteristics. Although, as Hamilton points out, by mid-nineteenth century there were a number of French and German novels which dealt with love between women in a manner which suggested decadence and corruption, those novels—and even the late nineteenth century 'discoveries' of medical men—were unfamiliar to the mass of the population. Thus it was that popular magazine fiction, well into the twentieth century, could depict female-female love relationships with an openness that later became, as I shall discuss, impossible." Faderman, "Lesbian Magazine Fiction in the Early Twentieth Century," *Journal of Popular Culture* 11, no. 4 (Spring 1978): 802. As Faderman suggests, midcentury French and German texts were instrumental in making love between women familiar to a wide readership. But at the same time that Honoré de Balzac, Émile Zola, and others were being read by many Americans, American writers themselves were producing texts in English that read sexual illicitness back into those European contexts—even as they borrowed the stylistics of realism (particularly from France) to produce

their own indigenous literature (this literary nationalism ironically was also arguably the effect of a French writer, Hippolyte Taine, whose 1863 *Histoire de la littérature anglaise* began to see literature in terms of national boundaries).

40. Thanet explained in interviews that the first name of her pseudonym had been derived from that of her roommate at Andover Academy, Octavia Putnam. The last name she took from the printing on a boxcar she once saw. She liked the name because it could be taken as either male or female. Lillian Faderman averred that "Octave seemed to view humanity as having three sexes—men, women, and Octave Thanet," even though Faderman also suggests that "Thanet saw only the model of heterosexuality around her and never questioned its morality." Faderman, *Surpassing the Love of Men: Romantic Friendship and Love between Women from the Renaissance to the Present* (New York: Morrow, 1981), 215–16. Thanet was reasonably prolific in her time: she wrote six novels, published nine volumes of stories—none of which reprinted "My Lorelei"—some essays, and also edited a collection of *The Best Letters of Lady Mary Wortley Montagu* (1890). According to her biographer, George McMichael, "For thirty years, she was one of the highest paid authors in the United States." McMichael, *Journey to Obscurity: The Life of Octave Thanet* (Lincoln: University of Nebraska Press, 1965), 1. The title of McMichael's biography would prove apt: to date, few critical commentaries of her work exist. Thanet's persistent obscurity can be explained by the fact that, however intimate she became with the dialects of poor white and black workers in Clover Bend, Arkansas (dialects that featured prominently in her later writings and strongly situate them within the local color tradition), she was profoundly conservative when it came to questions of race and gender. She was a staunch advocate of traditional roles for women and spoke out against both suffrage and pacifism. Susan Koppelman summarizes Thanet as "anti-labor union, a xenophobic who portrayed foreigners as sinister figures, and a racist caricaturist; she opposed Prohibition and helped to organize against the suffragists, whom she saw as in league with all those whom she opposed." Koppelman, *Two Friends*, 78. Later in her work, Thanet would become fascinated with social and national types: her writings in the 1890s included essays such as "The Tramp in Four Centuries," "The English Workingman and the Commercial Crises," and "The Contented Masses." She published her first story in 1878, "Communists and Capitalists."

It seems plausible, therefore, to assume that either Thanet herself or her editors might have found "My Lorelei" inconsistent with or unrelated to her later political views. I think an argument could be made, however, that

Thanet's literary conservatism played a strong role in the writing of this story, just as it would for other writers grasping toward familiar forms to make sense of content that had fewer literary conventions to call its own.

41. Thanet's papers are housed at the Newberry Library in Chicago. Her journals have never been published, and there is no other source for this information in print. I have not been able to verify this claim, although it hardly seems unreasonable, and McMichael's biography relies heavily on this archive. See McMichael, *Journey to Obscurity*.

42. References to the famous Lorelei tale could be found in just about any nineteenth-century periodical. In fact, during the decades preceding the publication of "My Lorelei," such references abounded in literary and artistic magazines, not only in places one might expect, like *The Eclectic Magazine of Foreign Literature*. During the 1870s, Lady Blanche Murphy published a series of stories set on the Rhine in magazines such as *Frank Leslie's Popular Monthly* and *Lippincott's*. Indeed, Thanet could never resist making at least one reference to the Lorelei at some point in these stories. Heinrich Heine and his Lorelei seemed to appeal particularly to women: Emma Lazarus translated and published some of Heine's poems in 1867. Some, like Rachel Pomeroy, published poems titled "Lorelei," while countless others regularly dropped in references to Lorelei without ever feeling the need to explain the reference itself; it was presumed to be so widely known that neither its origin nor its author needed to be identified. I have an entire file of periodical pieces from American magazines that refer to the Lorelei story, some more casually than others. No others that I've been able to find insist on any lesbian reading of the story, although most treat that tale as an exotic myth.

43. Octave Thanet, "My Lorelei," in *Two Friends and Other Nineteenth-Century Lesbian Stories by American Women Writers,* ed. Susan Koppelman (New York: Meridian, 1994), 81; subsequent references to this edition will be parenthetical.

44. The rough translation of these lines is as follows: "You have diamonds and pearls, / Have everything that Men desire, / And have the most beautiful eyes— / My sweetheart, what else can you want/desire?" The original German is odd, however: what Thanet records as "Menchenbegehr" should be two words—a subject and a verb, *Menschen begehren*. Any grammatical or orthographic mistakes in the German passages are quoted as they appear in the original English publication.

45. Again, the German would appear to be either transcribed incorrectly by the editor or written incorrectly by Thanet. This phrase should read "soll es bedeuten / Dass ich so Traurig bin!"

46. These conceptualizations of exotic otherness (embodied here in the figure of Lorelei) in turn infused the terms of American self-reference beyond the fantasy realm of fiction. Consider the following piece of writing submitted to the *Art Amateur*. Published only a few months after Thanet's story, Viola Alpina's "The Lorelei's Den—A New England Studio" outlines, in several detailed paragraphs, the transformation of a friend's studio into a den of exoticism:

"It is a square, uncarpeted room, with Persian rugs before the door and between the two north windows, and a large, soft crimson rug in the middle of the floor. Brass andirons shine in a cheerful open fireplace, hemmed in by a brass-rimmed wire fender. The chimney-piece is decorated with a row of tiles, studies in wild-flowers—and two relief medallions, portraits of Napoleon I and Josephine—the latter especially beautiful. On the high wooden mantel-shelf are several plates of dark-blue India ware, a Chinese salver with red flowers on a dull blue ground, and two jointed Chinese dolls, in blue and yellow native dresses, executing a fantastic dance in the friendly shade of an immense red-flowered pitcher. A small, quaintly-shaped iron lamp (like an antique chafing-dish) hangs by its high, curved handle just before Napoleon's stern face, and across the stone front of the fireplace, above the tiles, is fastened the long, black, polished stem of a Turkish meerschaum smoked by Louis Kossuth one night, years ago, as he sat in the library downstairs. Another relic is this curious old yellow and green box, upon which stands an unframed oil painting of a pert little darkey in a blue shirt; in front of him, on the box cover, is perched the sauciest and tiniest of Chinese slippers, with a turned-up toe!

"Leaving the fascinating fireplace, we come to a closet-door, above which are three bamboo canes and some Japanese fans. The door itself is covered with unframed oil paintings. The corner of the wall between closet and window is also covered with oil sketches, dried grasses and bits of queer Chinese paper. A walnut bracket with a bust of Minerva, a key, a large, old-fashioned blue umbrella, and a green one to match, complete this bewildering corner.

"Then comes the secretary—at which I am writing—its four shelves filled with bric-à-brac and books—the latter mostly German, including the works of Schiller, Goethe, Uhland and Heine. On the corner of the secretary hang three gay chatelaine bags of yellow silk, embroidered with flowers; twined carelessly around them are some charming mementoes of the Lorelei's foreign travel—rosaries, carved in amber, in coral, in white and red ivory, in olive-wood, and one, perfumed, of Turkish pressed rose-leaves. The window corner beyond the secretary is adorned with an exquisite dreamy little water-color sketch of 'Mythenstein,' and the 'lake of the four cantons,' in which the purple shadow of distant mountains falls across the deep, blue water. All along the wall are more paintings, mostly of French peasant women. Above these hang a framed photograph of a public garden in Hanover; a bunch of dried cat-tails, fastened to the wall; and a sketch of golden-rod, and purple asters.

"Continuing our 'voyage around the room,' we come next to an open cabinet, its five shelves filled with dainty china. Above, is draped a wide India scarf, against whose dark crimson folds, an alabaster statuette of the Gladiator, and of Ariadne, stand out finely. Two shelves hold China plaques, decorated by the Lorelei's artist pencil; tête-à-tête sets, coffee-cups and saucers, and some beautiful spode plates. Below are pieces of undecorated china, sketches and portfolios of engravings, screened from view by two exquisite scarfs, or veils, of Canton crape—one, white striped with yellow satin; the other brilliant with crimson and blue flowers. Alpina, "The Lorelei's Den—A New England Studio," *Art Amateur* (July 1880): 44.

"The Lorelei's Den" is a small-scale Crystal Palace, containing tchotchkes not only from Germany, but also from India, China, France, and Turkey. The story suggests the degree to which local color eccentricities are defined by global exoticism. The New England woman's creation of space is fused with the Lorelei myth, indexing the flow of textual traffic not just from the rural localities to the cities but from the cities back to the regions again. By the 1890s, local color writing would acquire a self-consciousness about the conditions of its circulation that, as Brad Evans has argued, produced the concept of the "chic" within its own fictional boundaries—chic, that is, as the cachet that the movement of both people and texts from rural to urban settings came to generate. See Evans, "Howellsian Chic: The Local Color of Cosmopolitanism," *ELH* 71, no. 3 (Fall 2004): 775–812.

47. Here, I think it might be helpful to contrast this analysis against a piece of literature that trades in such social type language. I've thought of perhaps the "tommy"—in, say, Willa Cather's "Tommy the Unsentimental"—but it seems too late to work in the context of the Cooke and Thanet analysis. There is also the nineteenth-century Sappho, but this is more of a poetry tradition.

48. As I suggest in my chapter on Henry James, there is a stronger tradition of response to pornography about sexual love between women in France—which only further highlights for English writers the foreign exoticism of the project.

49. Ralph Waldo Emerson, "The Poet," in his *Essays and Lectures,* ed. Joel Porte (New York: Library of America, 1983), 453.

50. John Ruskin, *Modern Painters*, vol. 3, *Of Many Things* (Sunnyside, Orpington, Kent: George Allen, 1888), 160.

51. Ibid., 158.

52. Ibid., 159–60.

53. See J. Hillis Miller, "Catachresis, Prosopopoeia, and the Pathetic Fallacy: The Rhetoric of Ruskin," in *Poetry and Epistemology: Turning Points in the History of Poetic Knowledge,* ed. Roland Hagenbüchle and Laura E. Skandera-Trombley (Regensburg: Verlag Friedrich Pustet, 1986), 398–407.

54. See Leo Bersani, *The Freudian Body: Psychoanalysis and Art* (New York: Columbia University Press, 1986); and *A Future for Astyanax: Character and Desire in Literature* (Boston: Little, Brown, 1976).

55. Regularly, the narrator describes Harriet watching both Helena's and Martha's routines and emotions: "Cousin Harriet looked on at a succession of ingenious and, on the whole, innocent attempts at pleasure" (204); "Miss Harriet, who presently came to the garden steps to watch like a hen at the water's edge" (206); "Martha scattered crumbs" to the birds that Helena once fed "while Miss Pyne watched from the dining-room window" (216).

56. Hamlin Garland, *Crumbling Idols: Twelve Essays on Art Dealing Chiefly with Literature, Painting, and the Drama* (Chicago: Stone and Kimball, 1894), 64.

57. Judith Fetterley and Marjorie Pryse, *Writing Out of Place.*

58. Amy Kaplan, "Nation, Region, and Empire," in *The Columbia History of the American Novel,* ed. Emory Elliott et al. (New York: Columbia University Press, 1991), 252.

59. Richard H. Brodhead, *Cultures of Letters: Scenes of Reading and Writing in Nineteenth-Century America* (Chicago: University of Chicago Press, 1993), 141, 120.

60. Gertrude Stein, *Q.E.D.,* in *Three Lives and Q.E.D.,* ed. Marianne DeKoven (New York: Norton, 2006), 179.

4. Reading *The Bostonians*'s History of Sexuality from the Outside In

1. Henry James, *The Bostonians*, in *Novels, 1881–1886,* ed. William T. Stafford (New York: Library of America, 1985), 1061; subsequent references to this edition will be parenthetical.

2. "Olive would whisk Verena off to these appointments directly after lunch; she flattered herself that she could arrange matters so that there would not be half an hour in the day during which Basil Ransom, complacently calling, would find the Bostonians in the house" (1062); "He knew that the Bostonians had been drawn thither [Cape Cod], for the hot weeks,

by its sedative influence" (1120); "He reflected that it would hardly do to begin his attack that night; he ought to give the Bostonians a certain amount of notice of his appearance on the scene" (1123).

3. Readers might be forgiven for making this assumption, not only because James has not distinguished some Bostonians from others but also because readers would have been long used to reading about characters situated in Boston. What distinguishes James's treatment of the city, from the perspective of his critics, is what they saw as the scathingly ironic treatment of his characters, which for some verged on a satire of Boston itself. Indeed, we might not recognize *The Bostonians* that we read today from the reviews it received. These reviews were so overwhelmingly unfavorable that James ultimately decided not to issue a New York edition (with preface) of this novel among his collected works (Scribner's, 1907–9). He would later say that he regretted the decision not to include it, claiming that "I would have liked to write that preface." At the time of the book's publication, he wrote to his brother, "If I have displeased people, as I hear, by calling the book *The Bostonians*—this was done wholly without invidious intention. I hadn't a dream of generalizing . . . . I shall write another: 'The Other Bostonians.'" James, *Letters*, ed. Leon Edel, vol. 3, *1883–1895* (Cambridge, Mass.: Belknap Press, 1980), 121. None of the reviews that I have found comments extensively on the sexuality of the characters. For a sense of what nineteenth-century readers might have expected in novels about Boston, see Frances Weston Carruth, *Fictional Rambles in and about Boston* (New York: McClure, Phillips, 1902). Carruth charts the way most nineteenth-century fiction incorporated Boston's monuments, buildings, and landscapes.

4. David Van Leer, "A World of Female Friendship: *The Bostonians*," in *Henry James and Homo-erotic Desire*, ed. John R. Bradley (New York: St. Martin's, 1999), 93.

5. It is commonly claimed, by scholars such as Lillian Faderman, Jonathan Ned Katz, and others, that *Boston marriage* was the term in circulation to describe passionate, if sometimes asexual, companionships between women—usually very educated women—at the end of the nineteenth century. Famous Boston marriages include those between Sarah Orne Jewett and Annie Fields. I have had trouble, however, finding documentation that confirms the use of this precise term during the time period and wonder whether James's novel did not in fact help to consolidate this "type" of relationship. The earliest print source to describe these relationships is usually taken to be the *Atlantic Monthly*, whose editor Mark DeWolfe Howe suggested that such a relationship between women was "a union—there is no truer word for it." Howe's daughter, Helen Huntington Howe, cites her father's words

in a long passage about the relationship between Jewett and Fields, noting the connection between their intimate connection and their literary output. This letter appears in Helen Huntington Howe's *The Gentle Americans, 1864–1960: Biography of a Breed* (New York: Harper and Row, 1965), 83. But debate about whether these "marriages" were sexual or asexual in nature seems to be a recent concern and, notably, one that does not preoccupy scholars of heterosexual unions. Benjamin Kahan has identified a print appearance of the term *Boston marriage* some fifteen years prior to Howe's usage, a usage that identifies an excess of putatively celibate old maids as the condition of possibility for Boston marriages themselves. See Benjamin Kahan, *Celibacies*, 39–42. For more information about the specifically "homosexual" history of Boston and on Boston marriages in particular, see the History Project, *Improper Bostonians: Lesbian and Gay History from the Puritans to Playland* (Boston: Beacon Press, 1998); and Lillian Faderman, *Surpassing the Love of Men*.

   6. Coviello, *Tomorrow's Parties: Sex and the Untimely in Nineteenth-Century America* (New York: New York University Press, 2013), 171.

   7. In *Celibacies*, Kahan points to what he sees as the "constitutive role of celibacy in the Boston Marriage" (41). In conversation with both Coviello and Kahan, Makoda Kishi returns to celibacy as a hermeneutic problem that haunts any anticipatory reading of this text as lesbian dating back at least to Phillip Rahv's first use of the term in the context of *The Bostonians* in 1945, identified as "the lack of explicit articulation of their sexual relationship in the novel." Holding on to both Coviello's caution against reading with anticipation and to Kahan's foregrounding of celibacy at the heart of the text, Kishi argues that "the shape of Olive Chancellor's erotic economy is illegible, not because the author and the protagonist fail to—or even refuse to—find a proper articulation for her same-sex desire. Rather, I would argue, it is because her eroticism is metaphysical, eschewing the physicality of sex in its quasi-theological desire." Makoda Kishi, "'The Ecstasy of the Martyr': Lesbianism, Sacrifice, and Morbidness in *The Bostonians*," *Henry James Review* 37, no. 1 (Winter 2016): 101, 103.

   8. In the case of *The Bostonians* the very indeterminate nature of this past life is reflected in the contemporary reviews of James's novel, most of which either ignore what today's critics see as the lesbian bond between Olive and Verena or, interestingly enough, import a quotation from the novel to let it speak for itself. The *Boston Evening Traveler* cites Ransom's assessment of Olive as "a single old maid" and then cites the narrator's description of Olive as "unmarried by every implication of her being . . . she was a spinster as Shelley was a lyric poet or as the month of August is

sultry"; another reviewer suggests mildly that "both Miss Chancellor and Ransom fall in love with the fascinating Verena" but does not belabor the point in any meaningful fashion. If the relationship between the Bostonians was one reason for the reviewers' dislike, they never articulated this reason as such. See *Henry James: The Contemporary Reviews,* ed. Kevin J. Hayes (Cambridge: Cambridge University Press, 1996), 157, 166.

9. In a related analysis, Lauren Berlant argues for reading feminism/ sexual identity as a genre. See Berlant, *The Female Complaint: The Unfinished Business of Sentimentality in American Culture* (Durham, N.C.: Duke University Press, 2008). In a way, I am interested in inverting the terms of her argument here: rather than read feminism/sexual identity as genre, I am interested in the ways genre organizes both.

10. See again Michel Foucault's famous pronouncement that "the sodomite had been a temporary aberration; the homosexual was now a species." Foucault, *The History of Sexuality,* vol. 1, 43. See also Jonathan Ned Katz, *The Invention of Heterosexuality* (New York: Dutton, 1995); and David M. Halperin, *One Hundred Years of Homosexuality and Other Essays on Greek Love* (New York: Routledge, 1990).

11. Some examples: Valerie Traub, *The Renaissance of Lesbianism in Early Modern England* (Cambridge: Cambridge University Press, 2002); Terry Castle, ed., *The Literature of Lesbianism: A Historical Anthology from Ariosto to Stonewall* (New York: Columbia University Press, 2003); Martha Vicinus, *Intimate Friends: Women Who Loved Women, 1778–1928* (Chicago: University of Chicago Press, 2004); John D'Emilio and Estelle B. Freedman, *Intimate Matters: A History of Sexuality in America,* 3rd ed. (Chicago: University of Chicago Press, 2012); Lillian Faderman, *Surpassing the Love of Men*; and Kathryn R. Kent, *Making Girls into Women: American Women's Writing and the Rise of Lesbian Identity* (Durham, N.C.: Duke University Press, 2003).

12. While most such readings turn on analyses of the dynamic between Olive and Verena, one of the more creative readings of Olive's queerness is Denis Flannery's assessment of Mrs. Luna. Flannery argues that "Adeline Luna is part of a complex and disjunctive affective structure, and a long tradition in American literature—one that overlaps sibling love and queer, specifically homoerotic, attachment." It is, in other words, Olive's sister who enables us to see the homosexuality of the text. Denis Flannery, "The Appalling Mrs Luna: Sibling Love, Queer Attachment, and Henry James's *The Bostonians,*" *Henry James Review* 26, no. 1 (Winter 2005): 5.

13. The *Oxford English Dictionary* indicates that at the end of the nineteenth century *morbid* referred to disease or physical ailments. In recorded

examples, however, *morbid* more often gestures less to physical states than it does to mental states. For instance, M. O. Warren (1775) refers to the "morbid brain," William Wordsworth to "morbid pleasure" (1798), and Kingsley to "morbid melancholy" (1942). William James writes, "The athletic attitude tends ever to break down, and it inevitably does break down even in the most stalwart when . . . morbid fears invade the mind." James, *The Varieties of Religious Experience: A Study in Human Nature: Being the Gifford Lectures on Natural Religion Delivered at Edinburgh in 1901–1902* (New York: Longmans, Green, 1902), 46. Frequently, but not always, the word *morbid* is applied to women. In T. H. Hall Caine's *Son of Hagar,* we read, "You morbid little woman, you shall be happy again." Caine, *A Son of Hagar: A Romance of Our Time,* vol. 2 (London: Chatto and Windus, 1887), 147. The *OED* does not confirm Stokes's reading of *morbid* as a euphemism for lesbianism, although Martha Vicinus provides several examples of *morbid* being used in the late nineteenth century to indicate gender crossing in men as well as in women. See Vicinus, *Intimate Friends,* 148, 199, 206, 221.

14. See John Stokes, *In the Nineties* (Chicago: University of Chicago Press, 1989), 26. See also Makoda Kishi, "'The Ecstasy of the Martyr.'"

15. See Judith Butler, "Imitation and Gender Insubordination," in *Inside/Out: Lesbian Theories, Gay Theories,* ed. Diana Fuss (New York: Routledge, 1991), 13–31; and Susan Sontag, "Notes on Camp," *Partisan Review* 31, no. 4 (Fall 1964): 515–30.

16. In her discussion of the debates about James's sexuality, Graham writes: "My intent . . . is to provide a better understanding of James's participation in the construction of homosexuality at the fin de siècle, particularly the way in which his effeminacy anticipated the majority of late-nineteenth-century medical, psychiatric, and legal representations of homosexuals." Graham's nuanced account of James as suspended between his reflexive acquaintance with his own pleasures and his fundamental chastity is indeed worthy of James himself. On the matter of Olive Chancellor, Graham is equally sanguine in her attention to her "morbidity," positioning it within the context of emerging psychological discourses that locate morbidness and New Englandness within the realm of psychological disturbance. Wendy Graham, *Henry James's Thwarted Love* (Stanford, Calif.: Stanford University Press, 1999), 9, 165.

17. Jeremy Bentham, *The Works of Jeremy Bentham,* vol. 8 (Edinburgh: William Tait, 1843), 334.

18. "Aesthetics of Dress," part 4, *Blackwood's Edinburgh Magazine,* June 1845, 731.

19. Arthur Baker, *A Plea for "Romanizers" in the Anglican Communion* (London: Joseph Masters, 1850), 26.

20. In the *OED* entries for *type* and *typify*, we can see the ways in which these words prefigure typification without fully embodying it. Earlier definitions of *type* and *typify* suggest a relationship between a thing and its class or a thing and a class of things that it inaugurates into being. The word *type* is used as far back as the Renaissance to designate a symbol or representative of a class. Examples come from the likes of Edmund Spenser's *Fairie Queene* ("That fare Ilands right, Which thou dost vayle in Type of Faery land, Elizas blessed field, that Albion hight"). *Type* extends back just as far as a verb, meaning not only to "be the type or symbol of" something, but also, in its theological sense, to "prefigure or foreshadow something as a type." In 1596, for instance, H. Claphams points out how the Bible "specially typed out Our spotless Priest Jesus."

21. See, for instance, William G. Madsen, *From Shadowy Types to Truth: Studies in Milton's Symbolism* (New Haven, Conn.: Yale University Press, 1968); and Ursula Brumm, *American Thought and Religious Typology* (New Brunswick, N.J.: Rutgers University Press, 1970); as well as Eric Auerbach, *Figura* (Paris: Belin, 1993).

22. Frank Kermode, *The Classic: Literary Images of Permanence and Change* (Cambridge, Mass.: Harvard University Press, 1983), 89–90.

23. Ibid., 90.

24. Recent studies of Henry James have unearthed his veritable obsession with type. Scholars have observed the ways in which the complexity of James's writing amounts to an undoing of types without really facilitating their disappearance. Two examples of this scholarship focus on the way types permeate James's realism. Stuart Burrows in his treatment of "The Real Thing" offers what he sees as a critical corrective to readings of the story: commentators often see photography in James's story as establishing "the real thing," but Burrows suggests that "'The Real Thing' insists on the impossibility of clear-cut distinctions between the real and the represented thing." In Burrows's estimation, "The Real Thing" "acknowledges its reliance on stock national and racial types in order to reveal the importance of the stereotype to all forms of representation"; his characters experience the world through the "already seen" of the stereotype. James also utilizes this screen of the "already seen" throughout his novel (in the production of "the Bostonians"). Burrows, "Stereotyping Henry James," *Henry James Review* 23, no. 3 (Fall 2002): 257, 260, 261. Sara Blair argues that James negotiates without overturning racial and national types, evincing the complicated ways in which such types can operate. See Blair, *Henry James and*

the Writing of Race and Nation (Cambridge: Cambridge University Press, 1996).

A large body of work also treats questions of gender and sexuality, often in terms that see James as deconstructing types. Leo Bersani has argued that social encounters dissolve the boundaries of individual types for Henry James's characters. In her highly influential discussion of "The Beast in the Jungle," Eve Kosofsky Sedgwick observes that even through the forms of the unspeakable and across a thematics of absence, homosexual types persist, defined by structures of preterition and the unspoken. Leland S. Person argues that James subverts stereotypes of masculinity, though in doing so he also acknowledges that types operate as an implied foil for James's writing. One thing all of these disparate works might be seen to have in common is an interest in the encounter of the apparent flatness of social types with the formal complexity of James's fiction, such that through the Jamesian prism types persist through and in new, highly wrought forms of literary expression. See Bersani, *A Future for Astyanax*; Sedgwick, "The Beast in the Closet: James and the Writing of Homosexual Panic," in *Epistemology of the Closet*, 182–212; and Person, *Henry James and the Suspense of Masculinity* (Philadelphia: University of Pennsylvania Press, 2003).

25. Another way to see this would be in light of Mary Poovey's work that describes how as a by-product of the rise of statistical thinking induction would come to be seen as interconnected with deduction. Poovey points out that by the 1830s, through the work of John Stuart Mill and John Herschel, a shift occurred in scientific thinking and its relationship to social policy: "It was no longer sufficient simply to celebrate induction. Instead, [Herschel] wanted to demonstrate that induction was actually dependent on deduction, just as a responsible application of deduction required induction. . . . By suggesting that induction and deduction are stages in a single method, he laid the groundwork for specifying the steps by which one moved back and forth between observed particulars and theoretical generalization to produce ever more inclusive versions of knowledge." Poovey, *A History of the Modern Fact: Problems of Knowledge in the Sciences of Wealth and Society* (Chicago: University of Chicago Press, 1998), 318. It would not be a stretch to think about Henry James as a novelist interested in pressing the limits of this particular dialectic, the laboratory of the social realm.

26. For articles on the treatment of place in James, see Janet Wolf Bowen, "Architectural Envy: 'A Figure Is Nothing without a Setting' in Henry James's *The Bostonians*," *New England Quarterly* 65, no. 1 (March 1992): 3–23; Mark McGurl, "Social Geometries: Taking Place in Henry James," *Representations* 68 (1999): 59–83; and John D. Ballam, "Henry James and

a 'Sense' of Place: The Modalities of Perception," *Henry James E-Journal,* March 6, 2004. http://www2.newpaltz.edu/~hathawar/ejourn8.html.

27. Hannah Arendt, *The Human Condition,* 2nd ed. (Chicago: University of Chicago Press, 1998), 41–42.

28. Ibid., 42.

29. Ibid., 39.

30. Henry James, "The Art of Fiction," in *The Art of Fiction,* by Walter Besant and Henry James (Boston: Cupples, Upham, 1885), 66.

31. This is precisely the argument that Walter Benn Michaels makes about James's representation of Ransom in "Local Colors," *MLN* 113, no. 4 (September 1998): 734–56. In conjuring up the image of (but never actually giving us) Ransom's dialect as connected to the plantation, James, according to Michaels, refuses the conventions of local color fiction. *The Bostonians,* he maintains vehemently, is not local color fiction, although the novel does implicitly respond to this body of literature.

32. Henry James, *The Notebooks of Henry James,* ed. F. O. Matthiessen and Kenneth B. Murdock (Chicago: University of Chicago Press, 1974), 47.

33. Lyall H. Powers suggests that this period begins with James's essay "The Art of Fiction" and from among his major fictional works includes *The Bostonians, The Princess Cassamassima,* and *The Tragic Muse.* His earliest work of literary criticism, *French Poets and Novelists,* registers James's long-standing interest in the group of French realists and naturalists that he called "the grandsons of Balzac." James, *Literary Criticism,* 2:1012. See also Powers, *Henry James and the Naturalist Movement* (East Lansing: Michigan State University Press, 1971). For more on the relationship of Henry James to naturalism, see Lyall H. Powers, "James's Debt to Alphonse Daudet," *Comparative Literature* 24, no. 2 (Spring 1972): 150–62; and Marie-Reine Garnier, *Henry James et la France* (Paris: H. Champion, 1927).

34. For further discussion of the Oneida community, see George Wallingford Noyes, *Free Love in Utopia: John Humphrey Noyes and the Origin of the Oneida Community,* ed. Lawrence Foster (Urbana: University of Illinois Press, 2001). See also Lawrence Foster, *Women, Family, and Utopia: Communal Experiments of the Shakers, the Oneida Community, and the Mormons* (Syracuse, N.Y.: Syracuse University Press, 1991); Tirzah Miller Herrick, *Desire and Duty at Oneida: Tirzah Miller's Intimate Memoir,* ed. Robert S. Fogarty (Bloomington: Indiana University Press, 2000); Victor Hawley, *Special Love/Special Sex: An Oneida Community Diary,* ed. Robert S. Fogarty (Syracuse, N.Y.: Syracuse University Press, 1994); and Lawrence Foster, *Religion and Sexuality: The Shakers, the Mormons, and the Oneida Community* (Oxford: Oxford University Press, 1981).

35. Henry James [Sr.], Horace Greeley, and Stephen Pearl Andrews, *Love, Marriage, and Divorce, and the Sovereignty of the Individual: A Discussion* (Boston: Benjamin R. Tucker, 1889), 28–29.

36. See Alfred Habegger, "The Lessons of the Father: Henry James, Sr., on Sexual Difference," in *Henry James and the "Woman Business"* (Cambridge: Cambridge University Press, 1989), 27–62.

37. Henry James [Sr.], Horace Greeley, and Stephen Pearl Andrews, *Love, Marriage, and Divorce,* 94.

38. Henry James, *Literary Criticism,* vol. 1, *Essays on Literature, American Writers, English Writers* (New York: Library of America, 1984), 567.

39. James, *Notebooks,* 47.

40. Henry James, *Literary Criticism,* vol. 2, *French Writers, Other European Writers, the Preface to the New York Edition* (New York: Library of America, 1984), 230.

41. Sigmund Freud would use the stair-climbing sequence from Daudet's *Sappho* to meditate on dreams arising from repressed homosexual impulses. In the scene, the lover carries a woman up the stairs, finding her quite light at first, but the higher he goes and the closer he gets to the bedroom, the more burdened he feels by the weight. Freud interprets the burden as the burden of heterosexuality, which increases the closer the analysand gets to the bedroom. Freud, *The Standard Edition of the Complete Psychological Works of Sigmund Freud,* vol. 4, *The Interpretation of Dreams (First Part),* ed. and trans. James Strachey (London: Hogarth Press and Institute of Psycho-Analysis, 1953), 285–89.

42. James, "Art of Fiction," 68.

43. Joan DeJean argues that *L'école des filles* does not properly belong to this tradition of French pornography because it doesn't really fit the generic categories, but the text was certainly treated as pornography by many readers. See DeJean, "The Politics of Pornography: *L'Ecole des Filles,*" in *The Invention of Pornography: Obscenity and the Origins of Modernity, 1500–1800,* ed. Lynn Hunt (New York: Zone, 1993), 109–23.

44. Janet Todd, *The Sign of Angellica: Women, Writing, and Fiction, 1660–1800* (New York: Columbia University Press, 1989), 30. See also Margaret Cavendish, *The Convent of Pleasure and Other Plays,* ed. Anne Shaver (Baltimore: Johns Hopkins University Press, 1999); Mary Astell, *A Serious Proposal to the Ladies,* ed. Patricia Springborg (Peterborough, Ontario: Broadview Press, 2002); and John Cleland, *Fanny Hill; or, Memoirs of a Woman of Pleasure* (New York: Modern Library, 2001).

45. Denslow Lewis, *The Gynecologic Consideration of the Sexual Act* (Chicago: Henry O. Shepard, 1900), 13.

46. A veritable subgenre of short fiction set in women's colleges emerges in the United States in the early twentieth century along precisely these lines. See, for instance, Josephine Daskam Dodge's *Smith College Stories* (1900), Mary MacLane's *The Story of Mary MacLane* (1902), Mary Constance Dubois's "The Lass of the Silver Sword" (1908–9), and Jennette Lee's "The Cat and the King" (1919).

47. M[ikhail] M. Bakhtin, "The Problem of Speech Genres," 65.

48. James sees his own preoccupations reflected in Hawthorne, when he writes that Hawthorne "testifies to the sentiments of the society in which he flourished almost as pertinently (proportions observed) as Balzac and some of his descendents—MM. Flaubert and Zola—testify to the manners and morals of the French people." James, *Hawthorne* (New York: Harper and Brothers, 1879), 4.

On the question of Alice and Katherine, Leon Edel, who remains the most authoritative among the many commentators on the significance of James's life to his writing, says: "[James] nevertheless noted the extent to which Alice leaned upon her powerful friend, Katherine Loring. Miss Loring had quite taken over the foreground of Alice's life; quite entered into her daily well-being and her nervous prostrations. Alice had described Miss Loring shortly after meeting her . . . [as having] 'all the mere brute superiority which distinguishes man from woman, combined with all the distinctively feminine virtues. There is nothing she cannot do from hewing wood and drawing water to driving runaway horses and educating all the women in North America.' . . . [James] was to observe closely this relationship. One might say that the figure of Olive Chancellor of *The Bostonians* had appeared upon the novelist's very doorstep." Leon Edel, *Henry James: The Middle Years, 1882–1895* (Philadelphia: Lippincott, 1962), 67–68.

49. James, "Art of Fiction," 52. James published an amended version of the essay in *Partial Portraits,* published in 1888.

5. Worlds Inside

1. On *The Well of Loneliness* see, for instance, Heather Love, "'Spoiled Identity': Stephen Gordon's Loneliness and the Difficulties of Queer History," *GLQ: A Journal of Lesbian and Gay Studies* 7, no. 4 (2001): 487–519; Julie Abraham, *Are Girls Necessary?* 1–40.

2. See Judith Butler, *Gender Trouble: Feminism and the Subversion of Sex* (New York: Routledge, 1990); Siobhan Somerville, *Queering the Color Line: Race and the Invention of Homosexuality in American Culture* (Durham: Duke University Press, 2000); and Eve Kosofsky Sedgwick,

"How to Bring Your Kids Up Gay: The War on Effeminate Boys," in *Tendencies* (Durham, N.C.: Duke University Press, 1993), 154–64.

3. Margaret Fuller, *Woman in the Nineteenth Century,* 85.

4. "Martha's Lady" was later collected in Jewett's compendium of stories *The Queen's Twin and Other Stories* (Boston: Houghton Mifflin, 1899), 135–69, and included as well in Willa Cather's collection *The Best Stories of Sarah Orne Jewett,* vol. 2 (Boston: Houghton Mifflin, 1925), 158–92. Since that time, the story has also been featured in anthologies of lesbian writing including Susan Koppelman's *Two Friends and Other Nineteenth-Century Lesbian Stories,* 198–219; and Margaret Reynolds, ed., *The Penguin Book of Lesbian Short Stories* (New York: Viking, 1993), 1–19.

5. Sarah Orne Jewett, "Dear Friend," in *Letters of Sarah Orne Jewett,* ed. Annie Fields (Boston: Houghton Mifflin, 1911), 112. This letter is cited in the following articles, among others: Glenda Hobbs, "Pure and Passionate: Female Friendship in Sarah Orne Jewett's 'Martha's Lady,'" *Studies in Short Fiction* 17, no. 1 (1980): 26; Susan Koppelman's headnote to the story in *Two Friends,* 198; and Melanie Kisthardt, "Reading Lives, Writing to Transgress: Sarah Orne Jewett's 'Unwritable Things,'" *Colby Quarterly* 34, no. 2 (June 1998): 134–35.

6. Heather Love, "Gyn/Apology: Sarah Orne Jewett's Spinster Aesthetics," *ESQ: A Journal of the American Renaissance* 55, nos. 3–4 (2009): 319.

7. Sarah Orne Jewett, "Martha's Lady," in Koppelman, ed., *Two Friends,* 202; subsequent references to this edition will be parenthetical.

8. Jaime Hovey, "Sapphic Primitivism in Gertrude Stein's *Q.E.D.,*" *MFS* 42, no. 3 (Fall 1996): 547–68.

9. Here is the story of *Q.E.D.*'s publication, according to Ann Charters: "After Leo Stein disapproved of this autobiographical story, which Gertrude asked him to read in manuscript, she put it away and it did not resurface publicly until after her death in 1946, when Alice B. Toklas sent the manuscript notebooks to Carl Van Vechten, who presented them for deposit in the Stein archives in the Beinecke Library at Yale University.

"*Q.E.D.* was first published in 1950 with the title *Things as They Are,* a phrase from the end of the book chosen by her literary executors. Twenty years later, it was reissued by the scholar Leon Katz, who restored Stein's original title. Katz also uncovered evidence of the homosexual triangle among Gertrude Stein ("Adele"), May Bookstaver ("Helen"); and Mabel Haynes ("Sophie Neathe")." Charters, headnote to appendix, in Stein, *Three Lives* (New York: Penguin, 1990), 201. In the later edition of the text, "Sophie" becomes "Mabel."

10. Carolyn Faunce Copeland, *Language & Time & Gertrude Stein* (Iowa City: University of Iowa Press, 1975), 10.

11. William James, *The Principles of Psychology,* vol. 1 (New York: Dover, 1950 [1890]), 6.

12. Gertrude Stein, *Q.E.D.,* in *Three Lives and Q.E.D.,* ed. Marianne DeKoven (New York: Norton, 2006), 178; subsequent references to this edition will be parenthetical.

13. Kobena Mercer and Isaac Julien, "Race, Sexual Politics, and Black Masculinity: A Dossier," in *Male Order: Unwrapping Masculinity,* ed. Rowena Chapman and Jonathan Rutherford (London: Lawerence and Wishart, 1988), 106.

14. Dimuro's introduction to Henry Blake Fuller, *Bertram Cope's Year,* ed. Joseph A. Dimuro (Peterborough, Ontario: Broadview Press, 2010), 17.

15. Fuller, *Bertram Cope's Year,* 152; subsequent references to this edition will be parenthetical.

16. See Edmund Wilson, "Henry B. Fuller: The Art of Making It Flat," *New Yorker,* May 23, 1970; Kenneth Scambray, *A Varied Harvest: The Life and Works of Henry Blake Fuller* (Pittsburgh, Penn.: University of Pittsburgh Press, 1987), 150; and Dimuro, introduction to *Bertram Cope's Year,* 9–34.

17. Carl Van Vechten, *Excavations: A Book of Advocacies* (New York: Knopf, 1926), 140.

18. Dimuro, introduction to *Bertram Cope's Year,* 18, 20.

19. Wilson, "Henry B. Fuller," 132, 134.

20. In her tribute to Fuller, Ella M. Saunders lauds "so fine a realism," in Anna Morgan, ed., *Tributes to Henry B.: From Friends in Whose Minds and Hearts He Will Live Always* (Chicago: Ralph Fletcher Seymour, 1929), 78.

21. Dimuro, introduction to *Bertram Cope's Year,* 25.

22. The Newberry Library holds Henry Blake Fuller's papers, which reveal the extent to which Fuller relied on psychological discourses at the time. I have read through this material, which is summarized best in print (see ibid.). See also Joseph Dimuro's account of the process of editing the book in "The Salient Angle: Revising the Queer Case of Henry Blake Fuller's 'Bertram Cope's Year,'" *Textual Cultures* 2, no. 1 (2007): 136–54.

23. Wilson, "Henry B. Fuller," 131.

24. Sedgwick, "How to Bring Your Kids Up Gay."

25. See George Chauncey, *Gay New York: Gender, Urban Culture, and the Making of the Gay Male World, 1890–1940* (New York: Basic Books, 1994).

26. There is a long history in English of representing the mind through the language of exteriors. See, for example, the ATT–Meta Project Databank,

available through the School of Computer Science at the University of Birmingham (http://www.cs.bham.ac.uk/). See also Mark S. Micale, ed., *The Mind of Modernism: Medicine, Psychology, and the Cultural Arts in Europe and America, 1880–1940* (Stanford, Calif.: Stanford University Press, 2004).

Some of the best examples during this period of the mind imagined as an exterior space appear in J. M. Barrie's *Peter and Wendy*. In one of these passages, Mrs. Darling is described as tidying up her children's minds at night. In another, Neverland itself is laid out as a place of the mind, replete with its imperial fantasy structure. See Barrie, *Peter and Wendy* (New York: Scribner's, 1911), 7–10.

27. Sigmund Freud, "On Beginning the Treatment," in *Standard Edition of the Complete Psychological Works of Sigmund Freud*, vol. 12, *The Case of Schreber, Papers on Technique and Other Works*, ed. and trans. James Strachey (London: Hogarth Press and Institute of Psycho-Analysis, 1958), 135. Freud used a similar metaphor to describe his own moods in an 1897 letter to Wilhelm Fleiss: "I live only for the 'inner work.' I am gripped and pulled through ancient times in quick association of thoughts: my moods change like landscapes seen by a traveler from a train." Freud, *The Complete Letters of Sigmund Freud to Wilhelm Fleiss, 1887–1904*, trans. Jeffrey Moussaieff Masson (Cambridge, Mass.: Belknap Press, 1985), 274.

Coda

1. Coviello takes the phrase "unspeakable past" from a 1914 letter from Henry James to Anne Adams Fields. See Peter Coviello, *Tomorrow's Parties*, 1–7.

2. Mark Mitchell and David Leavitt, introduction to *Pages Passed from Hand to Hand*, xv–xvi.

3. See Coviello, *Tomorrow's Parties*; and Elizabeth Freeman, *Time Binds: Queer Temporalities, Queer Histories* (Durham, N.C.: Duke University Press, 2010).

4. Roger Austen, *Playing the Game*, xi.

5. Edward Prime-Stevenson, "From *The Intersexes*," in *Glances Backward: An Anthology of American Homosexual Writing, 1830–1920*, ed. James J. Gifford (Peterborough, Ontario: Broadview Press, 2007), 4. See also Austen, *Playing the Game*, 21.

6. Austen, *Playing the Game*, 49, note 1.

7. See Jasbir K. Puar, *Terrorist Assemblages: Homonationalism in Queer Times* (Durham, N.C.: Duke University Press, 2007).

8. See Arnaldo Cruz-Malavé and Martin F. Manalansan IV, eds., *Queer Globalizations: Citizenship and the Afterlife of Colonialism* (New York: New York University Press, 2002).

9. Raymond Williams, *The Sociology of Culture* (Chicago: University of Chicago Press, 1981).

10. See, for example, the work of scholars such as Lara Langer Cohen and Jordan Stein, eds., *Early African American Print Culture* (Philadelphia: University of Pennsylvania Press, 2012); Lloyd Pratt, *The Strangers Book: The Human of African American Literature* (Philadelphia: University of Pennsylvania Press, 2016); Ivy Wilson, *Spectres of Democracy: Blackness and the Aesthetics of Nationalism* (New York: Oxford University Press, 2011); Siobhan Somerville, *Queering the Color Line*; Robert Reid-Pharr, *Black Gay Man* (New York: New York University Press, 2001); Robin Bernstein, *Racial Innocence: Performing American Childhood from Slavery to Civil Rights* (New York: New York University Press, 2011); Kyla Wazana Tompkins, *Racial Indigestion: Eating Bodies in the Nineteenth Century* (New York: New York University Press, 2012); and Aliyyah I. Abdur-Rahman, *Against the Closet: Black Political Longing and the Erotics of Race* (Durham, N.C.: Duke University Press, 2012).

11. Nancy Bentley, "The Fourth Dimension: Kinlessness and African American Narrative," *Critical Inquiry* 35, no. 2 (2009): 271.

12. Jordan Stein, "Queering Abolition," 11. Unpublished essay, cited here with the permission of the author.

13. Mark Rifkin, *When Did Indians Become Straight? Kinship, the History of Sexuality, and Native Sovereignty* (Oxford: Oxford University Press, 2011). Note as well Leslie Feinberg's deployment of the history of two-spirit people as a portal to understanding modern transgender identity—a representation that Rifkin critiques for the ways it fetishizes Indigenous gender for the purposes of white enlightenment—not unlike the ways someone like Charles Warren Stoddard idealizes the Indigenous cultures of the South Sea Islands as sites of sexual possibility. See Leslie Feinberg, *Transgender Warriors: Making History from Joan of Arc to Dennis Rodman* (Boston: Beacon Presss, 1996); Robert Fulton and Steven W. Anderson, "The Amerindian 'Man-Woman': Gender, Liminality, and Cultural Continuity," *Current Anthropology* 33, no. 5 (December 1992): 603–10; Charles Callender and Lee M. Kochems, "The North American Berdache," *Current Anthropology* 24, no. 4 (August–October 1983): 443–70; Walter L. Williams, *The Spirit and the Flesh: Sexual Diversity in American Indian Culture* (Boston: Beacon Press, 1986); and Richard C. Trexler, *Sex and Conquest: Gendered Violence, Political Order, and the European Conquest of the Americas* (Ithaca, N.Y.: Cornell University Press, 1995). For more on the history of the berdache in early American writing, see William Benemann, *Male-Male Intimacy in Early America: Beyond Romantic Friendships* (Binghamton, N.Y.:

Harrington Park Press, 2006). Benemann quotes William Clark's 1805 observation, as recorded by Nicholas Biddle: "Among Minitarees if a boy shows any symptoms of effeminacy or girlish inclinations he is put among the girls, dressed in their way, brought up with them, & sometimes married to men. They submit as women to all the duties of a wife. I have seen them— the French call them Birdashes" (ibid., 7); Donald Jackson, ed., *Letters of the Lewis and Clark Expedition with Related Documents 1783–1854,* 2nd ed., vol. 2 (Urbana: University of Illinois Press, 1978), 531. Benemann also charts the history of negative reaction to this figure dating back to the sixteenth century (8–9). See also Will Roscoe, *Changing Ones: Third and Fourth Genders in Native North America* (New York: St. Martin's Press, 1998); and *The Zuni Man-Woman* (Albuquerque: University of New Mexico Press, 1991); Birgit Brander Rasmussen, *Queequeg's Coffin: Indigenous Literacies and Early American Literature* (Durham, N.C.: Duke University Press, 2012); Zitkala-Ša, *American Indian Stories* (Washington, D.C.: Hayworth Publishing House, 1921), composed almost entirely of turn-of-the-century pieces; Qwo-Li Driskill et al., eds., *Sovereign Erotics: A Collection of Two-Spirit Literature* (Tucson: University of Arizona Press, 2011); and Will Roscoe, ed., *Living the Spirit: A Gay American Indian Anthology* (New York: St. Martin's, 1988).

14. Elizabeth Povinelli, *The Empire of Love: Toward a Theory of Intimacy, Genealogy, and Carnality* (Durham, N.C.: Duke University Press, 2006), 17, 226.

15. Terry Castle, introduction to *The Literature of Lesbianism: A Historical Anthology from Ariosto to Stonewall,* 6.

16. Axel Nissen, *Manly Love: Romantic Friendship in American Fiction* (Chicago: University of Chicago Press, 2009), 58.

17. See, for example, Jay A. Gertzman, *Bookleggers and Smuthounds: The Trade in Erotica, 1920–1940* (Philadelphia: University of Pennsylvania Press, 1999); and Guy Davidson, *Queer Commodities: Contemporary US Fiction, Consumer Capitalism, and Gay and Lesbian Subcultures* (New York: Palgrave Macmillan, 2012).

18. See Ramzi Fawaz and Shanté Paradigm Smalls, "Queers Read This: LGBTQ Literature Now," special issue of *GLQ* (forthcoming).

19. Sarah Schulman, *Stagestruck: Theatre, AIDS, and the Marketing of Gay America* (Durham, N.C.: Duke University Press, 1998).

20. E. D. Hirsch, *Validity in Interpretation* (New Haven, Conn.: Yale University Press, 1967).

INDEX

fairy, 136, 255n54, 256n55. *See also* gay men; insult

fantasy, xvii–xviii, 2, 13, 16–17, 39, 55, 57, 116, 130, 146, 157, 167, 208–9, 218, 279n26, 283n46. *See also* Freud, Sigmund; psychoanalysis

fashion, 2, 74, 204

Feinberg, Leslie, 260n13

female sexuality, 15, 116, 142, 182

femininity, 70, 219

feminism, xv, 150, 248n6, 288n9; feminist critics, 113; feminist scholarship, 114

feminotopias, 279n38

fetishism, 146, 225

Fetterley, Judith, 115, 146

Fiedler, Leslie, 22, 44

Fielding, Henry, 7

Fields, Annie, 114

Fish, Stanley, 261n10

flatness, 6, 116, 180, 184, 210, 226, 291n24

Flaubert, Gustave, 181, 250n18

Floyd, Kevin, 234

forgiveness, 212

Forster, E. M., xii–xiii, 44, 198, 199

Foster, Edward, 113, 275n8

Foster, Jeannette H., 2, 227, 254n50

Foucault, Michel, xiv, 7, 32, 46–47, 224, 244n13, 245n18, 288n10; *The History of Sexuality,* 32, 244n13

Freeman, Elizabeth, 227, 245n18

Freeman, Mary Eleanor Wilkins, 12, 112, 152, 275n4; "A New England Nun," 12–13, 112–13, 115, 146, 275n4

French, Alice. *See* Thanet, Octave

French literature, 180, 182; French writers, 181, 183; naturalism in, 181, 183; naturalist fiction,

151. *See also* national literature; world literature

Freud, Sigmund, 29, 189, 197, 200, 256n55; Ego-Id-Superego, 221. *See also* psychoanalysis

friendship, xii–xiii, 4, 7, 44, 61, 76, 88, 102, 153, 175–76, 182, 233, 251n30, 262n13; romantic, 4, 153, 233, 255n50, 266n40, 270n13

frigidity, 113

Frye, Northrop, 29, 32, 247n5

Fuller, Henry Blake, 12, 191, 210, 231; *Bertram Cope's Year,* 12, 38, 191, 192, 210–20, 296nn14–16, 296nn18–23

Fuller, Margaret, 50, 122, 193

Gale, Robert, 81

Gaonkar, Dilip, 10

Garland, Hamlin, 146

Garrett, Matthew, 7, 249n11

Gauguin, Paul, 267n49

gay and lesbian studies, xv, 2, 19–20, 26–27, 227–28, 254n50

gayety, 195

gay men, 4, 22, 218, 243n3

gay social life, xviii

genderphobic, 212, 219

genderqueer, 4, 254n50

genealogy, 17, 24, 187, 202, 230–31

genre, x–xi, xvii, 3–4, 6, 9–10, 12, 17–18, 21–22, 24–25, 28, 31–32, 38, 81, 107, 120, 151, 185, 187, 222, 224, 226, 229, 234–35, 246n21, 249n17, 264n25, 288n9; formation of, 32; theory of, 249n17

ghosts, xvi, 229

Gifford, James, xii, 227

gift, 60, 102, 180, 196, 244n7, 261n13

Leavitt, David, xi, 7, 225, 243n1,
    249n12, 297n2
Lee, Benjamin, 10, 34–35, 258n78;
    and Edward LiPuma, 250n21
leitmotif, 135
lesbianism, xi–xii, xv, 2–5, 8, 12,
    14–15, 17–24, 26–32, 37–38,
    107, 109–11, 114–16, 125,
    127–28, 138, 145–47, 150–51,
    153–57, 164, 181–83, 185–87,
    192–93, 200–201, 227–29,
    231–32, 234, 244n7, 247nn5–
    6, 249n17, 253n43, 253n45,
    253–55nn47–50, 257n61,
    257n65, 275n4, 276n18,
    276n21, 278n35, 279n36,
    280nn38–39, 282n42, 287nn7–8,
    288n11, 289n13, 295n4
lesbian salon culture, xii
letters, xvii, 7, 14, 82, 85, 88–90,
    102, 104, 112, 120, 178, 182,
    189, 197, 209, 211, 213, 215–
    17, 227, 233, 247n23, 252n31,
    254n50, 268n2, 269nn8–9,
    271–72nn17–26, 272n28,
    273n39, 286n3, 287n5, 295n5,
    297n27
Lewis, Denslow, 182, 293n45
library, ix–xiii, xvii, 4, 11–12, 16,
    42, 84, 96–97, 189, 225, 228
licentiousness, 51, 55–56, 58
linguistic anthropology, 33–34
location, xi, xvi–xvii, 4, 13–14, 41,
    62, 75, 101, 117, 121, 123–24,
    126, 130, 139, 175, 194, 199,
    208, 221–22, 224
locus amoenus, 94
loneliness, 5, 147, 150, 191–92
Longfellow, Henry Wadsworth,
    268n7, 270n10
Looby, Christopher, 5, 24, 227,
    248n7, 256n54, 257n62, 267n46

Loring, Katherine, 185, 294n48
Love, Heather, xv–xvi, 192, 194,
    274n1, 294n1, 295n6
Loving, Jerome, 96
Luciano, Dana, 245n18
lynching, 15
lyric, 8, 9, 91–95, 97, 104, 112,
    154, 287n8; apostrophe, 91, 94;
    speaker, 92

Mackenzie, Compton, 21
Manley, Delarivier, 6
Marcus, Sharon, xv, 246n20
Marquesas, 42–43, 51, 53, 76; Mar-
    quesans, 47, 51, 55
marriage, 4, 18, 25, 62–63, 69–
    72, 90, 114–15, 120–22, 125,
    129, 131, 137–38, 146, 150,
    170, 177–78, 211, 233–34,
    244n7, 262n21, 274n2, 276n18,
    278n32, 286n5, 287n7
Martin, Jay, 113, 275n7
Martin, Robert K., 43, 44
Marvell, Andrew, 8, 249n15
Marx, Karl, 10, 250n22
masculinity, 16, 252n39, 255n54,
    266n44, 291n24, 296n13;
    manhood, 79, 267n46; masculine
    women, 254n50
materialism, xiv–xv, 9, 11, 13, 19,
    82, 94, 99, 200, 203, 221
materiality, xvi, 13, 35, 76, 224,
    267n48
maternalism, 134
Maufort, Marc, 261n8
melancholy, 62, 75, 89, 133, 194,
    208, 234, 289n13; melancholic
    incorporation, 192, 197. *See also*
    affect; emotion
Melville, Herman, xvii, 12, 37,
    41, 45, 47, 60–61, 63, 67, 82,
    93–94, 190, 225, 228, 252n31,

xvii, 85, 298n13; South Seas,
xvii, 13, 16, 41–43, 46, 48–50,
52–53, 56, 60–61, 64, 66, 68–69,
79, 81, 84–86, 91, 93–94, 98,
101–3, 225, 261n8, 262n21,
263n24, 264n28, 265n35,
266n41, 266n43, 267n49,
269n9, 272nn26–27

spinster, xi, xvii, 16, 62, 112–14,
121, 124–25, 147, 154, 193–95,
202, 225, 233, 274–75nn1–3,
275n10, 276n18, 277n24,
287n8, 295n6. *See also* old maid

Spivak, Gayatri Chakravorty, xvii,
247n24

Stanton, Michael N., 21–22,
256n46, 256n55

Stein, Gertrude, xiii, 12, 15–17, 26,
38–39, 147, 191–92, 199–200,
202, 204, 206, 208–10, 221, 224,
230–31, 233, 252n36, 285n60,
295n8, 296n10, 296n12; *Q.E.D.*,
12, 15, 38, 147, 191–92, 199–
202, 205, 207–9, 220, 252n36,
285n60, 295nn8–9, 296n12

Stein, Jordan Alexander, xiii, 26,
230, 231, 244n10, 257n64,
298n10, 298n12

Stephens, Anna Sophia, 260n4

Stevenson, Robert Louis, 86

Stewart, Charles (C. S.), 46, 57–59,
67, 265n35, 266n43

Stimpson, Catharine R., 23, 227,
253n49, 256n56

Stoddard, Charles Warren, xvii, 3,
12–13, 16, 27–28, 31, 37, 41–44,
64–67, 76–77, 79, 81–107, 211,
225–26, 233, 244n9, 259n1,
266nn40–41, 267n49, 268–
74nn1–46, 298n13; "Cherries
and Grapes," 93; "Chumming

with a Savage," 104, 266n40,
270n13, 273n42; *For the Pleasure of His Company*, 3, 12, 13,
105–7, 269n9, 273n43, 274n44,
274n46; "In a Transport," 41–
42, 259n1, 272n27, 273n29;
"A South-Sea Idyl," 91–94,
98–101, 103, 104–5, 272n37;
South-Sea Idyls, 12, 31, 41,
65, 79, 84–86, 91–94, 98–101,
105, 259n1, 266n41, 268n2,
269n9, 270–71nn11–13, 272n17,
271n27, 273n42

Stokes, John, 154

Stowe, Harriet Beecher, 112, 275n4;
Uncle Tom's Cabin, 275n5,
277n27

stranger, 10, 39, 82–83, 87, 90–93,
95, 105, 217, 222; lyricized, 83,
92

Stroven, Carl, 81, 268n3

Stryker, Susan, 257n65

style, xii–xiii, 2, 8–9, 27, 45, 50–51,
84, 106–7, 199–200, 211, 218,
244nn10–11, 252n32, 257n64,
270n13

subculture, x, 9, 13, 97, 125, 220,
225, 243n3, 255n50, 266n44,
299n17. *See also* queer cultures

subject formation, 156

subjectivity, x–xi, xiii, 8, 31, 73, 75–
76, 139, 165, 170, 232

sublimation, 113

suffrage movement, 176

Sutherland, Howard, 89, 271n18

Symonds, John Addington, 96, 233

Taaroa, Marau, 268n49

taboo, 63, 67

Tahiti, 54, 86, 102, 263n22,
267n49, 268n1

Natasha Hurley is associate professor of English at the University of Alberta, where she works in American literature, childhood studies, critical theory, and queer studies. She is coeditor, with Steven Bruhm, of *Curiouser: On the Queerness of Children* (Minnesota, 2004).

Made in the USA
Monee, IL
02 November 2020